THE WHEEL OF FIRE

THE
WHEEL OF FIRE

INTERPRETATIONS OF SHAKESPEARIAN TRAGEDY

WITH THREE NEW ESSAYS

By G. WILSON KNIGHT

Emeritus Professor of English Literature
in the University of Leeds

Formerly Chancellors' Professor of English at
Trinity College, Toronto

You do me wrong to take me out o' the grave:
Thou art a soul in bliss; but I am bound
Upon a wheel of fire, that mine own tears
Do scald like molten lead.   KING LEAR, IV. vii. 45

Two truths are told,
As happy prologues to the swelling act
Of the imperial theme.   MACBETH, I, iii. 127

METHUEN & CO. LTD. LONDON
11 New Fetter Lane, E.C.4

Originally published by the Oxford University Press in
July 1930
Reprinted twice
This (fourth) revised and enlarged edition first published
by Methuen & Co. Ltd. in 1949
Reprinted with minor corrections 1954, 1956, 1959, 1962, 1965 *and* 1972
I.S.B.N. 0 416 50930 4

Published as a University Paperback 1961
Reprinted 1964, 1965, 1967, 1968, 1969, 1970, 1972 and 1974
I.S.B.N. 0 416 67620 0

PRINTED IN GREAT BRITAIN BY
BUTLER AND TANNER LTD, FROME AND LONDON

Distributed in the U.S.A. by
HARPER & ROW PUBLISHERS INC.
BARNES & NOBLE IMPORT DIVISION

PREFATORY NOTE

THIS re-issue of what was—except for my monograph *Myth and Miracle* (lately reprinted in *The Crown of Life*) —my first book, contains the original text complete with only some insignificant, mainly typographical, alterations. My two original essays on *Hamlet*, 'Hamlet's Melancholia' and 'The Embassy of Death', are, for neatness, grouped as one. I have tidied up some mannerisms, but made no attempt at correction of matter, preferring to let the various essays stand as documents of their time 'with all their imperfections on their heads', while hoping that they may be found to have worn not too badly during the years since their first publication in 1930. Where there are additions, as with my 'additional notes' and my three new essays, I have dated them. Of these essays, the first, on 'Tolstoy's Attack', was originally published as an English Association pamphlet and is reprinted here by kind permission of the Association. The other two, '*Hamlet* Reconsidered' and 'Two Notes on the Text of *Hamlet*' are quite new. I give line-references to the Oxford Shakespeare.

On looking back over the last two decades I feel that a short retrospective comment may help to clear up certain misunderstandings. My animadversions as to 'character' analysis were never intended to limit the living human reality of Shakespeare's people. They were, on the contrary, expected to loosen, to render flexible and even fluid, what had become petrified. Nor was I at all concerned to repudiate the work of A. C. Bradley. Though Bradley certainly on occasion pushed 'character' analysis to an unnecessary extreme, yet he it was who first subjected the atmospheric, what I have called the 'spatial', qualities of the Shakespearian play to a considered, if rudimentary, comment. Indeed, my own first published manifesto concerning my general aims in Shakespearian interpretation, an article in the year 1928 in the old *Shakespeare Review* under the editorship of A. K. Chesterton, defined those aims as the application to Shakespeare's work in general of the methods already applied by Bradley to certain outstanding plays. It was, and is, my hope that my own labours will be eventually regarded as a natural development within the classic tradition of Shakespearian study.[1]

But here again a distinction is necessary. It has been objected that I write of Shakespeare—as indeed did Coleridge, Hazlitt and Bradley—as a philosophic poet rather than a man of the stage. That is, in its way, true: and it is true that I would not regard the well-known commentaries of Harley Granville-Barker as properly within this central, more imaginative and metaphysical, tradition. Nevertheless, my own major interest has always been Shakespeare in the theatre; and to that my written work has been, in my own mind, subsidiary. But my experience as actor, producer and play-goer leaves me uncompromising in my assertion that the literary analysis of great drama in terms of theatrical technique accomplishes singularly little. Such technicalities should be confined to the theatre from which their terms are drawn. The proper thing to do about a play's dramatic quality is to produce it, to act in it, to attend performances; but the penetration of its deeper meanings is a different matter, and such a study, though the commentator should certainly be dramatically aware, and even wary, will not itself speak in theatrical terms. There is, of course, an all-important relation (which I discuss fully in my *Principles of Shakespearian Production*); and indeed the present standard of professional Shakespearian production appears to me inadequate precisely because these deeper meanings have not been exploited. The play's surface has been merely translated from book to stage, it has not been re-created from within; and that is why our productions remain inorganic.

So much, then, for what this new 'poetic interpretation' is not. What, in short, can we say that it *is*?

A recent account by Mr. Lance L. Whyte of modern developments in physics, which appeared in *The Listener* of July 17th, 1947, can help us here. Mr. Whyte explains how the belief in rigid 'particles' with predictable motions has been replaced by concepts of 'form, pattern and symmetry'; and not by these as static categories only but rather

[1] Parts of my essay 'The *Lear* Universe' constitute an expansion under changed focal length of material first indicated by Bradley (1953).

by something which he calls the 'transformation of patterns'. For 'particles' put 'characters' and we have a clear Shakespearian analogy. Even the dates, roughly, fit: 'From about 1870 to 1910' these 'particles' were thought to hold the key 'to all the secrets of nature'; but since then the conception has been found inadequate. Rigidly distinct and unchanging atoms have become 'patterns' occupying certainly a 'measurable region of space' but yet themselves, as patterns, dynamic, self-transforming. The pattern itself moves; space and time coalesce; such is the mysterious 'design of nature'. But, as too with Shakespeare, the old theories are not to be peremptorily dismissed. They are merely to be regarded as 'less than the utterly complete explanations they were once thought to be':

> They have therefore to be re-interpreted as part of some more comprehensive approach. The answer may be that we must not think of patterns as if they were built out of particles, but that what we have called particles, may ultimately be better explained as components of patterns.

The argument against excessive 'character' study could not be more concisely expressed.

Most important of all, however, is Mr. Whyte's stress on the 'development and transformation of patterns'. Though the 'causal analysis of detailed parts' must be continued as before, we are henceforth to 'pay more attention to certain aspects of phenomena which have been neglected till now, like pattern-tendency and transformation'. So 'the task before physics is to discover a new principle *which can unite permanence and change*'; and here, in the words I have italicized, we have our key to the literary problem.

Long before reading this article I had felt a certain similarity between the methods of what I call 'poetic interpretation' and what I vaguely understood by the theory of Einstein. Mr. Whyte observes that Einstein's relativity theory served to shift emphasis from individual entities to their observable 'relationships'; just as, in my early essays on *Hamlet*, I tried, at the risk of offending those who had (very reasonably) taken the play's hero to their hearts, to see that hero not merely as an isolated 'character' rigidly conceived, but in direct and living relation to his own dramatic environment. That, too, has been my method with other plays; and it is precisely such a 'relationship' that lies regularly behind Shakespeare's use of symbolism as distinct from persons. As for Mr. Whyte's closely similar thought of uniting permanence and change, the analogies are yet more obvious. My own investigations have continually forced me to speak, directly or metaphorically, in terms of a space-time unity, which is yet only to be properly known as a unity in so far as it has first been accepted as a duality. It is, as it were, the space-time 'relationship' that is central and so all-important: as with the interaction of spatial atmosphere and plot-sequence in any one Shakespearian play; the single tempest-music opposition binding and interpenetrating the whole succession of plays; the 'dome' and 'river' symbolisms of the Romantics and all that this implies (especially for the understanding of Keats, whose peculiar artistry can be shown to mature from an exquisite fusion of these, or similar, impressions). When actual stage-production is our argument, we have the fitting of action to setting. Poetry itself may be defined as pre-eminently a blend of the dynamic and the static, of motion and form; and, at the limit, the perfectly integrated man, or superman, is to be conceived as a creature of superb balance, poise and grace. Interpretation is, then, merely the free use of a faculty that responds with ease, and yet with full consciousness of the separate elements involved, to this space-time fusion, or relationship, this eternity, of art, in which every point on the sequence is impregnated by the whole. It is, moreover, something which, once admitted, can be applied widely to literature of consequence: it is as much at home with the *Agamemnon* of Aeschylus as with *Hassan* and *Journey's End*. There is nothing peculiarly Shakespearian about it.

Mr. Whyte himself sees the developments he describes as part of a general movement of the twentieth-century mind, noting similar tendencies in both biology and psychology. It would be sad were literary investigation to be allowed to lag too far behind these more virile sciences. Properly handled it might go some way towards meeting Mr. Whyte's expectation of a newly comprehensive system of knowledge 'covering the organic as well as the inorganic world, and therefore relevant also to man himself'.

Exactly what started me, personally, on this quest it would be hard to say. I was whole-heartedly devoted to Shakespeare—especially to Shakespeare acted—from a very early age. Perhaps what Mr. Eliot calls the 'restless demon' to interpret dates from a question posed suddenly by my brother during a performance of *The Tempest* to which I had persuaded him to accompany me: 'What does it mean?' For many years I have been labouring at the answer.

This note must not be allowed to grow into an essay of reminiscence. Let me conclude by expressing my thanks to Messrs. Methuen & Co. for being willing, at so difficult a time as this, to offer me the privilege and advantage of their imprint.

Leeds, 1947   G. W. K.

Among the writings that appear in retrospect to have influenced my Shakespearian investigations I would list John Masefield's 1924 Romanes Lecture *Shakespeare and Spiritual Life*; and also the pages on *Macbeth* in the chapter 'On the Ghosts in the Tragedies of Shakespeare' in Edward Gordon Craig's *On the Art of the Theatre*, which I had probably read. My remarks on 'character' might be compared with Strindberg's similar arguments in his preface to *Lady Julia*.

My thoughts on the dramas treated in the following pages have been amplified in *The Golden Labyrinth* (1962), *Shakespearian Production* (enlarged 1964), *Byron and Shakespeare* (1966), and *Shakespeare and Religion* (1967). These contain much on *Timon of Athens*, and some new thoughts on the personality of Othello and on his handkerchief (for the handkerchief *Shakespearian Production*, pp. 100–101, and *Byron and Shakespeare*, p. 250). For *King Lear*, I would point to my articles 'Tragedies of Love', *Books and Bookmen*, February 1971 (Vol. 16, No. 5), and 'Gloucester's Leap', *Essays in Criticism*, July 1972 (XXII, 3).

I would draw attention to Harold Fisch's impressive

study, *Hamlet and the Word: the Covenant Pattern in Shakespeare* (New York, Frederick Ungar Publishing Company, 1972).

Exeter, 1972

An important acknowledgement was made to J. Middleton Murry in the preface, not since reprinted, to my first publication, *Myth and Miracle*, in 1929. Among the following essays, especially the second essays on *Macbeth* and *King Lear*, the influence of A. C. Bradley is clearly apparent. Of this I shall say more in my forthcoming book *Shakespeare's Dramatic Challenge*.

Exeter, 1974

CONTENTS

INTRODUCTION

IT has taken me a long time to recognize the justification of what Mr. Wilson Knight calls 'interpretation'. In my previous scepticism I am quite ready to admit the presence of elements of pure prejudice, as well as of some which I defend. I have always maintained, not only that Shakespeare was not a philosophical poet in the sense of Dante and Lucretius; but also, what may be more easily overlooked, that 'philosophical poets' like Dante and Lucretius are not really philosophers at all. They are poets who have presented us with the emotional and sense equivalent for a definite philosophical system constructed by a philosopher—even though they may sometimes take little liberties with the system. To say that Shakespeare is not a philosophical poet like these is not to say anything very striking or important. It is more worth while to point out that my notion of Dante or Lucretius as providing the 'emotional equivalent' for a philosophical system expressed by someone else, is not to be pressed to a literal point for point parallelism, as in the old theory of mind and body. The poet has something to say which is not even necessarily implicit in the system, something which is also over and above the verbal beauty. In other words, the pattern of Cyrene or that of the Schools is not the whole of the pattern of the carpet of Lucretius or of Dante. This other part of the pattern is something to be found in the work of other great poets than those who are 'philosophical'—I say of other, not of all—for that would exclude Horace or Dryden or Malherbe. It is also to be found in the work of some (again, not of all) of the greatest novelists: certainly of George Eliot, and of Henry James who gave the phrase its currency. And of this sort of 'pattern' the most elaborate, the most extensive, and probably the most inscrutable is that of the plays of Shakespeare. For one thing, in Dante the pattern is interwoven chiefly with the systematic pattern which he set himself, and the mystery and excitement lies in trying to trace its relations and differences—the relation, and the personal variations in another mode, between for example the Thomist doctrine of Love, the poetic provencal tradition, and the direct experience of Dante with its modifications under philosophical and literary influences. But the philosophic pattern is far more a help than a hindrance, it is indeed *a priori* a help. Furthermore, Dante in his kind of poetry was doing exactly what he liked with his own material; and the practical exigencies of a badly paid playwright, popular entertainer, sometimes actor, and sometimes busy producer, can only confuse us in our study of Shakespeare. Then again, with Dante the philosophic system gives us a kind of criterion of *consciousness*, and the letter to Can Grande confirms it; just as of a lesser writer, but no less genuine a pattern-maker, Henry James, we have some gauge of consciousness in his very nearness to us in time and civilization, in the authors he studied and the constant play of his criticism upon his own work. But with Shakespeare we seem to be moving in an air of Cimmerian darkness. The conditions of his life, the conditions under which dramatic art was then possible, seem even more remote from us than those of Dante. We dare not treat him as completely isolated from his contemporary dramatists, as we can largely isolate Dante. We see his contemporaries for the most part as busy hack writers of untidy genius, sharing a particular sense of the tragic mood: this sense, such as it is, merging into the mere sense of what the public wanted. They confuse us by the fact that what at first appears to be their 'philosophy of life' sometimes turns out to be only a felicitous but shameless lifting of a passage from almost any author, as those of Chapman from Erasmus. This, indeed, is a habit which Shakespeare shares; he has his Montaigne, his Seneca, and his Machiavelli, or his Anti-Machiavel like the others. And they adapted, collaborated, and overlaid each other to the limits of confusion.

Nevertheless, they do seem, the best of Shakespeare's contemporaries, to have more or less faint or distinct patterns. (I was tempted to use the word 'secret' as an alternative to 'pattern', but that I remembered the unlucky example of Matthew Arnold, who said much about the 'secret of Jesus', a secret which having been revealed only and finally to Arnold himself, turned out to be a pretty poor secret after all.) In Marlowe, surely, we feel the search for one; in Chapman a kind of blundering upon one; in Jonson the one clear and distinct, slight but much more serious than it looks, pattern. There is something in the *Revenger's Tragedy*, but one play does not make a pattern; and Middleton completely baffles me; and as for Ford and Shirley, I suspect them of belonging to that class of poets not unknown to any age, which has all of the superficial qualities, and none of the internal organs, of poetry. But a study of these dramatists only renders our study of Shakespeare more difficult. The danger of studying him alone is the danger of working into the essence of Shakespeare what is just convention and the dodges of an overworked and underpaid writer; the danger of studying him together with his contemporaries is the danger of reducing a unique vision to a mode.

I once affirmed that Dante made great poetry out of a great philosophy of life; and that Shakespeare made equally great poetry out of an inferior and muddled philosophy of life. I see no reason to retract that assertion: but I ought to elucidate it. When I say 'great poetry' I do not suggest that there is a pure element in poetry, the right use of words and cadences, which the real amateur of poetry can wholly isolate to enjoy. The real amateur of poetry certainly enjoys, is thrilled by, uses of words which to the untrained reader seem prosaic. I would say that *only* the real amateur of poetry, perhaps, if this is not too presumptuous, only the real practitioner, can enjoy a great deal of poetry which the untrained reader dismisses as clever paraphrase of prose; certainly, to enjoy Pope, to have an analytic enough mind to enjoy even *second* rate eighteenth-century poetry, is a better test of 'love of poetry' than to like Shakespeare, which is no test at all: I can tell nothing from the fact that you enjoy Shakespeare, unless I know exactly *how* you enjoy him. But the greatest poetry, like the greatest prose, has a doubleness; the poet is talking to you on two planes at once. So I mean not merely that Shakespeare had as refined a sense for words as Dante; but that he also has this doubleness of speech.

Now it is only a personal prejudice of mine, that I prefer

poetry with a clear philosophical pattern, if it has the other pattern as well, to poetry like Shakespeare's. But this preference means merely a satisfaction of more of my own needs, not a judgement of superiority or even a statement that I *enjoy* it more as poetry. I like a definite and dogmatic philosophy, preferably a Christian and Catholic one, but alternatively that of Epicurus or of the Forest Philosophers of India; and it does not seem to me to obstruct or diminish either the 'poetry' or the other pattern. Among readers, probably both types, that of Dante and that of Shakespeare, suffer equal transformation. Dante will be taken as a mere paraphraser of Aquinas, occasionally bursting through his rigid frame into such scenes as Paolo and Francesca, but neither by his admirers nor by his detractors credited with anything like the freedom of Shakespeare. Shakespeare will be still worse traduced, in being attributed with some patent system of philosophy of his own, esoteric guide to conduct, yoga-breathing or key to the scriptures. Thus are the planes of order and pattern confounded.

It is also the prejudice or preference of any one who practises, though humbly, the art of verse, to be sceptical of all 'interpretations' of poetry, even his own interpretations; and to rely upon his sense of power and accomplishment in language to guide him. And certainly people ordinarily incline to suppose that in order to enjoy a poem it is necessary to 'discover its meaning'; so that their minds toil to discover a meaning, a meaning which they can expound to any one who will listen, in order to prove that they enjoy it. But for one thing the possibilities of meaning of 'meaning' in poetry are so extensive, that one is quite aware that one's knowledge of the meaning even of what oneself has written is extremely limited, and that its meaning to others, at least so far as there is some consensus of interpretation among persons apparently qualified to interpret, is quite as much a part of it as what it means to oneself. But when the meaning assigned is too clearly formulated, then one reader who has grasped *a* meaning of a poem may happen to appreciate it less exactly, enjoy it less intensely, than another person who has the discretion not to inquire too insistently. So, finally, the sceptical practitioner of verse tends to limit his criticism of poetry to the appreciation of vocabulary and syntax, the analysis of line, metric and cadence; to stick as closely to the more trustworthy senses as possible.

Or rather, tends to *try* to do this. For this exact and humble appreciation is only one ideal never quite arrived at or even so far as approximated consistently maintained. The restless demon in us drives us also to 'interpret' whether we will or not; and the question of the meaning of 'interpretation' is a very pretty problem for Mr. I. A. Richards, with which neither Mr. Wilson Knight nor myself in this context can afford to be too narrowly concerned. But our impulse to interpret a work of art (by 'work of art' I mean here rather the work of one artist as a whole) is exactly as imperative and fundamental as our impulse to interpret the universe by metaphysics. Though we are never satisfied by any metaphysic, yet those who insist dogmatically upon the impossibility of knowledge of the universe, or those who essay to prove to us that the term 'universe' is meaningless, meet, I think, with a singularly unanimous rejection by those who are curious about the universe; and their counsels fall more flat than the flimsiest constructions of metaphysics. And Bradley's apothegm that 'metaphysics is the finding of bad reasons for what we believe upon instinct; but to find these reasons is no less an instinct', applies as precisely to the interpretation of poetry.

To interpret, then, or to seek to pounce upon the secret, to elucidate the pattern and pluck out the mystery, of a poet's work, is 'no less an instinct'. Nor is the effort altogether vain; for as the study of philosophy, and indeed the surrendering ourselves, with adequate knowledge of other systems, to some system of our own or of someone else, is as needful part of a man's life as falling in love or making any contract, so is it necessary to surrender ourselves to some interpretation of the poetry we like. (In my own experience, a writer needs less to 'interpret' the work of some minor poet who has influenced him, and whom he has assimilated, than the work of those poets who are too big for anyone wholly to assimilate. But I dare say tha if one was as great a poet as Shakespeare, and was also his 'spiritual heir', one would feel no need to interpret him;

interpretation is necessary perhaps only in so far as one is passive, not creative, oneself.)

And I do not mean that *nothing* solid and enduring can be arrived at in interpretation: but to me it seems that there must be, as a matter of fact, in every effort of interpretation, some part which can be accepted and necessarily also some part which other readers can reject. I believe that there is a good deal in the interpretation of Shakespeare by Mr. Wilson Knight which can stand indefinitely for other people; and it would be a waste of time for me to pronounce judicially on the two elements in Mr. Knight's work. For that would be merely a re-interpretation of my own; and the reader will have to perform that operation for himself anyway. But I confess that reading his essays seems to me to have enlarged my understanding of the Shakespeare pattern; which, after all, is quite the main thing. It happened, fortunately for myself, that when I read some of his papers I was mulling over some of the later plays, particularly *Pericles*, *Cymbeline*, and *The Winter's Tale*; and reading the later plays for the first time in my life as a separate group, I was impressed by what seemed to me important and very serious recurrences of mood and theme. The old theory, current in my youth, of a Shakespeare altering and deteriorating his form and style to suit a new romantic taste, would not do; or if Shakespeare did this, then it became a remarkable coincidence that he should be able in middle life to turn about and give the public what it wanted—if these strange plays could conceivably be what any public would want— and at the same time remain steadfast in such integrity of exploration. And the mastery of language, I was sure, was quite undiminished.

To take Shakespeare's work as a whole, no longer to single out several plays as the greatest, and mark the others only as apprenticeship or decline—is I think an important and positive step in modern Shakespeare interpretation. More particularly, I think that Mr. Wilson Knight has shown insight in pursuing his search for the pattern below the level of 'plot' and 'character'. There are plots and there are characters: the question of 'sources' has its rights, and we must, if we go into the matter at all, inform ourselves

of the exact proportion of invention, borrowing, and adap-
tation in the plot; and so far as possible we must separate
the lines written by Shakespeare from those written by
collaborators, or taken over from an earlier hand or inter-
polated by a later. This sort of work must be done to pre-
pare for the search for the real pattern. But I think that
Mr. Knight, among other things, has insisted upon the right
way to interpret poetic drama. The writer of poetic drama
is not merely a man skilled in two arts and skilful to weave
them in together; he is not a writer who can decorate a
play with poetic language and metre. His task is different
from that of the 'dramatist' or that of the 'poet', for his
pattern is more complex and more dimensional; and with
the subtraction which I have noted above, that Dante's
pattern is the richer by a serious philosophy, and Shakespeare's the poorer by a rag-bag philosophy, I should say
that Shakespeare's pattern was more complex, and his
problem more difficult, than Dante's. The genuine poetic
drama must, at its best, observe all the regulations of the
plain drama, but will weave them *organically* (to mix a
metaphor and to borrow for the occasion a modern word)
into a much richer design. But our first duty as either
critics or 'interpreters', surely, must be to try to grasp the
whole design, and read *character* and *plot* in the understanding of this subterrene or submarine music. Here I say Mr.
Knight has pursued the right line for his own plane of
investigation, not hypostasizing 'character' and 'plot'. For
Shakespeare is one of the rarest of dramatic poets, in that
each of his characters is most nearly adequate both to the
requirements of the real world and to those of the poet's
world. If we can apprehend this balance in *Pericles*, we can
come to apprehend it even in Goneril and Regan. And here
Mr. Knight seems to me to be very helpful in expressing the
results of the passive, and more critical, poetic understanding.

My fear is, that both what I say in this prefatory way,
and what Mr. Wilson Knight has to say, may be misunderstood. It is a little irony that when a poet, like Dante,
sets out with a definite philosophy and a sincere determination to guide conduct, his philosophical and ethical pattern
is discounted, and our interpreters insist upon the pure

poetry which is to be disassociated from this reprehensible effort to do us good. And that when a poet like Shakespeare, who has no 'philosophy' and apparently no design upon the amelioration of our behaviour, sets forth his experience and reading of life, he is forthwith saddled with a 'philosophy' of his own and some esoteric hints towards conduct. So we kick against those who wish to guide us, and insist on being guided by those who only aim to show us a vision, a dream if you like, which is beyond good and evil in the common sense. It is all a question of our willingness to pursue any path to the end. For the very Catholic philosophy of Dante, with its stern judgement of morals, leads us to the same point beyond good and evil as the pattern of Shakespeare. Morality, we need to be told again and again, is not itself to be judged by moral standards: its laws are as 'natural' as any discovered by Einstein or Planck: which is expounded by, among others, Piccarda. Well: we must settle these problems for ourselves, provisionally, as well as we can.

Without pursuing that curious and obscure problem of the meaning of interpretation farther, it occurs to me as possible that there may be an essential part of error in all interpretation, without which it would not be interpretation at all: but this line of thought may be persevered in by students of *Appearance and Reality*. Another point, more immediately relevant, is that in a work of art, as truly as anywhere, reality only exists in and through appearances. I do not think that Mr. Wilson Knight himself, or Mr. Colin Still in his interesting book on *The Tempest* called *Shakespeare's Mystery Play*, has fallen into the error of presenting the work of Shakespeare as a series of mystical treatises in cryptogram, to be filed away once the cipher is read; poetry is poetry, and the surface is as marvellous as the core. A mystical treatise is at best a poor substitute for the original experience of its author; and a poem, or the life's work of a poet, is a very different document from that. The work of Shakespeare is like life itself something to be lived through. If we lived it completely we should need no interpretation; but on our plane of appearances our interpretations themselves are a part of our living.

T. S. ELIOT

1930

ON THE PRINCIPLES OF
SHAKESPEARE INTERPRETATION

THE following essays present an interpretation of
Shakespeare's work which may tend at first to confuse
and perhaps even repel the reader: therefore I here try to
clarify the points at issue. In this essay I outline what I
believe to be the main hindrances to a proper understanding
of Shakespeare; I also suggest the path which I think a
sound interpretation should pursue. My remarks are, however, to be read as a counsel of perfection. Yet, though I cannot claim to follow them throughout in practice, this preliminary discussion, in showing what I have been at pains to do
and to avoid, will serve to indicate the direction of my attempt.

At the start, I would draw a distinction between the
terms 'criticism' and 'interpretation'. It will be as well to
define, purely for my immediate purpose, my personal uses
of the words. 'Criticism' to me suggests a certain process
of deliberately objectifying the work under consideration;
the comparison of it with other similar works in order
especially to show in what respects it surpasses, or falls
short of, those works; the dividing its 'good' from its 'bad';
and, finally, a formal judgement as to its lasting validity.
'Interpretation', on the contrary, tends to merge into the
work it analyses; it attempts, as far as possible, to understand
its subject in the light of its own nature, employing external
reference, if at all, only as a preliminary to understanding;
it avoids discussion of merits, and, since its existence depends
entirely on its original acceptance of the validity of the
poetic unit which it claims, in some measure, to translate
into discursive reasoning, it can recognize no division of
'good' from 'bad'. Thus criticism is active and looks ahead,
often treating past work as material on which to base future
standards and canons of art; interpretation is passive, and
looks back, regarding only the imperative challenge of a
poetic vision. Criticism is a judgement of vision; interpretation a reconstruction of vision. In practice, it is probable

that neither can exist, or at least has yet on any comprehensive scale existed, quite divorced from the other. The greater part of poetic commentary pursues a middle course between criticism and interpretation. But sometimes work is created of so resplendent a quality, so massive a solidity of imagination, that adverse criticism beats against it idly as the wind that flings its ineffectual force against a mountain-rock. Any profitable commentary on such work must necessarily tend towards a pure interpretation.

The work of Shakespeare is of this transcendent order. Though much has already been written on it, only that profitably survives which in its total effect tends to interpretation rather than criticism. Coleridge, repelled by one of the horrors in *King Lear*, admitted that the author's judgement, being so consistently faultless, was here probably superior to his own: and he was right. That is the interpretative approach. Hazlitt and A. C. Bradley both developed that approach: their work is primarily interpretative. But to-day there is a strong tendency to 'criticize' Shakespeare, to select certain aspects of his mature works and point out faults. These faults are accounted for in various ways: it is said that Shakespeare, though a great genius, was yet a far from perfect artist; that certain elements were introduced solely to please a vulgar audience; or even, if the difficulty be extreme, that they are the work of another hand. Now it will generally be found that when a play is understood in its totality, these faults automatically vanish. For instance, Hamlet's slowness to avenge his father, the forgiveness of Angelo, Macbeth's vagueness of motive, Timon's universal hate—all these, which have continually baffled commentators, instead of projecting as ugly curiosities, will, when once we find the true focus demanded by the poet's work, appear not merely as relevant and even necessary, but as crucial, and themselves the very essence of the play concerned. It is, then, a matter of correct focal length; nor is it the poet's fault if our focus is wrong. For our imaginative focus is generally right enough. In reading, watching, or acting Shakespeare for pure enjoyment we accept everything. But when we think 'critically' we see faults which are not implicit in the play nor our enjoyment of it, but merely figments of our own minds. We should not, in fact, think critically at all: we should interpret our original imaginative experience into the slower consciousness of logic and intellect, preserving something of that child-like faith which we possess, or should possess, in the theatre. It is exactly this translation from one order of consciousness to another that interpretation claims to perform. Uncritically, and passively, it receives the whole of the poet's vision; it then proceeds to re-express this experience in its own terms.

To receive this whole Shakespearian vision within the intellectual consciousness demands a certain and very definite act of mind. One must be prepared to see the whole play in space as well as in time. It is natural in analysis to pursue the steps of the tale in sequence, noticing the logic that connects them, regarding those essentials that Aristotle noted: beginning, middle, and end. And yet by giving supreme attention to this temporal nature of drama we omit what, in Shakespeare, is at least of equivalent importance. A Shakespearian tragedy is set spatially as well as temporally in the mind. By this I mean that there are throughout the play a set of correspondences which relate to each other independently of the time-sequence which is the story: such are the intuition-intelligence opposition active within and across *Troilus and Cressida*, the death-theme in *Hamlet*, the nightmare evil of *Macbeth*. This I have sometimes called the play's 'atmosphere'. In interpretation of *Othello* it has to take the form of an essential relation, abstracted from the story, existing between the Othello, Desdemona, and Iago conceptions. Generally, however, there is unity, not diversity. Perhaps it is what Aristotle meant by 'unity of idea'. Now if we are prepared to see the whole play laid out, so to speak, as an area, being simultaneously aware of these thickly-scattered correspondences in a single view of the whole, we possess the unique quality of the play in a new sense. 'Faults' begin to vanish into thin air. Immediately we begin to realize necessity where before we saw irrelevance and beauty dethroning ugliness. For the Shakespearian person is intimately fused with this atmospheric quality; he obeys a spatial as well as a temporal necessity. Gloucester's mock-suicide, Malcolm's detailed confession of crimes,

Ulysses' long speech on order, are cases in point. But because we, in our own lives and those of our friends, see events most strongly as a time-sequence—thereby blurring our vision of other significances—we next, quite arbitrarily and unjustly, abstract from the Shakespearian drama that element which the intellect most easily assimilates; and, finding it not to correspond with our own life as we see it, begin to observe 'faults'. This, however, is apparent only after we try to rationalize our impressions; what I have called the 'spatial' approach is implicit in our imaginative pleasure to a greater or a less degree always. It is, probably, the ability to see larger and still larger areas of a great work spatially with a continual widening of vision that causes us to appreciate it more deeply, to own it with our minds more surely, on every reading; whereas at first, knowing it only as a story, much of it may have seemed sterile, and much of it irrelevant. A vivid analogy to this Shakespearian quality is provided by a fine modern play, *Journey's End*. Everything in the play gains tremendous significance from war. The story, which is slight, moves across a stationary background: if we forget that background for one instant parts of the dialogue fall limp; remember it, and the most ordinary remark is tense, poignant—often of shattering power. To study *Measure for Measure* or *Macbeth* without reference to their especial 'atmospheres' is rather like forgetting the war as we read or witness *Journey's End*; or the cherry orchard in Tchehov's famous play. There is, however, a difference. In *Journey's End* the two elements, the dynamic and static, action and background, are each firmly actualized and separated except in so far as Stanhope, rather like Hamlet, bridges the two. In *The Cherry Orchard* there is the same division. But with Shakespeare a purely spiritual atmosphere interpenetrates the action, there is a fusing rather than a contrast; and where a direct personal symbol growing out of the dominating atmosphere is actualized, it may be a supernatural being, as the Ghost, symbol of the death-theme in *Hamlet*, or the Weird Sisters, symbols of the evil in *Macbeth*.

Since in Shakespeare there is this close fusion of the temporal, that is, the plot-chain of event following event, with the spatial, that is, the omnipresent and mysterious reality brooding motionless over and within the play's movement, it is evident that my two principles thus firmly divided in analysis are no more than provisional abstractions from the whole. However, since to make the first abstraction with especial crudity, that is, to analyse the sequence of events, the 'causes' linking dramatic motive to action and action to result in time, is a blunder instinctive to the human intellect, I make no apology for restoring balance by insistence on the other. My emphasis is justified, in that it will be seen to clarify many difficulties. It throws neglected beauties into strong relief, and often resolves the whole play with a sudden revelation. For example, the ardour of Troilus in battle against the Greeks at the close of *Troilus and Cressida*, Mariana's lovely prayer for Angelo's life, the birth of love in Edmund at the close of *King Lear*, and the stately theme of Alcibiades' revenge in *Timon of Athens*—all these cannot be properly understood without a clear knowledge of the general themes which vitalize the action of those plays.

These dual elements seem perfectly harmonized in *Troilus and Cressida*, *Measure for Measure*, *Macbeth*, and *King Lear*. In *Hamlet* the spatial element is mainly confined to the theme of Hamlet and the Ghost, both sharply contrasted with their environment: thus the play offers a less unified statement as a whole, and interpretation is rendered difficult and not wholly satisfactory. With *Othello*, too, there is difficulty. Unless the play is to be considered as purely a sequence of events, if we are to find a spatial reality, we must view the qualities of the three chief persons together and in their essential relation to each other expect to find the core of the metaphysical significance: for the primary fact of the play is not, as in *Macbeth* and *King Lear*, a blending, but rather a differentiating, a demarcation, and separation, of essence from essence. In *Timon of Athens* both elements appear, but the temporal predominates in that the imaginative atmosphere itself changes with the play's progress: which fact here seems to reflect the peculiar clarity and conscious mastery of the poet's mind. With the poet, as with the reader, the time-sequence will be uppermost in consciousness, the pervading atmosphere or static background tending to be unconsciously apprehended or created, a half-realized significance, a vague all-inclusive deity of the dramatic universe. In respect of this atmospheric suggestion we find a sense of mystery in *King Lear* which cannot be found in *Othello*; and, in so far as the Shakespearian play lacks mystery, it seems, as a rule, to lack profundity. But in *Timon of Athens* the mystery of *King Lear* is, as it were, mastered, and yet re-expressed with the clarity of *Othello*. Here the poet explicates the atmospheric quality of former plays in a philosophic tragedy whose dominant temporal quality thus mirrors the clarity, in no sense the sterility, of the poet's vision. The spatial, that is, the spiritual, quality uses the temporal, that is, the story, lending it dominance in order to express itself the more clearly: *Timon of Athens* is essentially an allegory or parable. My suggestion as to the poet's 'consciousness' must, however, be considered as either pure hazard or useful metaphor, illuminating the play's nature and perhaps hitting the truth of Shakespeare's mind in composition. Certainly Hazlitt thought that in *Timon of Athens* the poet was of all his plays the most 'in earnest'. Elsewhere I am not concerned with the poet's 'consciousness', or his 'intentions'. Nor need the question arise; but, since a strong feeling exists that no subtlety or profundity can be born from a mind itself partly unconscious of such things, and since Shakespeare's life appears not to have been mainly concerned with transcendental realities—except in that he was born, loved, was ambitious, and died—it will be as well to refer briefly to the matter of 'intentions'. This I shall do next, and will afterwards deal with two other critical concepts which, with 'intentions', have helped to work chaos with our understanding of poetry.

There is a maxim that a work of art should be criticized according to the artist's 'intentions': than which no maxim could be more false. The intentions of the artist are but clouded forms which, if he attempt to crystallize them in consciousness, may prefigure a quite different reality from that which eventually emerges in his work,

> not answering the aim
> And that unbodied figure of the thought
> That gave't surmised shape.

In those soliloquies where Brutus and Macbeth try to clarify their own motives into clean-cut concepts, we may see good examples of the irrelevance born by 'intentions' to the instinctive power which is bearing the man towards his fate: it is the same with the poet. Milton's puritanical 'intentions' bear little relevance to his Satan. 'Intentions' belong to the plane of intellect and memory: the swifter consciousness that awakens in poetic composition touches subtleties and heights and depths unknowable by intellect and intractable to memory. That consciousness we can enjoy at will when we submit ourselves with utmost passivity to the poet's work; but when the intellectual mode returns it often brings with it a troop of concepts irrelevant to the nature of the work it thinks to analyse, and, with its army of 'intentions', 'causes', 'sources', and 'characters', and its essentially ethical outlook, works havoc with our minds, since it is trying to impose on the vivid reality of art a logic totally alien to its nature. In interpretation we must remember not the facts but the quality of the original poetic experience; and, in translating this into whatever concepts appear suitable, we find that the facts too fall into place automatically when once the qualitative focus is correct. Reference to the artist's 'intentions' is usually a sign that the commentator—in so far as he is a commentator rather than a biographer—has lost touch with the essentials of the poetic work. He is thinking in terms of the time-sequence and causality, instead of allowing his mind to be purely receptive. It will be clear, then, that the following essays say nothing new as to Shakespeare's 'intentions'; attempt to shed no light directly on Shakespeare the man; but claim rather to illuminate our own poetic experiences enjoyed whilst reading, or watching, the plays. In this sense, they are concerned only with realities, since they claim to interpret what is generally admitted to exist: the supreme quality of Shakespeare's work.

Next as to 'sources'. This concept is closely involved with that of 'intentions'. Both try to explain art in terms of causality, the most natural implement of intellect. Both fail empirically to explain any essential whatsoever. There is, clearly, a relation between Shakespeare's plays and the work of Plutarch, Holinshed, Vergil, Ovid, and the Bible; but not one of these, nor any number of them, can be considered a cause of Shakespeare's poetry and therefore the word 'source', that is, the origin whence the poetic reality flows, is a false metaphor. In Shakespeare's best known passage of aesthetic philosophy we hear that the poet's eye glances 'from heaven to earth, from earth to heaven', and that the poet's pen turns to 'shapes' the 'forms of things unknown'. It 'gives to airy nothing a local habitation and a name'. That is, the source of poetry is rooted in the otherness of mental or spiritual realities; these, however, are a 'nothing' until mated with earthly shapes. Creation is thus born of a union between 'earth' and 'heaven', the material and the spiritual. Without 'shapes' the poet is speechless; he needs words, puppets of the drama, tales. But the unknown 'forms' come first. In another profound but less known passage (*Richard II*, v. v. 6) we hear that in creation the brain is 'the female to the soul'. The spiritual then is the masculine, the material the feminine, agent in creation. The 'source' of *Antony and Cleopatra*, if we must indeed have a 'source' at all, is the transcendent erotic imagination of the poet which finds its worthy bride in an old world romance. It seems, moreover, that a great poet must, if he is to forgo nothing of concreteness and humanity, lose himself in contemplation of an actual tale or an actual event in order to find himself in supreme vision; otherwise he will tend to philosophy, to the divine element unmated to the earthly. Therefore 'sources', as usually understood, have their use for the poet: they have little value for the interpreter. The tale of Cleopatra married to a Hardy's imagination would have given birth to a novel very different from Shakespeare's play: the final poetic result is always a mystery. That result, and not vague hazards as to its 'source', must be the primary object of our attention. It should further be observed that, although the purely 'temporal' element of Shakespearian drama may sometimes bear a close relation to a tale probably known by Shakespeare, what I have called the 'spatial' reality is ever the unique child of his mind; therefore interpretation, concerned, as in the following essays, so largely with that reality, is clearly working outside and beyond the story alone. Now, whereas the spatial quality of these greater plays is different in each, they nearly all turn on the same plot. It is therefore reasonable to conclude that the poet has chosen a series of tales to whose life-rhythm he is spontaneously attracted, and has developed them in each instance according to his vision.

And finally, as to 'character'. In the following essays the term is refused, since it is so constantly entwined with a false and unduly ethical criticism. So often we hear that 'in *Timon of Athens* it was Shakespeare's intention to show how a generous but weak character may come to ruin through an unwise use of his wealth'; that 'Shakespeare wished in *Macbeth* to show how crime inevitably brings retribution'; that, 'in *Antony and Cleopatra* Shakespeare has given us a lesson concerning the dangers of an uncontrolled passion'. These are purely imaginary examples, coloured for my purpose, to indicate the type of ethical criticism to which I refer. It continually brings in the intention-concept, which our moral-philosophy, rightly or wrongly, involves. Hence, too, the constant and fruitless search for 'motives' sufficient to account for Macbeth's and Iago's actions: since the moral critic feels he cannot blame a 'character' until he understands his 'intentions', and without the opportunity of praising and blaming he is dumb. It is not, clearly, possible to avoid ethical considerations; nor is it desirable. Where one person within the drama is immediately apparent as morally good and another as bad, we will note the difference: but we should follow our dramatic intuitions. A person in the drama may act in such a way that we are in no sense antagonized but are aware of beauty and supreme interest only; yet the analogy to that same action may well be intolerable to us in actual life. When such a divergence occurs the commentator must be true to his artistic, not his normal, ethic. Large quantities of Shakespeare criticism have wrecked themselves on the teeth of this dualism. In so far as moral values enter into our appreciation of the poetic work, they will tend to be instinctive to us: Shakespeare here, as in his other symbols, speaks our own language. I mean, it is as natural to us to like Cordelia better than Goneril with a liking which may be said to depend partly on moral values as it is for us to recognize the power of Shakespeare's tempest-symbol as suggesting human tragedy, or his use of jewel-metaphors to embody the costly riches of love. In ages hence, when perhaps tempests are controlled by science and communism has replaced wealth, then the point of Shakespeare's symbolism may need explanation; and then it may, from a new ethical view-point, be necessary to analyse at length the moral values implicit in the Cordelia and Edmund conceptions. But in these matters Shakespeare speaks almost the same language as we, and ethical terms, though they must frequently occur in interpretation, must only be allowed in so far as they are used in absolute obedience to the dramatic and aesthetic significance: in which case they cease to be ethical in the usual sense.

This false criticism is implied by the very use of the word 'character'. It is impossible to use the term without any tinge of a morality which blurs vision. The term, which in ordinary speech often denotes the degree of moral control exercised by the individual over his instinctive passions, is altogether unsuited to those persons of poetic drama whose life consists largely of passion unveiled. *Macbeth* and *King Lear* are created in a soul-dimension of primal feeling, of which in real life we may be only partly conscious or may be urged to control by a sense of right and wrong. In fact, it may well seem that the more we tend away from the passionate and curbless life of poetic drama, the stronger we shall be as 'characters'. And yet, in reading *Macbeth* or *King Lear* we are aware of strength, not weakness. We are not aware of failure: rather we 'let determined things to destiny hold unbewailed their way'. We must observe, then, this paradox: the strong protagonist of poetic drama would probably appear a weakling if he were a real man; and, indeed, the critic who notes primarily Macbeth's weakness is criticizing him as a man rather than a dramatic person. Ethics are essentially critical when applied to life; but if they hold any place at all in art, they will need to be modified into a new artistic ethic which obeys the peculiar nature of art as surely as a sound morality is based on the nature of man. From a true interpretation centred on the imaginative qualities of Shakespeare, certain facts will certainly emerge which bear relevance to human life, to human morals: but interpretation must come first. And interpretation must be metaphysical rather than ethical. We shall gain nothing by applying to the delicate symbols of the poet's imagination the rough machinery of an ethical philosophy created to control the turbulences of actual life. Thus when a critic adopts the ethical attitude, we shall generally find that he is unconsciously lifting the object of his attention from his setting and regarding him as actually alive. By noting 'faults' in Timon's 'character' we are in effect saying that he would not be a success in real life: which is beside the point, since he, and Macbeth, and Lear, are evidently dramatic successes. Now, whereas the moral attitude to life is positive and dynamic and tells us what we ought to do, that attitude applied to literature is invariably negative and destructive. It is continually thrusting on our attention a number of 'failures', 'mistakes', and 'follies' in connexion with those dramatic persons from whom we have consistently derived delight and a sense of exultation. Even when terms of negation, such as 'evil', necessarily appear—as with *Hamlet* and *Macbeth*—we should so employ them that the essence they express is felt to be something powerful, autonomous, and grand. Our reaction to great literature is a positive and dynamic experience. Crudely, sometimes ineffectually, interpretation will attempt to translate that experience in a spirit also positive and dynamic.

To do this we should regard each play as a visionary whole, close-knit in personification, atmospheric suggestion, and direct poetic-symbolism: three modes of transmission, equal in their importance. Too often the first of these alone receives attention: whereas, in truth, we should not be content even with all three, however clearly we have them in our minds, unless we can work back through them to the original vision they express. Each incident, each turn of thought, each suggestive symbol throughout *Macbeth* or *King Lear* radiates inwards from the play's circumference to the burning central core without knowledge of which we shall miss their relevance and necessity: they relate primarily, not directly to each other, nor to the normal appearances of human life, but to this central reality alone. The persons of

Shakespeare have been analysed carefully in point of psychological realism, yet in giving so detailed and prolix a care to any one element of the poet's expression, the commentator, starting indeed from a point on the circumference, instead of working into the heart of the play, pursues a tangential course, riding, as it were, on his own life-experiences farther and farther from his proper goal. Such is the criticism that finds fault with the Duke's decisions at the close of *Measure for Measure*: if we are to understand the persons of Shakespeare we should consider always what they do rather than what they might have done. Each person, event, scene, is integral to the poetic statement: the removing, or blurring, of a single stone in the mosaic will clearly lessen our chance of visualizing the whole design.

Too often the commentator discusses Shakespeare's work without the requisite emotional sympathy and agility of intellect. Then the process of false criticism sets in: whatever elements lend themselves most readily to analysis on the analogy of actual life, these he selects, roots out, distorting their natural growth; he then praises or blames according to their measure of correspondence with his own life-experiences, and, creating the plaster figures of 'character', searches everywhere for 'causes' on the analogy of human affairs, noting that Iago has no sufficient reason for his villainy, executing some strange transference such as the statement that Lady Macbeth would have done this or that in Cordelia's position; observing that there appears to have been dull weather on the occasion of Duncan's murder. But what he will not do is recapture for analysis his own original experience, concerned, as it was, purely with a dramatic and artistic reality: with Iago the person of motiveless and instinctive villainy, with Cordelia known only with reference to the *Lear* universe, with the vivid extravagant symbolism of abnormal phenomena in beast and element and the sun's eclipse which accompanies the unnatural act of murder. These, the true, the poetic, realities, the commentator too often passes over. He does not look straight at the work he would interpret, is not true to his own imaginative reaction. My complaint is, not that such a commentator cannot appreciate the imaginative nature of Shakespeare—that would be absurd and unjustifiable—but that he falsifies his own experience when he begins to criticize. Part of the play —and that the less important element of story—he tears out ruthlessly for detailed analysis on the analogy of human life: with a word or two about 'the magic of poetry' or 'the breath of genius' he dismisses the rest. Hence the rich gems of Shakespeare's poetic symbolism have been left untouched and unwanted, whilst Hamlet was being treated in Harley Street. Hence arises the criticism discovering faults in Shakespeare. But when a right interpretation is offered it will generally be seen that both the fault and the criticism which discovered it are without meaning. The older critics drove psychological analysis to unnecessary lengths: the new school of 'realistic' criticism, in finding faults and explaining them with regard to Shakespeare's purely practical and financial 'intentions', is thus in reality following the wrong vision of its predecessors. Both together trace the process of my imaginary critic, who, thinking to have found an extreme degree of realism in one place, ends by complaining that he finds too little in another. Neither touch the heart of the Shakespearian play.

Nor will a sound knowledge of the stage and the especial theatrical technique of Shakespeare's work render up its imaginative secret. True, the plays were written as plays, and meant to be acted. But that tells us nothing relevant to our purpose. It explains why certain things cannot be found in Shakespeare: it does not explain why the finest things, the fascination of *Hamlet*, the rich music of *Othello*, the gripping evil of *Macbeth*, the pathos of *King Lear*, and the gigantic architecture of *Timon of Athens* came to birth. Shakespeare wrote in terms of drama, as he wrote in English. In the grammar of dramatic structure he expresses his vision: without that, or some other, structure he could not have expressed himself. But the dramatic nature of a play's origin cannot be adduced to disprove a quality implicit in the work itself. True, when there are any faults to be explained, this particular pursuit and aim of Shakespeare's poetry may well be noted to account for their presence. Interpretation, however, tends to resolve all but minor difficulties in connexion with the greater plays:

therefore it is not necessary in the following essays to remember, or comment on, the dramatic structure of their expression, though from another point of view such comment and analysis may well be interesting. It illuminates one facet of their surface: but a true philosophic and imaginative interpretation will aim at cutting below the surface to reveal that burning core of mental or spiritual reality from which each play derives its nature and meaning.

The soul-life of a Shakespearian play is an enduring power of divine worth. Its perennial fire is as mysterious, as near and yet as far, as that of the sun, and, like the sun, it burns on while generations pass. If interpretation attempts to split the original beam into different colours for inspection and analysis it does not claim, any more than will the scientist, that its spectroscope reveals the whole reality of its attention. It discovers something: exactly what it discovers, and whether that discovery be of ultimate value, cannot easily be demonstrated. But, though we know the sun better in the spring fields than in the laboratory, yet we might remember that the spectroscope discovered Helium first in the solar ray, which chemical was after sought and found on earth. So, too, the interpretation of poetic vision may have its use. And if it seems sometimes to bear little relevance to its original, if its mechanical joints creak and its philosophy lumber clumsily in attempt to follow the swift arrow-flight of poetry, it is, at least, no less rational a pursuit than that of the mathematician who writes a rhythmic curve in the stiff symbols of an algebraic equation.

I shall now shortly formulate what I take to be the main principles of right Shakespearian interpretation:

(i) Before noticing the presence of faults we should first regard each play as a visionary unit bound to obey none but its own self-imposed laws. To do this we should attempt to preserve absolute truth to our own imaginative reaction, whithersoever it may lead us in the way of paradox and unreason. We should at all costs avoid selecting what is easy to understand and forgetting the superlogical.

(ii) We should thus be prepared to recognize what I have called the 'temporal' and the 'spatial' elements: that is, to relate any given incident or speech either to the time-sequence of story or the peculiar atmosphere, intellectual or imaginative, which binds the play. Being aware of this new element we should not look for perfect verisimilitude to life, but rather see each play as an expanded metaphor, by means of which the òriginal vision has been projected into forms roughly correspondent with actuality, conforming thereto with greater or less exactitude according to the demands of its own nature. It will then usually appear that many difficult actions and events become coherent and, within the scope of their universe, natural.

(iii) We should analyse the use and meaning of direct poetic symbolism—that is, events whose significance can hardly be related to the normal processes of actual life. Also the minor symbolic imagery of Shakespeare, which is extremely consistent, should receive careful attention. Where certain images continually recur in the same associative connexion, we can, if we have reason to believe that this associative force is strong enough, be ready to see the presence of the associative value when the images occur alone. Nor should we neglect the symbolic value of aural effects such as the discharge of cannon in *Hamlet* and *Othello* or the sound of trumpets in *Measure for Measure* and *King Lear*.

(iv) The plays from *Julius Caesar* (about 1599) to *The Tempest* (about 1611) when properly understood fall into a significant sequence. This I have called 'the Shakespeare Progress'. Therefore in detailed analysis of any one play it may sometimes be helpful to have regard to its place in the sequence, provided always that thought of this sequence be used to illuminate, and in no sense be allowed to distort, the view of the play under analysis. Particular notice should be given to what I have called the 'hate-theme', which is turbulent throughout most of these plays: an especial mode of cynicism toward love, disgust at the physical body, and dismay at the thought of death; a revulsion from human life caused by a clear sight of its limitations—more especially limitations imposed by time. This progress I have outlined in *Myth and Miracle*, being concerned there especially with the Final Plays. The following essays are ordered according to the probable place in the Shakespeare Progress of the plays concerned. The order is that given by the late Professor

Henry Norman Hudson in *The New Hudson Shakespeare*. Though I here compare one theme in *Julius Caesar* with *Macbeth*, I postpone a comprehensive analysis of the play, since its peculiar quality relates it more directly to the later tragedies than to those noticed in this treatment.

These arguments I have pursued at some length, since my interpretation reaches certain conclusions which may seem somewhat revolutionary. Especially will this be apparent in my reading of the Final Plays as mystical representations of a mystic vision. A first sketch of this reading I have already published in *Myth and Miracle*. Since the publication of my essay, my attention has been drawn to Mr. Colin Still's remarkable book *Shakespeare's Mystery Play: A Study of The Tempest* (Cecil Palmer, 1921). Mr. Still's interpretation of *The Tempest* is very similar to mine. His conclusions were reached by a detailed comparison of the play in its totality with other creations of literature, myth, and ritual throughout the ages; mine are reached solely through seeing *The Tempest* as the conclusion to the Shakespeare Progress. *The Tempest* is thus exactly located as a work of mystic insight with reference to the cross-axes of universal and Shakespearian vision. It would seem, therefore, that my method of interpretation as outlined in this essay has already met with some degree of empirical proof.

In conclusion, I would emphasize that I here lay down certain principles and make certain objections for my immediate purpose only. I would not be thought to level complaint against the value of 'criticism' in general. My private and personal distinction between 'criticism' and 'interpretation' aims at no universal validity. It can hardly be absolute. No doubt I have narrowed the term 'criticism' unjustly. Much of the critical work of to-day is, according to my distinction, work of a high interpretative order. Nor do I suggest that true 'criticism' in the narrow sense I apply to it is of any lesser order than true interpretation: it may well be a higher pursuit, since it is, in a sense, the more creative and endures a greater burden of responsibility. The relative value of the two modes must vary in exact proportion to the greatness of the literature they analyse: that is why I believe the most profitable approach to Shakespeare to be interpretation rather than criticism.

II

THE EMBASSY OF DEATH:
AN ESSAY ON *HAMLET*

I

IN this first section I shall indicate the nature of Hamlet's mental suffering. It will then be clear that many of the scenes and incidents which have proved difficult in the past may be considered as expressions of that unique mental or spiritual experience of the hero which is at the heart of the play. In thus isolating this element for analysis I shall attempt to simplify at least one theme—and that the most important one—in a play baffling and difficult in its totality. My purpose will therefore be first limited strictly to a discussion, not of the play as a whole, nor even of Hamlet's mind as a whole, but of this central reality of pain, which, though it be necessarily related, either as effect or cause, to the events of the plot and to the other persons, is itself ultimate, and should be the primary object of our search.

Our attention is early drawn to the figure of Hamlet. Alone in the gay glitter of the court, silhouetted against brilliance, robustness, health, and happiness, is the pale, black-robed Hamlet, mourning. When first we meet him, his words point the essential inwardness of his suffering:

> But I have that within which passeth show;
> These but the trappings and the suits of woe.   (i. ii. 85)

When he is alone he reveals his misery more clearly:

> O, that this too too solid flesh would melt,
> Thaw and resolve itself into a dew!
> Or that the Everlasting had not fix'd
> His canon 'gainst self-slaughter! O God! O God!
> How weary, stale, flat, and unprofitable
> Seem to me all the uses of this world!
> Fie on't! ah fie! 'tis an unweeded garden,
> That grows to seed; things rank and gross in nature
> Possess it merely.   (i. ii. 129)

17

The mood expressed by these lines is patent. To Hamlet
the light has been extinguished from the things of earth.
He has lost all sense of purpose. We already know one
reason for Hamlet's state: his father's death. Claudius
and his mother have already urged him to

> throw to earth
> This unprevailing woe . . .   (1. ii. 106)

Now, during Hamlet's soliloquy, we see another reason:
disgust at his mother's second marriage:

> . . . within a month:
> Ere yet the salt of most unrighteous tears
> Had left the flushing in her galled eyes,
> She married. O, most wicked speed, to post
> With such dexterity to incestuous sheets!   (1. ii. 153)

These two concrete embodiments of Hamlet's misery are
closely related. He suffers from misery at his father's
death and agony at his mother's quick forgetfulness: such
callousness is infidelity, and so impurity, and, since Claudius
is the brother of the King, incest. It is reasonable to
suppose that Hamlet's state of mind, if not wholly caused
by these events, is at least definitely related to them. Of
his two loved parents, one has been taken for ever by
death, the other dishonoured for ever by her act of
marriage. To Hamlet the world is now an 'unweeded
garden'.

Hamlet hears of his father's Ghost, sees it, and speaks
to it. His original pain is intensified by knowledge of the
unrestful spirit, by the terrible secrets of death hinted by
the Ghost's words:

> I could a tale unfold whose lightest word
> Would harrow up thy soul, freeze thy young blood . . .
>   (1. v. 15)

This is added to Hamlet's sense of loss: this knowledge of
the father he loved suffering in death:

> Doom'd for a certain term to walk the night,
> And for the day confin'd to fast in fires . . .   (1. v. 10)

Nor is this all. He next learns that his father's murderer
now wears the crown, is married to his faithless mother.

Both elements in his original pain are thus horribly intensified. His hope of recovery to the normal state of healthy mental life depended largely on his ability to forget his father, to forgive his mother. Claudius advised him well. Now his mother's honour is more foully smirched than ever; and the living cause and symbol of his father's death is firmly placed on Denmark's throne. Forgetfulness is impossible, forgetfulness that might have brought peace. The irony of the Ghost's parting word is terrible:

> Adieu, adieu! Hamlet, remember me.   (I. v. 91)

If the spirit had been kind, it would have prayed that Hamlet might forget. This is the Ghost's last injunction, the one most indelibly printed in Hamlet's mind:

> Remember thee!
> Ay, thou poor ghost, while memory hold a seat
> In this distracted globe. Remember thee!
> Yea, from the table of my memory
> I'll wipe away all trivial fond records . . .   (I. v. 95)

Confronted by his irrevocable fate Hamlet repeats the words:

> Now to my word,
> It is 'Adieu, Adieu! remember me.'
> I have sworn 't.   (I. v. 110)

And he keeps his oath throughout the play.

When Horatio and Marcellus join him he relieves the unnatural tension of his mind by joking and laughter. As in *King Lear*, extreme mental agony tends towards expression in the region of the essentially comic. He makes his friends swear secrecy, thereby ensuring his future loneliness in the knowledge of the King's crime. He suggests that he may 'put an antic disposition on' (I. v. 172) to deceive the court. He cries out against the cruel fate that has laid on him, whose own soul is in chaos, the command of righting the evil in the state:

> O cursed spite,
> That ever I was born to set it right!   (I. v. 188)

Hamlet, when we first meet him, has lost all sense of life's significance. To a man bereft of the sense of purpose there is no possibility of creative action, it has no meaning.

No act but suicide is rational. Yet to Hamlet comes the command of a great act—revenge: therein lies the unique quality of the play—a sick soul is commanded to heal, to cleanse, to create harmony. But good cannot come of evil: it is seen that the sickness of his soul only further infects the state—his disintegration spreads out, disintegrating.

Hamlet's soul is sick to death—and yet there was one thing left that might have saved him. In the deserts of his mind, void with the utter vacuity of the knowledge of death —death of his father, death of his mother's faith—was yet one flower, his love of Ophelia.

> He hath, my lord, of late made many tenders
> Of his affection to me.   (1. iii. 99)

So speaks Ophelia to Polonius. Again:

> *Ophelia.* My lord, he hath importun'd me with love
>   In honourable fashion.
> *Polonius.* Ay, fashion you may call it; go to, go to.
> *Ophelia.* And hath given countenance to his speech, my lord,
>   With almost all the holy vows of Heaven.   (1. iii. 110)

This was before Hamlet saw the Ghost: perhaps before his father's death. Now there is one supreme enemy to the demon of neurotic despair, its antithesis and bright antagonist: romantic love. For this has assured power, it can recreate the sense of purpose, it inspires to heroism and action. And it is self-creative. The lonely flower can soon overspread the desert with a multiplicity of colour and delight. The love of Ophelia is thus Hamlet's last hope. This, too, is taken from him. Her repelling of his letters and refusing to see him, in obedience to Polonius' command, synchronizes unmercifully with the terrible burden of knowledge laid on Hamlet by the revelation of the Ghost. The result is given to us indirectly—but with excruciating vividness:

> *Ophelia.* My lord, as I was sewing in my closet,
>   Lord Hamlet, with his doublet all unbrac'd;
>   No hat upon his head; his stockings foul'd,
>   Ungarter'd, and down-gyved to his ankle;
>   Pale as his shirt; his knees knocking each other;
>   And with a look so piteous in purport
>   As if he had been loosed out of Hell
>   To speak of horrors—he comes before me.   (11. i. 77)

This is no mock-madness. To see it as such is to miss the power of the central theme of the play. Hamlet would not first try the practical joke of pretended madness on Ophelia whom he loved. That pallor was clearly no cosmetic. Hamlet was in truth 'loosed out of Hell to speak of horrors': on top of the Ghost's revelation has come Ophelia's unreasonable repulsion of that his last contact with life, his love for her. Therefore

> He took me by the wrist and held me hard;
> Then goes he to the length of all his arm;
> And, with his other hand thus o'er his brow,
> He falls to such perusal of my face
> As he would draw it. Long stay'd he so;
> At last, a little shaking of mine arm,
> And thrice his head thus waving up and down,
> He raised a sigh so piteous and profound
> As it did seem to shatter all his bulk
> And end his being . . .   (ii. i. 87)

From henceforth he must walk alone within the prison of mental death. There is surely no more pitiful thing in literature than this description. Polonius sees the truth. 'This is the very ecstasy of love . . .' he says. And he is right. If we remember that Hamlet loves Ophelia; that he has just seen his father's ghost; and that now Ophelia has refused to admit him—we need search no further for an explanation of Hamlet's behaviour. The suggestion that in these circumstances, at this moment in his history, he has the presence of mind to pretend madness to Ophelia is a perversion of commentary.

It is, however, certain that Hamlet does simulate madness before the court, and the King and Queen are both rightly unwilling to relate this madness to Hamlet's love of Ophelia. Says the Queen, when she hears that Polonius thinks he has traced the true cause:

> I doubt it is no other but the main;
> His father's death, and our o'erhasty marriage.
>
>   (ii. ii. 56)

The King later decides that love is not the cause of Hamlet's trouble:

> Love! his affections do not that way tend.   (iii. i. 171)

This is after Hamlet's meeting with Ophelia. Here the King is partly wrong, and again there is truth in Polonius' words:

> ... but yet do I believe
> The origin and commencement of his grief
> Sprung from neglected love ...   (III. i. 185)

It is not the whole truth. Hamlet's pain is a complex of different themes of grief. But absolute loss of control is apparent only in his dealings with Ophelia. Three times after the Ghost scene he utterly loses mental control: first, in the incident narrated by Ophelia; second, in his meeting with her in III. i.; and third, in the Graveyard scene, with Laertes over Ophelia's body. On all other occasions his abnormal behaviour, though it certainly tends towards, and might even be called, madness in relation to his environment, is yet rather the abnormality of extreme melancholia and cynicism.

Throughout the middle scenes of the play we become more closely acquainted with Hamlet's peculiar disease. He is bitterly cynical:

> ... to be honest, as this world goes, is to be one man picked out of ten thousand.   (II. ii. 179)

And

> Use every man after his desert, and who should 'scape whipping?   (II. ii. 561)

To Hamlet the world is a 'goodly' prison

> in which there are many confines, wards, and dungeons, Denmark being one o' the worst.   (II. ii. 255)

His mind is drawn to images in themselves repellent, and he dwells on the thought of foulness as the basis of life:

> For if the sun breed maggots in a dead dog ...   (II. ii. 183)

Hamlet reads, or says he is reading, a satirical book, which observes that

> ... old men have grey beards, that their faces are wrinkled, their eyes purging thick amber and plum-tree gum, and that they have a plentiful lack of wit, together with most weak hams.   (II. ii. 202)

The body of an old man is shown as something stupid, unpleasant: and Hamlet means it. Now all this is integral to Hamlet's state of mind. He is well described in a passage by William James in another connexion:

> ... you see how the entire consciousness of the poor man is so choked with the feeling of evil that the sense of there being any good in the world is lost for him altogether. His attention excludes it, cannot admit it: the sun has left his heaven.
>
> (*The Varieties of Religious Experience*, p. 149)

Hamlet's soul is sick. The symptoms are, horror at the fact of death and an equal detestation of life, a sense of uncleanliness and evil in the things of nature; a disgust at the physical body of man; bitterness, cynicism, hate. It tends towards insanity. All these elements are insistent in Hamlet. He can describe the glories of heaven and earth—but for him those glories are gone. And he knows not why. The disease is deeper than his loss of Ophelia, deeper than his mother's sexual impurity and his father's death. These are, like his mourning dress, the 'trappings and the suits of woe'. They are the outward symbols of it, the 'causes' of it: but the thing itself is ultimate, beyond causality. That is why the theme is here related to the supernatural, to the Ghost. He describes it thus:

> I have of late—but wherefore I know not—lost all my mirth, forgone all custom of exercises; and indeed it goes so heavily with my disposition that this goodly frame, the earth, seems to me a sterile promontory; this most excellent canopy, the air, look you, this brave o'erhanging firmament, this majestical roof fretted with golden fire, why, it appears no other thing to me than a foul and pestilent congregation of vapours.   (II. ii. 313)

It will be clear that Hamlet's outstanding peculiarity in the action of this play may be regarded as a symptom of this sickness in his soul. He does not avenge his father's death, not because he dare not, not because he hates the thought of bloodshed, but because his 'wit's diseased' (III. ii. 341); his will is snapped and useless, like a broken leg. Nothing is worth while. After the player has worked himself into a tragic passion in the recitation of 'Aeneas' Tale to Dido', Hamlet looks inward and curses and hates himself for his lack of passion, and then again he hates himself the

more for his futile self-hatred. He cannot understand
himself:

> ... it cannot be
> But I am pigeon-liver'd and lack gall
> To make oppression bitter.   (ii. ii. 612)

Aware of his own disease, he wonders if the spirit he has
seen may be an evil spirit:

> The spirit that I have seen
> May be the Devil: and the Devil hath power
> To assume a pleasing shape; yea, and perhaps
> Out of my weakness and my melancholy,
> As he is very potent with such spirits,
> Abuses me to damn me.   (ii. ii. 635)

This fear strikes nearer the truth than the comments of
many Shakespearian scholars.

In Hamlet's interview with Ophelia we are again brought
up against obvious symptoms of his spiritual atrophy. At
first sight of her his love wells up instinctively:

> Nymph, in thy orisons
> Be all my sins remember'd.   (iii. i. 89)

But he quickly recovers. The stupidity of love can have no
place in his mind. Ophelia offers him back some old gifts.
The voice of cynicism answers:

> No, not I;
> I never gave you aught.   (iii. i. 95)

This is true. The Hamlet that gave those 'remembrances'
is dead—dead as his father. The ghost of him alone hovers
pathetically over this dialogue. His past love seems now to
Hamlet a childish and absurd thing: he cannot admit he
was ever so puerile as to be cheated by it. Between the sick
soul and the knowledge of love there are all the interstellar
spaces that divide Hell from Heaven: for Hell and Heaven
are but spatial embodiments of these two modes of the
spirit. Therefore:

> *Hamlet.* Ha, ha! are you honest?
> *Ophelia.* My lord?
> *Hamlet.* Are you fair?
> *Ophelia.* What means your lordship?

Hamlet. That if you be honest and fair, your honesty should admit no discourse to your beauty.
Ophelia. Could beauty, my lord, have better commerce than with honesty?
Hamlet. Ay, truly; for the power of beauty will sooner transform honesty from what it is to a bawd than the force of honesty can translate beauty into his likeness: this was sometime a paradox, but now the time gives it proof. I did love you once.
Ophelia. Indeed, my lord, you made me believe so.
Hamlet. You should not have believed me; for virtue cannot so inoculate our old stock but we shall relish of it: I loved you not.

(III. i. 103)

Hamlet denies the existence of romantic values. Love, in his mind, has become synonymous with sex, and sex with uncleanness. Therefore beauty is dangerous and unclean. Sick of the world, of man, of love, Hamlet denies the reality of his past romance: 'I loved you not'. This statement alone fits coherently into his diseased mind, and so it is, to him, the truth. He cannot have loved, since love is unreal: if it were real, there would be meaning, passion, purpose in existence. These things are gone and love must go too.

Next he curses himself, accuses himself of all the crimes he can think of. This, too, is what we expect. He has seen through all things, including himself, to the foulness within. In self-hatred he cries:

What should such fellows as I do crawling between earth and heaven?

(III. i. 132)

Therefore why should Ophelia be a 'breeder of sinners'? Why should anyone carry on the stupid act of procreation? Hamlet denies the significance of humanity. There is only one course for Ophelia whose beauty perhaps yet echoes in Hamlet's mind some faint rhythm, as from a different existence, of his old love—to cut herself off from contact with an unclean and aimless world:

. . . Go thy ways to a nunnery.   (III. i. 134)

At this point it seems that Hamlet becomes aware of the spies behind the arras. He realizes that Ophelia is a decoy. He breaks out into uncontrollable hatred and fury. He cries:

Go to, I'll no more on't; it hath made me mad.

(III. i. 155)

His words at the end of this scene are indeed 'wild and whirling'. He loses control and gives voice to the loathing that is in him, the cynicism that borders on madness. He has seen through love. Ophelia—once a goddess—is a stupid doll who 'lisps', 'ambles', and paints her face. Unjust, no doubt. It is truth to Hamlet's mind.

Hamlet in this scene is cruel to Ophelia: so too he is cruel to his mother later. He tortures both of them, because he once loved them. They agonize him with the remembrance of what they once were to him, of what he himself is now. There are often moments when reincarnations of what must have been his former courteous and kindly nature—of which we hear, but which we only see by fits and starts—break through the bitterness of Hamlet as he appears in the play, but they do not last: cynicism and consequent cruelty, born of the burden of pain within him, blight the spontaneous gentleness that occasionally shows itself, strangle it. There is a continual process of self-murder at work in Hamlet's mind. He is cruel to Ophelia and his mother. He exults in tormenting the King by the murder of Gonzago, and when he finds him conscience-stricken, at prayer, takes a demoniac pleasure in the thought of preserving his life for a more damning death:

> Up, sword; and know thou a more horrid hent:
> When he is drunk asleep, or in his rage,
> Or in the incestuous pleasure of his bed;
> At gaming, swearing, or about some act
> That has no relish of salvation in't;
> Then trip him, that his heels may kick at Heaven,
> And that his soul may be as damn'd and black
> As Hell, whereto it goes.   (III. iii. 88)

With a callousness and a most evident delight that shocks Horatio he sends his former school-friends to an undeserved death, 'not shriving time allowed', again hoping to compass the eternal damnation of his enemy (v. ii. 47):

> *Horatio.* So Guildenstern and Rosencrantz go to't.
> *Hamlet.* Why, man, they did make love to this employment;
> They are not near my conscience; their defeat
> Does by their own insinuation grow:
> 'Tis dangerous when the baser nature comes
> Between the pass and fell incensed points
> Of mighty opposites.   (v. ii. 56)

Hamlet thus takes a devilish joy in cruelty towards the end of the play: he is like Iago. It is difficult to see the conventional courtly Prince of Denmark in these incidents. We have done ill to sentimentalize his personality. We have paid for it—by failing to understand him; and, failing to understand, we have been unable to sympathize with the demon of cynicism, and its logical result of callous cruelty, that has Hamlet's soul in its remorseless grip. Sentiment is an easy road to an unprofitable and unreal sympathy. Hamlet is cruel. He murders Polonius in error:

> Thou wretched, rash, intruding fool, farewell!
> I took thee for thy better: take thy fortune;
> Thou find'st to be too busy is some danger. (III. iv. 31)

He proceeds from this to vile abuse of his own mother:

> *Hamlet.*   Nay, but to live
> In the rank sweat of an enseamed bed,
> Stew'd in corruption, honeying and making love
> Over the nasty sty—
> *Queen.*   O, speak to me no more;
> These words, like daggers, enter in mine ears;
> No more, sweet Hamlet! (III. iv. 91)

At the end of his scene with his mother there is one beautiful moment when Hamlet gains possession of his soul:

> For this same lord,
> I do repent: but Heaven hath pleased it so,
> To punish me with this, and this with me. (III. iv. 172)

And his filial love wells up in:

> So, again, good-night.
> I must be cruel only to be kind:
> Thus bad begins and worse remains behind. (III. iv. 177)

But it is short-lived. Next comes a long speech of the most withering, brutal, and unnecessary sarcasm:

> Let the bloat king tempt you again to bed;
> Pinch wanton on your cheek; call you his mouse . . .
> (III. iv. 182)

Even more horrible are his disgusting words about Polonius, whom he has unjustly killed, to the King:

> *King.* Now, Hamlet, where's Polonius?
> *Hamlet.* At supper.

King. At supper! where?

Hamlet. Not where he eats, but where he is eaten: a certain convocation
of politic worms are e'en at him. Your worm is your only emperor for
diet: we fat all creatures else to fat us, and we fat ourselves for maggots:
your fat king and your lean beggar is but variable service, two dishes,
but to one table: that's the end.

King. Alas, alas!

Hamlet. A man may fish with the worm that hath eat of a king, and eat of
the fish that hath fed of that worm.

King. What dost thou mean by this?

Hamlet. Nothing but to show you how a king may go a progress through
the guts of a beggar.

King. Where is Polonius?

Hamlet. In Heaven; send thither to see: if your messenger find him not
there, seek him i' the other place yourself. But indeed, if you find him
not within this month, you shall nose him as you go up the stairs into
the lobby.   (iv. iii. 17)

A long and unpleasant quotation, I know. But it is necessary.
The horror of humanity doomed to death and decay has
disintegrated Hamlet's mind. From the first scene to the
last the shadow of death broods over this play. In the
exquisite prose threnody of the Graveyard scene the thought
of physical death is again given utterance. There its pathos,
its inevitability, its moral, are emphasized: but also its
hideousness. Death is truly the theme of this play, for
Hamlet's disease is mental and spiritual death. So Hamlet,
in his most famous soliloquy, concentrates on the terrors
of an after life. The uninspired, devitalized intellect of a
Hamlet thinks pre-eminently in terms of time. To him, the
body disintegrates in time; the soul persists in time too;
and both are horrible. His consciousness, functioning in
terms of evil and negation, sees Hell but not Heaven. But the
intuitive faith, or love, or purpose, by which we must live
if we are to remain sane, of these things, which are drawn
from a timeless reality within the soul, Hamlet is unmercifully bereft. Therefore he dwells on the foul appearances
of sex, the hideous decay of flesh, the deceit of beauty
either of the spirit or of the body, the torments of eternity if
eternity exist. The universe is an 'unweeded garden', or a
'prison', the canopy of the sky but a 'pestilent congregation
of vapours', and man but a 'quintessence of dust', waiting
for the worms of death.

It might be objected that I have concentrated unduly on the unpleasant parts of the play. It has been my intention to concentrate. They are the most significant parts. I have tried by various quotations and by suggestive phrases to indicate this sickness which eats into Hamlet's soul. Its nature is pointed further in the chapter entitled 'The Sick Soul' in *The Varieties of Religious Experience.* Now by emphasizing these elements in the figure of Hamlet I have essayed to pluck out the heart of his mystery. And it will be clear that the elements which I have emphasized, the matter of Hamlet's madness, his patent cruelty, his coarse humour, his strange dialogue with Ophelia, his inability to avenge his father's death, are all equally related to the same sickness within. The coherence of these elements in the play must be evident. Creative action; love; passion—all these can find none but a momentary home in Hamlet's paralysed mind. Before the action of the play, Hamlet was, no doubt

The glass of fashion and the mould of form. (III. i. 162)

But that is over—or nearly over—when Ophelia speaks her lovely words. When we first meet Hamlet the poison has started its disintegrating work. During the rest of the play the outstanding peculiarities of him are his bitterness, his disillusionment, his utter loss of purpose: and many of his humorous speeches which are often performed as pleasant witticisms, or as playful mock-madness, would be more truly rendered with the scornful stare and grating voice of cynicism.

The impression of the play, as a whole, is not so gloomy as the main theme: if it were, it would not have been so popular. There are many individual scenes of action, passion, humour, and beauty, that take our thoughts from the essentially morbid impact of Hamlet's melancholia. Hamlet himself at times recovers his old instinctive friendliness, humour, and gentleness. We can guess what he was like before. That side of his nature which never quite dies, appearing intermittently until the end, is important: it lends point and pathos to the inroads of his cynicism and disgust. His mind wavers between the principle of good, which is love, and that of evil, which is loathing and cruelty. But too

much emphasis has been laid on this element of Hamlet.
The popularity of the play is not innocent of misunderstanding. To ignore the unpleasant aspects of Hamlet blurs
our vision of the protagonist, the play as a whole, and its
place in Shakespeare's work. The matter of the disease-
theme in relation to the rest of the play is difficult. The total
impression, the imaginative impact of the whole, leaves us
with a sense of gaiety, health, superficiality, and colour,
against which is silhouetted the pale black-robed figure of
Hamlet who has seen what lies behind the smiles of
benevolence, who has broken free of the folly of love because
he has found its inward tawdriness and deceit, who knows
that king and beggar alike are bound for the same disgusting 'convocation of worms', and that even an 'indifferent
honest' man is too vile to be 'crawling between heaven and
earth'.

There is no fallacy in Hamlet's reasoning. We cannot
pick on this or that of his most bitter words, and prove them
false. The solitary and inactive figure of Hamlet is contrasted
with the bustle and the glitter of the court, the cancer of
cynicism in his mind, himself a discordant and destructive
thing whose very presence is a poison and a menace to the
happiness and health of Denmark, fulfilling to the letter the
devilish command of the Ghost:

> Adieu, Adieu, Hamlet, remember me.   (I. v. 91)

Hamlet does not neglect his father's final behest—he obeys
it, not wisely but only too well. Hamlet remembers—not
alone his father's ghost, but all the death of which it is a
symbol. What would have been the use of killing Claudius?
Would that have saved his mother's honour, have brought
life to his father's mouldering body, have enabled Hamlet
himself, who had so long lived in death, to have found again
childish joy in the kisses of Ophelia? Would that have
altered the universal scheme? To Hamlet, the universe
smells of mortality; and his soul is sick to death.

II

It is usual in Shakespeare's plays for the main theme to be reflected in subsidiary incidents, persons, and detailed suggestion throughout. Now the theme of *Hamlet* is death. Life that is bound for the disintegration of the grave, love that does not survive the loved one's life—both, in their insistence on death as the primary fact of nature, are branded on the mind of Hamlet, burned into it, searing it with agony. The bereavement of Hamlet and his consequent mental agony bordering on madness is mirrored in the bereavement of Ophelia and her madness. The death of the Queen's love is reflected in the swift passing of the love of the Player-Queen, in the 'Murder of Gonzago.' Death is over the whole play. Polonius and Ophelia die during the action, and Ophelia is buried before our eyes. Hamlet arranges the deaths of Rosencrantz and Guildenstern. The plot is set in motion by the murder of Hamlet's father, and the play opens with the apparition of the Ghost:

> What may this mean,
> That thou, dead corse, again in complete steel
> Revisit'st thus the glimpses of the moon,
> Making night hideous; and we fools of nature
> So horridly to shake our dispositions
> With thoughts beyond the reaches of our souls?   (I. iv. 51)

Those first scenes strike the note of the play—death. We hear of terrors beyond the grave, from the Ghost (I. v.) and from the meditations of Hamlet (III. i.). We hear of horrors in the grave from Hamlet whose mind is obsessed with hideous thoughts of the body's decay. Hamlet's dialogue with the King about the dead Polonius (IV. iii. 17) is painful; and the graveyard meditations, though often beautiful, are remorselessly realistic. Hamlet holds Yorick's skull:

> *Hamlet.* . . . Now, get you to my lady's chamber and tell her, let her paint an inch thick, to this favour she must come; make her laugh at that. Prithee, Horatio, tell me one thing.
> *Horatio.* What's that, my lord?
> *Hamlet.* Dost thou think Alexander looked o' this fashion i' the earth?
> *Horatio,* E'en so.
> *Hamlet.* And smelt so? pah!   (v. i. 211)

The general thought of death, intimately related to the predominating human theme, the pain in Hamlet's mind, is thus suffused through the whole play. And yet the play, as a whole, scarcely gives us that sense of blackness and the abysms of spiritual evil which we find in *Macbeth*; nor is there the universal gloom of *King Lear*. This is due partly to the difference in the technique of *Hamlet* from that of *Macbeth* or *King Lear*. Macbeth, the protagonist and heroic victim of evil, rises gigantic from the murk of an evil universe; Lear, the king of suffering, towers over a universe that itself toils in pain. Thus in *Macbeth* and *King Lear* the predominating imaginative atmospheres are used not to contrast with the mental universe of the hero, but to aid and support it, as it were, with similarity, to render realistic the extravagant and daring effects of volcanic passion to which the poet allows his protagonist to give voice. We are forced by the attendant personification, the verbal colour, the symbolism and events of the play as a whole, to feel the hero's suffering, to see with his eyes. But in *Hamlet* this is not so. We need not see through Hamlet's eyes. Though the idea of death is recurrent through the play, it is not implanted in the minds of other persons as is the consciousness of evil throughout *Macbeth* and the consciousness of suffering throughout *King Lear*. Except for the original murder of Hamlet's father, the *Hamlet* universe is one of healthy and robust life, good-nature, humour, romantic strength, and welfare: against this background is the figure of Hamlet pale with the consciousness of death. He is the ambassador of death walking amid life. The effect is at first one of separation. Nevertheless it is to be noted that the consciousness of death, and consequent bitterness, cruelty, and inaction, in Hamlet not only grows in his own mind disintegrating it as we watch, but also spreads its effects outward among the other persons like a blighting disease, and, as the play progresses, by its very passivity and negation of purpose, insidiously undermines the health of the state, and adds victim to victim until at the end the stage is filled with corpses. It is, as it were, a nihilistic birth in the consciousness of Hamlet that spreads its deadly venom around. That Hamlet is originally blameless, that the King is originally guilty, may well be granted. But, if we refuse to be diverted from a clear vision by questions of praise and blame, responsibility and causality, and watch only the actions and reactions of the persons as they appear, we shall observe a striking reversal of the usual commentary.

If we are to attain a true interpretation of Shakespeare we must work from a centre of consciousness near that of the creative instinct of the poet. We must think less in terms of causality and more in terms of imaginative impact. Now Claudius is not drawn as wholly evil—far from it. We see the government of Denmark working smoothly. Claudius shows every sign of being an excellent diplomatist and king. He is troubled by young Fortinbras, and dispatches ambassadors to the sick King of Norway demanding that he suppress the raids of his nephew. His speech to the ambassadors bears the stamp of clear and exact thought and an efficient and confident control of affairs:

> . . . and we here dispatch
> You, good Cornelius, and you, Voltimand,
> For bearers of this greeting to old Norway;
> Giving to you no further personal power
> To business with the king, more than the scope
> Of these delated articles allow.
> Farewell, and let your haste commend your duty.
>
> (I. ii. 33)

The ambassadors soon return successful. Claudius listens to their reply, receives the King of Norway's letter, and hears that young Fortinbras desires a free pass through Denmark to lead his soldiers against the Poles. Claudius answers:

> It likes us well;
> And at our more consider'd time we'll read,
> Answer, and think upon this business.
> Meantime we thank you for your well-took labour:
> Go to your rest; at night we'll feast together:
> Most welcome home! (II. ii. 80)

Tact has found an easy settlement where arms and opposition might have wasted the strength of Denmark. Notice his reservation of detailed attention when once he knows the main issues are clear; the courteous yet dignified attitude to his subordinates and the true leader's consideration for their comfort; and the invitation to the feast. The impression given by these speeches is one of quick efficiency—the efficiency of the man who can dispose of business without unnecessary circumstance, and so leaves himself time for enjoying the good things of life: a man kindly, confident, and fond of pleasure.

Throughout the first half of the play Claudius is the typical kindly uncle, besides being a good king. His advice to Hamlet about his exaggerated mourning for his father's death is admirable common sense:

> Fie! 'Tis a fault to Heaven,
> A fault against the dead, a fault to nature,
> To reason most absurd; whose common theme
> Is death of fathers, and who still hath cried,
> From the first corse, till he that died to-day,
> 'This must be so.'   (I. ii. 101)

It is the advice of worldly common sense opposed to the extreme misery of a sensitive nature paralysed by the facts of death and unfaithfulness. This contrast points the relative significance of the King and his court to Hamlet. They are of the world—with their crimes, their follies, their shallownesses, their pomp and glitter; they are of humanity, with all its failings, it is true, but yet of humanity. They assert the importance of human life, they believe in it, in themselves. Whereas Hamlet is inhuman, since he has seen through the tinsel of life and love, he believes in nothing, not even himself, except the memory of a ghost, and his black-robed presence is a reminder to everyone of the fact of death. There is no question but that Hamlet is right. The King's smiles hide murder, his mother's love for her new consort is unfaithfulness to Hamlet's father, Ophelia has deserted Hamlet at the hour of his need. Hamlet's philosophy may be inevitable, blameless, and irrefutable. But it is the negation of life. It is death. Hence Hamlet is a continual fear to Claudius, a reminder of his crime. It is a mistake to consider Claudius as a hardened criminal. When Polonius remarks on the hypocrisy of mankind, he murmurs to himself:

> O, 'tis too true!
> How smart a lash that speech doth give my conscience!
> The harlot's cheek, beautied with plastering art,

Is not more ugly to the thing that helps it
Than is my deed to my most painted word:
O heavy burthen!   (III. i. 49)

Again, Hamlet's play wrenches his soul with remorse—
primarily not fear of Hamlet, as one might expect, but a
genuine remorse—and gives us that most beautiful prayer
of a stricken soul beginning, 'O, my offence is rank, it smells
to Heaven' (III. iii. 36):

> . . . What if this cursed hand
> Were thicker than itself with brother's blood,
> Is there not rain enough in the sweet heavens
> To wash it white as snow? Whereto serves mercy
> But to confront the visage of offence?

He fears that his prayer is worthless. He is still trammelled
by the enjoyment of the fruits of his crime. 'My fault is
past,' he cries. But what does that avail, since he has his
crown and his queen still, the prizes of murder? His
dilemma is profound and raises the problem I am pointing
in this essay. Claudius, as he appears in the play, is not a
criminal. He is—strange as it may seem—a good and
gentle king, enmeshed by the chain of causality linking him
with his crime. And this chain he might, perhaps, have
broken except for Hamlet, and all would have been well.
Now, granted the presence of Hamlet—which Claudius at
first genuinely desired, persuading him not to return to
Wittenberg as he wished—and granted the fact of his
original crime which cannot now be altered, Claudius can
hardly be blamed for his later actions. They are forced on
him. As King, he could scarcely be expected to do otherwise.
Hamlet is a danger to the state, even apart from his knowledge of Claudius' guilt. He is an inhuman—or superhuman
—presence, whose consciousness—somewhat like Dostoievsky's Stavrogin—is centred on death. Like Stavrogin, he is
feared by those around him. They are always trying in vain
to find out what is wrong with him. They cannot understand
him. He is a creature of another world. As King of Denmark
he would have been a thousand times more dangerous than
Claudius. The end of Claudius' prayer is pathetic:

> What then?   What rests?
> Try what repentance can: what can it not?

> Yet what can it when one can not repent?
> O wretched state! O bosom black as death!
> O limed soul, that, struggling to be free,
> Art more engag'd! Help, angels! make assay!
> Bow, stubborn knees; and, heart with strings of steel,
> Be soft as sinews of the new-born babe!
> All may be well.   (III. iii. 64)

Set against this lovely prayer—the fine flower of a human soul in anguish—is the entrance of Hamlet, the late joy of torturing the King's conscience still written on his face, his eye a-glitter with the intoxication of conquest, vengeance in his mind; his purpose altered only by the devilish hope of finding a more damning moment in which to slaughter the King, next hastening to his mother to wring her soul too. Which then, at this moment in the play, is nearer the Kingdom of Heaven? Whose words would be more acceptable of Jesus' God? Which is the embodiment of spiritual good, which of evil? The question of the relative morality of Hamlet and Claudius reflects the ultimate problem of this play.

Other eminently pleasant traits can be found in Claudius. He hears of Hamlet's murder of Polonius:

> O Gertrude, come away!
> The sun no sooner shall the mountains touch,
> But we will ship him hence: and this vile deed
> We must, with all our majesty and skill,
> Both countenance and excuse.   (IV. i. 28)

Though a murderer himself, he has a genuine horror of murder. This does not ring hypocritical. He takes the only possible course. Hamlet is a danger:

> His liberty is full of threats to all.   (IV. i. 14)

To hurry him from Denmark is indeed necessary: it is the only way of saving himself, and, incidentally, the best line of action in the interests of the state. During the scene of Ophelia's madness (IV. v.) Claudius shows a true and sensitive concern, exclaiming, 'How do you, pretty lady?' and 'Pretty Ophelia!' and after he has told Horatio to look after her, he speaks in all sincerity to his Queen:

> O, this is the poison of deep grief; it springs
> All from her father's death. O Gertrude, Gertrude,

> When sorrows come, they come not single spies,
> But in battalions. First, her father slain:
> Next, your son gone; and he most violent author
> Of his most just remove . . .   (IV. V. 76)

He continues the catalogue of ills. The people are dis-
satisfied, Laertes has returned. The problems are over-
whelming. When Laertes enters, Claudius rouses our
admiration by his cool reception of him:

> What is the cause, Laertes,
> That thy rebellion looks so giant-like?
> Let him go, Gertrude; do not fear our person:
> There's such divinity doth hedge a king,
> That treason can but peep to what it would,
> Acts little of his will. Tell me, Laertes,
> Why thou art thus incens'd. Let him go, Gertrude.
> Speak, man.   (IV. V. 120)

When he hears of Hamlet's return he plots treachery with
Laertes. Everything considered, one can hardly blame him.
He has, it is true, committed a dastardly murder, but in the
play he gives us the impression of genuine penitence and a
host of good qualities. After the murder of Polonius we
certainly feel that both the King and the Queen are sane and
doing their level best to restrain the activities of a madman.
That is the impression given by the play at this point, as we
read. If we think in terms of logic, we remember at once that
we must side with Hamlet; and we perhaps remember the
continual and sudden emergences of a different Hamlet, a
Hamlet loving and noble and sane. But intermittent madness
is more dangerous by far than obvious insanity. At the best
we only prove that Hamlet's madness is justifiable, a statement which makes nonsense; for Hamlet's behaviour, so
utterly out of harmony with his environment of eminently
likeable people, in that relation may well be called a kind
of madness. Whatever it is, it is extremely dangerous and
powerful.

I have concentrated on Claudius' virtues. They are
manifest. So are his faults—his original crime, his skill in
the less admirable kind of policy, treachery, and intrigue.
But I would point clearly that, in the movement of the play,
his faults are forced on him, and he is distinguished by

creative and wise action, a sense of purpose, benevolence, a
faith in himself and those around him, by love of his Queen:

> . . . and for myself—
> My virtue or my plague, be it either which—
> She's so conjunctive to my life and soul,
> That as the star moves not but in his sphere,
> I could not but by her.   (IV. vii. 12)

In short he is very human. Now these are the very qualities
Hamlet lacks. Hamlet is inhuman. He has seen through
humanity. And this inhuman cynicism, however justifiable
in this case on the plane of causality and individual responsibility, is a deadly and venomous thing. Instinctively the
creatures of earth, Laertes, Polonius, Ophelia, Rosencrantz
and Guildenstern, league themselves with Claudius: they
are of his kind. They sever themselves from Hamlet. Laertes
sternly warns Ophelia against her intimacy with Hamlet, so
does Polonius. They are, in fact, all leagued against him,
they are puzzled by him or fear him: he has no friend except
Horatio, and Horatio, after the Ghost scenes, becomes a queer
shadowy character who rarely gets beyond 'E'en so, my
lord', 'My lord——', and such-like phrases. The other persons are firmly drawn, in the round, creatures of flesh and
blood. But Hamlet is not of flesh and blood, he is a spirit
of penetrating intellect and cynicism and misery, without
faith in himself or anyone else, murdering his love of
Ophelia, on the brink of insanity, taking delight in cruelty,
torturing Claudius, wringing his mother's heart, a poison in
the midst of the healthy bustle of the court. He is a superman
among men. And he is a superman because he has walked
and held converse with death, and his consciousness works
in terms of death and the negation of cynicism. He has seen
the truth, not alone of Denmark, but of humanity, of the
universe: and the truth is evil. Thus Hamlet is an element
of evil in the state of Denmark. The poison of his mental
existence spreads outwards among things of flesh and blood,
like acid eating into metal. They are helpless before his very
inactivity and fall one after the other, like victims of an
infectious disease. They are strong with the strength of
health—but the demon of Hamlet's mind is a stronger thing
than they. Futilely they try to get him out of their country;

anything to get rid of him, he is not safe. But he goes with a cynical smile, and is no sooner gone than he is back again in their midst, meditating in graveyards, at home with death. Not till it has slain all, is the demon that grips Hamlet satisfied. And last it slays Hamlet himself:

> The spirit that I have seen
> May be the Devil ...   (II. ii. 635)

It was.

It was the devil of the knowledge of death, which possesses Hamlet and drives him from misery and pain to increasing bitterness, cynicism, murder, and madness. He has truly bought converse with his father's spirit at the price of enduring and spreading Hell on earth. But however much we may sympathize with Ophelia, with Polonius, Rosencrantz, Guildenstern, the Queen, and Claudius, there is one reservation to be made. It is Hamlet who is right. What he says and thinks of them is true, and there is no fault in his logic. His mother is certainly faithless, and the prettiness of Ophelia does in truth enclose a spirit as fragile and untrustworthy as her earthly beauty; Polonius is 'a foolish prating knave'; Rosencrantz and Guildenstern are time-servers and flatterers; Claudius, whose benevolence hides the guilt of murder, is, by virtue of that fact, 'a damned smiling villain'. In the same way the demon of cynicism which is in the mind of the poet and expresses itself in the figures of this play, has always this characteristic: it is right. One cannot argue with the cynic. It is unwise to offer him battle. For in the warfare of logic it will be found that he has all the guns.

In this play we are confronted by a curious problem of technique. I pointed out early in this section that the effects are gained by contrast, and it will be seen from my analysis that this contrast has its powerful imaginative effects. But it is also disconcerting. Though we instinctively tend at first to adopt the view-point of Hamlet himself, we are not forced to do so throughout. My analysis has shown that other methods of approach are possible; and, if they are possible, they are, in objective drama, legitimate. It is, clearly, necessary that we should be equally prepared to adopt the point of view of either side, otherwise we are offering a biassed interpretation. And though the Hamlet-theme preponderates over that of any one other individual in the play, it will be clear that Hamlet has set in contrast to him all the other persons: they are massed against him. In the universe of this play—whatever may have happened in the past—he is the only discordant element, the only hindrance to happiness, health, and prosperity: a living death in the midst of life. Therefore a balanced judgement is forced to pronounce ultimately in favour of life as contrasted with death, for optimism and the healthily second-rate, rather than the nihilism of the superman: for he is not, as the plot shows, safe; and he is not safe, primarily because he is right— otherwise Claudius could soon have swept him from his path. If we think primarily of the state of Denmark during the action of the play, we are bound to applaud Claudius, as he appears before us: he acts throughout with a fine steadiness of purpose. By creating normal and healthy and lovable persons around his protagonist, whose chief peculiarity is the abnormality of extreme melancholia, the poet divides our sympathies. The villain has become a kindly uncle, the princely hero is the incarnation of cynicism. It is true that if Hamlet had promptly avenged his father, taken the throne, forgotten his troubles, resumed a healthy outlook on life, he would have all our acclamations. Laertes entering in wrath at the death of his father, daring 'damnation' (iv. v. 132) and threatening Claudius, comes on us like a blast of fresh air, after the stifling, poisonous atmosphere of Hamlet's mind. Laertes and Hamlet struggling at Ophelia's grave are like symbols of life and death contending for the prize of love. Laertes is brave in his course of loyalty. But to expect such a course from Hamlet is to misunderstand him quite and his place in the play. The time is out of joint, he is thrown out of any significant relation with his world. He cannot bridge the gulf by rational action. Nor can he understand the rest any more than they understand him. His ideals— which include an insistent memory of death—are worth nothing to them, and, most maddening fact of all, they get on perfectly well as they are—or would do if Hamlet were out of the way. Thus, through no fault of his own, Hamlet has been forced into a state of evil: Claudius, whose crime originally placed him there, is in a state of healthy and robust spiritual life. Hamlet, and we too, are perplexed.

So Hamlet spends a great part of his time in watching, analysing, and probing others. He unhesitatingly lances each in turn in his weakest spot. He is usually quite merciless. But all he actually accomplishes is to torment them all, terrorize them. They are dreadfully afraid of him. Hamlet is so powerful. He is, as it were, the channel of a mysterious force, a force which derives largely from his having seen through them all. In contact with him they know their own faults: neither they nor we should know them otherwise. He exposes faults everywhere. Yet he is not tragic in the usual Shakespearian sense; there is no surge and swell of passion pressing onward through the play to leave us, as in *King Lear*, with the mighty crash and backwash of a tragic peace. There is not this direct rhythm in Hamlet—there is no straight course. Instead of being dynamic, the force of Hamlet is, paradoxically, static. Its poison is the poison of negation, nothingness, threatening a world of positive assertion. This element is not, however, the whole of Hamlet. He can speak lovingly to his mother at one moment, and the next, in an excess of revulsion, torment her with a withering and brutal sarcasm. One moment he can cry:

> I loved Ophelia: forty thousand brothers
> Could not, with all their quantity of love,
> Make up my sum. (v. i. 291)

Shortly after he scorns himself for his outbreak. His mind reflects swift changes. He may for a moment or two see with the eyes of humour, gentleness, love—then suddenly the whole universe is blackened, goes out, leaves utter vacancy. This is, indeed, the secret of the play's fascination and its lack of unified and concise poetic statement. Hamlet is a dualized personality, wavering, oscillating between grace and the hell of cynicism. The plot reflects this see-saw motion; it lacks direction, pivoting on Hamlet's incertitude, and analysis holds the fascination of giddiness. Nor can Hamlet feel anything passionately for long, since passion implies purpose, and he has no one purpose for any length of time. One element in Hamlet, and that a very important one, is

the negation of any passion whatsoever. His disease—or
vision—is primarily one of negation, of death. Hamlet is
a living death in the midst of life; that is why the play sounds
the note of death so strong and sombre at the start. The
Ghost was conceived throughout as a portent not kind but
sinister. That sepulchral cataclysm at the beginning is the
key to the whole play. *Hamlet* begins with an explosion in
the first act; the rest of the play is the reverberation thereof.
From the first act onwards Hamlet is, as it were, blackened,
scorched by that shattering revelation. The usual process is
reversed and the climax is at the start. Hamlet, already in
despair, converses early with death: through the remaining
acts he lives within that death, remembering the Ghost,
spreading destruction wherever he goes, adding crime to
crime,[1] like Macbeth, and becoming more and more callous,
until his detestable act of sending his former friends to un-
merited death 'not shriving-time allow'd' (v. ii. 47). Finally
'this fell sergeant, death' (v. ii. 350) arrests him too. This
is his mysterious strength, ghost-begotten, before which the
rest succumb. That is why this play is so rich in death—why
its meaning is analysed by Hamlet in soliloquy, why Hamlet
is so fascinated by the skulls the Grave-digger unearths; why
so many 'casual slaughters' and 'deaths put on by cunning
and forced cause' (v. ii. 393) disrupt the action, till we are
propelled to the last holocaust of mortality and Fortinbras'
comment:

> This quarry cries on havoc. O proud death,
> What feast is toward in thine eternal cell,
> That thou so many princes at a shot
> So bloodily hast struck?   (v. ii. 378)

The Ghost may or may not have been a 'goblin damned'; it
certainly was no 'spirit of health' (i. iv. 40). The play ends
with a dead march. The action grows out of eternity, closes
in it. The ominous discharge of ordnance thus reverberates
three times: once, before Hamlet sees the Ghost, and twice
in Act v. The eternity of death falls as an abyss at either
end, and Hamlet crosses the stage of life aureoled in its
ghostly luminance.

---

[1] An exaggeration. Hamlet's 'crimes' are, properly, two only. See my essay '*Hamlet Reconsidered*' (1947).

III

This contrast between Hamlet and his world is of extreme importance, for it is repeated in different forms in the plays to follow. *Hamlet* contains them all in embryo. They are to reflect the contest between (i) human life, and (ii) the principle of negation. That principle may be subdivided into love-cynicism and death-consciousness, which I elsewhere call 'hate' and 'evil', respectively. *Troilus and Cressida* is concerned with love alone; *Othello*—and also *King Lear*—with love until the end, which, by the tragic climax, throws the love problem into relation with eternity. *Measure for Measure* is concerned with both death and love. In *Macbeth*, the death-consciousness, as in *Hamlet*, works chaos and destruction on earth. As Hamlet does not know why he cannot, or does not, slay Claudius, so Macbeth is quite unable to understand why he murders Duncan. The analogy is close, since the slaying of Claudius is, to Hamlet at least, an act in the cause of life. In *Timon of Athens* the contrast is especially clear. First we have the world of humanity in all its glitter and superficial delight: repelled thence the hero moves, as it were, with full purposive assurance, within the halls of death. In the curious juxtaposition of Hamlet and his environment we shall find much of what follows implicit, but not unless we concentrate on the main elements of Hamlet's mental pain without letting our sympathy for him as the hero blur our vision of the gentler qualities of other persons. If in our attempt to see with Hamlet's eyes, we are prepared to regard Claudius as the blackest of criminals, Gertrude as an adulteress, Polonius as a fool, and Ophelia as a deceit and a decoy—there is no other way—we only blur our vision of them and consequently our understanding of him. The technique of *Hamlet* is not as that of *Macbeth* or *King Lear*, or *Timon of Athens*. We are forced by the poet to suffer the terrors of Macbeth, the agonies of Lear, the hate of Timon. But *Hamlet* has no dominating atmosphere, no clear purposive technique to focus our vision. Macbeth and Lear, in their settings, are normal; Hamlet, in his, abnormal. Hamlet is a creature of a different world, a different kind of poetic vision, from the other persons: he is incommensurable with them—himself of quality akin to Macbeth and Lear, he is let loose in the world of Hotspur and Henry V. He is thus too profound to be consistently lovable. Therefore, unless we forget or cut or distort some of the most significant parts of the play—as is so often done —we cannot feel the disgust and nausea that Hamlet feels at the wise and considerate Claudius, the affectionate mother, Gertrude, the eminently lovable old Polonius, and the pathetic Ophelia. Now the technical problem here reflects a universal problem: that of a mind of 'more than ordinary sensibility' revolted by an insensate but beautiful world which denies his every aspiration. Which is right? The question is asked in *Hamlet* not by discourse of reason or argument, but by two different modes of poetic vision and technique: one for Hamlet, one for the other persons. They are placed together, and our sympathies are divided.

A comprehensive view of the whole throws the play into significant relation with human affairs. Claudius is a murderer. The ghost of the dead king will not tolerate that he so easily avoid the consequences proper to crime, so readily build both firmly and well on a basis of evil. This spirit speaks to Hamlet alone both because he is his son and because his consciousness is already tuned to sympathize with death. Two things he commands Hamlet: (i) vengeance, and (ii) remembrance. The latter, but not the former, is, from the first, branded most deep on Hamlet's mind—this is apparent from his soliloquy, 'Remember thee! Ay, thou poor ghost . . .' (I. v. 95). Hamlet's soul is wrung with compassion's agony. He does not obey the command:

> Pity me not, but lend thy serious hearing
> To what I shall unfold.   (I. v. 5)

The contrast between pity and revenge is clearly pointed later:

> Do not look upon me
> Lest with this piteous action you convert
> My stern effects: then what I have to do
> Will want true colour, tears perchance, for blood.
>   (III. iv. 126)

While Hamlet pities he cannot revenge, for his soul is then

sick with knowledge of death and that alone. Now, at the start, we hear that

Something is rotten in the state of Denmark. (I. iv. 90)

Claudius must be cast out, as a thing unclean—that is the Ghost's command. Were Hamlet the possessor of spiritual harmony, he might have struck once, and restored perfect health to Denmark. That would have been a creative act, in the cause of life. But pity enlists Hamlet in the cause not of life, but of death; and we are shown how sickness and death-consciousness cannot heal sickness, cannot prescribe to life. Hence Hamlet's disordered soul symbolizes itself in acts of destruction: he thinks so closely in terms of death that he can perform no life-bringing act. So thoughts of the King's eternal damnation prevent Hamlet from the life-bringing act of slaying him as he prays. The destructive symbols of his inner disintegration are evident in the inno-cent blood he sheds, passing by the thing of guilt. Himself the ambassador of death, tormented with 'thoughts beyond the reaches of our souls' (I. iv. 56), in that dread eminence he deals destruction around him. The lesson of the play as a whole is something like this—Had Hamlet forgotten both the Ghost's commands, it would have been well, since Claudius is a good king, and the Ghost but a minor spirit; had he remembered both it would have been still better—Hamlet would probably have felt his fetters drop from his soul, he would have stepped free, then—but not till then—have been a better king than Claudius, and, finally, the un-restful spirit would know peace. But, remembering only the Ghost's command to remember, he is paralysed, he lives in death, in pity of hideous death, in loathing of the life that breeds it. His acts, like Macbeth's, are a commentary on his negative consciousness: he murders all the wrong people, exults in cruelty, grows more and more dangerous. At the end, fate steps in, forces him to perform the act of creative assassination he has been, by reason of his inner disintegra-tion, unable to perform. Not Hamlet, but a greater principle than he or the surly Ghost, puts an end to this continual slaughter.

But we properly know Hamlet himself only when he is

alone with death: then he is lovable and gentle, then he is beautiful and noble, and, there being no trivial things of life to blur our mortal vision, our minds are tuned to the exquisite music of his soul. We know the real Hamlet only in his address to the Ghost, in his 'To be or not to be . . .' soliloquy, in the lyric prose of the Graveyard scene:

> Here hung those lips that I have kissed I know not how oft . . .
> (v. i. 206)

These touch a melody that holds no bitterness. Here, and when he is dying, we glimpse, perhaps, a thought wherein death, not life, holds the deeper assurance for humanity. Then we will understand why Hamlet knows death to be felicity:

> Absent thee from felicity awhile,
> And in this harsh world draw thy breath in pain
> To tell my story . . .   (v. ii. 361)

The story of a 'sweet prince' (v. ii. 373) wrenched from life and dedicate alone to death.

ADDITIONAL NOTES

1947. For further remarks on *Hamlet*, see my chapters 'Symbolic Personification' and '*Hamlet* Reconsidered' in this volume and 'Rose of May' in *The Imperial Theme*.

1953. I find that my reading of *Hamlet* may be profitably compared with that outlined by Nietzsche in *The Birth of Tragedy*, VII.

THE PHILOSOPHY OF *TROILUS*
AND CRESSIDA

TROILUS AND CRESSIDA is more peculiarly analytic in language and dramatic meaning than any other work of Shakespeare. Often it has been called difficult, incoherent. It may be superficially difficult, but it is not incoherent. The difficulties, moreover, being essentially those of intellectual complexity, lend themselves naturally to intellectual interpretation. When once we see clearly the central idea—it is almost a 'thesis'—from which the play's thought and action derive their significance, most of the difficulties vanish.

The theme is this. Human values are strongly contrasted with human failings. In Shakespeare there are two primary values, love and war. These two are vividly present in *Troilus and Cressida*. But they exist in a world which questions their ultimate purpose and beauty. The love of Troilus, the heroism of Hector, the symbolic romance which burns in the figure of Helen—these are placed beside the 'scurril jests' and lazy pride of Achilles, the block-headed stupidity of Ajax, the mockery of Thersites. The Trojan party stands for human beauty and worth, the Greek party for the bestial and stupid elements of man, the barren stagnancy of intellect divorced from action, and the criticism which exposes these things with jeers. The atmospheres of the two opposing camps are thus strongly contrasted, and the handing over of Cressida to the Greeks, which is the pivot incident of the play, has thus a symbolic suggestion. These two primary aspects of humanity can next be provisionally equated with the concepts 'intuition' and 'intellect', or 'emotion' and 'reason'. In the play this distinction sometimes assumes the form of an antinomy between 'individualism' and 'social order'. Now human values rest on an intuitive faith or an intuitive recognition: the denial of them—which may itself be largely emotional—if not directly caused by intellectual reasoning, is very easily related to such reasoning, and often looks to it for its own defence. Cynicism is eminently logical to the modern, post-Renaissance, mind. Therefore, though aware that my terms cannot be ultimately justified as exact labels for the two faculties under discussion, I use them for my immediate purpose to point the peculiar dualism that persists in the thought of this play. Thus 'intellect' is considered here as tending towards 'cynicism', and 'intuition' in association with 'romantic faith'—a phrase chosen to suggest the dual values, love and war. We can then say that the root idea of *Troilus and Cressida* is the dynamic opposition in the mind of these two faculties: intuition and intellect.

The language of the play is throughout pregnant with close reasoning. Many of the persons think hard and deep: the most swift and fleeting of love's glances are subjected to piercing intellectual analysis, and the profoundest questions of human fate discussed, analysed, dissected. The metaphoric phraseology is often rich in philosophic meaning; the primary persons, though not alive with the warm humanity of an Othello, yet enjoy a strangely vivid vitality of burning thought. Those who adhere to the cause of intuition think out their intuitions, try to explicate them in terms of intellect. Intelligence here is a primary quality: fools are jeered at for their blunt wits, wise men display their prolix wisdom, the lover analyses the metaphysical implications of his love. We are in a metaphysical universe. In the usual Shakespearian fashion, the problem of the main theme—the rational untrustworthiness in conflict with the intuitive validity of romantic sight—is reflected throughout the play. We are shown throughout different varieties of human vision and different grades of human intellect, insensibly merging into one another, illustrating the numerous mental reactions of man to the realities of love and war. I shall now consider: first, two subsidiary scenes of importance illustrating different forms of the intuition-intelligence opposition underlying the play's movement; second, the general significance of the Greek Party, with especial notice of Thersites; and, third, the dominant love-theme of Troilus and Cressida.

In Act I, Scene iii, the Greek generals discuss the military situation. No scene in the play more clearly illustrates and more closely defines the peculiar analytic quality here obtaining. Agamemnon chides the generals for their depression. The Greeks, he says, have had ill-luck; their plans have not resulted in the looked-for success. But these are God's trials. Not in human success, but in human failure, is the essential nobility of man made manifest. When fortune smiles all men are alike:

> But, in the wind and tempest of her frown,
> Distinction, with a broad and powerful fan,
> Puffing at all, winnows the light away;
> And what hath mass or matter, by itself
> Lies rich in virtue and unmingled. (I. iii. 26–30)

Agamemnon urges, not stoically but with warmth and feeling, that men should rejoice, not sorrow, at the storms of adversity: an admirable philosophy—but is its logical result likely to win the war? Next Nestor, from whose age the thought comes more appropriately, expands the same idea. Any frail boat dare sail on a smooth sea; but only a 'strong-ribb'd bark' dare adventure on a stormy one. He continues:

> Even so
> Doth valour's show and valour's worth divide
> In storms of fortune; for in her ray and brightness
> The herd hath more annoyance by the breese
> Than by the tiger; but when the splitting wind
> Makes flexible the knees of knotted oaks,
> And flies fled under shade, why, then the thing of courage
> As rous'd with rage with rage doth sympathize,
> And with an accent tun'd in selfsame key
> Retorts to chiding fortune. (I. iii. 45–54)

The imagery and phraseology in both these speeches inevitably call to mind Shakespeare's view of human tragedy. The 'bark' and the 'tempest' are recurring symbols of tragedy, to be found in numerous passages throughout the plays. Storms are symbolic of tragedy when they occur in stage directions. Its 'tempest' is, in fact, an integral part of the Shakespearian tragedy; and Shakespeare's final mystic play, *The Tempest*, primarily owes its plot and name, not to Sir George Somer's shipwreck (with which it may at the same time bear a certain secondary relation), but to the very fact of this poetic symbol. So Agamemnon and Nestor have expressed quite clearly a significant but baffling truth: the purely mystic grandeur of tragedy. The view of tragedy as essentially a victory—which is at the root of our mystic understanding of the Christian cross—though its validity to our imaginations need not be questioned, is yet very difficult if we seek for a practical application: logically, it would seem to lead to chaos or paralysis of action. Hence Ulysses' prolix reply. He answers, not Agamemnon's speech alone, but its ultimate implications. Agamemnon's words imply a philosophy of life which in turn implies a somewhat impractical mind in his conduct of the campaign. Ulysses answers with an opposing philosophy which insists on 'order' and suggests that Agamemnon has been remiss—that the Greeks fail through lack of discipline and unity. His reply is that of reason directed against the irrational grandeur of tragedy. For the tragic view of human existence, if carried to a logical conclusion and correctly symbolized in action, will, it would appear, lead to chaos. Order is essential. This thought Ulysses expands at great length. Again, Nestor counselled the nobility of tragic passion—a Lear's or a Timon's passion whose accent is tuned to 'retort' to chiding fortune in language tempestuous as man's tempestuous fate. But if tragic passion be the highest good, if discipline and order be not man's ideal—and the choice ultimately rests between these two—then there is an end of natural harmony and human civilization:

> And, hark, what discord follows! each thing meets
> In mere oppugnancy: the bounded waters
> Should lift their bosoms higher than the shores
> And make a sop of all this solid globe:
> Strength should be lord of imbecility,
> And the rude son should strike his father dead:
> Force should be right; or rather, right and wrong,
> Between whose endless jar justice resides,
> Should lose their names and so should justice too.
>
> (I. iii. 110)

So, indeed, 'justice' does in truth 'lose its name' in *King Lear:* and not in *King Lear* only, but in all high tragedy properly understood.

Ulysses' speech forms a perfect statement of the case for the moral order against the high mystic philosophy of tragedy and passion. Nor is this to twist the natural meaning of a dramatic speech; for we must observe that the speeches in *Troilus and Cressida* are primarily analytic rather than dramatic, and, if we are to understand its peculiar meaning we must be ready, as are the persons of the play, to respond to the lightest tones and shades of its philosophy. This reading of the argument as a discussion of tragedy does not conflict with the dramatic situation. Agamemnon has expressed a profound and sympathetic commentary on the progress of the war. He has spoken like a mystic; but mystics seldom make good generals. Agamemnon is thus closely analogous to the Duke in *Measure for Measure*. Both speak wisdom, especially the profound mystic wisdom of the tragic philosophy. Both are, however, impractical in the ordinary sense. From the view-point of Thersites Agamemnon is an honest man enough, but a fool (v. i. 56–8). Ulysses answers Agamemnon's gentle and noble acceptance of misfortune by suggesting that his actual conduct of the war lacks the co-ordinating and directing quality of regal discipline. This we can well believe from what we see of the Greek army. There are, then, two layers of thought here: the purely dramatic and the profoundly universal and philosophic meanings. They are not properly separate, but rather two aspects of the same thing. We have an illuminating instance of what often happens here: the persons are all obsessed with the desire of analysis, and, in the process of their search for truth, continually raise the particular into the realm of the universal. Here the crucial problem of the play is at issue: since intuition and faith accept the tragic philosophy, reason and intellect reject it. In this instance, the intuition-intellect opposition is obviously one with that of individualism and order. Ulysses, exponent always throughout the play of reason, statecraft, and order, attacks the intuitional and emotional—one might almost say the 'sentimental'—arguments of Agamemnon and Nestor. And it must be observed that both sides use the peculiar Shakespearian symbols of disorder and tempest which are fundamental in tragedies of the *Macbeth* and *King Lear* type. For, besides the tempest-imagery of the passages already quoted, there is, in Ulysses' speech, a reference to unnatural, disorderly phenomena in earth and sky such as I discuss elsewhere in relation to *Julius Caesar* and *Macbeth*:

>   . . . but when the planets
> In evil mixture to disorder wander,
> What plagues, and what portents! what mutiny!
> What raging of the sea! shaking of earth!
> Commotion in the winds! fights, changes, horrors,
> Divert and crack, rend and deracinate
> The unity and married calm of states
> Quite from their fixure!   (I. iii. 94)

The relevance of this to Shakespearian tragedy is obvious; nor could a better commentary be found on Shakespeare's disorder-symbolism than this carefully constructed order-speech of Ulysses. It should be observed that Ulysses' arguments win the day.

 The next scene I would notice is Act II, Scene ii. The Trojans discuss the question of restoring Helen to the Greeks and so ending the war. Hector counsels such a course. Helen, he says, is not worth the terrific cost in Trojan lives. But Troilus—always the ardent exponent of absolute faith in a supreme value, and the necessity of translating that faith into action—argues that the King's honour is a thing 'infinite' in comparison with 'reasons'. The 'infinity' of such values as love is in different forms a usual space-metaphor in Shakespeare, suggesting the incommensurability of quality in terms of quantity. This dialogue—and indeed the whole play—is an interesting antidote to the commentary that observes no original philosophic thought in Shakespeare:

> *Troilus.*   Fie, fie, my brother!
> Weigh you the worth and honour of a king
> So great as our dread father in a scale
> Of common ounces? will you with counters sum
> The past proportion of his infinite?
> And buckle in a waist most fathomless
> With spans and inches so diminutive
> As fear and reasons? fie, for godly shame!
>   (II. ii. 25)

To which Helenus answers:

> No marvel, though you bite so sharp at reasons,
> You are so empty of them. Should not our father
> Bear the great sway of his affairs with reasons,
> Because your speech hath none that tells him so?
>   (II. ii. 33)

Troilus' answer is withering. Reasons, he says, will always counsel cowardice:

> . . . Nay, if we talk of reason,
> Let's shut our gates and sleep; manhood and honour
> Should have hare-hearts, would they but fat their thoughts
> With this cramm'd reason: reason and respect
> Make livers pale and lustihood deject.
>
> (II. ii. 46)

From this point the argument gets into deep waters:

> *Hector.* Brother, she is not worth what she doth cost
>   The holding.
> *Troilus.* What is aught, but as 'tis valued?
> *Hector.* But value dwells not in particular will;
>   It holds his estimate and dignity
>   As well wherein 'tis precious of itself
>   As in the prizer: 'tis mad idolatry
>   To make the service greater than the god;
>   And the will dotes that is attributive
>   To what infectiously itself affects,
>   Without some image of the affected merit.
>
> (II. ii. 51)

Hector takes his stand on the objectivity of pure value: subjective emotion by itself weighs nothing—it is sentimentalism, idolatry. The passion ('will')[1] which infects an object in imagination with those very qualities for which it worships it is clearly absurd: it must have at least some clear-cut and objective image or concept of the quality which it adores. The word 'image' is chosen for its clear suggestion of objectivity.

Troilus' answer is of extreme importance. It is difficult. The first pregnant eight lines are as follows:

> I take to-day a wife and my election
> Is led on in the conduct of my will;
> My will enkindled by mine eyes and ears,
> Two traded pilots 'twixt the dangerous shores
> Of will and judgement; how may I avoid,
> Although my will distaste what it elected,
> The wife I chose? there can be no evasion
> To blench from this and to stand firm by honour.
>
> (II. ii. 61)

[1] 'Will' is often to be equated with 'passion' in Shakespeare: see *Antony and Cleopatra,* III. xi. 3, and *Othello,* III. iii. 232. In these passages 'will' is contrasted with 'reason' and 'judgement'. The emotional quality implicit in the 'will' concept of Shakespeare is important.

This outlines a metaphysic of symbolism—which is suggested by other passages of Shakespeare and especially in the imagery of this play—a philosophy which seems to regard the shapes of materiality as bodies infused into life by the vitality of the regarding mind: matter the symbol of spirit. First, we must see clearly that 'will' stands for instinctive, unconscious passion. Troilus' meaning then is: To-day I take a wife, and my choice of her is directed by the urging power of instinctive 'will', erotic desire; this unconscious instinct having been kindled to self-expression by my senses, which serve as skilled pilots to navigate the dangerous waters between unconscious instinct and conscious judgement. That is, dormant desire in me has been awakened by my discovering a sensuous image or symbol of that desire, which image serves to bridge the gulf between consciousness and unconsciousness, between mind and soul. The suggestion is that the lover sees his own soul reflected in what he loves. He awakes to self-knowledge by seeing. His sensuous perception allows his nameless unconscious desire to reach fulfilment in self-consciousness, or 'judgement'. In this speech we have a careful analysis of love's intuition: and thence, perhaps, we may deduce a corresponding though less vivid process of ordinary sensuous perception. It will be clear that the reasoning and analysis of this play go deep: it will be clear that the mind of Shakespeare is here intensely engaged with purely philosophic issues. So Troilus champions the cause of intuition, of immediate values. But he is not consistent. For, once having made a choice, he says, it must be a point of honour to keep to it. Yet, we might ask, if immediate values are everything, why not let one value succeed another? When the 'will' does 'distaste what it elected', why not find a new sensuous image to satisfy it? To argue otherwise seems to call in the aid of the much-despised 'reason'. This is, indeed, at the root of Troilus' love-tragedy. His nature must be loyal to the dictates of a supreme intuition: but the stream of events takes its logical course in hideous reversal of his faith.

The question of Helen is discussed throughout the scene: throughout the scene the thinking is intricate and subtle, yet voiced with fervour and poetic colour. Paris, like Troilus, takes his stand on points of 'honour'. Hector quotes Aristotle, and sums up the discussion, urging the sanctity of marriage, the moral imperative of Helen's restoration, and then, after a speech of cogent reasoning, curiously concludes by asserting:

> Hector's opinion
> Is thus in way of truth: yet ne'ertheless,
> My spritely brethren, I propend to you
> In resolution to keep Helen still,
> For 'tis a cause that has no mean dependence
> Upon our joint and several dignities.   (ii. ii. 188)

The balance is just. Troilus' argument of immediate values does not altogether satisfy our practical reason. Hector's is eminently logical—but he himself does not act on it. And just in this indecisive fashion do human acts and judgements interpenetrate and preclude each other. Here, we should note, the adherents of intuition win against the rationalists.

I have noticed these two scenes in order to point the peculiar nature of this play: its analytic and metaphysical quality. In both scenes the argument may be said to concern some form of the intuition-intellect opposition: the opposition from which is struck the spark of the central love-theme of Troilus. But before I pass to this the central theme of the play, I shall indicate briefly certain important strata of the life-view expressed in some other subsidiary scenes and persons on the side of the Greek party. This view is pre-eminently analytic and critical: and where it is critical, criticism is levelled, not as in *Measure for Measure*, against moral failings, but rather against lack of wisdom and intellect. This critical attitude extends from the studied commentary of Ulysses to the violent invectives of Thersites. The figures of Achilles and Ajax are selected for especial satire, and their behaviour shown not so much as immoral as essentially stupid.

Achilles sulking in his tent is conceived as a man of bodily strength, supreme egotism, and lack of intellect. Ulysses describes the lazy and licentious amusements of Achilles and Patroclus 'mocking the designs' of the leaders and breaking 'scurril jests' (i. iii. 146). He concludes:

> And in this fashion,
> All our abilities, gifts, natures, shapes,

> Severals and generals of grace exact,
> Achievements, plots, orders, preventions,
> Excitements to the field, or speech for truce,
> Success or loss, what is or is not, serves
> As stuff for these two to make paradoxes.   (I. iii. 178)

Satire here is two-edged: Achilles, proud only of his personal strength, is a creature essentially absurd; but so, also, his criticisms of the generals, and their own laboured and long-winded annoyance at his mockery, render their prided authority and intellect itself ridiculous. We cannot but enjoy the keen satire of Achilles' speech to Patroclus:

> To him, Patroclus; tell him I humbly desire the valiant Ajax to invite the most valorous Hector to come unarmed to my tent, and to procure safe-conduct for his person of the magnanimous and most illustrious six-or-seven-times-honoured captain-general of the Grecian Army, Agamemnon, &c.
> (III. iii. 277)

Achilles, says Ulysses, recognizes no value in intellect. He and Patroclus

> Forestall prescience and esteem no act
> But that of hand: the still and mental parts,
> That do contrive how many hands shall strike,
> When fitness calls them on, and know by measure
> Of their observant toil the enemies' weight—
> Why this hath not a finger's dignity:
> They call this bed-work, mappery, closet-war;
> So that the ram that batters down the wall,
> For the great swing and rudeness of his poise,
> They place before his hand that made the engine,
> Or those that with the fineness of their souls
> By reason guide his execution.   (I. iii. 199)

Nestor's conclusion is unanswerable:

> Let this be granted, and Achilles' horse
> Makes many Thetis' sons.   (I. iii. 211)

But neither Agamemnon, with his companions Nestor and Ulysses, nor Achilles seem worthy of admiration. The staff are incapable of anything but futile and prolix talk; Achilles and Ajax are both hopelessly spoilt by egotism and pride.

This theme is continued by the staff's choice of Ajax to oppose Hector, thus enabling them to pretend that they rely no more on Achilles: which plan succeeds in rousing Achilles from his swelled-headed laziness and insolence. The scene

(III. iii) where Ulysses broaches the matter to Achilles deserves attention. The nature of pride is keenly analysed. No man is 'the lord of anything' till he sees his qualities reflected among others. Just as beauty is visible not to the owner but to those around, just as the eye needs a mirror if it is to see itself, so all human qualities are practically non-existent until expressed, and not known by the originator until seen to be reflected. Individual pride is thus condemned, not as wicked, but as metaphysically unsound, and the shallowness of Achilles' behaviour exposed as a thing of folly. The insistence here is always on things of the mind, the criticism and satire directed against folly. Ulysses, too, points out that Achilles does ill to rest on his past laurels. Time will destroy past glories and there is no continued honour save to the man whose acts keep pace with time. All fine qualities are subject to 'envious and calumniating time' (III. iii. 174). With these arguments Ulysses has his way. Again, Ulysses' victory is a victory of intellect over intuition: he shows individualism to be not merely wrong, or even unwise, but non-existent. For, since he attacks (i) individualism and (ii) faith in an immediate reality without reference to time, with the arguments of man's social dependence and the validity of the time-sequence, he is clearly pursuing his former philosophy of reason and order against a form of intuition. This is further shown by his fine words on the 'soul of state' which, he says, knows all the details of Achilles' love passages with Polyxena of Troy (III. iii. 195–207). This scene exposes the weakness of individualism, its rational absurdity. Achilles is convinced. He decides to bestir himself, his folly exposed.

Both Achilles and Ajax—the latter conceived as a hopeless blockhead—are butts for the invectives of Thersites. Thersites grows naturally enough from this intellectual satirical atmosphere. He is cynicism incarnate: a demoniac spirit of keen critical apprehension, who sees the stupid and sordid aspects of mankind, fit only for jeers with which he salutes them in full measure. His critical intellect measures man always by intellectual standards. He sees folly everywhere, and finds no wisdom in mankind's activity. He sees one side of the picture only: man's stupidity. He is blind to man's nobility. The choice is between these two. For, if values of beauty, love, goodness, honour, be subtracted from our view of man, what is left is profoundly stupid: a critical intellect can prove almost any endeavour to be meaningless, any end illogical, any passionate hope a delusion. What is left is an animal aping something which he cannot attain, with no inherent reason for his absurd pride. Thersites' satire is thus eminently comparable with Swift's: *Gulliver's Travels* is an illuminating and exquisitely apt commentary on this especial mode of the Shakespearian hate-theme which sets the stage for *Troilus and Cressida*. As Achilles says:

> My mind is troubled, like a fountain stirr'd;
> And I myself see not the bottom of it ...   (iii. iii. 314)

Thersites comments to himself,

> Would the fountain of your mind were clear again, that I might water an ass at it! I had rather be a tick in a sheep than such a valiant ignorance.
> (iii. iii. 316)

His favourite target is Ajax. The others recognize Ajax' stupidity and Ulysses especially makes wit-capital of it; but Thersites glories in it:

> ... thou art here but to thrash Trojans; and thou art bought and sold among those of any wit, like a barbarian slave.   (ii. i. 50)

Ajax, says Thersites, 'wears his wit in his belly and his guts in his head' (ii. i. 78). Thersites' hate of man is, however, universal: it so warps his mind that he levels a sweeping condemnation of their miserable stupidity wholesale. He addresses Patroclus:

> ... The common curse of mankind, folly and ignorance, be thine in great revenue! Heaven bless thee from a tutor, and discipline come not near thee! Let thy blood be thy direction to thy death!
> (ii. iii. 30)

This last sentence illustrates the positive side of Thersites' hate: he is disgusted at man's uncontrolled instincts and passions ('blood') which assume proportion to his lack of intellect. The whole matter of the war is absurd to him: 'all the argument is a cuckold and a whore' (ii. iii. 79). He includes Agamemnon and Menelaus in his category of despisal (v. i. 53–75); also Diomed (v. i. 98–110). Patroclus

is thought to be Achilles' 'masculine whore' (v. i. 20).
Lechery, pride, stupidity, wars—this is Thersites' vision
of human activity. These are the rock-bottom realities
glossed over by the film of irrational supposed 'values'. As
the play's action speeds up in the fierce fighting at the end,
when passion burns high in war, Thersites stands behind
the fight of Paris and Menelaus, mocking:

> The cuckold and the cuckold-maker are at it. Now, bull! now, dog!
> 'Loo, Paris, 'loo! now my double-henned sparrow! 'loo Paris, 'loo!
> The bull has the game: ware horns, ho!   (v. vii. 9)

One should observe how well Thersites succeeds: he here
makes the contestants look blatantly ridiculous. But he, too,
is distorted, deformed, absurd. He knows it:

> I am a bastard, too: I love bastards: I am a bastard begot, bastard in-
> structed, bastard in mind, bastard in valour, in everything illegitimate.
>   (v. vii. 17)

It is true. So, too, the critical intellect by itself, unaided and
unimpelled by intuition or some mode of faith, contains the
seeds of its own destruction: it is self-contradictory, un-
creative, deformed.

   Thersites is the extreme personification of the view of life
developed in the Greek party of *Troilus and Cressida*. We
partly endorse his opinion, without countenancing his
manners. Mankind and their loves and wars are successfully
satirized. The whole business of this war, indeed, seems
particularly pointless. This is emphasized by Diomed in
conversation with Paris. Paris asks who deserves Helen best,
he or Menelaus. Diomed replies bitterly that both merit
alike who seek her 'with such a hell of pain and world of
charge' (iv. i. 57), continuing with the thought that she is
already dishonoured and utterly valueless:

> *Paris.* You are too bitter to your countrywoman.
> *Diomed.* She's bitter to her country: hear me, Paris:
> For every false drop in her bawdy veins
> A Grecian's life hath sunk; for every scruple
> Of her contaminated carrion weight,
> A Trojan hath been slain: since she could speak,
> She hath not given so many good words breath
> As for her Greeks and Trojans suffer'd death.   (iv. i. 67)

The military action of the play is here shown to be rotten at
its core.

Though the Greek camp is throughout under the shadow of cynicism—we must remember that Agamemnon and Nestor cannot escape our satiric sense, since there is something strangely ineffectual in their acts and words—the Trojans are presented very differently. Whereas the Greeks represent 'intellect' in our crude division, the Trojans stand for 'intuition'. True, on each side there are verbal conflicts between points of view corresponding to these labels, as I have shown: yet in the Greek discussion the rationalist, and in the Trojan the emotional, argument gains the ascendency. The contrast between the two camps is marked by the Pandarus and Thersites conceptions. Pandarus' humour is always kindly and sympathetic, Thersites' cynical and mocking. From the start Pandarus' fussy interest in his young friends' love-adventure is truly delightful:

> Go to, a bargain made: seal it, seal it; I'll be the witness. Here I hold
> your hand, here my cousin's.   (III. ii. 204)

We must not be repelled by Pandarus' lax morality in helping these two to illicit love: since, in so far as we regard their love as illicit, we are clearly missing the whole point of this theme. We must see clearly that no such moral criticism may be levelled against Troilus as he is presented and depicted within the action of this play. Troilus' love is throughout hallowed by his constancy, his fire, his truth:

> I am as true as truth's simplicity
> And simpler than the infancy of truth.   (III. ii. 176)

It is conceived and presented throughout as a thing essentially pure and noble. Pandarus' part in this love-story exactly corresponds, at the start, to that of the Nurse in *Romeo and Juliet*. But when tragedy overtakes the lovers, he is nearer akin to the Fool in *King Lear*. Like the Fool, he attempts to relieve the tension by a strained comedy:

> What a pair of spectacles is here! Let me embrace too. 'O heart', as the
> goodly saying is,
>
>> '. . . O heart, heavy heart,
>> Why sigh'st thou without breaking?'
>
> Where he answers again,
>
>> 'Because thou canst not ease thy smart
>> By friendship nor by speaking.'

There was never a truer rhyme. Let us cast away nothing for we may live to have need of such a verse: we see it, we see it. How now, lambs?

(IV. iv. 14)

Towards the end, he is deeply sympathetic. He hands Troilus a letter from the faithless Cressid:

> *Pandarus.* Here's a letter come from yond poor girl.
> *Troilus.* Let me read.
> *Pandarus.* A whoreson tisick, a whoreson rascally tisick so troubles me, and the foolish fortune of this girl; and what one thing, what another, that I shall leave you one o' these days: and I have a rheum in mine eyes too, and such an ache in my bones, that, unless a man were cursed, I cannot tell what to think on't. What says she there?   (v. iii. 99)

That holds the true pathos of humour vanquished by tragedy. The conception of Pandarus is one of the most exquisite things in this play. But not only is Pandarus' humour like health-bringing sunshine compared with the sickly eclipsing cynicism of Thersites' jeers: the Trojans are conceived throughout on an heroic and chivalrous plane.

Troilus is a 'prince of chivalry' (I. ii. 246), and Hector 'in the vein of chivalry' (v. iii. 32); phrases which point a quality ever present among the Trojans. Honour is their creed, they hold beauty as a prize, and behave and speak like men dedicate to high purposes:

> Life every man holds dear; but the brave man
> Holds honour far more precious dear than life.   (v. iii. 27)

This is typical:

>   Can it be
> That so degenerate a strain as this
> Should once set footing in your generous bosoms?
> There's not the meanest spirit on our party
> Without a heart to dare or sword to draw
> When Helen is defended, nor none so noble
> Whose life were ill-bestow'd, or death unfam'd
> Where Helen is the subject.   (II. ii. 153)

With them there is room for romance, sacrifice, love. Their world is conceived imaginatively, picturesquely: knights of valour pass one by one returning from battle, praised in turn by Pandarus; Cassandra's prophecies and Andromache's dreams suggest the infinite and the unknown purposes of fate or God; the strains of music herald the entry of Helen, queen of romance. Among them we find love and honour of parents, humour, conviviality, patriotism: all which are lacking among the Greeks. The Trojans remain firm in their mutual support. Their cause is worthy, if only because they believe in it. They speak glittering words of honour, generosity, bravery, love. Here is a strange and happy contrast with the shadowed world of the Greek camp, where all seems stagnant, decadent, paralysed. Troy is a world breathing the air of medieval, storied romance; the Greek camp exists on that of Renaissance satire and disillusion. There is thus a sharp dualism of two world-views: the romantic contrasted with the cynical. Between these two modes of consciousness Troilus' mind is drawn asunder until he finds no 'rule in unity itself': Cressida passes from Troy and his love over to the Greeks and the loose wantonness of Diomed. So between the glancing lights of romance and the shadows of cynicism is worked out the philosophic love-story of Troilus and Cressida. The larger dualism reflects the central one: and both may be roughly equated with the intuition-intellect opposition.

Troilus is shown to us as an ardent and faithful lover, faithful as he more than once says to 'simplicity'. Cressida is shallow and indirect in her thinking and behaviour, though we need not suppose her love for Troilus, whilst it lasts, to be insincere. Now Troilus' love is from the first unrestful. In *Romeo and Juliet* the adverse forces work from without: here they are implicit within long before the separation of the lovers. This is the primary difference between the early and the later play. When we first meet Troilus he is in agonies of unsatisfied aspiration; and he seems throughout the play aware that his love-aspiration is such that it probably cannot be satisfied. In the first scene we see him deserting the value of war for that of love, and analysing this new and potent reality that has claimed his heart:

> Peace, you ungracious clamours! peace, rude sounds!
> Fools on both sides! Helen must needs be fair,
> When with your blood you daily paint her thus.
> I cannot fight upon this argument;
> It is too starved a subject for my sword.
> But Pandarus—Oh gods, how do you plague me!

I cannot come to Cressid but by Pandar;
And he's as tetchy to be woo'd to woo,
As she is stubborn-chaste against all suit.
Tell me, Apollo, for thy Daphne's love,
What Cressid is, what Pandar, and what we?
Her bed is India; there she lies, a pearl:
Between our Ilium and where she resides,
Let it be call'd the wild and wandering flood,
Ourself the merchant, and this sailing Pandar
Our doubtful hope, our convoy, and our bark.   (I. i. 94)

This is Shakespeare's usual love-symbolism. The loved one
is costly merchandise or a rich stone, across the sea.[1] The
tempestuous waves of temporal conditions sever the lover
from the impossible fruition of his love. On these waters of
tragedy the frail bark of the individual mind must set its
sails to the rough seas and the winds of time (see p. 53,
II. ii. 64–5). Troilus in love pauses to ask what exactly are
the elements which make up this overpowering reality. There
are three: (i) the lover, (ii) the objective image of love to
which he aspires, (iii) the flux of chance and change in the
temporal scheme which parts the first two. This speech is an
instance of purely metaphysical thought given the concrete
forms of poetry: or, more truly, an instance of pure poetic
thought which lends itself to a clear intellectual paraphrase.
From the very start we are aware of the peculiarly analytic cast of Troilus' love: he is throughout a metaphysical
lover.

Next Troilus' suit prospers: hence his vigorous defence
of values and heroic action in the cause of Troy which I
have already noted. The successful lover sees all life's adventure in terms of romance, and is strong in the glistening
armour of vision. But when the time comes for him to
encounter Cressid his mind again recoils in dismay from the
feared impossibility of actual fruition:

> *Troilus.* I am giddy; expectation whirls me round.
>   The imaginary relish is so sweet
>   That it enchants my sense: what will it be,

[1] *Romeo and Juliet*, I. v. 50; II. ii. 83–4; *Othello*, II. i. 83; *The Merchant of Venice*, II.
vii. 44–8; *Troilus and Cressida*, II. ii. 81–3, Sonnet LXXXVI. 1–2. Love, merchandise or rich
stones, and dangerous sea journeys appear to be related in Shakespeare's imagination. The
metaphor of 'jewel' or 'pearl' occurs frequently in Shakespeare's love-imagery: *Othello*, I. iii.
195, V. ii. 346; *Cymbeline*, I. iv. 82–7, and 170; *A Midsummer-Night's Dream*, IV. i. 197; *The
Two Gentlemen of Verona*, II. iv. 170–2—and elsewhere throughout the plays and sonnets.

When that the watery palate tastes indeed
Love's thrice-repured nectar? death, I fear me,
Swooning destruction, or some joy too fine,
Too subtle-potent, tuned too sharp in sweetness,
For the capacity of my ruder powers:
I fear it much; and I do fear besides,
That I shall lose distinction in my joys:
As doth a battle, when they charge on heaps
The enemy flying.   (III. ii. 17)

Troilus fears that love's reality is a thing essentially beyond
the capacity of the individual mind: that the mind must
break in the attempt to compass it in all its infinity of delight.
Here again we see the difference from the time of Romeo:
Romeo had no such fears—he was the instinctive and boyish
lover thwarted by fate. Troilus is by way of being a metaphysical lover thwarted inwardly by the fine knowledge of
human limitations. For Troilus' mind in love aspires only
to the infinite, as he says in his dialogue with Cressid a little
further on:

. . . This is the monstruosity in love, lady, that the will is infinite and
the execution confined; that the desire is boundless, and the act a slave
to limit.   (III. ii. 85)

The prose dialogue of the lovers' first meetings is, indeed,
throughout pregnant with meaning. And its studied, courteous manner is noteworthy. After the fiery imaginations
of Troilus' love-thoughts, comes the impact of actuality—
he meets Cressid in the flesh, and is embarrassed. All he
can say on first meeting her is:

O Cressida, how often have I wished me thus!   (III. ii. 63)

—an exquisite touch of psychology. But they soon warm to
more poetic ardour—yet even then Troilus is beset with
anxiety. He is never at ease, in all the course of his love:

O that I thought it could be in a woman—
As, if it can, I will presume in you—
To feed for aye her lamp and flames of love;
To keep her constancy in plight and youth,
Outliving beauty's outward, with a mind
That doth renew swifter than blood decays!
Or that persuasion could but thus convince me,
That my integrity and truth to you
Might be affronted with the match and weight
Of such a winnow'd purity in love;

How were I then uplifted! but, alas!
I am as true as truth's simplicity
And simpler than the infancy of truth.   (III. ii. 165)

Such a desire is irrational: it is trying to make infinite a
thing which is 'a slave to limit'. The mystic apprehension
of romantic love cannot be perfectly bodied into symbols
of sex throughout a lifetime: yet this is Troilus' desire—the
desire of all who love passionately, while they love passionately. The immediate experience is all-conquering: an
experience of something ineffable and infinite. But no finite
symbols can contain it through the stretch of years—and if
they could, it would be limited in time by death. And here
we are at the core of this play's philosophy.

It is the arch-enemy, Time, that kills values. When we
next meet the lovers, they have reached the physical fruition
of love. It is early morning, and they part to the notes of the
morning lark, like Romeo and Juliet. Romeo was forced to
leave Juliet by the laws of Verona: but, before ever Troilus
and Cressida are forced to part, Troilus shows us that no
physical act can sate his aspiration—and his complaint is
levelled against time, the destroyer of love-moments:

Troilus. O Cressida! but that the busy day,
  Waked by the lark, hath rous'd the ribald crows,
  And dreaming night will hide our joys no longer,
  I would not from thee.
Cressida.   Night hath been too brief.
Troilus. Beshrew the witch! with venomous wights she stays
  As tediously as hell, but flies the grasps of love
  With wings more momentary swift than thought.
  You will catch cold, and curse me.   (IV. ii. 8)

Notice how, with the last line, we are aware of the cold
realism which succeeds the faery consciousness of love;
notice, too, the time-thought—the thought of the swift
passage of intuitions, the swift passing of love's enjoyment.[1]

Time-imagery is recurrent and magnificent in *Troilus and
Cressida* beyond any other of Shakespeare's plays. Cressida
speaks a noble passage in swearing her love:

If I be false, or swerve a hair from truth,
When time is old and hath forgot itself,

---

[1] The swiftness of intuitive thoughts in the mind is to be related to the swift-passing of
love's enjoyment in the flux of time. See below, 'Notes on the Text of *Hamlet*', Note B.

> When waterdrops have worn the stones of Troy,
> And blind oblivion swallow'd cities up,
> And mighty states characterless are grated
> To dusty nothing, yet let memory,
> From false to false, among false maids in love,
> Upbraid my falsehood!   (III. ii. 191)

And, later, she says:

> Time, force, and death
> Do to this body what extremes you can.   (IV. ii. 108)

Troilus curses time when Cressida is taken from him:

> Injurious time, now with a robber's haste
> Crams his rich thievery up, he knows not how:
> As many farewells as be stars in heaven,
> With distinct breath and consign'd kisses to them,
> He fumbles up into a loose adieu,
> And scants us with a single famish'd kiss,
> Distasted with the salt of broken tears.   (IV. iv. 42)

Hector tells us

> . . . The end crowns all,
> And that old common arbitrator, Time,
> Will one day end it.   (IV. v. 223)

Nestor is a

> . . . good old chronicle
> That hast so long walked hand in hand with time.   (IV. v. 201)

The creating mind of the poet seems to have been obsessed in the writing of this play by the concept of time: it keeps recurring in one form or another. Agamemnon—though a Greek, we remember he hankers after 'intuition'—welcomes Hector as a guest, and gives him offer of immediate and present love irrespective of future and past events, again working on the negative aspect of the same idea:

> What's past and what 's to come is strew'd with husks
> And formless ruin of oblivion,
> But in this extant moment, faith and troth,
> Strain'd purely from all hollow bias-drawing,
> Bids thee with most divine integrity
> From heart of very heart, great Hector, welcome.   (IV. v. 165)

We have, too, Ulysses' long and elaborate speech on time, commencing

> Time hath, my lord, a wallet at his back,
> Wherein he puts alms for oblivion,
> A great-siz'd monster of ingratitudes;
> Those scraps are good deeds past: which are devour'd
> As fast as they are made, forgot as soon
> As done. (III. iii. 145)

Again, further on:

> O, let not virtue seek
> Remuneration for the thing it was;
> For beauty, wit,
> High birth, vigour of bone, desert in service,
> Love, friendship, charity, are subjects all
> To envious and calumniating time.

But if time is the destroyer, it is also that in which 'shapes' of actuality are born. Says Ulysses:

> I have a young conception in my brain;
> Be you my time to bring it to some shape. (I. iii. 312)

This is a usual Shakespearian phraseology: 'shapes' or 'bodies' are given to things of the mind or spirit, 'born' in 'time'. More 'time' references occur in this play at IV. v. 2, where Agamemnon talks of 'anticipating time with starting courage', and at I. ii. 82, where Pandarus says, 'Time must friend or end'. The time-thinking in this play is inextricably twined with the central love-theme. Troilus is throughout half-conscious of the fact that his love is destined to disaster in the world of flesh: it is a spiritual and delicate thing incapable of continued expression and satisfaction among the rough chaotic and temporal symbols of actuality. Hence his reference to Pandarus—love's medium—as 'our doubtful hope, our convoy, and our bark': in the seas of time the frail bark of the soul's desire is to steer a dangerous course. Hence, too, his analysis of love's intuition, in which the senses are 'the traded pilots twixt the dangerous shores of will and judgement'. The most fleeting of love's glances has to put out on the waters of sense-perception, that is of materiality, and so of time—for time and materiality as normally understood must be considered as interfused and intrinsicate. Throughout this play, in compressed metaphor, in self-conscious and detailed analysis, and thence to dialogue and incident, we have a philosophy of love which regards

it as essentially un-at-home in time and incapable of continued concrete embodiment in the difficult flux of events.
The love-interest turns on this theme: the theme of immediate value, killed, or apparently killed, by time; which is
again the purest form of the intuition-intellect opposition,
since intellect and the time concept are interdependent, and
irrational or super-rational faith of some kind or another can
alone open to the mind a consciousness beyond the temporal,
knowledge of a timeless reality.

Troilus has to part with Cressid: the course of events now
leagues itself with Troilus' metaphysical difficulties against
his love-aspiration. Or, to put it more crudely—from the
view of Pandarus—he at last has a real and honest reason for
complaining against the difficulties and limitations of his
love. Just before she leaves him, Aeneas calls, and Troilus
says:

> Hark! you are call'd: some say the Genius so
> Cries 'Come' to him that instantly must die.   (iv. iv. 50)

This is important. In one sense, Cressid does at this moment
die for Troilus, as I shall show; but in another, we may say
that it would have been well for her and Troilus if she had
—then, like Antony and Cleopatra, whose loves are also
tossed tempestuously on the sea of time, they might enjoy
a transcendent immortality in the time-vanquishing experience of death-in-love. The greater love-tragedy to come
is foreshadowed. The tragic answer to the problem of this
play is already implicit: and this is not the only instance
where the difficulties of the problem plays are directly or
indirectly answered by the great tragedies that follow them.

And then Troilus watches Cressid's inconstancy. He
literally doubts his senses—'the attest of eyes and ears'
(v. ii. 119). He tells Ulysses that it was not Cressida they
have been watching. And then he breaks out passionately
into a speech which tries in vain to resolve the hopeless
dualism in his mind:

> *Troilus.* This she? No, this is Diomed's Cressida;
>   If beauty have a soul, this is not she;
>   If souls guide vows, if vows be sanctimonies,
>   If sanctimony be the gods' delight,
>   If there be rule in unity itself,

This is not she. O madness of discourse,
That cause sets up with and against itself!
Bi-fold authority! where reason can revolt
Without perdition, and loss assume all reason
Without revolt: this is, and is not, Cressid.
Within my soul there doth conduce a fight
Of this strange nature that a thing inseparate
Divides more wider than the sky and earth,
And yet the spacious breadth of this division
Admits no orifex for a point as subtle
As Ariachne's broken woof to enter.   (v. ii. 134)

'This is, and is not, Cressid.' The moral, or the problem, of this play. One has only to compare this speech with similar parts of *Othello* to see the peculiarly analytic and intellectual cast of the play's language. Othello may and does doubt Desdemona's faithlessness: but to question her identity with herself in solemn earnest—he does do so once, purely ironically—would seem an absurdity to him. But it is exactly this questioning of Cressida's identity with herself that we are concerned with here. Must Troilus deny his love-faith, and say, like Hamlet, 'I loved you not'? Or, if he is to stand by his faith in Cressid, must he deny the evidence of his eyes? He cannot love her faithless, yet he loves her—the Cressida of his imagination—still. He still holds fast to his love-vision: it is so deeply rooted in his soul, he may not, dare not, deny it. 'Never did young man fancy with so eternal and so fixed a soul' (v. ii. 162). Are there two Cressids? One of yesterday, one of to-day? That is, it seems, the nearest to a solution. 'Injurious time' 'calumniator time', 'that old common arbitrator time'—has killed the former Cressid. Herein lies the tragedy of Troilus. He puts his faith in an immediately apprehended irrational—or super-rational—experience, and expects it to stand the test of time and reason. It does not do so. To Troilus, whose nature must keep faith with a supreme romantic value, there is now no 'rule in unity itself'. Cressid, with a butterfly temperament flitting from one faith to another, is consistent. She lives emotionally. Thersites, the creature of satire and cynicism, is consistent:

> . . . Lechery, lechery; still, wars and lechery; nothing else holds fashion:
> a burning devil take them!   (v. ii. 192)

He lives critically. But Troilus, who would champion to the uttermost throughout time with all his resources of reason and action his once plighted faith in a timeless experience, who would never 'turn back the silks upon the merchant' (ii. ii. 69), is wrenched torturingly by the tug of two diverging principles. There is now only one hope for Troilus if he is to keep his sanity intact. In the play we have seen him recognize two values: love, and the honour of Priam's cause in war; the same two realities which Thersites curses—'wars and lechery'. At the opening of the play we saw Troilus' love drive out his warriorship: now he transfers his allegiance back to his other value, and passionately throws himself, body and soul, into the war. In the final scenes he fights like one possessed:

> I do not speak of flight, of fear, of death,
> But dare all imminence that gods and men
> Address their dangers in.   (v. x. 12)

He, compact of simplicity and faith and valour, makes the whole host of decadent and absurd Greeks the symbols of his mortal fury. Now, to avenge the knightly and courteous Hector, he launches the cataracts of his hate against Achilles:

> You vile abominable tents,
> Thus proudly pight upon our Phrygian plains,
> Let Titan rise as early as he dare,
> I'll through and through you! and, thou great-siz'd coward,
> No space of earth shall sunder our two hates:
> I'll haunt thee like a wicked conscience still,
> That mouldeth goblins swift as frenzy's thoughts.   (v. x. 23)

This dynamic and positive passion of Troilus is not understood in all its power, purpose, and direction, till we have a clear sight of all that is involved here in the opposition of the Greeks and Troy: Troilus champions, not only Troy, but the fine values of humanity, fighting against the demon powers of cynicism.

The universe of this play is one of love and war. The most nauseating person in the play exposes the futility and stupidity of these activities so ardently and irrationally pursued by mankind: but the beautiful and the heroic are bound to the fiery wheel of these tormenting calls on their instinctive allegiance. So curiously in *Troilus and Cressida* are intertwined the profitless and ugly event with the aspiring and noble endeavour: here we see the infinite cruelly made 'slave to limit'; it is a world of incommensurables, a world of gleaming beauties, and ardent, fiery desires, pitted against the cynic snarl of Thersites, the stupidity of Ajax, and the cold reason of Ulysses. Above all, it is a world of value and vision ruled by murderous and senseless time, who, ignorant and inexorable, pursues his endless course of destruction and slavery, cramming up his rich thievery, 'he knows not how'. The less noble and beautiful seem to win. Time slays the love of Cressid. Hector, symbol of knighthood and generosity, is slain by Achilles, lumbering giant of egotism, lasciviousness, and pride: but all the fires of human nobility and romance yet light Troilus to the last.

In emphasizing the intellectual quality of *Troilus and Cressida* I have implied no adverse criticism of its poetry. Its poetry is exquisite. Metaphysical poetry is not necessarily the less poetry for being metaphysical. And it is too common an error to allot definite provinces of the mind to the rainbow colours of prose and poetry, science, philosophy, and religious mysticism. The human mind is capable of an infinity of varying states of consciousness, merging into one another, some of which demand and some exclude the separate mechanisms of logic, of imagery, of music; and there are border-states where it is impossible to distinguish clearly one faculty from another. *Troilus and Cressida* induces and appeals to a consciousness of sensitive poetic activity which is yet not independent of the forms of abstract conceptual thought nor of the close reasoning of the philosopher. It is, in fact, an instance of a philosophical argument perfectly bodied into poetry and the forms and fictional incidents of drama. Itself analytic, it lends itself easily to philosophic analysis and interpretation. In no play of Shakespeare is there a more powerful unity of idea: throughout *Troilus and Cressida* we meet the same dualism at issue. The dramatic compression is remarkable. There is no waste. The texture of personification, incident, argument, and analysis is close-woven. Envenomed cynicism, with its food, ignorant stupidity, are thrown into relation with the profound philosophy of the Greek leaders: both contrast with the romantic chivalry of Troy and the humour of Pandarus. The symbolic setting for the main theme is, indeed, masterly. Two views of human life are pitted against each other in the opposing armies, and in the continual and lengthy discussions. Always we find it to be fundamentally the same dualism of (i) immediate and personal experience, intuition, the infinite, the timeless; and (ii) the concepts of order and social system, intellect, the finite world, the time-concept. Between these two modes the consciousness of Troilus is wrenched, divided. There is no rule in unity itself.

IV

MEASURE FOR MEASURE AND THE GOSPELS

IN *Measure for Measure* we have a careful dramatic pattern, a studied explication of a central theme: the moral nature of man in relation to the crudity of man's justice, especially in the matter of sexual vice. There is, too, a clear relation existing between the play and the Gospels, for the play's theme is this:

> Judge not, that ye be not judged. For with what judgement ye judge, ye shall be judged: and with what measure ye mete, it shall be measured to you again. (Matthew, vii. 1)

The ethical standards of the Gospels are rooted in the thought of *Measure for Measure*. Therefore, in this analysis we shall, while fixing attention primarily on the play, yet inevitably find a reference to the New Testament continually helpful, and sometimes essential.

Measure for Measure is a carefully constructed work. Not until we view it as a deliberate artistic pattern of certain pivot ideas determining the play's action throughout shall we understand its peculiar nature. Though there is consummate psychological insight here and at least one person of most vivid and poignant human interest, we must first have regard to the central theme, and only second look for exact verisimilitude to ordinary processes of behaviour. We must be careful not to let our human interest in any one person distort our single vision of the whole pattern. The play tends towards allegory or symbolism. The poet elects to risk a certain stiffness, or arbitrariness, in the directing of his plot rather than fail to express dramatically, with variety and precision, the full content of his basic thought. Any stiffness in the matter of human probability is, however, more than balanced by its extreme fecundity and compacted significance of dramatic symbolism. The persons of the play tend to illustrate certain human qualities chosen with careful reference to the main theme. Thus Isabella stands for sainted purity, Angelo for Pharisaical righteousness, the Duke for a psychologically sound and enlightened ethic. Lucio represents indecent wit, Pompey and Mistress Overdone professional immorality. Barnardine is hard-headed, criminal, insensitiveness. Each person illumines some facet of the central theme: man's moral nature. The play's attention is confined chiefly to sexual ethics: which in isolation is naturally the most pregnant of analysis and the most universal of all themes. No other subject provides so clear a contrast between human consciousness and human instinct; so rigid a distinction between the civilized and the natural qualities of man; so amazing, yet so slight, a boundary set in the public mind between the foully bestial and the ideally divine in humanity. The atmosphere, purpose, and meaning of the play are throughout ethical. The Duke, lord of this play in the exact sense that Prospero is lord of *The Tempest*, is the prophet of an enlightened ethic. He controls the action from start to finish, he allots, as it were, praise and blame, he is lit at moments with divine suggestion comparable with his almost divine power of fore-knowledge, and control, and wisdom. There is an enigmatic, other-worldly, mystery suffusing his figure and the meaning of his acts: their results, however, in each case justify their initiation; wherein we see the allegorical nature of the play, since the plot is so arranged that each person receives his deserts in the light of the Duke's—which is really the Gospel—ethic.

The poetic atmosphere is one of religion and critical morality. The religious colouring is orthodox, as in *Hamlet*. Isabella is a novice among 'the votarists of St. Clare' (I. iv. 5); the Duke disguises himself as a Friar, exercising the divine privileges of his office towards Juliet, Barnardine, Claudio, Pompey. We hear of 'the consecrated fount a league below the city' (IV. iii. 106). The thought of death's eternal damnation, which is prominent in *Hamlet*, recurs in Claudio's speech:

> Ay, but to die and go we know not where;
> To lie in cold obstruction and to rot;
> This sensible warm motion to become
> A kneaded clod; and the delighted spirit

To bathe in fiery floods, or to reside
In thrilling region of thick-ribbed ice;
To be imprison'd in the viewless winds,
And blown with restless violence round about
The pendant world; or to be worse than worst
Of those that lawless and incertain thoughts
Imagine howling: 'tis too horrible!
The weariest and most loathed worldly life
That age, ache, penury, and imprisonment
Can lay on nature is a paradise
To what we fear in death.   (III. i. 116)

So powerful can orthodox eschatology be in *Measure for
Measure*: it is not, as I shall show, all-powerful. Nor is the
play primarily a play of death-philosophy: its theme is rather
that of the Gospel ethic. And there is no more beautiful
passage in all Shakespeare on the Christian redemption than
Isabella's lines to Angelo:

Alas! Alas!
Why, all the souls that were, were forfeit once;
And He, that might the vantage best have took,
Found out the remedy. How would you be,
If He which is the top of judgement, should
But judge you as you are? O, think on that;
And mercy then will breathe within your lips,
Like man new made.   (II. ii. 72)

This is the natural sequence to Isabella's earlier lines:

Well, believe this,
No ceremony that to great ones 'longs,
Not the king's crown, nor the deputed sword,
The marshal's truncheon, nor the judge's robe,
Become them with one half so good a grace
As mercy does.   (II. ii. 58)

These thoughts are a repetition of those in Portia's famous
'mercy' speech. There they come as a sudden, gleaming,
almost irrelevant beam of the ethical imagination. But here
they are not irrelevant: they are intrinsic with the thought
of the whole play, the pivot of its movement. In *The Merchant
of Venice* the Gospel reference is explicit:

. . . We do pray for mercy;
And that same prayer doth teach us all to render
The deeds of mercy.   (IV. i. 200)

And the central idea of *Measure for Measure* is this:

> And forgive us our debts as we forgive our debtors. (Matthew, vi, 12)

Thus 'justice' is a mockery: man, himself a sinner, cannot presume to judge. That is the lesson driven home in *Measure for Measure*.

The atmosphere of Christianity pervading the play merges into the purely ethical suggestion implicit in the inter-criticism of all the persons. Though the Christian ethic be the central theme, there is a wider setting of varied ethical thought, voiced by each person in turn, high or low. The Duke, Angelo, and Isabella are clearly obsessed with such ideas and criticize freely in their different fashions. So also Elbow and the officers bring in Froth and Pompey, accusing them. Abhorson is severely critical of Pompey:

> A bawd? Fie upon him! He will discredit our mystery.
>
> (IV. ii. 29)

Lucio traduces the Duke's character, Mistress Overdone informs against Lucio. Barnardine is universally despised. All, that is, react to each other in an essentially ethical mode: which mode is the peculiar and particular vision of this play. Even music is brought to the bar of the ethical judgement:

> . . . music oft hath such a charm
> To make bad good, and good provoke to harm.   (IV. i. 16)

Such is the dominating atmosphere of this play. Out of it grow the main themes, the problem and the lesson of *Measure for Measure*. There is thus a pervading atmosphere of orthodoxy and ethical criticism, in which is centred the mysterious holiness, the profound death-philosophy, the enlightened human insight and Christian ethic of the protagonist, the Duke of Vienna.

The satire of the play is directed primarily against self-conscious, self-protected righteousness. The Duke starts the action by resigning his power to Angelo. He addresses Angelo, outspoken in praise of his virtues, thus:

> Angelo,
> There is a kind of character in thy life,
> That to the observer doth thy history
> Fully unfold. Thyself and thy belongings
> Are not thine own so proper, as to waste
> Thyself upon thy virtue, they on thee.

Heaven doth with us as we with torches do;
Not light them for themselves; for if our virtues
Did not go forth of us, 'twere all alike
As if we had them not. Spirits are not finely touch'd
But to fine issues, nor Nature never lends
The smallest scruple of her excellence,
But, like a thrifty goddess, she determines
Herself the glory of a creditor,
Both thanks and use.   (1. i. 27)

The thought is similar to that of the Sermon on the Mount:

Ye are the light of the world. A city that is set on an hill cannot be hid.
Neither do men light a candle, and put it under a bushel, but on a candle-
stick; and it giveth light unto all that are in the house.
                                                         (Matthew, v. 14)

Not only does the Duke's 'torch' metaphor clearly recall
this passage, but his development of it is vividly paralleled
by other of Jesus' words. The Duke compares 'Nature' to
'a creditor', lending qualities and demanding both 'thanks
and use'. Compare:

For the Kingdom of Heaven is as a man travelling into a far country,
who called his own servants, and delivered unto them his goods.

And unto one he gave five talents, to another two, and to another one;
to every man according to his several ability; and straightway took his
journey.   (Matthew, xxv. 14)

The sequel needs no quotation. Now, though Angelo
modestly refuses the honour, the Duke insists, forcing it on
him. Later, in conversation with Friar Thomas, himself disguised as a Friar now, he gives us reason for his strange act:

We have strict statutes and most biting laws,
The needful bits and curbs to headstrong steeds,
Which for this nineteen years we have let slip;
Even like an o'ergrown lion in a cave,
That goes not out to prey. Now, as fond fathers,
Having bound up the threatening twigs of birch,
Only to stick it in their children's sight
For terror, not to use, in time the rod
Becomes more mock'd than fear'd; so our decrees,
Dead to infliction, to themselves are dead;
And liberty plucks justice by the nose;
The baby beats the nurse, and quite athwart
Goes all decorum.   (1. iii. 19)

Therefore he has given Angelo power and command to
'strike home'. Himself he will not exact justice, since he has

already, by his laxity, as good as bade the people sin by his
'permissive pass': the people could not readily understand
such a change in himself—with a new governor it would be
different. But these are not his only reasons. He ends:

> Moe reasons for this action
> At our more leisure shall I render you;
> Only, this one: Lord Angelo is precise;
> Stands at a guard with envy; scarce confesses
> That his blood flows, or that his appetite
> Is more to bread than stone: hence shall we see
> If power change purpose, what our seemers be.   (I. iii. 48)

The rest of the play slowly unfolds the rich content of the
Duke's plan, and the secret, too, of his lax rule.

Escalus tells us that the Duke was

> One that, above all other strifes, contended especially to know himself.
> (III. ii. 252)

But he has studied others, besides himself. He prides himself
on his knowledge:

> There is written in your brow, provost, honesty and constancy: if I read
> it not truly, my ancient skill beguiles me . . .   (IV. ii. 161)

Herein are the causes of his leniency. His government
has been inefficient, not through an inherent weakness or
laxity in him, but rather because meditation and self-
analysis, together with profound study of human nature,
have shown him that all passions and sins of other men have
reflected images in his own soul. He is no weakling: he has
been 'a scholar, a statesman, and a soldier' (III. ii. 158). But
to such a philosopher government and justice may begin to
appear a mockery, and become abhorrent. His judicial
method has been original: all criminals were either executed
promptly or else freely released (IV. ii. 136–9). Nowhere is
the peculiar modernity of the Duke in point of advanced
psychology more vividly apparent. It seems, too, if we are
to judge by his treatment of Barnardine (IV. iii. 71–88), that
he could not tolerate an execution without the criminal's own
approval! The case of Barnardine troubles him intensely:

> A creature unprepar'd, unmeet for death;
> And to transport him in the mind he is
> Were damnable.   (IV. iii. 74)

The Duke's sense of human responsibility is delightful throughout: he is like a kindly father, and all the rest are his children. Thus he now performs the experiment of handing the reins of government to a man of ascetic purity who has an hitherto invulnerable faith in the rightness and justice of his own ideals—a man of spotless reputation and self-conscious integrity, who will have no fears as to the 'justice' of enforcing precise obedience. The scheme is a plot, or trap: a scientific experiment to see if extreme ascetic righteousness can stand the test of power.

The Duke, disguised as the Friar, moves through the play, a dark figure, directing, watching, moralizing on the actions of the other persons. As the play progresses and his plot on Angelo works he assumes an ever-increasing mysterious dignity, his original purpose seems to become more and more profound in human insight, the action marches with measured pace to its appointed and logical end. We have ceased altogether to think of the Duke as merely a studious and unpractical governor, incapable of office. Rather he holds, within the dramatic universe, the dignity and power of a Prospero, to whom he is strangely similar. With both, their plot and plan is the plot and plan of the play: they make and forge the play, and thus are automatically to be equated in a unique sense with the poet himself—since both are symbols of the poet's controlling, purposeful, combined, movement of the chess-men of the drama. Like Prospero, the Duke tends to assume proportions evidently divine. Once he is actually compared to the Supreme Power:

> O my dread lord,
> I should be guiltier than my guiltiness,
> To think I can be undiscernible,
> When I perceive your grace, like power divine,
> Hath look'd upon my passes. (v. i. 367)

So speaks Angelo at the end. We are prepared for it long before. In the rhymed octosyllabic couplets of the Duke's soliloquy in iii. ii. there is a distinct note of supernatural authority, forecasting the rhymed mystic utterances of divine beings in the Final Plays. He has been talking with Escalus and the Provost, and dismisses them with the words:

> Peace be with you!

They leave him and he soliloquizes:

He who the sword of Heaven will bear
Should be as holy as severe ;
Pattern in himself to know
Grace to stand and virtue go;
More nor less to other paying
Than by self-offences weighing.
Shame to him whose cruel striking
Kills for faults of his own liking !
Twice treble shame on Angelo,
To weed my vice and let his grow !
O what may man within him hide,
Though angel on the outward side !
How may likeness made in crimes,
Making practice on the times,
To draw with idle spiders' strings
Most ponderous and substantial things !
Craft against vice I must apply :
With Angelo to-night shall lie
His old betrothed but despis'd ;
So disguise shall, by the disguis'd,
Pay with falsehood false exacting,
And perform an old contracting.   (iii. ii. 283)

This fine soliloquy gives us the Duke's philosophy: the philosophy that prompted his original plan. And it is important to notice the mystical, prophetic tone of the speech.

The Duke, like Jesus, is the prophet of a new order of ethics. This aspect of the Duke as teacher and prophet is also illustrated by his cryptic utterance to Escalus just before this soliloquy:

Escalus. Good even, good father.
Duke. Bliss and goodness on you.
Escalus. Of whence are you?
Duke. Not of this country, though my chance is now
     To use it for my time : I am a brother
     Of gracious order, late come from the See
     In special business from his Holiness.
Escalus. What news abroad i' the world?
Duke. None, but that there is so great a fever on goodness, that the dis-
     solution of it must cure it : novelty is only in request ; and it is as dangerous
     to be aged in any kind of course, as it is virtuous to be constant in any
     undertaking. There is scarce truth enough alive to make societies secure ;
     but security enough to make fellowships accurst : much upon this riddle
     runs the wisdom of the world. This news is old enough, yet it is every
     day's news. I pray you, sir, of what disposition was the Duke?

Escalus. One that, above all other strifes, contended especially to know himself. (III. ii. 233)

This remarkable speech, with its deliberate, incisive, cryptic sentences, has a profound quality and purpose which reaches the very heart of the play. It deserves exact attention. Its expanded paraphrase runs thus:

> No news, but that goodness is suffering such a disease that a complete dissolution of it (goodness) is needed to cure it. That is, our whole system of conventional ethics should be destroyed and rebuilt. A change (novelty) never gets beyond request, that is, is never actually put in practice. And it is as dangerous to continue indefinitely a worn-out system or order of government, as it is praiseworthy to be constant in any individual undertaking. There is scarcely enough knowledge of human nature current in the world to make societies safe; but ignorant self-confidence (i.e. in matters of justice) enough to make human intercourse within a society a miserable thing. This riddle holds the key to the wisdom of the world (probably, both the false wisdom of the unenlightened, and the true wisdom of great teachers). This news is old enough, and yet the need for its understanding sees daily proof.

I paraphrase freely, admittedly interpreting difficulties in the light of the recurring philosophy of this play on the blindness of men's moral judgements, and especially in the light of the Duke's personal moral attitude as read from his other words and actions. This speech holds the poetry of ethics. Its content, too, is very close to the Gospel teaching, the insistence on the blindness of the world, its habitual disregard of the truth exposed by prophet and teacher:

> And this is the condemnation, that light is come into the world, and men loved darkness rather than light, because their deeds were evil.
>
> (John, iii. 19)

The same almost divine suggestion rings in many of the Duke's measured prose utterances. There are his supremely beautiful words to the Provost (iv. ii. 219):

> Look, the unfolding star calls up the shepherd. Put not yourself into amazement how these things should be: all difficulties are but easy when they are known.

The first lovely sentence—a unique beauty of Shakespearian prose, in a style peculiar to this play—derives part of its appeal from New Testament associations, and the second sentence holds the mystic assurance of Matthew, x. 26:

> . . . for there is nothing covered, that shall not be revealed; and hid, that shall not be known.

The Duke exercises the authority of a teacher throughout his disguise as a friar. He speaks authoritatively on repentance to Juliet:

> *Duke.*　　　... but lest you do repent,
>   As that the sin hath brought you to this shame,
>   Which sorrow is always towards ourselves, not Heaven,
>   Showing we would not spare Heaven as we love it,
>   But as we stand in fear—
> *Juliet.* I do repent me as it is an evil,
>   And take the shame with joy.
> *Duke.* There rest ...　　　　　　　　　　(II. iii. 30)

After rebuking Pompey the bawd very sternly but not unkindly, he concludes:

> Go mend, go mend.　　　　　　　　　　(III. ii. 28)

His attitude is that of Jesus to the woman taken in adultery:

> Neither do I condemn thee: go, and sin no more.　(John, viii. 11)

Both are more kindly disposed towards honest impurity than light and frivolous scandal-mongers, such as Lucio, or Pharisaic self-righteousness such as Angelo's.

The Duke's ethical attitude is exactly correspondent with Jesus': the play must be read in the light of the Gospel teaching, if its full significance is to be apparent. So he, like Jesus, moves among men suffering grief at their sins and deriving joy from an unexpected flower of simple goodness in the deserts of impurity and hardness. He finds softness of heart where he least expects it—in the Provost of the prison:

> *Duke.* This is a gentle provost: seldom when
>   The steeled gaoler is the friend of men.　　(IV. ii. 89)

So, too, Jesus finds in the centurion,

> a man under authority, having soldiers under me ...
> 　　　　　　　　　　　　　　　(Matthew, viii. 9)

a simple faith where he least expects it:

> ... I say unto you, I have not found so great faith, no, not in Israel.

The two incidents are very similar in quality. Now, in that he represents a perfected ethical philosophy joined to supreme authority, the Duke is, within the dramatic universe, automatically comparable with Divinity; or we may suggest that he progresses by successive modes, from worldly power through the prophecy and moralizing of the middle scenes, to the supreme judgement at the end, where he exactly reflects the universal judgement as suggested by many Gospel passages. There is the same apparent injustice, the same tolerance and mercy. The Duke is, in fact, a symbol of the same kind as the Father in the Parable of the Prodigal Son (Luke xv) or the Lord in that of the Unmerciful Servant (Matthew xviii). The simplest way to focus correctly the quality and unity of *Measure for Measure* is to read it on the analogy of Jesus' parables.

Though his ethical philosophy is so closely related to the Gospel teaching, yet the Duke's thoughts on death are devoid of any explicit belief in immortality. He addresses Claudio, who is to die, and his words at first appear vague, agnostic: but a deeper acquaintance renders their profundity and truth. Claudio fears death. The Duke comforts him by concentrating not on death, but on life. In a series of pregnant sentences he asserts the negative nature of any single life-joy. First, life is slave to death and may fail at any chance moment; however much you run from death, yet you cannot but run still towards it; nobility in man is inextricably twined with 'baseness' (this is, indeed, the moral of *Measure for Measure*), and courage is ever subject to fear; sleep is man's 'best rest', yet he fears death which is but sleep; man is not a single independent unit, he has no solitary self to lose, but rather is compounded of universal 'dust'; he is always discontent, striving for what he has not, forgetful of that which he succeeds in winning; man is a changing, wavering substance; his riches he wearily carries till death unloads him; he is tortured by disease and old age. The catalogue is strong in unremittent condemnation of life:

> Thou hast nor youth nor age,
> But, as it were, an after-dinner's sleep,
> Dreaming on both; for all thy blessed youth
> Becomes as aged, and doth beg the alms
> Of palsied eld; and when thou art old and rich,
> Thou hast neither heat, affection, limb, nor beauty,
> To make thy riches pleasant. What's yet in this
> That bears the name of life? Yet in this life
> Lie hid moe thousand deaths: yet death we fear,
> That makes these odds all even. (III. i. 32)

Life is therefore a sequence of unrealities, strung together in a time-succession. Everything it can give is in turn killed. Regarded thus, it is unreal, a delusion, a living death. The thought is profound. True, the Duke has concentrated especially on the temporal aspect of life's appearances, regarding only the shell of life and neglecting the inner vital principle of joy and hope; he has left deeper things untouched. He neglects love and all immediate transcendent intuitions. But since it is only this temporal aspect of decayed appearances which death is known to end, since it is only the closing of this very time-succession which Claudio fears, it is enough to prove this succession valueless. Claudio is comforted. The death of such a life is not death, but rather itself a kind of life:

> I humbly thank you.
> To sue to live, I find I seek to die;
> And seeking death, find life: let it come on.   (III. i. 41)

Now he 'will encounter darkness as a bride', like Antony (III. i. 82). The Duke's death-philosophy is thus the philosophy of the great tragedies to follow—of *Timon of Athens*, of *Antony and Cleopatra*. So, too, his ethic is the ethic of *King Lear*. In this problem play we find the profound thought of the supreme tragedies already emergent and given careful and exact form, the Duke in this respect being analogous to Agamemnon in *Troilus and Cressida*. Both his ethical and his death thinking are profoundly modern. But Claudio soon reverts to the crude time-thinking (and fine poetry) of his famous death-speech, in which he regards the after-life in terms of orthodox eschatology, thinking of it as a temporal process, like Hamlet:

> Ay, but to die, and go we know not where . . .   (III. i. 116)

In the Shakespearian mode of progressive thought it is essential first to feel death's reality strongly as the ender of what we call 'life': only then do we begin to feel the tremendous pressure of an immortality not known in terms of time. We then begin to attach a different meaning to the words 'life' and 'death'. The thought of this scene wavers between the old and the new death-philosophies.

The Duke's plot pivots on the testing of Angelo. Angelo is a man of spotless reputation, generally respected. Escalus says

> If any in Vienna be of worth
> To undergo such ample grace and honour,
> It is Lord Angelo.   (1. i. 22)

Angelo, hearing the Duke's praise, and his proposed trust, modestly declines, as though he recognizes that his virtue is too purely idealistic for the rough practice of state affairs:

> Now, good my lord,
> Let there be some more test made of my metal,
> Before so noble and so great a figure
> Be stamp'd upon it.   (1. i. 47)

Angelo is not a conscious hypocrite: rather a man whose chief faults are self-deception and pride in his own righteousness—an unused and delicate instrument quite useless under the test of active trial. This he half-recognizes, and would first refuse the proffered honour. The Duke insists: Angelo's fall is thus entirely the Duke's responsibility. So this man of ascetic life is forced into authority. He is

> a man whose blood
> Is very snow-broth; one who never feels
> The wanton stings and motions of the sense,
> But doth rebate and blunt his natural edge
> With profits of the mind, study and fast.   (1. iv. 57)

Angelo, indeed, does not know himself: no one receives so great a shock as he himself when temptation overthrows his virtue. He is no hypocrite. He cannot, however, be acquitted of Pharisaical pride: his reputation means much to him, he 'stands at a guard with envy' (1. iii. 51). He 'takes pride' in his 'gravity' (11. iv. 10). Now, when he is first faced with the problem of Claudio's guilt of adultery—and commanded, we must presume, by the Duke's sealed orders to execute stern punishment wholesale, for this is the Duke's ostensible purpose—Angelo pursues his course without any sense of wrongdoing. Escalus hints that surely all men must know sexual desire—how then is Angelo's procedure just? Escalus adopts the Duke's ethical point of view, exactly:

> Let but your honour know
> (Whom I believe to be most strait in virtue),

> That, in the working of your own affections,
> Had time coher'd with place, or place with wishing,
> Or that the resolute acting of your blood
> Could have attain'd the effect of your own purpose,
> Whether you had not, some time in your life,
> Err'd in this point, which now you censure him,
> And pull'd the law upon you.   (II. i. 8)

Which reflects the Gospel message:

> Ye have heard that it was said by them of old time, Thou shalt not commit adultery:
> But I say unto you, that whosoever looketh on a woman to lust after her hath committed adultery with her already in his heart.
>
> (Matthew, v. 27)

Angelo's reply is sound sense:

> 'Tis one thing to be tempted, Escalus,
> Another thing to fall.   (II. i. 17)

Isabella later uses the same argument as Escalus:

> . . . Go to your bosom;
> Knock there, and ask your heart what it doth know
> That 's like my brother's fault: if it confess
> A natural guiltiness, such as is his,
> Let it not sound a thought upon your tongue
> Against my brother's life.   (II. ii. 136)

We are reminded of Jesus' words to the Scribes and Pharisees concerning the woman 'taken in adultery':

> He that is without sin among you, let him first cast a stone at her.
>
> (John, viii. 7)

Angelo is, however, sincere: terribly sincere. He feels no personal responsibility, since he is certain that he does right. We believe him when he tells Isabella:

> It is the law, not I, condemn your brother:
> Were he my kinsman, brother, or my son,
> It should be thus with him.   (II. ii. 80)

To execute justice, he says, is kindness, not cruelty, in the long run.

Angelo's arguments are rationally conclusive. A thing irrational breaks them: his passion for Isabella. Her purity, her idealism, her sanctity enslave him—she who speaks to him of

> true prayers
> That shall be up at heaven and enter there
> Ere sun-rise, prayers from preserved souls,
> From fasting maids whose minds are dedicate
> To nothing temporal. (II. ii. 151)

Angelo is swiftly enwrapped in desire. He is finely shown as falling a prey to his own love of purity and asceticism:

> What is't I dream on?
> O cunning enemy, that, to catch a saint,
> With saints dost bait thy hook! (II. ii. 179)

He 'sins in loving virtue'; no strumpet could ever allure him; Isabella subdues him utterly. Now he who built so strongly on a rational righteousness, understands for the first time the sweet unreason of love:

> Ever till now,
> When men were fond, I smil'd and wonder'd how.
> (II. ii. 186)

Angelo struggles hard: he prays to Heaven, but his thoughts 'anchor' on Isabel (II. iv. 4). His gravity and learning—all are suddenly as nothing. He admits to himself that he has taken 'pride' in his well-known austerity, adding 'let no man hear me'—a pathetic touch which casts a revealing light both on his shallow ethic and his honest desire at this moment to understand himself. The violent struggle is short. He surrenders, his ideals all toppled over like ninepins:

> Blood, thou art blood:
> Let's write good angel on the Devil's horn,
> 'Tis not the Devil's crest. (II. iv. 15)

Angelo is now quite adrift: all his old contacts are irrevocably severed. Sexual desire has long been anathema to him, so his warped idealism forbids any healthy love. Good and evil change places in his mind, since this passion is immediately recognized as good, yet, by every one of his stock judgements, condemned as evil. The Devil becomes a 'good angel'. And this wholesale reversion leaves Angelo in sorry plight now: he has no moral values left. Since sex has been synonymous with foulness in his mind, this new love, reft from the start of moral sanction in a man who 'scarce confesses that his blood flows', becomes swiftly a devouring and curbless lust:

> I have begun,
> And now I give my sensual race the rein.   (ii. iv. 160)

So he addresses Isabella. He imposes the vile condition of
Claudio's life. All this is profoundly true: he is at a loss with
this new reality—embarrassed as it were, incapable of
pursuing a normal course of love. In proportion as his moral
reason formerly denied his instincts, so now his instincts
assert themselves in utter callousness of his moral reason. He
swiftly becomes an utter scoundrel. He threatens to have
Claudio tortured. Next, thinking to have had his way with
Isabella, he is so conscience-stricken and tortured by fear that
he madly resolves not to keep faith with her: he orders
Claudio's instant execution. For, in proportion as he is
nauseated at his own crimes, he is terror-struck at exposure.
He is mad with fear, his story exactly pursues the Macbeth
rhythm:

> This deed unshapes me quite, makes me unpregnant
> And dull to all proceedings. A deflower'd maid!
> And by an eminent body that enforc'd
> The law against it! But that her tender shame
> Will not proclaim against her maiden loss,
> How might she tongue me! Yet reason dares her no;
> For my authority bears so credent bulk,
> That no particular scandal once can touch
> But it confounds the breather. He should have lived,
> Save that his riotous youth, with dangerous sense,
> Might in the times to come have ta'en revenge,
> By so receiving a dishonour'd life
> With ransome of such shame. Would yet he had lived!
> Alack, when once our grace we have forgot,
> Nothing goes right: we would, and we would not.
>
> (iv. iv. 23)

This is the reward of self-deception, of pharisaical pride, of
an idealism not harmonized with instinct—of trying, to use
the Duke's pregnant phrase:

> To draw with idle spiders' strings
> Most ponderous and substantial things.   (iii. ii. 297)

Angelo has not been overcome with evil. He has been en-
snared by good, by his own love of sanctity, exquisitely

symbolized in his love of Isabella: the hook is baited with a saint, and the saint is caught. The cause of his fall is this and this only. The coin of his moral purity, which flashed so brilliantly, when tested does not ring true. Angelo is the symbol of a false intellectualized ethic divorced from the deeper springs of human instinct.

The varied close-inwoven themes of *Measure for Measure* are finally knit in the exquisite final act. To that point the action—reflected image always of the Ducal plot—marches

> By cold gradation and well-balanced form.   (iv. iii. 108)

The last act of judgement is heralded by trumpet calls:

> Twice have the trumpets sounded;
> The generous and gravest citizens
> Have hent the gates, and very near upon
> The Duke is entering.   (iv. vi. 12)

So all are, as it were, summoned to the final judgement. Now Angelo, Isabella, Lucio—all are understood most clearly in the light of this scene. The last act is the key to the play's meaning, and all difficulties are here resolved. I shall observe the judgement measured to each, noting retrospectively the especial significance in the play of Lucio and Isabella.

Lucio is a typical loose-minded, vulgar wit. He is the product of a society that has gone too far in condemnation of human sexual desires. He keeps up a running comment on sexual matters. His very existence is a condemnation of the society which makes him a possibility. Not that there is anything of premeditated villainy in him: he is merely superficial, enjoying the unnatural ban on sex which civilization imposes, because that very ban adds point and spice to sexual gratification. He is, however, sincerely concerned about Claudio, and urges Isabella to plead for him. He can be serious—for a while. He can speak sound sense, too, in the full flow of his vulgar wit:

> Yes, in good sooth, the vice is of a great kindred; it is well allied: but it is impossible to extirp it quite, friar, till eating and drinking be put down. They say this Angelo was not made by man and woman after this downright way of creation: is it true, think you?   (iii. ii. 110)

This goes to the root of our problem here. Pompey has voiced the same thought (ii. i. 248–63). This is, indeed, what the Duke has known too well: what Angelo and Isabella do not know. Thus Pompey and Lucio here at least tell down-right facts—Angelo and Isabella pursue impossible and valueless ideals. Only the Duke holds the balance exact throughout. Lucio's running wit, however, pays no consistent regard to truth. To him the Duke's leniency was a sign of hidden immorality:

> Ere he would have hanged a man for getting a hundred bastards, he would have paid for the nursing of a thousand : he had some feeling of the sport; he knew the service, and that instructed him to mercy.
>
> (III. ii. 126)

He traduces the Duke's character wholesale. He does not pause to consider the truth of his words. Again, there is no intent to harm—merely a careless, shallow, truthless wit-philosophy which enjoys its own sex-chatter. The type is common. Lucio is refined and vulgar, and the more vulgar because of his refinement; whereas Pompey, because of his natural coarseness, is less vulgar. Lucio can only exist in a society of smug propriety and self-deception : for his mind's life is entirely parasitical on those insincerities. His false—because fantastic and shallow—pursuit of sex, is the result of a false, fantastic, denial of sex in his world. Like so much in *Measure for Measure* he is eminently modern. Now Lucio is the one person the Duke finds it all but impossible to forgive:

> I find an apt remission in myself;
> And yet here 's one in place I cannot pardon.　　(v. i. 499)

All the rest have been serious in their faults. Lucio's condemnation is his triviality, his insincerity, his profligate idleness, his thoughtless detraction of others' characters:

> You, sirrah, that knew me for a fool, a coward,
> One all of luxury, an ass, a madman;
> Wherein have I so deserv'd of you,
> That you extol me thus?　　(v. i. 501)

Lucio's treatment at the close is eminently, and fittingly, undignified. He is threatened thus: first he is to marry the mother of his child, about whose wrong he formerly boasted; then to be whipped and hanged. Lucio deserves some credit, however : he preserves his nature and answers with his characteristic wit. He cannot be serious. The Duke, his sense of humour touched, retracts the sentence:

> *Duke*. Upon mine honour, thou shalt marry her.
>   Thy slanders I forgive; and therewithal
>   Remit thy other forfeits. Take him to prison;
>   And see our pleasure herein executed.
> *Lucio*. Marrying a punk, my lord, is pressing to death, whipping, and hanging.
> *Duke*. Slandering a prince deserves it.   (v. i. 520)

Idleness, triviality, thoughtlessness receive the Duke's strongest condemnation. The thought is this:

> But I say unto you, That every idle word that men shall speak, they shall give account thereof in the day of judgement.
> > (Matthew xii. 36)

Exactly what happens to Lucio. His wit is often illuminating, often amusing, sometimes rather disgusting. He is never wicked, sometimes almost lovable, but terribly dangerous.[1]

Isabella is the opposite extreme. She is more saintly than Angelo, and her saintliness goes deeper, is more potent than his. When we first meet her, she is about to enter the secluded life of a nun. She welcomes such a life. She even wishes

> a more strict restraint
> Upon the sisterhood, the votarists of Saint Clare.   (I. iv. 4)

Even Lucio respects her. She calls forth something deeper than his usual wit:

> I would not—though 'tis my familiar sin
> With maids to seem the lapwing and to jest,
> Tongue far from heart—play with all virgins so:
> I hold you as a thing ensky'd and sainted,
> By your renouncement an immortal spirit,
> And to be talk'd with in sincerity,
> As with a saint.   (I. iv. 31)

Which contains a fine and exact statement of his shallow behaviour, his habitual wit for wit's sake. Lucio is throughout a loyal friend to Claudio: truer to his cause, in fact, than Isabella. A pointed contrast. He urges her to help. She shows a distressing lack of warmth. It is Lucio that talks of 'your poor brother'. She is cold:

[1] For Lucio, see also *The Imperial Theme*, p. 20.

Lucio.   Assay the power you have.
Isabella. My power? Alas, I doubt—
Lucio.   Our doubts are traitors
    And make us lose the good we oft might win,
    By fearing to attempt.   (I. iv. 76)

Isabella's self-centred saintliness is thrown here into strong contrast with Lucio's manly anxiety for his friend. So, contrasted with Isabella's ice-cold sanctity, there are the beautiful lines with which Lucio introduces the matter to her:

    Your brother and his lover have embrac'd:
    As those that feed grow full, as blossoming time
    That from the seedness the bare fallow brings
    To teeming foison, even so her plenteous womb
    Expresseth his full tilth and husbandry.   (I. iv. 40)

Compare the pregnant beauty of this with the chastity of Isabella's recent lisping line:

    Upon the sisterhood, the votarists of Saint Clare.   (I. iv. 5)

Isabella lacks human feeling. She starts her suit to Angelo poorly enough. She is luke-warm:

    There is a vice that most I do abhor,
    And most desire should meet the blow of justice;
    For which I would not plead but that I must;
    For which I must not plead, but that I am
    At war 'twixt will and will not.   (II. ii. 29)

Lucio has to urge her on continually. We begin to feel that Isabella has no real affection for Claudio; has stifled all human love in the pursuit of sanctity. When Angelo at last proposes his dishonourable condition she quickly comes to her decision:

    Then, Isabel, live chaste and, brother, die.
    More than our brother is our chastity.   (II. iv. 185)

When Shakespeare chooses to load his dice like this—which is seldom indeed—he does it mercilessly. The Shakespearian satire here strikes once, and deep: there is no need to point it further. But now we know our Isabel. We are not surprised that she behaves to Claudio, who hints for her sacrifice, like a fiend:

            Take my defiance!
    Die, perish! Might but my bending down
    Reprieve thee from thy fate, it should proceed:
    I'll pray a thousand prayers for thy death,
    No word to save thee.   (III. i. 141)

Is her fall any less than Angelo's? Deeper, I think. With whom is Isabel angry? Not only with her brother. She has feared this choice—terribly: 'O, I do fear thee, Claudio', she said (III. i. 72). Ever since Angelo's suggestion she has been afraid. Now Claudio has forced the responsibility of choice on her. She cannot sacrifice herself. Her sex inhibitions have been horribly shown her as they are, naked. She has been stung—lanced on a sore spot of her soul. She knows now that it is not all saintliness, she sees her own soul and sees it as something small, frightened, despicable, too frail to dream of such a sacrifice. Though she does not admit it, she is infuriated not with Claudio, but with herself. 'Saints' should not speak like this. Again, the comment of this play is terribly illuminating. It is significant that she readily involves Mariana in illicit love: it is only her own chastity which assumes, in her heart, universal importance.'[1]

Isabella, however, was no hypocrite, any more than Angelo. She is a spirit of purity, grace, maiden charm: but all these virtues the action of the play turns remorselessly against herself. In a way, it is not her fault. Chastity is hardly a sin —but neither, as the play emphasizes, is it the whole of virtue. And she, like the rest, has to find a new wisdom. Mariana in the last act prays for Angelo's life. Confronted by that warm, potent, forgiving, human love, Isabella herself suddenly shows a softening, a sweet humanity. Asked to intercede, she does so—she, who was at the start slow to intercede for a brother's life, now implores the Duke to save Angelo, her wronger:

> I partly think
> A due sincerity govern'd his deeds,
> Till he did look on me.   (v. i. 446)

There is a suggestion that Angelo's strong passion has itself moved her, thawing her ice-cold pride. This is the moment of her trial: the Duke is watching her keenly, to see if she has learnt her lesson—nor does he give her any help, but deliberately puts obstacles in her way. But she stands the test: she bows to a love greater than her own saintliness. Isabella, like Angelo, has progressed far during the play's action: from sanctity to humanity.

[1] I now doubt if Isabella's attitude to Mariana should be held against her (1955).

Angelo, at the beginning of this final scene, remains firm in denial of the accusations levelled against him. Not till the Duke's disguise as a friar is made known and he understands that deception is no longer possible, does he show outward repentance. But we know that his inward thoughts must have been terrible enough, for his earlier agonized soliloquies put this beyond doubt. Now, his failings exposed, he seems to welcome punishment:.

> Immediate sentence then and sequent death
> Is all the grace I beg.   (v. i. 374)

Escalus expresses sorrow and surprise at his actions. He answers:

> I am sorry that such sorrow I procure:
> And so deep sticks it in my penitent heart
> That I crave death more willingly than mercy;
> 'Tis my deserving and I do entreat it.   (v. i. 475)

To Angelo, exposure seems to come as a relief: the horror of self-deception is at an end. For the first time in his life he is both quite honest with himself and with the world. So he takes Mariana as his wife. This is just: he threw her over because he thought she was not good enough for him,

> Partly for that her promised proportions
> Came short of composition, but in chief
> For that her reputation was disvalued
> In levity.   (v. i. 213)

He aimed too high when he cast his eyes on the sainted Isabel: now, knowing himself, he will find his true level in the love of Mariana. He has become human. The union is symbolical. Just as his supposed love-contact with Isabel was a delusion, when Mariana, his true mate, was taking her place, so Angelo throughout has deluded himself. Now his acceptance of Mariana symbolizes his new self-knowledge. So, too, Lucio is to find his proper level in marrying Mistress Kate Keepdown, of whose child he is the father. Horrified as he is at the thought, he has to meet the responsibilities of his profligate behaviour. The punishment of both is this only: to know, and to be, themselves. This is both their punishment and at the same time their highest reward for their sufferings: self-knowledge being the supreme, perhaps the only, good. We remember the parable of the Pharisee and the Publican (Luke xviii).

So the Duke draws his plan to its appointed end. All, including Barnardine, are forgiven, and left, in the usual sense, unpunished. This is inevitable. The Duke's original leniency has been shown by his successful plot to have been right, not wrong. Though he sees 'corruption boil and bubble' (v. i. 316) in Vienna, he has found, too, that man's sainted virtue is a delusion: 'judge not that ye be not judged'. He has seen an Angelo to fall from grace at the first breath of power's temptation, he has seen Isabella's purity scarring, defacing her humanity. He has found more gentleness in 'the steeled gaoler' than in either of these. He has found more natural honesty in Pompey the bawd than in Angelo the ascetic; more humanity in the charity of Mistress Overdone than in Isabella condemning her brother to death with venomed words in order to preserve her own chastity. Mistress Overdone has looked after Lucio's illegitimate child:

> ... Mistress Kate Keepdown was with child by him in the Duke's time; he promised her marriage; his child is a year and a quarter old, come Philip and Jacob: I have kept it myself ... (III. ii. 215)

Human virtue does not flower only in high places: nor is it the monopoly of the pure in body. In reading *Measure for Measure* one feels that Pompey with his rough humour and honest professional indecency is the only one of the major persons, save the Duke, who can be called 'pure in heart'. Therefore, knowing all this, the Duke knows his tolerance to be now a moral imperative: he sees too far into the nature of man to pronounce judgement according to the appearances of human behaviour. But we are not told what will become of Vienna. There is, however, a hint, for the Duke is to marry Isabel, and this marriage, like the others, may be understood symbolically. It is to be the marriage of understanding with purity; of tolerance with moral fervour. The Duke, who alone has no delusions as to the virtues of man, who is incapable of executing justice on vice since he finds forgiveness implicit in his wide and sympathetic understanding—he alone wins the 'enskied and sainted' Isabel. More, we are not told. And we may expect her in future to learn from him wisdom, human tenderness, and love:

> What 's mine is yours and what is yours is mine.   (v. i. 539)

If we still find this universal forgiveness strange—and many have done so—we might observe Mariana, who loves Angelo with a warm and realistically human love. She sees no fault in him, or none of any consequence:

> O my dear lord,
> I crave no other nor no better man.   (v. i. 426)

She knows that

> best men are moulded out of faults,
> And, for the most, become much more the better
> For being a little bad.   (v. i. 440)

The incident is profoundly true. Love asks no questions, sees no evil, transfiguring the just and unjust alike. This is one of the surest and finest ethical touches in this masterpiece of ethical drama. Its moral of love is, too, the ultimate splendour of Jesus' teaching.

Measure for Measure is based firmly on that teaching. The lesson of the play is that of Matthew, v. 20:

> For I say unto you, That except your righteousness shall exceed the righteousness of the scribes and Pharisees, ye shall in no case enter into the Kingdom of Heaven.

The play must be read, not as a picture of normal human affairs, but as a parable, like the parables of Jesus. The plot is, in fact, an inversion of one of those parables—that of the Unmerciful Servant (Matthew, xviii); and the universal and level forgiveness at the end, where all alike meet pardon, is one with the forgiveness of the Parable of the Two Debtors (Luke, vii). Much has been said about the difficulties of *Measure for Measure*. But, in truth, no play of Shakespeare shows more thoughtful care, more deliberate purpose, more consummate skill in structural technique, and, finally, more penetrating ethical and psychological insight. None shows a more exquisitely inwoven pattern. And, if ever the thought at first sight seems strange, or the action unreasonable, it will be found to reflect the sublime strangeness and unreason of Jesus' teaching.

V

THE *OTHELLO* MUSIC

IN *Othello* we are faced with the vividly particular rather than the vague and universal. The play as a whole has a distinct formal beauty: within it we are ever confronted with beautiful and solid forms. The persons tend to appear as warmly human, concrete. They are neither vaguely universalized, as in *King Lear* or *Macbeth*, nor deliberately mechanized and vitalized by the poet's philosophic plan as in *Measure for Measure* and *Timon of Athens*, wherein the significance of the dramatic person is dependent almost wholly on our understanding of the allegorical or symbolical meaning. It is true that Iago is here a mysterious, inhuman creature of unlimited cynicism: but the very presence of the concrete creations around, in differentiating him sharply from the rest, limits and defines him. *Othello* is a story of intrigue rather than a visionary statement. If, however, we tend to regard Othello, Desdemona, and Iago as suggestive symbols rather than human beings, we may, from a level view of their interaction, find a clear relation existing between *Othello* and other plays of the hate-theme. Such an analysis will be here only in part satisfactory. It exposes certain underlying ideas, abstracts them from the original: it is less able to interpret the whole positive beauty of the play. With this important reservation, I shall push the interpretative method as far as possible.

Othello is dominated by its protagonist. Its supremely beautiful effects of style are all expressions of Othello's personal passion. Thus, in first analysing Othello's poetry, we shall lay the basis for an understanding of the play's symbolism: this matter of style is, indeed, crucial, and I shall now indicate those qualities which clearly distinguish it from other Shakespearian poetry. It holds a rich music all its own, and possesses a unique solidity and precision of picturesque phrase or image, a peculiar chastity and serenity of thought. It is, as a rule, barren of direct metaphysical content. Its thought does not mesh with the reader's: rather it is always

outside us, aloof. This aloofness is the resultant of an inward
aloofness of image from image, word from word. The
dominant quality is separation, not, as is more usual in
Shakespeare, cohesion. Consider these exquisite poetic movements:

> O heavy hour!
> Methinks it should be now a huge eclipse
> Of sun and moon, and that the affrighted globe
> Should yawn at alteration.   (v. ii. 97)

Or,

> It is the very error of the moon;
> She comes more near the earth than she was wont,
> And makes men mad.   (v. ii. 107)

These are solid gems of poetry which lose little by divorce
from their context: wherein they differ from the finest
passages of *King Lear* or *Macbeth*, which are as wild flowers
not to be uptorn from their rooted soil if they are to live. In
these two quotations we should note how the human drama
is thrown into sudden contrast and vivid, unexpected relation
with the tremendous concrete machinery of the universe,
which is thought of in terms of individual heavenly bodies:
'sun' and 'moon'. The same effect is apparent in:

> Nay, had she been true,
> If Heaven would make me such another world
> Of one entire and perfect chrysolite,
> I'd not have sold her for it.   (v. ii. 141)

Notice the single word 'chrysolite' with its outstanding and
remote beauty: this is typical of *Othello*.

The effect in such passages is primarily one of contrast.
The vastness of the night sky, and its moving planets, or
the earth itself—here conceived objectively as a solid, round,
visualized object—these things, though thrown momentarily
into sensible relation with the passions of man, yet remain
vast, distant, separate, seen but not apprehended; something
against which the dramatic movement may be silhouetted,
but with which it cannot be merged. This poetic use of
heavenly bodies serves to elevate the theme, to raise issues
infinite and unknowable. Those bodies are not, however,
implicit symbols of man's spirit, as in *King Lear*: they

remain distinct, isolated phenomena, sublimely decorative to the play. In *Macbeth* and *King Lear* man commands the elements and the stars: they are part of him. Compare the above quotations from *Othello* with this from *King Lear*:

> You nimble lightnings, dart your blinding flames
> Into her scornful eyes! Infect her beauty,
> You fen-suck'd fogs, drawn by the powerful sun,
> To fall and blast her pride. (II. iv. 167)

This is typical: natural images are given a human value. They are insignificant, visually: their value is only that which they bring to the human passion which cries out to them. Their aesthetic grandeur, in and for themselves, is not relevant to the *King Lear* universe. So, too, Macbeth cries

> Stars, hide your fires;
> Let not light see my black and deep desires. (I. iv. 50)

And Lady Macbeth:

> Come, thick night,
> And pall thee in the dunnest smoke of Hell,
> That my keen knife see not the wound it makes,
> Nor Heaven peep through the blanket of the dark,
> To cry 'Hold, hold!' (I. v. 51)

Here, and in the *King Lear* extract, there is no clear visual effect as in *Othello*: tremendous images and suggestions are evoked only to be blurred as images by the more powerful passion which calls them into being. Images in *Macbeth* are thus continually vague, mastered by passion; apprehended, but not seen. In Othello's poetry they are concrete, detached; seen but not apprehended. We meet the same effect in:

> Like to the Pontic sea,
> Whose icy current and conpulsive course
> Ne'er feels retiring ebb, but keeps due on
> To the Propontic and the Hellespont,
> Even so my bloody thoughts, with violent pace,
> Shall ne'er look back, ne'er ebb to humble love,
> Till that a capable and wide revenge
> Swallow them up. Now, by yond marble heaven,
> In the due reverence of a sacred vow
> I here engage my words. (III. iii. 454)

This is a strongly typical speech. The long comparison, explicitly made, where in *King Lear* or *Macbeth* a series of

swiftly evolving metaphors would be more characteristic, is
another example of the separateness obtaining throughout
Othello. There is no fusing of word with word, rather a
careful juxtaposition of one word or image with another.
And there are again the grand single words, 'Propontic',
'Hellespont', with their sharp, clear, consonant sounds, constituting defined aural solids typical of the *Othello* music:
indeed, fine single words, especially proper names, are a
characteristic of this play—Anthropophagi, Ottomites,
Arabian trees, 'the base Indian', the Egyptian, Palestine,
Mauretania, the Sagittary, Olympus, Mandragora, Othello,
Desdemona. This is a rough assortment, not all used by
Othello, but it points the Othello quality of rich, often
expressly consonantal, outstanding words. Now Othello's
prayer, with its 'marble heaven', is most typical and illus-
trative. One watches the figure of Othello silhouetted against
a flat, solid, moveless sky: there is a plastic, static suggestion
about the image. Compare it with a similar *King Lear* prayer:

> O heavens,
> If you do love old men, if your sweet sway
> Allow obedience, if yourselves are old,
> Make it your cause; send down and take my part!
>
> (II. iv. 192)

Here we do not watch Lear: 'We are Lear.' There is no
visual effect, no rigid subject-object relation between Lear
and the 'heavens', nor any contrast, but an absolute unspatial
unity of spirit. The heavens blend with Lear's prayer, each
is part of the other. There is an intimate interdependence,
not a mere juxtaposition. Lear thus identifies himself in kind
with the heavens to which he addresses himself directly:
Othello speaks of 'yond marble heaven', in the third person,
and swears by it, does not pray to it. It is conceived as outside
his interests.

This detached style, most excellent in point of clarity and
stateliness, tends also to lose something in respect of power.
At moments of great tension, the *Othello* style fails of a
supreme effect. Capable of fine things quite unmatched in
their particular quality in any other play, it nevertheless
sinks sometimes to a studied artificiality, nerveless and without force. For example, Othello thinks of himself as:

> . . . one whose subdued eyes,
> Albeit unused to the melting mood,
> Drop tears as fast as the Arabian trees
> Their medicinal gum.   (v. ii. 347)

Beside this we might place Macduff's

> O I could play the woman with mine eyes
> And braggart with my tongue! But, gentle heavens,
> Cut short all intermission . . .   (iv. iii. 229)

Othello's lines here have a certain restrained, melodic beauty, like the 'Pontic sea' passage; both speeches use the typical *Othello* picturesque image or word; both compare, by simile, the passion of man with some picture delightful in itself, which is developed for its own sake, slightly over-developed—so that the final result makes us forget the emotion in contemplation of the image. Beauty has been imposed on human sorrow, rather than shown to be intrinsic therein. But Macduff's passionate utterance has not time to paint word pictures of 'yond marble heaven', or to search for abstruse geographical images of the Hellespont or Arabia. There is more force in his first line than all Othello's slightly over-strained phraseology of 'subdued eyes' and 'melting mood'. Its strength derives from the compression of metaphor and the sudden heightened significance of a single, very commonplace, word ('woman'), whereas the other style deliberately refuses power in the level prolixity of simile, and searches always for the picturesque. The *Othello* style is diffuse, leisurely, like a meandering river; the *Macbeth* style compressed, concentrated, and explosive; often jerky, leaping like a mountain torrent. But metaphor is not essential to intensest Shakespearian power. Another, still finer, passage from *King Lear* on the same theme might be adduced:

> *Cordelia.* How does my royal lord? How fares your majesty?
> *Lear.* You do me wrong to take me out o' the grave:
>   Thou art a soul in bliss; but I am bound
>   Upon a wheel of fire, that mine own tears
>   Do scald like molten lead.   (iv. vii. 44)

The extraordinary force of that ending is gained by simile: but there is no diffusion of content, no accent that does not carry the maximum of emotion. It is even more powerful than Macduff's speech, since it lacks excitability: it has the control and dignity of Othello's with the compressed, explosive quality of Macduff's. The *Othello* style does not compass the overpowering effects of *Macbeth* or *King Lear*: nor does it, as a rule, aim at them. At the most agonizing moments of Othello's story, however, there is apparent weakness: we find an exaggerated, false rhetoric.

There is a speech in *Othello* that begins in the typical restrained manner, but degenerates finally to what might almost be called bombast. It starts:

> Where should Othello go?
> Now, how dost thou look now? O ill-starr'd wench!
> Pale as thy smock! When we shall meet at compt,
> This look of thine will hurl my soul from Heaven,
> And fiends will snatch at it. Cold, cold, my girl!
> Even like thy chastity.   (v. ii. 270)

Here we have the perfection of the *Othello* style. Concrete, visual, detached. Compare it with Lear's, 'Thou art a soul in bliss . . .', where the effect, though perhaps more powerful and immediate, is yet vague, intangible, spiritualized. Now this speech, started in a style that can in its own way challenge that of *King Lear*, rapidly degenerates as Othello's mind is represented as collapsing under the extreme of anguish:

> O cursed, cursed slave! Whip me, ye devils,
> From the possession of this heavenly sight!
> Blow me about in winds! roast me in sulphur!
> Wash me in steep-down gulfs of liquid fire!
> O Desdemona! Desdemona! dead!
> Oh! Oh! Oh!   (v. ii. 276)

There is a sudden reversal of poetic beauty: these lines lack cogency because they exaggerate rather than concentrate the emotion. Place beside these violent eschatological images the passage from *King Lear*:

> And my poor fool is hang'd! No, no, no life!
> Why should a dog, a horse, a rat have life,
> And thou no breath at all? Thou'lt come no more,
> Never, never, never, never, never!
> Pray you, undo this button: thank you, sir.
> Do you see this? Look on her, look, her lips,
> Look there, look there!   (v. iii. 307)

Notice by what rough, homely images the passion is transmitted—which are as truly an integral part of the naturalism of *King Lear* as the mosaic and polished phrase and the abstruse and picturesque allusion are, in its best passages, characteristic of Othello's speech. Thus the extreme, slightly exaggerated beauty of Othello's language is not maintained. This is even more true elsewhere. Othello, who usually luxuriates in deliberate and magnificent rhetoric, raves, falls in a trance:

> Lie with her! lie on her! We say lie on her, when they belie her. Lie with her! that 's fulsome. Handkerchief—confessions—handkerchief! To confess, and be hanged for his labour; first, to be hanged, and then to confess—I tremble at it. Nature would not invest herself in such shadowing passion without some instruction. It is not words that shake me thus. Pish! Noses, ears, and lips.—Is 't possible?—Confess—handkerchief!—O devil!   (IV. i. 35)

Whereas Lear's madness never lacks artistic meaning, whereas its most extravagant and grotesque effects are presented with imaginative cogency, Othello can speak words like these. This is the Iago-spirit, the Iago-medicine, at work, like an acid eating into bright metal. This is the primary fact of Othello and therefore of the play: something of solid beauty is undermined, wedged open so that it exposes an extreme ugliness.

When Othello is represented as enduring loss of control he is, as Macbeth and Lear never are, ugly, idiotic; but when he has full control he attains an architectural stateliness of quarried speech, a silver rhetoric of a kind unique in Shakespeare:

> It is the cause, it is the cause, my soul—
> Let me not name it to you, you chaste stars!—
> It is the cause. Yet I'll not shed her blood;
> Nor scar that whiter skin of hers than snow,
> And smooth as monumental alabaster.
> Yet she must die, else she'll betray more men.
> Put out the light, and then put out the light.
> If I quench thee, thou flaming minister,
> I can again thy former light restore,
> Should I repent me: but once put out thy light,
> Thou cunning'st pattern of excelling nature,
> I know not where is that Promethean heat
> That can thy light relume. When I have pluck'd the rose,
> I cannot give it vital growth again,
> It needs must wither: I'll smell it on the tree.   (V. ii. 1)

This is the noble *Othello* music: highly-coloured, rich in sound and phrase, stately. Each word solidifies as it takes its place in the pattern. This speech well illustrates the *Othello* style: the visual or tactile suggestion—'whiter skin of hers than snow', 'smooth as monumental alabaster'; the slightly over-decorative phrase, 'flaming minister'; the momentary juxtaposition of humanity and the vast spaces of the night, the 'chaste stars'; the concrete imagery of 'thou cunning'st pattern of excelling nature', and the lengthy comparison of life with light; the presence of simple forward-flowing clarity of dignified statement and of simile in place of the super-logical welding of thought with molten thought as in the more compressed, agile, and concentrated poetry of *Macbeth* and *King Lear*; and the fine outstanding single word, 'Promethean'. In these respects Othello's speech is nearer the style of the aftermath of Elizabethan literature, the settled lava of that fiery eruption, which gave us the solid image of Marvell and the 'marmoreal phrase' of Browne: it is the most Miltonic thing in Shakespeare.

This peculiarity of style directs our interpretation in two ways. First, the tremendous reversal from extreme, almost over-decorative, beauty, to extreme ugliness—both of a kind unusual in Shakespeare—will be seen to reflect a primary truth about thĕ play. That I will demonstrate later in my essay. Second, the concreteness and separation of image, word, or phrase, contrasting with the close-knit language elsewhere, suggests a proper approach to *Othello* which is not proper to *Macbeth* or *King Lear*. Separation is the rule throughout *Othello*. Whereas in *Macbeth* and *King Lear* we have one dominant atmospere, built of a myriad subtleties of thought and phraseology entwining throughout, subduing our minds wholly to their respective visions, whereas each has a single quality, expresses as a whole a single statement, *Othello* is built rather of outstanding differences. In *Othello* all is silhouetted, defined, concrete. Instead of reading a unique, pervading, atmospheric suggestion—generally our key to interpretation of what happens within that atmosphere —we must here read the meaning of separate persons. The persons here are truly separate. Lear, Cordelia, Edmund all grow out of the *Lear* universe, all are levelled by its characteristic atmosphere, all blend with it and with each other, so that they are less closely and vividly defined. They lack solidity. Othello, Desdemona, Iago, however, are clearly and vividly separate. All here—but Iago—are solid, concrete. Contrast is raised to its highest pitch. Othello is statuesque, Desdemona most concretely human and individual, Iago, if not human or in any usual sense 'realistic', is quite unique. Within analysis of these three persons and their interaction lies the meaning of *Othello*. In *Macbeth* or *King Lear* we interpret primarily a singleness of vision. Here, confronted with a significant diversity, we must have regard to the essential relation existing between the three main personal conceptions. Interpretation must be based not on unity but differentiation. Therefore I shall pursue an examination of this triple symbolism; which analysis will finally resolve the difficulty of Othello's speech, wavering as it does between what at first sight appear an almost artificial beauty and an equally inartistic ugliness.

Othello radiates a world of romantic, heroic, and pictur-esque adventure. All about him is highly coloured. He is a Moor; he is noble and generally respected; he is proud in the riches of his achievement. Now his prowess as a soldier is emphasized. His arms have spent 'their dearest action in the tented field' (I. iii. 85). Again,

> The tyrant custom, most grave Senators,
> Hath made the flinty and steel couch of war
> My thrice-driven bed of down.
>
> (I. iii. 230)

His iron warriorship is suggested throughout. Iago says:

> Can he be angry? I have seen the cannon,
> When it hath blown his ranks into the air,
> And, like the Devil, from his very arm
> Puff'd his own brother:—and can he be angry?
> Something of moment then: I will go meet him:
> There's matter in't indeed, if he be angry.
>
> (III. iv. 133)

And Lodovico:

> Is this the noble nature
> Whom passion could not shake? Whose solid virtue
> The shot of accident, nor dart of chance,
> Could neither graze nor pierce?
>
> (IV. i. 276)

But we also meet a curious discrepancy. Othello tells us:

> Rude am I in my speech,
> And little bless'd with the soft phrase of peace. (I. iii. 81)

Yet the dominant quality in this play is the exquisitely moulded language, the noble cadence and chiselled phrase, of Othello's poetry. Othello's speech, therefore, reflects not a soldier's language, but the quality of soldiership in all its glamour of romantic adventure; it holds an imaginative realism. It has a certain exotic beauty, is a storied and romantic treasure-house of rich, colourful experiences. He recounts his adventures, telling of

> antres vast and desarts idle,
> Rough quarries, rocks, and hills whose heads touch heaven,
> (I. iii. 140)

of Cannibals, and the Anthropophagi, and 'men whose heads do grow beneath their shoulders' (I. iii. 144). He tells Desdemona of the handkerchief given by 'an Egyptian' to his mother:

> 'Tis true: there 's magic in the web of it:
> A sibyl, that had number'd in the world
> The sun to course two hundred compasses,
> In her prophetic fury sew'd the work;
> The worms were hallow'd that did breed the silk,
> And it was dyed in mummy which the skilful
> Conserved of maidens' hearts. (III. iv. 70)

Swords are vivid, spiritualized things to Othello. There is his famous line:

> Keep up your bright swords, for the dew will rust them.
> (I. ii. 59)

And in the last scene, he says:

> I have another weapon in this chamber;
> It is a sword of Spain, the ice-brook's temper. (V. ii. 251)

In his address at the end, he speaks of himself as

> one whose hand,
> Like the base Indian, threw a pearl away
> Richer than all his tribe. (V. ii. 345)

His tears flow as the gum from 'Arabian trees' (V. ii. 349); he recounts how in Aleppo he smote 'a malignant and a turban'd Turk' (v. ii. 352) for insulting Venice. Finally there is his noble apostrophe to his lost 'occupation':

> Farewell the plumed troop and the big wars,
> That make ambition virtue! O, farewell!
> Farewell the neighing steed and the shrill trump,
> The spirit-stirring drum, the ear-piercing fife,
> The royal banner and all quality,
> Pride, pomp, and circumstance of glorious war!
> And, O you mortal engines, whose rude throats
> The immortal Jove's dread clamours counterfeit,
> Farewell! Othello's occupation 's gone.   (III. iii. 350)

Again, we have the addition of phrase to separate phrase, rather than the interdependence, the evolution of thought from thought, the clinging mesh of close-bound suggestions of other plays. This noble eulogy of war is intrinsic to the conception. War is in Othello's blood. When Desdemona accepts him, she knows she must not be 'a moth of peace' (I. iii. 258). Othello is a compound of highly-coloured, romantic adventure—he is himself 'coloured'—and war; together with a great pride and a great faith in those realities. His very life is dependent on a fundamental belief in the validity and nobility of human action—with, perhaps, a strong tendency towards his own achievement in particular. Now war, in Shakespeare, is usually a positive spiritual value, like love. There is reference to the soldiership of the protagonist in all the plays analysed in my present treatment. Soldiership is almost the condition of nobility, and so the Shakespearian hero is usually a soldier. Therefore Othello, with reference to the Shakespearian universe, becomes automatically a symbol of faith in human values of love, of war, of romance in a wide and sweeping sense. He is, as it were, conscious of all he stands for: from the first to the last he loves his own romantic history. He is, like Troilus, dedicate to these values, has faith and pride in both. Like Troilus he is conceived as extraordinarily direct, simple, 'credulous' (IV. i. 46). Othello, as he appears in the action of the play, may be considered the high-priest of human endeavour, robed in the vestments of romance, whom we watch serving in the temple of war at the altar of love's divinity.

Desdemona is his divinity. She is, at the same time, warmly human. There is a certain domestic femininity about

her. She is 'a maiden never bold' (I. iii. 94). We hear that
'the house affairs' (had Cordelia any?) drew her often from
Othello's narrative (I. iii. 147). But she asks to hear the
whole history:

> I did consent,
> And often did beguile her of her tears,
> When I did speak of some distressful stroke
> That my youth suffer'd. My story being done,
> She gave me for my pains a world of sighs:
> She swore, in faith, 'twas strange, 'twas passing strange,
> 'Twas pitiful, 'twas wondrous pitiful:
> She wish'd she had not heard it, yet she wish'd
> That heaven had made her such a man.   (I. iii. 155)

The same domesticity and gentleness is apparent throughout.
She talks of 'to-night at supper' (III. iii. 57) or 'to-morrow
dinner' (III. iii. 58); she is typically feminine in her attempt
to help Cassio, and her pity for him. This is how she describes her suit to Othello:

> Why, this is not a boon;
> 'Tis as I should entreat you wear your gloves,
> Or feed on nourishing dishes, or keep you warm,
> Or sue to you to do a peculiar profit
> To your own person . . .   (III. iii. 76)

—a speech reflecting a world of sex-contrast. She would
bind Othello's head with her handkerchief—that handkerchief which is to become a terrific symbol of Othello's
jealousy. The *Othello* world is eminently domestic, and
Desdemona expressly feminine. We hear of her needlework
(IV. i. 197), her fan, gloves, mask (IV. ii. 8). In the exquisite
willow-song scene, we see her with her maid, Emilia. Emilia
gives her 'her nightly wearing' (IV. iii. 16). Emilia says she
has laid on her bed the 'wedding-sheets' (IV. ii. 104) Desdemona asked for. Then there is the willow-song, brokenly
sung whilst Emilia 'unpins' (IV. iii. 34) Desdemona's dress:

> My mother had a maid called Barbara:
> She was in love, and he she loved proved mad
> And did forsake her . . .   (IV. iii. 26)

The extreme beauty and pathos of this scene are largely
dependent on the domesticity of it. *Othello* is eminently a
domestic tragedy. But this element in the play is yet to be

related to another more universal element. Othello is concretely human, so is Desdemona. Othello is very much the typical middle-aged bachelor entering matrimony late in life, but he is also, to transpose a phrase of Iago's, a symbol of human—especially masculine—'purpose, courage, and valour' (IV. ii. 218), and, in a final judgement, is seen to represent the idea of human faith and value in a very wide sense. Now Desdemona, also very human, with an individual domestic feminine charm and simplicity, is yet also a symbol of woman in general daring the unknown seas of marriage with the mystery of man. Beyond this, in the far flight of a transcendental interpretation, it is clear that she becomes a symbol of man's ideal, the supreme value of love. At the limit of the series of wider and wider suggestions which appear from imaginative contemplation of a poetic symbol she is to be equated with the divine principle. In one scene of *Othello*, and one only, direct poetic symbolism breaks across the vividly human, domestic world of this play.[1] As everything in *Othello* is separated, defined, so the plot itself is in two distinct geographical divisions: Venice and Cyprus. Desdemona leaves the safety and calm of her home for the stormy voyage to Cyprus and the tempest of the following tragedy. Iago's plot begins to work in the second part. The storm scene, between the two parts, is important.

Storms are continually symbols of tragedy in Shakespeare. This scene contains some most vivid imaginative effects, among them passages of fine storm-poetry of the usual kind:

> For do but stand upon the foaming shore,
> The chidden billow seems to pelt the clouds;
> The wind-shak'd surge, with high and monstrous mane,
> Seems to cast water on the burning bear,
> And quench the guards of the ever-fixed pole:
> I never did like molestation view,
> On the enchafed flood. (II. i. 11)

This storm-poetry is here closely associated with the human element. And in this scene where direct storm-symbolism occurs it is noteworthy that the figures of Desdemona and Othello are both strongly idealized:

[1] But note too the significance of the magic handkerchief *as both a symbol of domestic sanctity and the play's one link with the supernatural* (1947).

> *Cassio.* Tempests themselves, high seas and howling winds,
>   The gutter'd rocks and congregated sands—
>   Traitors ensteep'd to clog the guiltless keel—
>   As having sense of beauty, do omit
>   Their mortal natures, letting go safely by
>   The divine Desdemona.
> *Montano.*   What is she?
> *Cassio.* She that I spake of, our great captain's captain,
>   Left in the conduct of the bold Iago,
>   Whose footing here anticipates our thoughts
>   A se'nnight's speed. Great Jove, Othello guard,
>   And swell his sail with thine own powerful breath,
>   That he may bless this bay with his tall ship,
>   Make love's quick pants in Desdemona's arms,
>   Give renew'd fire to our extincted spirits,
>   And bring all Cyprus comfort!
>   *Enter Desdemona, &c.*
>   O, behold,
>   The riches of the ship is come on shore!
>   Ye men of Cyprus, let her have your knees.
>   Hail to thee, lady! and the grace of Heaven,
>   Before, behind thee, and on every hand,
>   Enwheel thee round!   (II. i. 68)

Desdemona is thus endued with a certain transcendent quality of beauty and grace. She 'paragons description and wild fame' says Cassio: she is

> One that excels the quirks of blazoning pens,
> And in the essential vesture of creation
> Does tire the ingener.   (II. i. 63)

And Othello enters the port of Cyprus as a hero coming to 'bring comfort', to 'give renewed fire' to men. The entry of Desdemona and that of Othello are both heralded by discharge of guns: which both merges finely with the tempest-symbolism and the violent stress and excitement of the scene as a whole, and heightens our sense of the warrior nobility of the protagonist and his wife, subdued as she is 'to the very quality' of her lord (I. iii. 253). Meeting Desdemona, he speaks:

> *Othello.* O my fair warrior!
> *Desdemona.*   My dear Othello!
> *Othello.* It gives me wonder great as my content
>   To see you here before me. O my soul's joy!
>   If after every tempest come such calms,
>   May the winds blow till they have waken'd death!

And let the labouring bark climb hills of seas
Olympus-high and duck again as low
As Hell's from Heaven! If it were now to die,
'Twere now to be most happy; for, I fear,
My soul hath her content so absolute
That not another comfort like to this
Succeeds in unknown fate.   (II. i. 185)

This is the harmonious marriage of true and noble minds. Othello, Desdemona, and their love are here apparent, in this scene of storm and reverberating discharge of cannon, as things of noble and conquering strength: they radiate romantic valour. Othello is essential man in all his prowess and protective strength; Desdemona essential woman, gentle, loving, brave in trust of her warrior husband. The war is over. The storm of sea or bruit of cannonade are powerless to hurt them: yet there is another storm brewing in the venomed mind of Iago. Instead of merging with and accompanying tragedy the storm here is to be contrasted with the following tragic events: as usual in *Othello*, contrast and separation take the place of fusion and unity. This scene is as a microcosm of the play, reflecting its action. Colours which are elsewhere softly toned are here splashed vividly on the play's canvas. Here especially Othello appears a prince of heroes, Desdemona is lit by a divine feminine radiance: both are transfigured. They are shown as coming safe to land, by Heaven's 'grace', triumphant, braving war and tempestuous seas, guns thundering their welcome. The reference of all this, on the plane of high poetic symbolism, to the play as a whole is evident.

Against these two Iago pits his intellect. In this scene too Iago declares himself with especial clarity:

O gentle lady, do not put me to't;
For I am nothing if not critical.   (II. i. 118)

His conversation with Desdemona reveals his philosophy. Presented under the cloak of fun, it exposes nevertheless his attitude to life: that of the cynic. Roderigo is his natural companion: the fool is a convenient implement, and at the same time continual food for his philosophy. Othello and Desdemona are radiant, beautiful: Iago opposes them, critical, intellectual. Like cold steel his cynic skill will run

through the warm body of their love. Asked to praise Desdemona, he draws a picture of womanly goodness in a vein
of mockery; and concludes:

> *Iago.* She was a wight if ever such wight were—
> *Desdemona.* To do what?
> *Iago.* To suckle fools and chronicle small beer.   (ii. i. 158)

Here is his reason for hating Othello's and Desdemona's
love: he hates their beauty, to him a meaningless, stupid
thing. That is Iago. Cynicism is his philosophy, his very life,
his 'motive' in working Othello's ruin. The play turns on
this theme: the cynical intellect pitted against a lovable
humanity transfigured by qualities of heroism and grace. As
Desdemona and Othello embrace he says:

> O you are well tuned now!
> But I'll set down the pegs that make this music,
> As honest as I am.   (ii. i. 202)

'Music' is apt: we remember Othello's rich harmony of
words. Against the *Othello* music Iago concentrates all the
forces of cynic villainy.

Iago's cynicism is recurrent:

> Virtue! a fig! 'tis in ourselves that we are thus or thus . . .
> (i. iii. 323)

Love to him is

> . . . merely a lust of the blood and a permission of the will.
> (i. iii. 339)

He believes Othello's and Desdemona's happiness will be
short-lived, since he puts no faith in the validity of love.
Early in the play he tells Roderigo:

> It cannot be that Desdemona should long continue her love to the Moor
> . . . nor he his to her . . . These Moors are changeable in their wills . . .
> the food that to him now is as luscious as locusts, shall be to him shortly
> as bitter as coloquintida. She must change for youth: when she is sated
> with his body, she will find the error of her choice: she must have
> change, she must.   (i. iii. 347)

This is probably Iago's sincere belief, his usual attitude to
love: he is not necessarily deceiving Roderigo. After this,
when he is alone, we hear that he suspects Othello with his
own wife: nor are we surprised. And, finally, his own cynical

beliefs suggest to him a way of spiting Othello. He thinks of
Cassio:

> After some time, to abuse Othello's ear
> That he is too familiar with his wife.   (1. iii. 401)

The order is important: Iago first states his disbelief in
Othello's and Desdemona's continued love, and next thinks
of a way of precipitating its end. That is, he puts his cynicism
into action. The same rhythmic sequence occurs later. Iago
witnesses Cassio's meeting with Desdemona at Cyprus, and
comments as follows:

> He takes her by the palm: ay, well said, whisper: with as little a web as
> this will I ensnare as great a fly as Cassio. Ay, smile upon her, do; I will
> gyve thee in thine own courtship . . .   (11. i. 168)

Iago believes Cassio loves Desdemona. He has another
cynical conversation with Roderigo as to Desdemona's
chances of finding satisfaction with Othello, and the probability of her love for Cassio (11. i. 223–79). A kiss, to Iago,
cannot be 'courtesy': it is

> Lechery, by this hand; an index and obscure prologue to the history of
> lust and foul thoughts.   (11. i. 265)

Iago is sincere enough and means what he says. Cynicism is
the key to his mind and actions. After Roderigo's departure,
he again refers to his suspicions of Othello—and Cassio too
—with his own wife. He asserts definitely—and here there
is no Roderigo to impress—his belief in Cassio's guilt:

> That Cassio loves her, I do well believe it;
> That she loves him, 'tis apt and of great credit.   (11. i. 298)

In this soliloquy he gets his plans clearer: again, they are
suggested by what he believes to be truth. I do not suggest
that Iago lacks conscious villainy: far from it. Besides, in
another passage he shows that he is aware of Desdemona's
innocence (1v. i. 48). But it is important that we observe how
his attitude to life casts the form and figure of his meditated
revenge. His plan arises out of the cynical depths of his
nature. When, at the end, he says, 'I told him what I thought'
(v. ii. 174), he is speaking at least a half-truth. He hates
the romance of Othello and the loveliness of Desdemona

because he is by nature the enemy of these things. Cassio, he says,

> hath a daily beauty in his life
> That makes mine ugly.   (v. i. 19)

This is his 'motive' throughout: other suggestions are surface deep only. He is cynicism loathing beauty, refusing to allow its existence. Hence the venom of his plot: the plot is Iago—both are ultimate, causeless, self-begotten. Iago is cynicism incarnate and projected into action.

Iago is utterly devilish: no weakness is apparent in his casing armour of unrepentant villainy. He is a kind of Mephistopheles, closely equivalent to Goethe's devil, the two possessing the same qualities of mockery and easy cynicism. He is called a 'hellish villain' by Lodovico (v. ii. 367), a 'demi-devil' by Othello (v. ii. 300). Othello says:

> I look down towards his feet; but that 's a fable.
> If that thou be'est a devil, I cannot kill thee.   (v. ii. 285)

Iago himself recognizes a kinship:

> Hell and night
> Must bring this monstrous birth to the world's sight.
> (i. iii. 409)

And,

> Divinity of Hell!
> When devils will the blackest sins put on,
> They do suggest at first with heavenly shows
> As I do now.   (ii. iii. 359)

He knows that his 'poison' (iii. iii. 326) will 'burn like the mines of sulphur' (iii. iii. 330) in Othello. Thus Iago is, to Othello, the antithesis of Desdemona: the relation is that of the spirit of denial to the divine principle. Desdemona 'plays the god' (ii. iii. 356) with Othello: if she is false, 'Heaven mocks itself' (iii. iii. 278). During the action, as Iago's plot succeeds, her essential divinity changes, for Othello, to a thing hideous and devilish—that is to its antithesis:

> Her name that was as fresh
> As Dian's visage, is now begrim'd and black
> As mine own face.   (iii. iii. 387)

She is now 'devil' (iv. i. 252, 255) or 'the fair devil' (iii. iii. 479); her hand, a 'sweating devil' (iii. iv. 43); the 'devils themselves' will fear to seize her for her heavenly looks (iv. ii. 35). Thus Iago, himself a kind of devil, insidiously eats his way into this world of romance, chivalry, nobility. The word 'devil' occurs frequently in the latter acts: devils are alive here, ugly little demons of black disgrace. They swarm over the mental horizon of the play, occurring frequently. Iago is directly or indirectly their author and originator. 'Devil', 'Hell', 'damnation'—these words are recurrent, and continually juxtaposed to thoughts of 'Heaven', prayer, angels. We are clearly set amid 'Heaven and men and devils' (v. ii. 219). Such terms are related here primarily to sexual impurity. In *Othello*, pure love is the supreme good; impurity damnation. This pervading religious tonal significance relating to infidelity explains lines such as:

> Turn thy complexion there,
> Patience, thou young and rose-lipp'd cherubin—
> Ay, there, look grim as Hell!   (iv. ii. 61)

Othello addresses Emilia:

> You, mistress,
> That have the office opposite to Saint Peter,
> And keep the gate of Hell!   (iv. ii. 89)

Here faithful love is to be identified with the divine, the 'heavenly'; unfaithful love, or the mistrust which imagines it, or the cynic that gives birth to that imagination—all these are to be identified with the devil. The hero is set between the forces of Divinity and Hell. The forces of Hell win and pure love lies slain. Therefore Othello cries to 'devils' to whip him from that 'heavenly' sight (v. ii. 276). He knows himself to have been entrapped by hell-forces. The Iago-Devil association is of importance.

It will be remembered that *Othello* is a play of concrete forms. This world is a world of visual images, colour, and romance. It will also be clear that the mesh of devil-references I have just suggested show a mental horizon black, formless, colourless. They contrast with the solid, chiselled, enamelled *Othello* style elsewhere. This devil-world is insubstantial, vague, negative. Now on the plane of personification we see that Othello and Desdemona are concrete, moulded of flesh and blood, warm. Iago contrasts with them

metaphysically as well as morally: he is unlimited, formless
villainy. He is the spirit of denial, wholly negative. He never
has visual reality. He is further blurred by the fact of his
being something quite different from what he appears to the
others. Is he to look like a bluff soldier, or Mephistopheles?
He is a different kind of being from Othello and Desdemona:
he belongs to a different world. They, by their very existence,
assert the positive beauty of created forms—hence Othello's
perfected style of speech, his strong human appeal, his faith
in creation's values of love and war. This world of created
forms, this sculptural and yet pulsing beauty, the Iago-spirit
undermines, poisons, disintegrates. Iago is a demon of
cynicism, colourless, formless, in a world of colours, shapes,
and poetry's music. Of all these he would create chaos.
Othello's words are apt:

> Excellent wretch! Perdition catch my soul
> But I do love thee! And when I love thee not,
> Chaos is come again.   (III. iii. 90)

Chaos indeed. Iago works at the foundations of human
values. Cassio is a soldier: he ruins him as a soldier, makes
him drunk. So he ruins both Othello's love and warrior-
heart. He makes him absurd, ugly. Toward the end of the
play there is hideous suggestion. We hear of 'cords, knives,
poison' (III. iii. 389), of lovers 'as prime as goats, as hot as
monkeys' (III. iii. 404); we meet Bianca, the whore, told by
Cassio to 'throw her vile guesses in the Devil's teeth' (III. iv
183); there are Othello's incoherent mutterings, 'Pish!
Noses, ears and lips!' (IV. i. 43), he will 'chop' Desdemona
'into messes' (IV. i. 210); she reminds him of 'foul toads'
(IV. ii. 60). Watching Cassio, he descends to this:

> O! I see that nose of yours, but not the dog I shall throw it to.
>   (IV. i. 144)

Othello strikes Desdemona, behaves like a raging beast.
'Fire and brimstone!' (IV. i. 246) he cries, and again, 'Goats
and monkeys!' (IV. i. 274). 'Heaven stops the nose' at Desdemona's impurity (IV. ii. 76). Othello in truth behaves like
'a beggar in his drink' (IV. ii. 120). In all these phrases I
would emphasize not the sense and dramatic relevance alone,
but the suggestion—the accumulative effect of ugliness,

hellishness, idiocy, negation. It is a formless, colourless essence, insidiously undermining a world of concrete, visual, richly-toned forms. That is the Iago-spirit embattled against the domesticity, the romance, the idealized humanity of the *Othello* world.

Here, too, we find the reason for the extreme contrast of Othello's two styles: one exotically beautiful, the other blatantly absurd, ugly. There is often no dignity in Othello's rage. There is not meant to be. Iago would make discord of the *Othello* music. Thus at his first conquest he filches something of Othello's style and uses it himself:

> Not poppy, nor mandragora,
> Nor all the drowsy syrups of the world,
> Shall ever medicine thee to that sweet sleep
> Which thou owed'st yesterday.   (III. iii. 331)

To him Othello's pride in his life-story and Desdemona's admiration were ever stupid:

> Mark me with what violence she first loved the Moor, but for bragging and telling her fantastical lies: and will she love him still for prating?
> (II. i. 225)

Iago, 'nothing if not critical', speaks some truth of Othello's style—it is 'fantastical'. As I have shown, it is somewhat over-decorative, highly-coloured. The dramatic value of this style now appears. In fact, a proper understanding of Othello's style reveals Iago's 'motive' so often questioned. There is something sentimental in Othello's language, in Othello. Iago is pure cynicism. That Iago should scheme —in this dramatic symbolism forged in terms of interacting persons—to undermine Othello's faith in himself, his wife, and his 'occupation', is inevitable. Logically, the cynic must oppose the sentimentalist: dramatically, he works his ruin by deceit and deception. That Othello often just misses tragic dignity is the price of his slightly strained emotionalism. Othello loves emotion for its own sake, luxuriates in it, like Richard II. As ugly and idiot ravings, disjointed and with no passionate dignity even, succeed Othello's swell and flood of poetry, Iago's triumph seems complete. The honoured warrior, rich in strength and experience, noble in act and repute, lies in a trance, nerveless, paralysed by the Iago-conception:

Work on, my medicine, work.   (iv. i. 45)

But Iago's victory is not absolute. During the last scene, Othello is a nobly tragic figure. His ravings are not final: he rises beyond them. He slays Desdemona finally not so much in rage, as for 'the cause' (v. ii. 1). He slays her in love. Though Desdemona fails him, his love, homeless, 'perplexed in the extreme' (v. ii. 345), endures. He will kill her and 'love her after' (v. ii. 19). In that last scene, too, he utters the grandest of his poetry. The Iago-spirit never finally envelops him, masters him, disintegrates his soul. Those gem-like miniatures of poetic movement quoted at the start of my essay are among Othello's last words. His vast love has, it is true, failed in a domestic world. But now symbols of the wide beauty of the universe enrich his thoughts: the 'chaste stars', the 'sun and moon', the 'affrighted globe', the world 'of one entire and perfect chrysolite' that may not buy a Desdemona's love. At the end we know that Othello's fault is simplicity alone. He is, indeed, 'a gull, a dolt' (v. ii. 161); he loves 'not wisely but too well' (v. ii. 343). His simple faith in himself endures: and at the end, he takes just pride in recalling his honourable service.

In this essay I have attempted to expose the underlying thought of the play. Interpretation here is not easy, nor wholly satisfactory. As all within *Othello*—save the Iago-theme—is separated, differentiated, solidified, so the play itself seems at first to be divorced from wider issues, a lone thing of meaningless beauty in the Shakespearian universe, solitary, separate, unyielding and chaste as the moon. It is unapproachable, yields itself to no easy mating with our minds. Its thought does not readily mesh with our thought. We can visualize it, admire its concrete felicities of phrase and image, the mosaic of its language, the sculptural outline of its effects, the precision and chastity of its form. But one cannot be lost in it, subdued to it, enveloped by it, as one is drenched and refreshed by the elemental cataracts of *King Lear*; one cannot be intoxicated by it as by the rich wine of *Antony and Cleopatra*. *Othello* is essentially outside us,

beautiful with a lustrous, planetary beauty. Yet the Iago-
conception is of a different kind from the rest of the play.
This conception alone, if no other reason existed, would point
the necessity of an intellectual interpretation. So we see
the Iago-spirit gnawing at the root of all the *Othello* values,
the *Othello* beauties; he eats into the core and heart of this
romantic world, worms his way into its solidity, rotting it,
poisoning it. Once this is clear, the whole play begins to have
meaning. On the plane of dramatic humanity, we see a story
of the cynic intriguing to ruin the soldier and his love. On
the plane of poetic conception, in matters of technique, style,
personification—there we see a spirit of negation, colourless,
and undefined, attempting to make chaos of a world of
stately, architectural, and exquisitely coloured forms. The
two styles of Othello's speech illustrate this. Thus the different technique of the Othello and Iago conceptions is
intrinsic with the plot of the play: in them we have the spirit
of negation set against the spirit of creation. That is why
Iago is undefined, devisualized, inhuman, in a play of consummate skill in concrete imagery and vivid human delineation. He is a colourless and ugly thing in a world of colour
and harmony. His failure lies in this: in the final scene, at
the moment of his complete triumph, Emilia dies for her
mistress to the words of Desdemona's willow-song, and the
Othello music itself sounds with a nobler cadence, a richer
flood of harmonies, a more selfless and universalized flight
of the imagination than before. The beauties of the *Othello*
world are not finally disintegrated: they make 'a swan-like
end, fading in music'.

Additional Note (1947)

Any valuable discussion of Othello's physical appearance and general status
as a 'noble Moor' must take full account of Morocco's self-description in *The
Merchant of Venice*. Imaginatively, the two conceptions are almost identical,
the one being a first sketch of the other.

1972: For the Handkerchief, see my note on p. 109; also p. ix above.

VI

BRUTUS AND MACBETH

FROM the crystal lucidity, even flow, and brilliant imagery of the style of *Julius Caesar* stand out two main personal themes: the Brutus-theme and the Cassius-theme. The one predominates at the start, the other at the finish. The two men are finely contrasted. But I shall not concern myself in this essay primarily with that contrast. Nor shall I consider the play as a whole in its romantic and spiritual significance. The *Julius Caesar* universe is one of high-spirited adventure and nobility, of heroic optimism, erotic emotion. It is differentiated sharply from the plays succeeding it. It is essentially a play of keen spiritual faith and vision, curiously preceding the sequence of the hate-theme which starts with *Hamlet*. These important elements I do not analyse here.[1] Rather I outline the imaginative nature of the Brutus-theme alone; and, in considering the figure of Brutus, I shall indicate how his soul-experience resembles that of Macbeth. The process is interesting, since it forces us to cut below the surface crust of plot and 'character', and to expose those riches of poetic imagination too often deep-buried in our purely unconscious enjoyment of Shakespeare's art. Moreover, it will serve as a valuable introduction to the complexities of the *Macbeth* vision itself.

Brutus is confronted with a task from which his nature revolts. He, like Macbeth, embarks on a line of action destructive rather than creative; directed against the symbol of established authority; at root, perhaps, selfish. For, though he may tell himself that his ideals force him to a work of secrecy, conspiracy, and destruction, he is not at peace. He suffers a state of spiritual or mental division. Two impulses diverge: one urges him to conspiracy and murder, the other reminds him of Caesar's goodness and the normal methods of upright men. He is thus divided—torn between a certain sense of duty and his instinct for peaceful and civilized behaviour. Now his state is very similar to that of Macbeth.

[1] My comprehensive analysis of *Julius Caesar* is presented in *The Imperial Theme*.

Though their motives at first sight appear to be very different, yet in each the resulting disharmony is almost identical
in imaginative impact. We should not let our sight of a
poetic reality be blurred by consideration of 'causes'. With
Macbeth it is almost impossible to fit clear terms of conceptual thought to the motives tangled in his mind or soul.
Therein lies the fine truth of the *Macbeth* conception: a deep,
poetic, psychology or metaphysic of the birth of evil. He
himself is hopelessly at a loss, and has little idea as to why
he is going to murder Duncan. He tries to fit names to his
reasons—'ambition', for instance—but this is only a name.
The poet's mind is here at grips with the problem of spiritual
evil—the inner state of disintegration, disharmony and fear,
from which is born an act of crime and destruction. And the
state of evil endured by Macbeth is less powerfully, but
similarly, experienced by Brutus. Its signs are loneliness,
a sense of unreality, a sickly vision of nightmare forms. It
contemplates murder and anarchy to symbolize outwardly
its own inner anarchy, and so, by forcibly creating itself in
things around it, to restore contact with its environment for
its severed and lonely individuality. Now one simple statement can be made of both Macbeth and Brutus: they both
suffer a state of division, due to conflicting impulses, for and
against murder. Their inner disharmony is given an almost
identical reflection in words—not only in terms of logical
statement, but in terms, too, of the more important verbal
colour and association, imagery, rhythm—in short, of poetry.
   Consider Brutus' speech:

> Since Cassius first did whet me against Caesar
> I have not slept.
> Between the acting of a dreadful thing
> And the first motion, all the interim is
> Like a phantasma or a hideous dream:
> The genius and the mortal instruments
> Are then in council; and the state of man,
> Like to a little kingdom, suffers then
> The nature of an insurrection.   (ii. i. 61)

Compare Macbeth's:

> This supernatural soliciting
> Cannot be good, cannot be ill: if ill,
> Why hath it given me earnest of success

> Commencing with a truth? I am Thane of Cawdor.
> If good, why do I yield to that suggestion
> Whose horrid image doth unfix my hair,
> And make my seated heart knock at my ribs
> Against the use of nature? Present fears
> Are less than horrible imaginings:
> My thought, whose murder yet is but fantastical,
> Shakes so my single state of man that function
> Is smother'd in surmise, and nothing is
> But what is not.   (1. iii. 130)

The second speech is more vivid, powerful, and tense: but in quality they are alike. One is only a more packed and pregnant verbal expression of the state of being expressed by the other. Each gives us a sickly sense of nightmare unreality. The ordinary forms of reality, to the self-contemplating mind in the grip of evil, have become 'nothing': and a ghastly negation, a black abyss of nothing, has usurped the significance of reality. Thus the mind endures 'horrible imaginings' which are 'like a phantasma or a hideous dream'. Both speeches use the metaphor, 'the state of man'. This 'state' is shaken from its normal balance of faculties, so that it endures anarchy and disorder. This anarchy of the soul reflects the outer anarchy which it is fated to impose by its act of murder, directed against the symbol of ordered community, the King, or Caesar: the soul mirrors as in a glass the disharmony and disruption to be brought about by its act of nihilism. All three realities are intertwined: the chaos in the 'state of man'; the act of murder; the resulting chaos in the state of the community.

The instigation in both plays comes partly from within, partly from without. Though Cassius' words 'whet' Brutus against Caesar we know that he has already suffered the beginnings of inward division. He is already, as he tells Cassius, 'with himself at war' (1. ii. 46). In the same way, though Macbeth is urged on by his wife, he has already been in contact with the Weird Sisters. Both Brutus and Macbeth find their own vague mental suggestions brought to rapid growth by outside influences. Both, too, promise to consider the matter further:

> *Brutus.*   . . . for this present
> I would not, so with love I might entreat you,

Be any further moved. What you have said
I will consider. What you have to say
I will with patience hear . . .   (i. ii. 164)

and,

Macbeth. We will speak further.   (i. v. 72)

In *Macbeth* the tragic tension is always more powerful than
in *Julius Caesar*; gained, too, within a minimum of space
either by the most perfect and powerful simplicity, or by the
complexity of highly-charged, compressed, and pregnant
metaphoric thought. The effects in the Brutus-theme are so
much more prolix, and therefore less powerful, especially
in the matter of blood-imagery, which I notice later.

Both Brutus and Macbeth meditate in solitude concerning
the proposed act (I quote only their first words):

Brutus. It must be by his death: and for my part
I know no personal cause to spurn at him,
But for the general . . .   (ii. i. 10)

and,

Macbeth. If it were done, when 'tis done, then 'twere well
It were done quickly. If the assassination
Could trammel up the consequence and catch
With his surcease success . . .   (i. vii. 1)

Though the intellectual meanings of these soliloquies are
different, their poetic qualities are similar. Each reflects
unrest, indecision; in a style of broken and disjointed, medi-
tative, flashes of thought. They give one the impression that
the personality of the thinker is momentarily relaxed, letting
arguments and reasons pass rapidly and automatically across
the screen of his own mind for the hundredth time: they
are merely chaotic shapes and shadows of the active intellect,
which the contemplating mind watches projected away from
its centre, trying to understand. They are not vitally immediate and concentrated thought-adventures, like Hamlet's
'To be or not to be. . .'. They reflect a mind trying to get
its own motives clear. Brutus' is throughout rhythmically
uneven and jerky; so is Macbeth's in the first half. Each of
them is characterized by a quite unexpected and, it would
seem, untrue method of presenting irrelevant arguments:
they are both getting their reasons and motives hopelessly

wrong. So Brutus tells himself that Caesar must be assassin-
ated to avoid the dangers contingent on his nature possibly
changing after he becomes king. Yet, he says, he has never
known him let passion master reason. There is a hopeless
confusion: Brutus' strongest method of justifying his act
is to assert that the Roman ideal of a commonwealth must
not be shattered by the accession of a king, good or bad.
Yet, in his confused desire to justify himself, he does not
do this, but falls back on a quite indefensible sophistry. He
does not understand himself. Who, at a really testing
moment, does? Similarly Macbeth, whose conscience revolts
from the crime, persuades himself that he is a most cold-
blooded villain, and only fears actual and personal punishment. How untrue this is may be apparent from the latter
half of his soliloquy where he begins to speak with a
passionate sincerity: then he miserably images to himself
the excellences of Duncan, as Brutus contemplates those of
Caesar, and sees that his virtues are as angels trumpet-
tongued to plead against the crime. He concludes by
crying:

> I have no spur
> To prick the sides of my intent, save only
> Vaulting ambition, which o'erleaps itself
> And falls on the other.   (I. vii. 25)

He is perfectly aware of the futility of such 'ambition': yet
he can find no better name. So, too, Brutus sighs:

> I know no personal cause to spurn at him,
> But for the general . . .   (II. i. 11)

And neither is, it seems, quite convinced: though Brutus
is much nearer peace of mind and clarity of motive than
Macbeth. But both are in the same kind of confusion. And
it may be noticed that Brutus' speech in point of complexity
and condensation of thought and phrase stands out remarkably from a play of a lucidity and crystal transparence of
diction unparalleled in Shakespeare: it has a typical *Macbeth*
ring.

Soon after both these soliloquies the impulse to assassinate
definitely wins. Both are appealed to on grounds of personal
pride: Brutus by the paper which Lucius brings him,

Macbeth by his wife. They assent at moments of dramatic intensity again remarkably similar in their sudden finality:

> *Brutus.* 'Speak, strike, redress!' Am I entreated
>   To speak and strike? O Rome, I make thee promise,
>   If the redress will follow, thou receivest
>   Thy full petition at the hand of Brutus!   (II. i. 55)

Macbeth likewise reaches decision with a similar finality:

> *Macbeth.*   I am settled and bend up
>   Each corporal agent to this terrible feat.
>   Away, and mock the time with fairest show.
>   False face must hide what the false heart doth know.   (I. vii. 79)

Why does Macbeth thus decide on a course repellant to his instinct and unsound to his own reasoning? One of the finest interpretative remarks ever made on Macbeth is A. C. Bradley's to the effect that Macbeth sets about the murder 'as an appalling duty'. This is profoundly true. Like Brutus he has to be appealed to on grounds of pride: like Brutus, he undertakes a terrible and appalling duty. So Macbeth counsels his wife to 'mock the time with fairest show'. This is a typical *Macbeth* thought and occurs in slightly different forms elsewhere (I. iv. 52; I. v. 65; I. v. 72). At first sight it seems far from a Brutus. But we have the same counsel given by Brutus:

>   O conspiracy,
>   Shamest thou to show thy dangerous brow by night,
>   When evils are most free? O, then by day,
>   Where wilt thou find a cavern dark enough
>   To mask thy monstrous visage? Seek none, conspiracy;
>   Hide it in smiles and affability . . .   (II. i. 77)

Again, he advises cunning as follows:

>   And let out hearts as subtle masters do,
>   Stir up their servants to an act of rage,
>   And after seem to chide 'em. This shall make
>   Our purpose necessary and not envious . . .   (II. i. 175)

And finally,

>   Good gentlemen, look fresh and merrily;
>   Let not our looks put on our purposes . . .   (II. i. 224)

The prolix and diffuse expression in *Julius Caesar* corresponds, as elsewhere, to a more packed and condensed

explosive poetry in *Macbeth*. This recurrent thought in both
plays emphasizes the essential isolation of the hero from
surrounding human reality: the act to be is an act of darkness
whose very conception bears the Ishmael stamp of outlawry
and tends to make the perpetrator a pariah from the ways
of men. Both Brutus and Macbeth endure this spiritual
loneliness: it is at the root of their suffering. Loneliness,
deception, and loss of that daily nurse of anguish, sleep.

Sleeplessness and nightmare vision are twined with this
loneliness, this severance of individual consciousness—consciousness feverishly awake and aware of its deception and
isolation due to—or urging towards—the proposed deed of
blood. There is insistence on sleep in both plays. Macbeth's
crime is a hideous murder of sleep: Caesar is waked from
sleep by Calpurnia's cries in nightmare—'Help, ho! they
murder Caesar!' (II. ii. 3). Calpurnia has a dream of Caesar's
statue spouting blood (II. ii. 76). Cinna the poet dreamt
that he feasted with Caesar and is next mobbed and, we
suppose, slain. He reminds us of Banquo:

> I dreamt to-night that I did feast with Caesar,
> And things unluckily charge my fantasy;
> I have no will to wander forth of doors,
> Yet something leads me forth.   (III. iii. 1)

Compare Banquo's:

> A heavy summons lies like lead upon me,
> And yet I would not sleep: merciful powers,
> Restrain in me the cursed thoughts that nature
> Gives way to in repose!   (II. i. 6)

There is a nightmare fear powerful throughout both plays.
Sleep-imagery is recurrent in the Brutus-theme and in
Macbeth to an extent paralleled in no other of Shakespeare's
tragedies. Brutus has not slept since Cassius first instigated
him against Caesar (II. i. 61). He calls:

> Boy! Lucius! Fast asleep? It is no matter;
> Enjoy the honey-heavy dew of slumber.
> Thou hast no figures nor no fantasies,
> Which busy care draws in the brains of men;
> Therefore thou sleep'st so sound.   (II. i. 229)

Again:

> I would it were my fault to sleep so soundly.   (II. i. 4)

And Portia, too, refers to Brutus' sleeplessnes (II. i. 252).
At the close of the tent-scene in Act IV, it is sleep and the
drowsy tune of Lucius' instrument that touches for a while
these latter hours with the faery wand of a gentleness and
beauty that are remorselessly shattered by the Ghost of
Caesar—the 'evil spirit' of Brutus; the evil that has gripped
him, symbolized itself in murder, and left him condemned,
like Macbeth, to 'sleep no more'. So, too, the most terrible
element in the punishment of Macbeth and Lady Macbeth
is a loss of sleep:

> *Macbeth.* Methought I heard a voice cry, 'Sleep no more!
>   Macbeth does murder sleep'—the innocent sleep,
>   Sleep that knits up the ravell'd sleeve of care,
>   The death of each day's life, sore labour's bath,
>   Balm of hurt minds, great nature's second course,
>   Chief nourisher in life's feast—
> *L. Macbeth.*   What do you mean?
> *Macbeth.* Still it cried 'Sleep no more!' to all the house.
>   'Glamis hath murder'd sleep, and therefore Cawdor
>   Shall sleep no more; Macbeth shall sleep no more.'
>
>   (II. ii. 36)

Again, later:

> But let the frame of things disjoint, both the worlds suffer,
> Ere we will eat our meal in fear and sleep
> In the affliction of these terrible dreams
> That shake us nightly: better be with the dead,
> Whom we, to gain our peace, have sent to peace,
> Than on the torture of the mind to lie
> In restless ecstasy. Duncan is in his grave;
> After life's fitful fever he sleeps well;
> Treason has done his worst; nor steel, nor poison,
> Malice domestic, foreign levy, nothing,
> Can touch him further.   (III. ii. 16)

There is the dread sleep-walking of Lady Macbeth: Macbeth
asks the doctor for some 'sweet oblivious antidote' (v. iii. 43)
to give rest to her agonized consciousness. One of the worst
terrors of the Macbeth and Brutus experience is imaged as
a loss of the sweet curative of sleep.

In so far as we regard Brutus as the hero of *Julius Caesar*,
it will be evident that the falling action continues to present
similarities to *Macbeth*. The act of blood looses chaos and
destruction on earth. So Antony prophesies:

> Domestic fury and fierce civil strife
> Shall cumber all the parts of Italy;
> Blood and destruction shall be so in use
> And dreadful objects so familiar
> That mothers shall but smile when they behold
> Their infants quarter'd with the hands of war;
> All pity chok'd with custom of fell deeds . . .   (iii. i. 263)

Similar is the description by Ross of the horrors alive in Scotland:

> Alas, poor country!
> Almost afraid to know itself. It cannot
> Be call'd our mother, but our grave; where nothing,
> But who knows nothing, is once seen to smile;
> Where sighs and groans and shrieks that rend the air
> Are made, not mark'd; where violent sorrow seems
> A modern ecstasy: the dead man's knell
> Is there scarce ask'd for who; and good men's lives
> Expire before the flowers in their caps,
> Dying or ere they sicken.   (iv. iii. 164)

These exaggerated speeches—tending away from realism to pure poetic symbolism, like the storms and strange behaviour of beasts that accompany the central actions—emphasize the essentially chaotic and destructive nature of the first murders. Also after the murder each hero experiences a purely subjective vision of a ghost. This suggests the continuance of the divided state of evil: though Brutus may continually refer to his high motives, the Ghost of Caesar introduces himself as 'Thy evil spirit, Brutus'.[1] The inward division tends to prevent any continued success. Both Brutus and Macbeth fail in their schemes not so much because of outward events and forces, but through the working of that part of their natures which originally forbade murder. Macbeth's additional and unnecessary crimes are in reality due to his agonized conscience. Had he from the first been a hardened and callous murderer, had he undertaken the act without any conflict of mind or soul, there was nothing to prevent his establishing himself safely on the throne. Conscience, which had urged him not to murder Duncan, now forces him to murder many others. With Brutus, much

---

[1] That this phrase comes from Plutarch is not relevant here. Shakespeare need not have used it. Nor, in any case, does its legendary survival prove its artistic sterility: rather the reverse.

the same cause produces the same final result by different means: his conscience, or instinct, or whatever it was which urged him not to assassinate Caesar, tells him not to risk further unnecessary bloodshed, and even to allow Antony's oration—all in the nature of a peace-offering to his own uneasy conscience. The result in both cases determines the downfall of the hero.

At the end Brutus and Macbeth are attacked each by two main enemies: the symbols of (i) their original deed of destruction, and (ii) their own trammelling and hindering conscience. Which has profound significance, since had either remained absolutely true to one side of his nature there would, probably, have been no failure. They are thus tracked down by this dual representation of their originally divided selves: it is apparent throughout that the same division is at the root of both their original state of evil and their eventual failure. So here the conquering forces are to be led against Brutus by the young Octavius, nephew of Caesar, and Antony, whom Brutus' conscience has indirectly placed in power; and against Macbeth by the young Malcolm, son of Duncan, and Macduff, whom Macbeth's tortured conscience has roused against him. And before the end, each is left more lonely than ever by the death of his nearest partner. Brutus finds Cassius dead soon after having heard of his wife's suicide. Macbeth, too, loses his wife. Each receives such news callously: for, after all, what has this new element of loneliness to add to that spiritual isolation that has been so long a torment? The death of each is unspectacular:

> *Brutus.* So fare you well at once; for Brutus' tongue
>   Hath almost ended his life's history:
>   Night hangs upon mine eyes; my bones would rest
>   That have but laboured to attain this hour.   (v. v. 39)

Macbeth meets Macduff and is killed. With each hero the sleepless agony of spiritual division finds rest and unity in the vaster sleep of death.

The similarities I have noticed between the Brutus-theme and *Macbeth* are essentially imaginative similarities: only in so far as we are submerged in the poetic quality of the plays will this similarity be powerfully and significantly in evidence. Therefore it is not strange that on the plane of pure poetic symbolism and attendant atmosphere there should be more, and striking, parallels. The most obvious forms of symbolism in these two plays are (i) storm-symbolism, (ii) blood-imagery, and (iii) animal-symbolism. The Brutus and Macbeth themes alone in Shakespeare are accompanied by these three forms of poetic atmosphere and suggestion in full force. They stand for contest, destruction, and disorder in the outer world and in the reader's mind, mirroring the contest, destruction, and disorder both in the soul of the hero and in that element of the poet's intuitive experience to which the plays concerned give vivid and concrete dramatic form.

The storm-imagery in the early scenes of *Julius Caesar* is insistent and lurid:

> *Casca.* Are you not moved when all the sway of earth
>   Shakes like a thing unfirm? O, Cicero,
>   I have seen tempests, when the scolding winds
>   Have rived the knotty oaks, and I have seen
>   The ambitious ocean swell and rage and foam,
>   To be exalted with the threatening clouds:
>   But never till to-night, never till now,
>   Did I go through a tempest dropping fire.
>   Either there is a civil strife in heaven,
>   Or else the world, too saucy with the gods,
>   Incenses them to send destruction.   (i. iii. 3)

More storm references occur throughout the scene. So, too, Lennox speaks to Macbeth on the night of the murder:

> The night has been unruly: where we lay,
>   Our chimneys were blown down; and, as they say,
>   Lamentings heard i' the air—strange screams of death;
>   And, prophesying with accents terrible
>   Of dire combustion and confus'd events
>   New-hatch'd to the woeful time, the obscure bird
>   Clamour'd the live-long night: some say the earth
>   Was feverous, and did shake.   (ii. iii. 60).

The storm-imagery in *Macbeth*, as, too, the whole imaginative atmosphere, is less fiery and bright and scintillating: more black, smoky, foul. There is nothing so vividly pictorial as the 'fierce fiery warriors' fighting in the heavens above Rome (ii. ii. 19). But the same order of imagery occurs, reflecting the same kind of theme. Macbeth answers to Lennox merely:

> 'Twas a rough night.

The storm itself has little meaning for him: it is merely a pale reflex—for our benefit—of the tempest conflicting in his soul. Nor is Brutus affected by it—it serves as a convenient method of illumination:

> The exhalations whizzing in the air
> Give so much light that I may read by them.   (ii. i. 44)

The phantasms that make terrible the skies of Rome, and drizzle blood upon the Capitol, are nothing to the phantasma and hideous dream in his own mind. He is, in fact, ignorant of them: they are for us, not for him. But their effect on the minor characters, and thence on the reader, is great. It is, however, noteworthy that Lady Macbeth and Cassius will not be shown to us as struck with any kind of awe: since, enduring no inward conflict and chaos of soul, it is inevitable that they should be presented as untouched by the symbol of conflict. Lady Macbeth is coldly realistic at the time of the murder:

> I heard the owl scream and the crickets cry.   (ii. ii. 17)

Cassius even revels in the storm. To him, it symbolizes not the act of destruction, but rather the present state of things which he whole-heartedly intends to alter:

> *Casca.*   Cassius, what night is this!
> *Cassius.* A very pleasing night to honest men.
> *Casca.* Who ever knew the heavens menace so?
> *Cassius.* Those that have known the earth so full of faults.
>   For my part, I have walked about the streets,
>   Submitting me unto the perilous night,
>   And, thus unbraced, Casca, as you see,
>   Have bared my bosom to the thunder-stone;
>   And when the cross-blue lightning seem'd to open
>   The breast of heaven, I did present myself
>   Even in the aim and very flash of it.   (i. iii. 42)

Cassius, in conspiring against Caesar, is being true to his own nature. Suffering no consciousness of evil in himself, being, that is, in harmony with himself, he can say that the night is pleasing 'to honest men'. The storm has no terrors

for Cassius, since to him the murder of Caesar is creative,
not destructive—the act is one to restore, not disturb, the
order of Rome. Now, though the storm effects in *Macbeth*
are, as are most other effects, less prolix than in *Julius Caesar*,
they are in their impact even more powerful. They are less
coloured and less varied, but more grim and thick with a
choking atmosphere of evil. Foul weather, thunder, and
lightning, accompany the Weird Sisters from the start. But,
though imaginatively the whole of the Brutus-theme is on
a more brilliant, optimistic, almost cheerfully heroic plane
than the action of *Macbeth*, one is only a more concentrated
and explosive development of the other: though one flower
be bright and the other dark, the roots are of the same
species—destruction, spiritual division, disharmony and
anarchy within and without.

The blood-imagery of *Julius Caesar* is flagrant and excessive. Images of blood and human wounds abound. Such lines
as the following are typical:

> O mighty Caesar! dost thou lie so low?
> Are all thy conquests, glories, triumphs, spoils,
> Shrunk to this little measure? Fare thee well.
> I know not, gentlemen, what you intend,
> Who else must be let blood, who else is rank:
> If I myself, there is no hour so fit
> As Caesar's death's hour, nor no instrument
> Of half that worth as those your swords, made rich
> With the most noble blood of all this world.
> I do beseech you, if you bear me hard,
> Now whilst your purpled hands do reek and smoke,
> Fulfil your pleasure.   (III. i. 148)

There is Brutus' elaborate and rather horrible description
of the proposed 'carving' of Caesar (II. i. 173); there are the
'fierce fiery warriors' who 'drizzled blood upon the Capitol'
(II. ii. 19); there is Caesar's dream of the statue

> Which like a fountain with a hundred spouts
> Did run pure blood.   (II. ii. 77)

'Blood' or 'bloody' occurs seventeen times in III. i. alone.
Brutus advises the conspirators to stoop and bathe their
swords and arms in Caesar's blood. Blood is again emphasized in Antony's oration—blood and Caesar's wounds.

The pages of this play are drenched in it. And yet the whole
of the blood-imagery here does not hold a quarter of the
terror and the misery of the blood-speeches in *Macbeth*; of
Lady Macbeth's

> Yet who would have thought the old man to have had so much blood in
> him?   (v. i. 42)

or Angus'

>   Now does he feel
> His secret murders sticking on his hands   (v. ii. 16)

—terrible bloodless metaphor! or of Macbeth's

> What hands are these? Ha! they pluck out mine eyes.
> Will all great Neptune's ocean wash this blood
> Clean from my hand? No, this my hand will rather
> The multitudinous seas incarnadine,
> Making the green one red.   (II. ii. 60)

In comparison with such lines those in *Julius Caesar* show
more of a blood-zest than a blood-horror: just as the storm
in *Julius Caesar* is lurid, fiery, bizarre, and picturesque—a
kind of tragic fireworks; whereas the atmosphere of *Macbeth*
is gloomy, black, and fearful. But in both plays the essentially murderous and destructive nature of the action is
emphasized by recurrent blood-imagery.

And, finally, there is the animal-symbolism. Many of the
creatures mentioned are either unnatural in form or unnatural in behaviour. They are creatures suggestive of a
disjointed and disorganized state, creatures of unnatural
disorder, reflecting the unnatural and disorderly acts of
Brutus and Macbeth: for it is, in the present era, now that
'human statute' has 'purged the general weal' (*Macbeth*,
III. iv. 76), as natural to man to aim at harmony and order
both without and within the individual 'state of man' as it
is to birds and beasts to follow the instinctive laws of their
kind. Hence the murder of Caesar is heralded by varied
unnatural phenomena. Not only do 'birds and beasts' break
from all habits of their 'quality and kind' (I. iii. 64); all laws
of nature are interrupted:

> *Casca.* A common slave—you know him well by sight—
> Held up his left hand, which did flame and burn
> Like twenty torches join'd, and yet his hand,

> Not sensible of fire, remain'd unscorch'd.
> Besides—I ha' not since put up my sword—
> Against the Capitol I met a lion,
> Who glared upon me and went surly by,
> Without annoying me.   (i. iii. 15)

He tells how

> Men all in fire walk up and down the streets.
> And yesterday the bird of night did sit
> Even at noon-day upon the market place,
> Hooting and shrieking.   (i. iii. 25)

A lioness 'hath whelped in the streets' (ii. ii. 17). Graves have opened, and the dead walk forth shrieking (ii. ii. 18, 24). All things seem to have changed

> from their ordinance
> Their natures and preformed faculties
> To monstrous quality.   (i. iii. 66)

There is no heart within the sacrificial offering (ii. ii 40). We are confronted with things apparently beyond the workings of causality. In *Julius Caesar* all order is inverted: 'old men fool and children calculate' (i. iii. 65). And all this shadows vaguely the terrors and dangers of an act against the symbol of order and authority: an act of destruction directed against the state, a rough tearing of the woven fabric of society and order and peace. Now the action of *Macbeth* is accompanied by similar extraordinary manifestations. Not only have we the familiars of the Weird Sisters and their references to animals of unnatural form as 'the rat without a tail'[1] and the numerous evil forms of life mentioned in the cauldron incantation scene, but, as in *Julius Caesar*, weird phenomena in the animal and stellar worlds strike fear and wonder into the minds of men. In both plays, the comparison of these outward forms to the central act of disorder is clearly pointed. Cassius tells us:

> And the complexion of the element
> In favour' s like the work we have in hand,
> Most bloody, fiery, and most terrible.   (i. iii. 128)

Calpurnia knows that 'when beggars die there are no comets seen' (ii. ii. 30). In *Macbeth* we are told clearly, in a short

---

[1] The fact that this was a popular superstition in no way lessens its imaginative value in *Macbeth*.

scene of choric commentary, that these strange events reflect
the essential unnaturalness of murder—that is, the essential
disorderliness of destruction: and this reflects—or is reflected
in—the unnatural disharmony in Macbeth's soul. Ross and
an Old Man talk:

> *Old Man.* Three score and ten I can remember well:
>   Within the volume of which time I have seen
>   Hours dreadful and things strange; but this sore night
>   Hath trifled former knowings.
> *Ross.*   Ah, good father,
>   Thou seest, the heavens, as troubled with man's act,
>   Threaten his bloody stage: by the clock, 'tis day,
>   And yet dark night strangles the travelling lamp;
>   Is't night's predominance, or the day's shame,
>   That darkness does the face of earth entomb,
>   When living light should kiss it?
> *Old Man.*   'Tis unnatural,
>   Even like the deed that's done. On Tuesday last,
>   A falcon, towering in her pride of place,
>   Was by a mousing owl hawk'd at and kill'd.
> *Ross.* And Duncan's horses—a thing most strange and certain—
>   Beauteous and swift, the minions of their race,
>   Turn'd wild in nature, broke their stalls, flung out,
>   Contending 'gainst obedience, as they would make
>   War with mankind.
> *Old Man.*   'Tis said they eat each other.
> *Ross.* They did so, to the amazement of mine eyes
>   That look'd upon't.   (ii. iv. 1)

Again the insistence on disorder: the suspension and interruption of natural laws corresponding to the unlawful and
so unnatural deed. Earlier in the play Lennox told us
that:

> . . . prophesying with accents terrible
> Of dire combustion and confus'd events
> New-hatch'd to the woeful time, the obscure bird
> Clamour'd the live-long night . . .   (ii. iii. 62)

—like 'the bird of night' in *Julius Caesar*, 'hooting and
shrieking' (i. iii. 26) in the market-place.
  Such portents are harbingers of 'confused events', of
disorder. So Macbeth, who has, like Brutus, 'let slip the
dogs of war' within himself, but determines not to return
but 'go o'er', tells the Weird Sisters that he must be satisfied

whatever confusion and disorder follow: again, an emphasis on chaos, disorder, 'confused events':

> I conjure you, by that which you profess,
> Howe'er you come to know it, answer me:
> Though you untie the winds and let them fight
> Against the churches; though the yesty waves
> Confound and swallow navigation up;
> Though bladed corn be lodg'd and trees blown down;
> Though castles topple on their warders' heads;
> Though palaces and pyramids do slope
> Their heads to their foundations; though the treasure
> Of nature's germens tumble all together,
> Even till destruction sicken; answer me
> To what I ask you.   (iv. i. 50)

These are the forces of destruction and disorder Macbeth must now loose—against himself. This speech is followed by the three 'apparitions'; and we see how the interruption of natural laws itself recoils on him—Birnam Wood is to move to Dunsinane, or appear to him to do so; and Macduff, not 'born of woman', will be the appointed angel of revenge. Brutus also finds he has released forces against himself and his party. Antony's prophecy is fulfilled:

> . . . Caesar's spirit, ranging for revenge,
> With Ate by his side, come hot from Hell,
> Shall in these confines, with a monarch's voice,
> Cry 'Havoc!' and let slip the dogs of war.   (iii. i. 270)

In both plays it is seen that good does not come from evil; order from disorder; harmony from conflict. But a new good must take the place of the old, a new order, like the old, must come back to Rome and Scotland; the new harmony will be as the old harmony that was shattered by the rash act of conflict.

The poetic symbolism and imaginative atmosphere of these two plays tend to mirror the spiritual significance. The outer conflict is a symbol of an inner conflict. The unnatural phenomena of earth and sky show a disorder in things: so, too, is there disorder in the souls—or minds—of Brutus and Macbeth. An exact reference of these disorder-symbols to the mental experience of the protagonists is most important. I shall next attempt to show why the disorder-symbols of *Julius Caesar* must be related to Brutus, and not elsewhere.

The horror of Caesar's assassination is apparent most strongly to two people in the play: Brutus and Antony. Its necessity is apparent most strongly to Brutus and Cassius. Cassius and Antony are both sure of themselves, and enjoy a oneness of vision, which results in clear and concise action. To neither does the act present a twofold and agonizingly inconsistent appearance. But it is exactly this incertitude, this wavering between two aspects of reality, which is at the root of disorder.[1] It is this which torments Brutus; it is this twofold fated necessity and yet rational absurdity of Caesar's assassination which the play, as a whole, gives the reader; it is this consciousness of the wrongness and unnaturalness of destruction in a mind that is yet involved automatically and half-willingly in that very destruction which forms the poetic experience of Brutus and Macbeth, and the poetic experience of the poet which created, and that in the reader which is induced by, the attendant symbolism of storm, blood, and chaos in nature. For the poet and the reader, like Brutus, see both sides of the question, and suffer a division of sympathy. And it is only in respect of this division of sympathy in the beholder that the murders can ultimately be considered unnatural. That they are 'unnatural' in themselves and absolutely cannot ultimately be asserted: they happened and were therefore natural. Absolute disorder is inconceivable. So though to Antony the murder is purely hateful, unnecessary and in a sense unnatural, and though he may prophesy external disorder, he is in no doubt as to his own course, he endures no division of sympathy, no unnatural experience, no spiritual conflict, and so, not suffering inward disorder, he promptly expresses himself by recreating 'order'. The murder of Caesar is natural to Antony in that it falls readily into his scheme of thought: he therefore knows just what to do about it. But Brutus, like the reader, is twined in the meshes of the immediately actual and impending—and so in one sense perfectly natural

[1] Cf. Bergson's contention (to which I am indebted) that the concept of disorder is the result of a mind oscillating between *two kinds of order*. In writing of 'orders' he says: 'There is not first the incoherent, then the geometrical, then the vital; there is only the geometrical and the vital and then, by a swaying of the mind between them, the idea of the incoherent' (*Creative Evolution*, translated A. Mitchell, p. 249). This appears to me to have relevance to the Brutus-theme and *Macbeth*; both of which turn on the idea of 'disorder' and that of a mind suffering division and conflict.

—fact of the murder, and yet sees all the time its essential breaking of the natural evolved laws of humanity. It is this twofold consciousness of the unnatural within the actual that creates disorder in the souls of Brutus and Macbeth. And we, in reading, are made to feel a similar symbolic disorder within the order of nature. The poetic symbolism accordingly forces us to see the central act of *Julius Caesar* more nearly through the vision of a Brutus than that of any other of the chief persons.

This is the peculiar technique of mature Shakespearian tragedy. The hero and his universe are interdependent. In *Macbeth* and *King Lear* this interdependence is obvious: in *Julius Caesar* it is only evident, perhaps, on the analogy of *Macbeth*. But, whether in *Macbeth* or *Julius Caesar*, this interpenetration of the protagonist with his environment is a supreme act of poetry. It not merely forces our vision to the focus of the hero's consciousness but is philosophically profound: for the play then contains more than an historical sequence of events. In so closely fusing protagonist with plot, the poet has created a living reality in that he shows us, not merely a series of persons and events, but a profound relation between the mind and its environment; a relation bridged by action. There is disorder in Brutus, in Macbeth: there is a disorderly act: there is disorder in the world. And yet this is not a purely logical sequence. The original spiritual disorder may equally be said either to cause, or to be caused by, the final disorder in the world: since, if the murderer were at peace with himself originally, his deed might not lead—as I have shown—to political chaos; and yet it is the fear of final disorder—that is, of crime—which originally seems to cause disorder in the hero's soul. Thus there is no rigid time-sequence of cause and effect between the hero and his environment: there is, however, a relation, and this relation is cemented and fused by the use of prophecy and poetic symbolism, merging subject with object, present with future. We are shown not merely the story of a murder; not merely the mind of a murderer; nor merely the effect of murder; but rather a single reality built of these three interacting, reciprocal, co-existent. The future disorder of Rome is mirrored in the skies before Caesar's death: the

Weird Sisters foreshadow the death of Duncan, the Sooth-sayer that of Caesar: the future is half felt as existing within the present and the time-sequence has a secondary reality only. In this way we are shown the essence of destruction, of evil. This essence is not purely human, though it uses humanity; it is contingent on human action, and it is therefore not inhuman either. It exists purely as a reciprocity, or relation: and in so far as the poetic symbolism alone directly expresses this relation it is of more importance than either the protagonist himself or the action of the play. It alone reflects an absolute reality. It is, in fact, the pivot and core of the drama. In this way *Julius Caesar* and *Macbeth* expose the nature of an evil reality: an abnormal and dynamic relation between a unit and its environment.

I do not claim in this essay to have done more than indicate wherein the Brutus and Macbeth conceptions are poetically alike. The divergences are readily apparent. I do not deny a difference on the plane of ethics. Brutus is more conscious of integrity and harmony in his aims—if not in himself—than Macbeth. And partly for this reason, the whole of the first part of *Julius Caesar* with its fire and blood imagery and its picturesque menagerie of beasts, is always heroic and romantic and colourful against the darkness, and contrasts with the gloom and murk of *Macbeth*; its muffled thunder; and the unclean rites of the Weird Sisters. But in essence the conflicts are similar. Though the contestants in the souls of the two heroes be not exactly commensurable with each other, the conflict is of the same nature. The courses of their tragedies follow channels of the same curves. The Brutus-theme, though pitched in a different ethical key, presents the same rhythm as *Macbeth*.

VII

MACBETH AND THE METAPHYSIC
OF EVIL

MACBETH is Shakespeare's most profound and mature vision of evil. In the ghost and death themes of *Hamlet* we have something of the same quality; in the Brutus-theme of *Julius Caesar* we have an exactly analogous rhythm of spiritual experience; in *Richard III* we have a parallel history of an individual's crime. In *Macbeth* all this, and the many other isolated poetic units of similar quality throughout Shakespeare, receive a final, perfected form. Therefore analysis of *Macbeth* is of profound value: but it is not easy. Much of *Hamlet*, and the *Troilus-Othello-Lear* succession culminating in *Timon of Athens*, can be regarded as representations of the 'hate-theme'. We are there faced by man's aspiring nature, unsatiated of its desire among the frailties and inconsistencies of its world. They point us to good, not evil, and their very gloom of denial is the shadow of a great assertion. They accordingly lend themselves to interpretation in terms of human thought, and their evil can be regarded as a negation of man's positive longing. In *Macbeth* we find not gloom, but blackness: the evil is not relative, but absolute. In point of imaginative profundity *Macbeth* is comparable alone to *Antony and Cleopatra*. There we have a fiery vision of a paradisal consciousness; here the murk and nightmare torment of a conscious hell. This evil, being absolute and therefore alien to man, is in essence shown as inhuman and supernatural, and is most difficult of location within any philosophical scheme. *Macbeth* is fantastical and imaginative beyond other tragedies. Difficulty is increased by that implicit blurring of effects, that palling darkness, that overcasts plot, technique, style. The persons of the play are themselves groping. Yet we are left with an overpowering knowledge of suffocating, conquering evil, and fixed by the basilisk eye of a nameless terror. This evil will be my subject. In parts of my treatment the influence of A. C. Bradley will be apparent.

It is dangerous to abstract the personal history of the protagonist from his environment as a basis for interpretation. The main theme is not primarily differentiated from that of the important subsidiary persons and cannot stand alone. Rather there is a similarity, and the evil in Banquo, Macduff, Malcolm, and the enveloping atmosphere of the play, all forms so many steps by which we may approach and understand the titanic evil which grips the two protagonists. The *Macbeth* universe is woven in a texture of a single pattern. The whole play is one swift act of the poet's mind, and as such must be interpreted, since the technique confronts us not with separated integers of 'character' or incident, but with a molten welding of thought with thought, event with event. There is an interpenetrating quality that subdues all to itself. Therefore I shall start by noticing some of the more important elements in this total imaginative effect, and thence I shall pass to the more purely human element. The story and action of the play alone will not carry us far. Here the logic of imaginative correspondence is more significant and more exact than the logic of plot.

Macbeth is a desolate and dark universe where all is befogged, baffled, constricted by the evil. Probably in no play of Shakespeare are so many questions asked. It opens with 'When shall we three meet again?' and 'Where the place?' (I. i. 1 and 6). The second scene starts with, 'What bloody man is that?' (I. ii. 1), and throughout it questions are asked of the Sergeant and Ross. This is followed by:

> *First Witch.* Where hast thou been, sister?
> *Second Witch.* Killing swine.
> *First Witch.* Sister, where thou? (I. iii. 1)

And Banquo's first words on entering are: 'How far is't called to Forres? What are these . . .?' (I. iii. 39). Questions succeed each other quickly throughout this scene. Amazement and mystery are in the play from the start, and are reflected in continual questions—there are those of Duncan to Malcolm in I. iv, and of Lady Macbeth to the Messenger and then to her lord in I. v. They continue throughout the play. In I. vii they are tense and powerful:

Macbeth.   . . . How now! What news?
L. Macbeth. He has almost supp'd: why have you left the chamber?
Macbeth. Hath he asked for me?
L. Macbeth.   Know you not he has?   (I. vii. 28)

This scene bristles with them. At the climax of the murder they come again, short stabs of fear: 'Didst thou not hear a noise?—Did not you speak?—When?—Now.—As I descended? . . .' (II. ii. 16). Some of the finest and most heart-rending passages are in the form of questions: 'But wherefore could I not pronounce Amen?' and, 'Will all great Neptune's ocean wash this blood clean from my hand?' (II. ii. 32; II. ii. 61). The scene of the murder and that of its discovery form a series of questions. To continue the list in detail would be more tedious than difficult: to quote a few—there are the amazed questions of the guests and Lady Macbeth at the Banquet (III. iii); Macbeth's continual questioning of the Weird Sisters in the Cauldron scene (IV. i); those of Macduff's son to Lady Macduff (IV. ii); of Macduff to Ross who brings him news of his family's slaughter (IV. iii); of the Doctor to the Gentlewoman (V. i).

These questions are threads in the fabric of mystery and doubt which haunts us in *Macbeth*. All the persons are in doubt, baffled. Duncan is baffled at the treachery of a man he trusted (I. iv. 11). Newcomers strike amaze:

What a haste looks through his eyes! So should he look
That seems to speak things strange.   (I. ii. 47)

Surprise is continual. Macbeth does not understand how he can be Thane of Cawdor (I. iii. 108). Lady Macbeth is startled at the news of Duncan's visit (I. v. 32); Duncan at the fact of Macbeth's arrival before himself (I. vi. 20). There is the general amazement at the murder; of Lennox, Ross, and the Old Man at the strange happenings in earth and heaven on the night of the murder (II. iii. 60–7; II. iv. 1–20). Banquo and Fleance are unsure of the hour (II. i. 1–4). No one is sure of Macduff's mysterious movements. Lady Macbeth is baffled by Macbeth's enigmatic hints as to the 'deed of dreadful note' (III. ii. 44). The two murderers are not certain as to who has wronged them, Macbeth or Banquo (III. i. 76–9); they do not understand

the advent of the 'third murderer' (III. iii. 1). Ross and
Lady Macduff are at a loss as to Macduff's flight, and
warning is brought to Lady Macduff by a mysterious
messenger who 'is not to her known' (IV. ii. 63). Malcolm
suspects Macduff, and there is a long dialogue due to his
'doubts' (IV. iii); and in the same scene Malcolm recognizes
Ross as his countryman yet strangely 'knows him not'
(IV. iii. 160). As the atmosphere brightens at the end of the
play, the contrast is aptly marked by reference to the stroke
of action which will finally dispel the fog of insecurity:

> The time approaches
> That will with due decision make us know
> What we shall say we have and what we owe.
> Thoughts speculative their unsure hopes relate,
> But certain issues strokes must arbitrate.   (V. iv. 17)

This blurring and lack of certainty is increased by the
heavy proportion of second-hand or vague knowledge reported during the play's progress. We have the two accounts
of the fighting, by the Sergeant and Ross: but the whole
matter of the rebellion is vague to us. Later, after Ross has
told Macbeth of his new honours, Angus says that he
'knows not' the exact crimes of the former Thane of Cawdor
(I. iii. 111–16). Malcolm has spoken with 'one that saw him
die' (I. iv. 4). Lady Macbeth hears amazedly of the Weird
Sisters' prophecy by letter (I. v.). Macbeth describes the voice
that bade him 'sleep no more' (II. ii. 36) and the dead body
of Duncan (II. iii. 118). People are continually receiving the
latest news from each other, the climax being Macduff's
hearing of his family's slaughter (II. iv; III. vi; IV. iii. 161–
239). Rumours are alive throughout:

> *Macbeth.* How say'st thou that Macduff denies his person
>   At our great bidding?
> *L. Macbeth.*   Did you send to him, Sir?
> *Macbeth.* I hear it by the way; but I will send.   (III. iv. 128)

We hear more rumours of Macduff in the dialogue between
Lennox and the Lord in III. vi. There is the 'galloping of
horses' with the mysterious 'two or three' who bring word
of Macduff's flight (IV. i. 141). It is a world of rumours
and fears:

Ross.   I dare not speak much further;
  But cruel are the times, when we are traitors
  And do not know ourselves; when we hold rumour
  From what we fear, yet know not what we fear,
  But float upon a wild and violent sea
  Each way and move.   (iv. ii. 17)

Ross has heard a 'rumour' of a rise in Scotland against
Macbeth (iv. iii. 182). In a hushed voice the Gentlewoman
describes Lady Macbeth's sleep-walking to the Doctor
(v. i.); and the Doctor says he has 'heard something' of
Macbeth's 'royal preparation' (v. iii. 57–8). Siward 'learns
no other' but that Macbeth is defending his castle (v. iv. 9),
and Lady Macbeth, 'as 'tis thought', commits suicide
(v. vii. 99). These are but a few random instances: questions,
rumours, startling news, and uncertainties are everywhere.
From the time when Banquo asks 'How far is't called to
Forres?' (i. iii. 39) until Siward's 'What wood is this before
us?' (v. iv. 3) we are watching persons lost, mazed.[1] They
do not understand themselves even:

Malcolm.   Why do we hold our tongues
  That most may claim this argument for ours?   (ii. iii. 126)

The persons of the drama can say truly, with Ross, 'we . . .
do not know ourselves' (iv. ii. 19). We too, who read, are in
doubt often. Action here is illogical. Why does Macbeth not
know of Cawdor's treachery? Why does Lady Macbeth
faint? Why do the King's sons flee to different countries
when a whole nation is ready in their support? Why does
Macduff move so darkly mysterious in the background
and leave his family to certain death? Who is the Third
Murderer? And, finally, why does Macbeth murder Duncan?
All this builds a strong sense of mystery and irrationality
within us. We, too, grope in the stifling dark, and suffer
from doubt and insecurity.

Darkness permeates the play. The greater part of the
action takes place in the murk of night. It is unnecessary to
detail more than a few of the numerous references to darkness. Lady Macbeth prays:

[1] Cf. Colin Still's *Shakespeare's Mystery Play: A Study of The Tempest* (Cecil Palmer,
1921; revised and reissued as *The Timeless Theme*, Nicholson and Watson, 1936). In his
interpretation, the Court Party are related to the maze in ancient ritual; and in my interpretation of *The Tempest*, I roughly equate the Antonio and Sebastian theme with *Macbeth*.

> Come, thick night,
> And pall thee in the dunnest smoke of Hell,
> That my keen knife see not the wound it makes,
> Nor Heaven peep through the blanket of the dark
> To cry, Hold! Hold!   (I. v. 51)

And Macbeth:

> Stars, hide your fires.
> Let not light see my black and deep desires;
> The eye wink at the hand; yet let that be,
> Which the eye fears, when it is done, to see.   (I. iv. 50)

During the play 'light thickens' (III. ii. 50), the 'travelling lamp' is 'strangled' (II. iv. 7), there is 'husbandry in heaven' (II. i. 4). This is typical:

> Now spurs the lated traveller apace
> To gain the timely inn.   (III. iii. 6)

Now this world of doubts and darkness gives birth to strange and hideous creatures. Vivid animal disorder-symbolism is recurrent in the play and the animals mentioned are for the most part of fierce, ugly, or ill-omened significance. We hear of 'the Hyrcan tiger' and the 'armed rhinoceros' (III. iv. 101), the 'rugged Russian bear' (III. iv. 100); the wolf, 'whose howl's his watch' (II. i. 54); the raven who croaks the entrance of Duncan under Lady Macbeth's battlements (I. v. 39); the owl, 'fatal bellman who gives the stern'st goodnight' (II. ii. 4). There are 'maggot-pies and choughs and rooks' (III. iv. 125), and

> . . . hounds and greyhounds, mongrels, spaniels, curs,
> Shoughs, water-rugs, and demi-wolves . . .   (III. i. 93)

We have the bat and his 'cloistered flight', the 'shard-borne beetle', the crow making wing to the 'rooky wood'; 'night's black agents' rouse to their preys; Macbeth has 'scotch'd the snake, not killed it'; his mind is full of 'scorpions' (III. ii. 13–53). All this suggests life threatening, ill-omened, hideous: and it culminates in the holocaust of filth prepared by the Weird Sisters in the Cauldron scene. But not only are animals of unpleasant suggestion here present: we have animals, like men, irrational and amazing in their acts. A falcon is attacked and killed by a 'mousing owl', and Duncan's horses eat each other (ii. iv. 11–18). There is a prodigious and ghastly tempest, with 'screams of death'; the owl clamoured through the night; the earth itself shook (ii. iii. 60–7). We are made aware of a hideous abnormality in this world; and again we feel its irrationality and mystery. In proportion as we let ourselves be receptive to the impact of all these suggestions we shall be strongly aware of the essential fearsomeness of this universe.

We are confronted by mystery, darkness, abnormality, hideousness: and therefore by fear. The word 'fear' is ubiquitous. All may be unified as symbols of this emotion. Fear is predominant. Everyone is afraid. There is scarcely a person in the play who does not feel and voice at some time a sickening, nameless terror. The impact of the play is analogous to nightmare, to which state there are many references:

> Now o'er the one-half world,
> Nature seems dead, and wicked dreams abuse
> The curtain'd sleep . . .　　　　　　　　　　(ii. i. 49)

Banquo cries:

> Merciful powers,
> Restrain in me the cursed thoughts that nature
> Gives way to in repose!　　　　　　　　　　(ii. i. 7)

Banquo has dreamed of 'the three weird sisters' (ii. i. 20), who are thus associated with a nightmare reality. There are those who cried in their sleep, and said their prayers after (ii. ii. 24). Macbeth may 'sleep no more' (ii. ii. 44); sleep, balm of hurt minds, 'shall neither night nor day hang upon his pent-house lid' (i. iii. 19)—if we may transfer the reference. He and his wife are condemned to live

> in the affliction of these terrible dreams
> That shake us nightly.　　　　　　　　　　(iii. ii. 18)

The central act of the play is a hideous murder of sleep. Finally, we have the extreme agony of sleep-consciousness depicted in Lady Macbeth's sleep-walking. Nor are there dreams only: the narrow gulf between nightmare and the abnormal actuality of the *Macbeth* universe—itself of nightmare quality—is bridged by phantasies and ghosts: the dagger of Macbeth's mind, the Ghost of Banquo, the Apparitions, the Vision of Scottish Kings, culminating in the three Weird Sisters. There is no nearer equivalent, in the experience of a normal mind, to the poetic quality of *Macbeth* than the consciousness of nightmare or delirium. That is why life is here a 'tale told by an idiot' (v. v. 27), a 'fitful fever' after which the dead 'sleep well' (iii. ii. 23); why the earth itself is 'feverous' (ii. iii. 67). The Weird Sisters are nightmare actualized; Macbeth's crime nightmare projected into action. Therefore this world is unknowable, hideous, disorderly, and irrational. The very style of the play has a mesmeric, nightmare quality, for in that dream-consciousness, hateful though it be, there is a nervous tension, a vivid sense of profound significance, an exceptionally rich apprehension of reality electrifying the mind: one is in touch with absolute evil, which, being absolute, has a satanic beauty, a hideous, serpent-like grace and attraction, drawing, paralysing. This quality is in the poetic style: the language is tense, nervous, insubstantial, without anything of the visual clarity of *Othello*, or the massive solemnity of *Timon of Athens*. The poetic effect of the whole, though black with an inhuman abysm of darkness, is yet shot through and streaked with vivid colour, with horrors that hold a mesmeric attraction even while they repel; and things of brightness that intensify the enveloping murk. There is constant reference to blood. Macbeth and Banquo 'bathe in reeking wounds' (i. ii. 40) in the fight reported by the 'bloody' Sergeant; Macbeth's sword 'smoked with bloody execution' (i. ii. 18); there is the blood on Macbeth's hands, and on Lady Macbeth's after she has 'smeared' the sleeping grooms with it (ii. ii). There is the description of Duncan's body, 'his silver skin lac'd with his golden blood' (ii. iii. 118). There is blood on the face of the Murderer who comes to tell of Banquo's 'trenched gashes' (iii. iv. 27); the 'gory locks' (iii. iv. 51) of the 'blood-bolter'd' Banquo; the 'bloody child' Apparition; the blood-nightmare of Lady Macbeth's sleep-walking. But though blood-imagery is rich, there is no brilliance in it; rather a sickly smear. Yet there is brilliance in the fire-imagery: the thunder and lightning which accompanies the Weird Sisters; the fire of the cauldron; the green glint of the spectral dagger; the glaring eyes which hold 'no speculation' of Banquo's Ghost, the insubstantial sheen of the three Apparitions, the ghastly pageant of kings unborn.

Macbeth has the poetry of intensity: intense darkness shot with the varied intensity of pure light or pure colour. In the same way the moral darkness is shot with imagery of bright purity and virtue. There is 'the temple-haunting martlet' (I. vi. 4) to contrast with evil creatures. We have the early personation of the sainted Duncan, whose body is 'the Lord's anointed temple' (II. iii. 74), the bright limning of his virtues by Macbeth (I. vii. 16–20), and Macduff (IV. iii. 108); the latter's lovely words on Malcolm's mother who, 'oftener upon her knees than on her feet, died every day she lived' (IV. iii. 110); the prayer of Lennox for 'some holy angel' (III. vi. 45) to fly to England's court for saving help; Macbeth's agonized vision of a starry good, of 'Heaven's cherubim' horsed in air, and Pity like a babe; those who pray that God may bless them in their fevered dream; above all, Malcolm's description of England's holy King, health-giver and God-elect who, unlike Macbeth, has power over 'the evil', in whose court Malcolm borrows 'grace' to combat the nightmare evil of his own land:

> *Malcolm.*   Comes the King forth, I pray you?
> *Doctor.* Ay, sir; there are a crew of wretched souls
>   That stay his cure: their malady convinces
>   The great assay of art; but at his touch—
>   Such sanctity hath Heaven given his hand—
>   They presently amend.
> *Malcolm.*   I thank you, doctor.
> *Macduff.* What's the disease he means?
> *Malcolm.*   'Tis call'd the evil.
>   A most miraculous work in this good king;
>   Which often, since my here-remain in England,
>   I have seen him do. How he solicits Heaven,
>   Himself best knows: but strangely visited people,
>   All swoln and ulcerous, pitiful to the eye,
>   The mere despair of surgery, he cures,
>   Hanging a golden stamp about their necks,
>   Put on with holy prayers: and 'tis spoken,
>   To the succeeding royalty he leaves
>   The healing benediction. With this strange virtue,
>   He hath a heavenly gift of prophecy,

And sundry blessings hang about his throne,
That speak him full of grace.   (IV. iii. 140)

This description is spoken just before Ross enters with the shattering narration of Macbeth's most dastardly and ruinous crime. The contrast at this instant is vivid and pregnant. The King of England is thus full of supernatural 'grace'. In *Macbeth* this supernatural grace is set beside the supernatural evil. Against such grace Macbeth first struck the blow of evil. Duncan was 'gracious' (III. i. 66); at his death 'renown and grace is dead' (II. iii. 101). By 'the grace of Grace' (V. vii. 101) alone Malcolm will restore health[1] to Scotland. The murk, indeed, thins towards the end. Bright daylight dawns and the green leaves of Birnam come against Macbeth. A world climbs out of its darkness, and in the dawn that panorama below is a thing of nightmare delusion. The 'sovereign flower' (V. ii. 30) is bright-dewed in the bright dawn, and the murk melts into the mists of morning: the Child is crowned, the Tree of Life in his hand.

I have indicated something of the imaginative atmosphere of this play. It is a world shaken by 'fears and scruples' (II. iii. 136). It is a world where 'nothing is but what is not' (I. iii. 141), where 'fair is foul and foul is fair' (I. i. 11). I have emphasized two complementary elements: (i) the doubts, uncertainties, irrationalities; (ii) the horrors, the dark, the abnormalities. These two elements repel respectively the intellect and the heart of man. And, since the contemplating mind is then powerfully unified in its immediate antagonism, our reaction holds the positive and tense fear that succeeds nightmare, wherein there is an experience of something at once insubstantial and unreal to the understanding and appallingly horrible to the feelings: this is the evil of *Macbeth*. In this equal repulsion of the dual attributes of the mind a state of singleness and harmony is induced in the recipient, and it is in respect of this that *Macbeth* forces us to a consciousness more exquisitely unified and sensitive than any of the great tragedies but its polar opposite, *Antony and Cleopatra*. This is how the *Macbeth* universe presents

[1] The 'evil' of *Macbeth* is symbolized in a nation's sickness. See v. ii. 27–9; v. iii. 49–56. The spiritual evil of *Macbeth* is directly related to the bodily evil of blood-destruction and sickness in the community.

to us an experience of absolute evil. Now, these two peculiarities of the whole play will be found also in the purely
human element. The two main characteristics of Macbeth's
temptation are (i) ignorance of his own motive, and (ii) horror
of the deed to which he is being driven. Fear is the primary
emotion of the *Macbeth* universe: fear is at the root of
Macbeth's crime. I shall next notice the nature of those
human events, actions, experiences to which the atmosphere
of unreality and terror bears intimate relation.

The action of the play turns on a deed of disorder. Following the disorderly rebellion which prologues the action we
have Macbeth's crime, and the disorder which it creates:

> Confusion now hath made his masterpiece!
> Most sacrilegious murder hath broke ope
> The Lord's anointed temple, and stole thence
> The life o' the building.   (II. iii. 72)

Duncan's murder and its results are felt as events of confusion and disorder, as interruptions of the even tenor of
human nature, and are therefore related to the disorder-
symbols and instances of unnatural behaviour in man or
animal or element throughout the play. The evil of atmospheric effect interpenetrates the evil of individual persons.
It has so firm a grip on this world that it fastens not only on
the protagonists, but on subsidiary persons too. This point I
shall notice before passing to the themes of Macbeth and his
wife.

Many minor persons are definitely related to evil: the two
—or three—Murderers, the traitors, Cawdor and Macdonald,
the drunken porter, doing duty at the gate of Hell. But the
major ones too, who are conceived partly as contrasts to
Macbeth and his wife, nevertheless succumb to the evil
down-pressing on the *Macbeth* universe. Banquo is early
involved. Returning with Macbeth from a bloody war, he
meets the three Weird Sisters. We may imagine that the
latter are related to the bloodshed of battle, and that they
have waited until after 'the hurly-burly's done' (I. i. 3) to
instigate a continuance of blood-lust in the two generals.
We must observe that the two generals' feats of arms are
described as acts of unprecedented ferocity:

> Except they meant to bathe in reeking wounds,
> Or memorize another Golgotha,
> I cannot tell.   (I. ii. 40)

This campaign strikes amaze into men. War is here a thing
of blood, not romance. Ross addresses Macbeth:

> Nothing afeard of what thyself didst make,
> Strange images of death.   (I. iii. 96)

Macbeth's sword 'smoked with bloody execution' (I. ii. 18).
The emphasis is important. The late wine of blood-destruction focuses the inward eyes of these two to the reality of the
sisters of blood and evil, and they in turn urge Macbeth to
add to those 'strange images of death' the 'great doom's
image' (II. iii. 85) of a murdered and sainted king. This
knowledge of evil implicit in his meeting with the three
Weird Sisters Banquo keeps to himself, and it is a bond of
evil between him and Macbeth. It is this that troubles him
on the night of the murder, planting a nightmare of unrest
in his mind: 'the cursed thoughts that nature gives way to in
repose.' He feels the typical *Macbeth* guilt: 'a heavy summons lies like lead' upon him (II. i. 6). He is enmeshed in
Macbeth's horror, and, after the coronation, keeps the guilty
secret, and lays to his heart a guilty hope. Banquo is thus
involved. So also is Macduff. His cruel desertion of his
family is emphasized:

> *L. Macduff.* His flight was madness; when our actions do not,
>   Our fears do make us traitors.
> *Ross.*   You know not
>   Whether it was his wisdom or his fear.
> *L. Macduff.* Wisdom! to leave his wife, to leave his babes,
>   His mansion and his titles in a place
>   From whence himself does flee?   (IV. ii. 3)

For this, or for some nameless reason, Macduff knows he
bears some responsibility for his dear ones' death:

> Sinful Macduff,
> They were all struck for thee! Naught that I am,
> Not for their own demerits, but for mine,
> Fell slaughter on their souls. Heaven rest them now!
>   (IV. iii. 223)

All the persons seem to share some guilt of the down-pressing
enveloping evil. Even Malcolm is forced to repeat crimes on

himself. He catalogues every possible sin, and accuses himself of all. Whatever be his reasons, his doing so yet remains part of the integral humanism of this play. The pressure of evil is not relaxed till the end. Not that the persons are 'bad characters'. They are not 'characters' at all, in the proper use of the word. They are but vaguely individualized, and more remarkable for similarity than difference. All the persons are primarily just this: men paralysed by fear and a sense of evil in and outside themselves. They lack will-power: that concept finds no place here. Neither we, nor they, know of what exactly they are guilty: yet they feel guilt.

So, too, with Lady Macbeth. She is not merely a woman of strong will: she is a woman possessed—possessed of evil passion. No 'will-power' on earth would account for her dread invocation:

> Come, you spirits
> That tend on mortal thoughts, unsex me here,
> And fill me from the crown to the toe, top-full
> Of direst cruelty!   (I. v. 41)

This speech, addressed to the 'murdering ministers' who 'in their sightless substances wait on nature's mischief' is demonic in intensity and passion. It is inhuman—as though the woman were controlled by an evil something which masters her, mind and soul. It is mysterious, fearsome, yet fascinating: like all else here, it is a nightmare thing of evil. Whatever it be it leaves her a pure woman, with a woman's frailty, as soon as ever its horrible work is done. She faints at Macbeth's description of Duncan's body. As her husband grows rich in crime, her significance dwindles: she is left shattered, a human wreck who mutters over again in sleep the hideous memories of her former satanic hour of pride. To interpret the figure of Lady Macbeth in terms of 'ambition' and 'will' is, indeed, a futile commentary. The scope and sweep of her evil passion is tremendous, irresistible, ultimate. She is an embodiment—for one mighty hour —of evil absolute and extreme.[1]

The central human theme—the temptation and crime of Macbeth—is, however, more easy of analysis. The crucial

---

[1] Iago is not absolutely evil in this sense. He is too purely intellectual to antagonize our emotions powerfully.

speech runs as follows:

> Why do I yield to that suggestion,
> Whose horrid image doth unfix my hair,
> And make my seated heart knock at my ribs
> Against the use of nature ? Present fears
> Are less than horrible imaginings.
> My thought whose murder yet is but fantastical
> Shakes so my single state of man that function
> Is smother'd in surmise, and nothing is
> But what is not.   (i. iii. 134)

These lines, spoken when Macbeth first feels the impending evil, expresses again all those elements I have noticed in the mass-effect of the play: questioning doubt, horror, fear of some unknown power; horrible imaginings of the supernatural and 'fantastical'; an abysm of unreality; disorder on the plane of physical life. This speech is a microcosm of the *Macbeth* vision: it contains the germ of the whole. Like a stone in a pond, this original immediate experience of Macbeth sends ripples of itself expanding over the whole play. This is the moment of the birth of evil in *Macbeth*—he may have had ambitious thoughts before, may even have intended the murder, but now for the first time he feels its oncoming reality. This is the mental experience which he projects into action, thereby plunging his land, too, in fear, horror, darkness, and disorder. In this speech we have a swift interpenetration of idea with idea, from fear and disorder, through sickly imaginings, to abysmal darkness, nothingness. 'Nothing is but what is not': that is the text of the play. Reality and unreality change places. We must see that Macbeth, like the whole universe of this play, is paralysed, mesmerized, as though in a dream. This is not merely 'ambition'—it is fear, a nameless fear which yet fixes itself to a horrid image. He is helpless as a man in a nightmare: and this helplessness is integral to the conception—the will-concept is absent. Macbeth may struggle, but he cannot fight: he can no more resist than a rabbit resists a weasel's teeth fastened in its neck, or a bird the serpent's transfixing eye. Now this evil in Macbeth propels him to an act absolutely evil. For, though no ethical system is ultimate, Macbeth's crime is as near absolute as may be. It is there-

fore conceived as absolute. Its dastardly nature is emphasized
clearly (I. vii. 12–25): Duncan is old, good; he is at once
Macbeth's kinsman, king, and guest; he is to be murdered
in sleep. No worse act of evil could well be found. So the
evil of which Macbeth is at first aware rapidly entraps him
in a mesh of events: it makes a tool of Duncan's visit, it
dominates Lady Macbeth. It is significant that she, like her
husband, is influenced by the Weird Sisters and their
prophecy. Eventually Macbeth undertakes the murder, as a
grim and hideous duty. He cuts a sorry figure at first, but,
once embarked on his allegiant enterprise of evil, his
grandeur grows. Throughout he is driven by fear—the fear
that paralyses everyone else urges him to an amazing and
mysterious action of blood. This action he repeats, again and
again.

By his original murder he isolates himself from humanity.
He is lonely, endures the uttermost torture of isolation. Yet
still a bond unites him to men: that bond he would 'cancel
and tear to pieces'—the natural bond of human fellowship
and love.[1] He further symbolizes his guilty, pariah soul by
murdering Banquo. He fears everyone outside himself but
his wife, suspects them. Every act of blood is driven by fear
of the horrible disharmony existent between himself and his
world. He tries to harmonize the relation by murder. He
would let 'the frame of things disjoint, both the worlds
suffer' (III. ii. 16) to win back peace. He is living in an
unreal world, a fantastic mockery, a ghoulish dream: he
strives to make this single nightmare to rule the outward
things of his nation. He would make all Scotland a nightmare thing of dripping blood. He knows he cannot return,
so determines to go o'er. He seeks out the Weird Sisters a
second time. Now he welcomes disorder and confusion,
would let them range wide over the earth, since they range
unfettered in his own soul:

> . . . though the treasure
> Of nature's germens tumble all together,
> Even till destruction sicken; answer me
> To what I ask you.   (IV. i. 58)

[1] Macbeth prays to night to 'cancel and tear to pieces that great bond which keeps me
pale' (III. ii. 49). This is the bond of *nature*, that which binds man to the good which is in
him; the bond of daylight, reality, life. 'Cancel his bond of life' occurs in *Richard III*, IV. iv. 77.

So he addresses the Weird Sisters. Castles, palaces, and pyramids—let all fall in general confusion, if only Macbeth be satisfied. He is plunging deeper and deeper into unreality, the severance from mankind and all normal forms of life is now abysmal, deep. Now he is shown Apparitions glassing the future. They promise him success in terms of natural law; no man 'of woman born' shall hurt him, he shall not be vanquished till Birnam Wood come against him. He, based firmly in the unreal, yet thinks to build his future on the laws of reality. He forgets that he is trafficking with things of nightmare fantasy, whose truth is falsehood, falsehood truth. That success they promise is unreal as they themselves. So, once having cancelled the bond of reality he has no home: the unreal he understands not, the real condemns him. In neither can he exist. He asks if Banquo's issue shall reign in Scotland: most horrible thought to him, since, if that be so, it proves that the future takes its natural course irrespective of human acts—that prophecy need not have been interpreted into crime: that he would in truth have been King of Scotland without his own 'stir' (I. iii. 144). Also the very thought of other succeeding and prosperous kings, some of them with 'twofold balls and treble sceptres' (IV. i. 121), is a maddening thing to him who is no real king but only monarch of a nightmare realm. The Weird Sisters who were formerly as the three Parcae, or Fates, foretelling Macbeth's future, now, at this later stage of his story, become the Erinyes, avengers of murder, symbols of the tormented soul. They delude and madden him with their apparitions and ghosts. Yet he does not give way, and raises our admiration at his undaunted severance from good. He contends for his own individual soul against the universal reality. Nor is his contest unavailing. He is fighting himself free from the nightmare fear of his life. He goes on 'till destruction sicken' (IV. i. 60): he actually does 'go o'er', is not lost in the stream of blood he elects to cross. It is true. He wins his battle. He adds crime to crime and emerges at last victorious and fearless:

> I have almost forgot the taste of fears:
> The time has been, my senses would have cool'd
> To hear a night-shriek; and my fell of hair

> Would at a dismal treatise rouse and stir
> As life were in't; I have supp'd full with horrors;
> Direness, familiar to my slaughterous thoughts,
> Cannot once start me.   (v. v. 9)

Again, 'Hang those that talk of fear!' (v. iii. 36) he cries, in
an ecstasy of courage. He is, at last, 'broad and general as
the casing air' (iii. iv. 23).

This will appear a strange reversal of the usual commentary; it is, however, true and necessary. Whilst Macbeth
lives in conflict with himself there is misery, evil, fear: when,
at the end, he and others have openly identified himself with
evil, he faces the world fearless: nor does he appear evil any
longer. The worst element of his suffering has been that
secrecy and hypocrisy so often referred to throughout the
play (i. iv. 12; i. v. 64; iii. ii. 34; v. iii. 27). Dark secrecy
and night are in Shakespeare ever the badges of crime. But at
the end Macbeth has no need of secrecy. He is no longer
'cabin'd, cribb'd, confined, bound in to saucy doubts and
fears' (iii. iv. 24). He has won through by excessive crime to
an harmonious and honest relation with his surroundings.
He has successfully symbolized the disorder of his lonely
guilt-stricken soul by creating disorder in the world, and
thus restores balance and harmonious contact. The mighty
principle of good planted in the nature of things then asserts
itself, condemns him openly, brings him peace. Daylight is
brought to Macbeth, as to Scotland, by the accusing armies
of Malcolm. He now knows himself to be a tyrant confessed,
and wins back that integrity of soul which gives us:

> I have lived long enough: my way of life
> Is fallen into the sere, the yellow leaf ...   (v. iii. 22)

Here he touches a recognition deeper than fear, more potent
than nightmare. The delirious dream is over. A clear daylight now disperses the imaginative dark that has eclipsed
Scotland. The change is remarkable. There is now movement,
surety and purpose, colour: horses 'skirr the country round'
(v. iii. 35), banners are hung out on the castle walls (v. v. 1),
soldiers hew down the bright leaves of Birnam (v. iv. 5).
There is, as it were, a paean of triumph as the *Macbeth*
universe, having struggled darkly upward, now climbs into
radiance. Though they oppose each other in fight, Macbeth

and Malcolm share equally in this relief, this awakening from horror. Of a piece with this change is the fulfilment of the Weird Sisters' prophecies. In bright daylight the nightmare reality to which Macbeth has been subdued is insubstantial and transient as sleep-horrors at dawn. Their unreality is emphasized by the very fact that they are nevertheless related to natural phenomena: they are thus parasitic on reality. To these he has trusted, and they fail. But he himself is, at the last, self-reliant and courageous. The words of the Weird Sisters ring true:

> Though his bark cannot be lost
> Yet it shall be tempest-toss'd.   (I. iii. 24)

Each shattering report he receives with redoubled life-zest; and meets the fate marked out by the daylight consciousness of normal man for the nightmare reality of crime. Malcolm may talk of 'this dead butcher and his fiend-like queen' (v. vii. 98). We, who have felt the sickly poise over the abysmal deeps of evil, the hideous reality of the unreal, must couch our judgement in a different phrase.

The consciousness of nightmare is a consciousness of absolute evil, presenting an heightened awareness of positive significance which challenges the goldenest dreams of blissful sleep: it is positive, powerful, autonomous. Whether this be ultimate truth or not, it is what our mental experience knows: and to deny it is to deny the aristocracy of mind. The 'sickly weal' of Scotland is in the throes of this delirious dream, which, whilst it lasts, has every attribute of reality. Yet this evil is not a native of man's heart: it comes from without. The Weird Sisters are objectively conceived: they are not, as are the dagger and ghost, the subjective effect of evil in the protagonist's mind. They are, within the *Macbeth* universe, independent entities; and the fact that they instigate Macbeth directly and Lady Macbeth indirectly tends to assert the objectivity of evil. This, however, is purely a matter of poetic impact: the word 'absolute' seems a just interpretation of the imaginative reality, in so far as an immediate interpretation only is involved. Its implications in a wider system might not be satisfactory. But, whatever be the evil here, we can say that we understand something of the psychological state which gives these extraneous things of horror their reality and opportunity. And if we are loth to believe in such evil realities, potentially at least alive and powerful, we might call to mind the words of Lafeu in *All's Well that Ends Well*:

> They say miracles are past; and we have our philosophical persons, to make modern and familiar things supernatural and causeless. Hence is it that we make trifles of terrors, ensconcing ourselves into seeming knowledge, when we should submit ourselves to an unknown fear.
>
> (II. iii. 1)

A profound commentary on *Macbeth*. But, though the ultimate evil remain a mystery, analysis of the play indicates something of its relation to the mind and the actions of men.

Such analysis must be directed not to the story alone, but to the manifold correspondencies of imaginative quality extending throughout the whole play. The *Macbeth* vision is powerfully superlogical. Yet it is the work of interpretation to give some logical coherence to things imaginative. To do this, it is manifestly not enough to abstract the skeleton of logical sequence which is the story of the play: that is to ignore the very quality which justifies our anxious attention. Rather, relinquishing our horizontal sight of the naked rock-line which is the story, we should, from above, view the whole as panorama, spatialized: and then map out imaginative similarities and differences, hills and vales and streams. Only to such a view does *Macbeth* reveal the full riches of its meaning. Interpretation must thus first receive the quality of the play in the imagination, and then proceed to translate this whole experience into a new logic which will not be confined to those superficialities of cause and effect which we think to trace in our own lives and actions, and try to impose on the persons of literature. In this way, we shall know that *Macbeth* shows us an evil not to be accounted for in terms of 'will' and 'causality'; that it expresses its vision, not to a critical intellect, but to the responsive imagination; and, working in terms not of 'character' or any ethical code, but of the abysmal deeps of a spirit-world untuned to human reality, withdraws the veil from the black streams which mill that consciousness of fear symbolized in actions of blood. *Macbeth* is the apocalypse of evil.

ADDITIONAL NOTE (1947)

In *Hamlet* and *Macbeth* supernatural figures are first objective; seen later by the hero alone; and, at the conclusion, clearly do not exist; as though some unrest in the outer universe has been satisfactorily projected and dispelled. Does this help to explain the gathering poetic force of Macbeth's speeches, culminating in the supreme pieces of Act V ? Note, too, Macbeth's courage in successfully dismissing the air-drawn dagger and, twice, Banquo's Ghost. Macbeth shows throughout a positive drive. For a further development of this reading, see my *Christ and Nietzsche*.

For a study of the more obvious, countering, positives (e.g. effects of social health, nature, Banquo's descendants and child-images rising to the child-apparitions) see my essay 'The Milk of Concord' in *The Imperial Theme*; and also my analysis of the Apparition scene in *The Shakespearian Tempest*. For Hecate see *The Shakespearian Tempest*, App. B.

VIII

KING LEAR AND THE COMEDY OF
THE GROTESQUE

IT may appear strange to search for any sort of comedy as a primary theme in a play whose abiding gloom is so heavy, whose reading of human destiny and human actions so starkly tragic. Yet it is an error of aesthetic judgement to regard humour as essentially trivial. Though its impact usually appears vastly different from that of tragedy, yet there is a humour that treads the brink of tears, and tragedy which needs but an infinitesimal shift of perspective to disclose the varied riches of comedy. Humour is an evanescent thing, even more difficult of analysis and intellectual location than tragedy. To the coarse mind lacking sympathy an incident may seem comic which to the richer understanding is pitiful and tragic. So, too, one series of facts can be treated by the artist as either comic or tragic, lending itself equivalently to both. Sometimes a great artist may achieve significant effects by a criss-cross of tears and laughter. Tchehov does this, especially in his plays. A shifting flash of comedy across the pain of the purely tragic both increases the tension and suggests, vaguely, a resolution and a purification. The comic and the tragic rest both on the idea of incompatibilities, and are also, themselves, mutually exclusive: therefore to mingle them is to add to the meaning of each; for the result is then but a new sublime incongruity.

King Lear is roughly analogous to Tchehov where *Macbeth* is analogous to Dostoievsky. The wonder of Shakespearian tragedy is ever a mystery—a vague, yet powerful, tangible, presence; an interlocking of the mind with a profound meaning, a disclosure to the inward eye of vistas undreamed, and but fitfully understood. *King Lear* is great in the abundance and richness of human delineation, in the level focus of creation that builds a massive oneness, in fact, a universe, of single quality from a multiplicity of differentiated units; and in a positive and purposeful working out

of a purgatorial philosophy. But it is still greater in the
perfect fusion of psychological realism with the daring
flights of a fantastic imagination. The heart of a Shakespearian tragedy is centred in the imaginative, in the unknown; and in *King Lear*, where we touch the unknown,
we touch the fantastic. The peculiar dualism at the root of
this play which wrenches and splits the mind by a sight of
incongruities displays in turn realities absurd, hideous, pitiful. This incongruity is Lear's madness; it is also the
demonic laughter that echoes in the *Lear* universe. In pure
tragedy the dualism of experience is continually being dissolved in the masterful beauty of passion, merged in the
sunset of emotion. But in comedy it is not so softly resolved
—incompatibilities stand out till the sudden relief of laughter
or its equivalent of humour: therefore incongruity is the
especial mark of comedy. Now in *King Lear* there is a
dualism continually crying in vain to be resolved either by
tragedy or comedy. Thence arises its peculiar tension of
pain: and the course of the action often comes as near to the
resolution of comedy as to that of tragedy. So I shall notice
here the imaginative core of the play, and, excluding much
of the logic of the plot from immediate attention, analyse
the fantastic comedy of *King Lear*.

From the start, the situation has a comic aspect. It has
been observed that Lear has, so to speak, staged an interlude,
with himself as chief actor, in which he grasps expressions
of love to his heart, and resigns his sceptre to a chorus of
acclamations. It is childish, foolish—but very human. So,
too, is the result. Sincerity forbids play-acting, and Cordelia
cannot subdue her instinct to any judgement advising tact
rather than truth. The incident is profoundly comic and
profoundly pathetic. It is, indeed, curious that so storm-
furious a play as *King Lear* should have so trivial a domestic
basis: it is the first of our many incongruities to be noticed.
The absurdity of the old King's anger is clearly indicated
by Kent:

> Kill thy physician, and the fee bestow
> Upon the foul disease.   (1. i. 166)

The result is absurd. Lear's loving daughter Cordelia is
struck from his heart's register, and he is shortly, old and

grey-haired and a king, cutting a cruelly ridiculous figure
before the cold sanity of his unloving elder daughters. Lear
is selfish, self-centred. The images he creates of his three
daughters' love are quite false, sentimentalized: he understands the nature of none of his children, and demanding an
unreal and impossible love from all three, is disillusioned by
each in turn. But, though sentimental, this love is not weak.
It is powerful and firm-planted in his mind as a mountain
rock embedded in earth. The tearing out of it is hideous,
cataclysmic. A tremendous soul is, as it were, incongruously
geared to a puerile intellect. Lear's senses prove his idealized
love-figments false, his intellect snaps, and, as the loosened
drive flings limp, the disconnected engine of madness spins
free, and the ungeared revolutions of it are terrible, fantastic.
This, then, is the basis of the play: greatness linked to
puerility. Lear's instincts are themselves grand, heroic—
noble even. His judgement is nothing. He understands
neither himself nor his daughters:

> *Regan.* 'Tis the infirmity of his age: yet he hath ever but slenderly known
> himself.
> *Goneril.* The best and soundest of his time hath been but rash . . .
>
> (I. i. 296)

Lear starts his own tragedy by a foolish misjudgement.
Lear's fault is a fault of the mind, a mind unwarrantably,
because selfishly, foolish. And he knows it:

> O Lear, Lear, Lear!
> Beat at this gate that let thy folly in,
> And thy dear judgement out!   (I. iv. 294)

His purgatory is to be a purgatory of the mind, of madness.
Lear has trained himself to think he cannot be wrong: he
finds he is wrong. He has fed his heart on sentimental knowledge of his children's love: he finds their love is not sentimental. There is now a gaping dualism in his mind, drawn
asunder by incongruities, and he endures madness. So the
meaning of the play is embodied continually into a fantastic
incongruity, which is implicit in the beginning—in the very
act of Lear's renunciation, retaining the 'title and addition'
of King, yet giving over a king's authority to his children.
As he becomes torturingly aware of the truth, incongruity

masters his mind, and fantastic madness ensues; and this peculiar fact of the Lear-theme is reflected in the *Lear* universe:

> *Gloucester.* These late eclipses in the sun and moon portend no good to us: though the wisdom of nature can reason it thus and thus, yet nature finds itself scourged by the sequent effects: love cools, friendship falls off, brothers divide: in cities, mutinies; in countries, discord; in palaces, treason; and the bond cracked 'twixt son and father. This villain of mine comes under the prediction; there 's son against father: the King falls from bias of nature; there 's father against child. We have seen the best of our time: machinations, hollowness, treachery, and all ruinous disorders, follow us disquietly to our graves.   (I. ii. 115)

Gloucester's words hint a universal incongruity here: the fantastic incongruity of parent and child opposed. And it will be most helpful later to notice the Gloucester-theme in relation to that of Lear.

From the first signs of Goneril's cruelty, the Fool is used as a chorus, pointing us to the absurdity of the situation. He is indeed an admirable chorus, increasing our pain by his emphasis on a humour which yet will not serve to merge the incompatible in a unity of laughter. He is not all wrong when he treats the situation as matter for a joke. Much here that is always regarded as essentially pathetic is not far from comedy. For instance, consider Lear's words:

> I will have such revenges on you both
> That all the world shall—I will do such things—
> What they are, yet I know not; but they shall be
> The terrors of the earth.   (II. iv. 282)

What could be more painfully incongruous, spoken, as it is, by an old man, a king, to his daughter? It is not far from the ridiculous. The very thought seems a sacrilegious cruelty, I know: but ridicule is generally cruel. The speeches of Lear often come near comedy. Again, notice the abrupt contrast in his words:

> But yet thou art my flesh, my blood, my daughter;
> Or rather a disease that 's in my flesh,
> Which I must needs call mine: thou art a boil,
> A plague-sore, an embossed carbuncle,
> In my corrupted blood. But I'll not chide thee . . .
>   (II. iv. 224)

This is not comedy, nor humour. But it is exactly the stuff of which humour is made. Lear is mentally a child; in passion a titan. The absurdity of his every act at the beginning of his tragedy is contrasted with the dynamic fury which intermittently bursts out, flickers—then flames and finally gives us those grand apostrophes lifted from man's stage of earth to heaven's rain and fire and thunder:

> Blow, winds, and crack your cheeks! rage! blow!
> You cataracts and hurricanoes, spout
> Till you have drench'd our steeples, drown'd the cocks!
>
> (III. ii. 1)

Two speeches of this passionate and unrestrained volume of Promethean curses are followed by:

> No, I will be the pattern of all patience;
> I will say nothing. (III. ii. 37)

Again we are in touch with potential comedy: a slight shift of perspective, and the incident is rich with humour. A sense of self-directed humour would have saved Lear. It is a quality he absolutely lacks.

Herein lies the profound insight of the Fool: he sees the potentialities of comedy in Lear's behaviour. This old man, recently a king, and, if his speeches are fair samples, more than a little of a tyrant, now goes from daughter to daughter, furious because Goneril dares criticize his pet knights, kneeling down before Regan, performing, as she says, 'unsightly tricks' (II. iv. 159)—the situation is excruciatingly painful, and its painfulness is exactly of that quality which embarrasses in some forms of comedy. In the theatre, one is terrified lest some one laugh: yet, if Lear could laugh—if the Lears of the world could laugh at themselves—there would be no such tragedy. In the early scenes old age and dignity suffer, and seem to deserve, the punishments of childhood:

> Now, by my life,
> Old fools are babes again; and must be used
> With checks as flatteries. (I. iii. 19)

The situation is summed up by the Fool:

> *Lear.* When were you wont to be so full of songs, sirrah?
> *Fool.* I have used it, nuncle, ever since thou madest thy daughters thy mother: for when thou gavest them the rod, and put'st down thine own breeches . . . (I. iv. 186)

The height of indecency in suggestion, the height of incongruity. Lear is spiritually put to the ludicrous shame endured bodily by Kent in the stocks: and the absurd rant of Kent, and the unreasonable childish temper of Lear, both merit in some measure what they receive. Painful as it may sound, that is, provisionally, a truth we should realize. The Fool realizes it. He is, too, necessary. Here, where the plot turns on the diverging tugs of two assurances in the mind, it is natural that the action be accompanied by some symbol of humour, that mode which is built of unresolved incompatibilities. Lear's torment is a torment of this dualistic kind, since he scarcely believes his senses when his daughters resist him. He repeats the history of Troilus, who cannot understand the faithlessness of Cressid. In *Othello* and *Timon of Athens* the transition is swift from extreme love to revenge or hate. The movement of Lear's mind is less direct: like Troilus, he is suspended between two separate assurances. Therefore Pandarus, in the latter acts of *Troilus and Cressida*, plays a part similar to the Fool in *King Lear*: both attempt to heal the gaping wound of the mind's incongruous knowledge by the unifying, healing release of laughter. They make no attempt to divert, but rather to direct the hero's mind to the present incongruity. The Fool sees, or tries to see, the humorous potentialities in the most heart-wrenching of incidents:

Lear. O me, my heart, my rising heart! but, down!
Fool. Cry to it, nuncle, as the cockney did to the eels when she put 'em i'
the paste alive; she knapped 'em o' the coxcombs with a stick, and cried
'Down, wantons, down!' 'Twas her brother that, in pure kindness to
his horse, buttered his hay. (II. iv. 122)

Except for the last delightful touch—the antithesis of the other—that is a cruel, ugly sense of humour. It is the sinister humour at the heart of this play: we are continually aware of the humour of cruelty and the cruelty of humour. But the Fool's use of it is not aimless. If Lear could laugh he might yet save his reason.

But there is no relief. Outside, in the wild country, the storm grows more terrible:

Kent.   . . . Since I was man
Such sheets of fire, such bursts of horrid thunder,
Such groans of roaring wind and rain, I never
Remember to have heard . . . (III. ii. 45)

Lear's mind keeps returning to the unreality, the impossibility of what has happened:

> Your old kind father, whose frank heart gave all—
> O, that way madness lies; let me shun that;
> No more of that. (III. iv. 20)

He is still self-centred; cannot understand that he has been anything but a perfect father; cannot understand his daughters' behaviour. It is

> as this mouth should tear this hand
> For lifting food to't . . . (III. iv. 15)

It is incongruous, impossible. There is no longer any 'rule in unity itself'.[1] Just as Lear's mind begins to fail, the Fool finds Edgar disguised as 'poor Tom'. Edgar now succeeds the Fool as the counterpart to the breaking sanity of Lear; and where the humour of the Fool made no contact with Lear's mind, the fantastic appearance and incoherent words of Edgar are immediately assimilated, as glasses correctly focused to the sight of oncoming madness. Edgar turns the balance of Lear's wavering mentality. His fantastic appearance and lunatic irrelevancies, with the storm outside, and the Fool still for occasional chorus, create a scene of wraith-like unreason, a vision of a world gone mad:

> . . . Bless thy five wits! Tom's a-cold—O, do de, do de, do de. Bless thee from whirlwinds, star-blasting, and taking! Do poor Tom some charity, whom the foul fiend vexes: there could I have him now—and there—and there again, and there. (III. iv. 57)

To Lear his words are easily explained. His daughters 'have brought him to this pass'. He cries:

> *Lear.* Is it the fashion that discarded fathers
> Should have thus little mercy on their flesh?
> Judicious punishment! 'twas this flesh begot
> Those pelican daughters.
> *Edgar.* Pillicock sat on Pillicock-hill:
> Halloo, halloo, loo, loo!
> *Fool.* This cold night will turn us all to fools and madmen.
> (III. iv. 71)

What shall we say of this exquisite movement? Is it comedy? Lear's profound unreason is capped by the blatant irrelevance

[1] *Troilus and Cressida*, v. ii. 138.

of Edgar's couplet suggested by the word 'pelican'; then the two are swiftly all but unified, for us if not for Lear, in the healing balm of the Fool's conclusion. It is the process of humour, where two incompatibles are resolved in laughter. The Fool does this again. Lear again speaks a profound truth as the wild night and Edgar's fantastic impersonation grip his mind and dethrone his conventional sanity:

> *Lear.* Is man no more than this? Consider him well. Thou owest the worm no silk, the beast no hide, the sheep no wool, the cat no perfume. Ha! Here 's three on 's are sophisticated! Thou art the thing itself: unaccommodated man is no more but such a poor, bare, forked animal as thou art. Off, off, you lendings! come unbutton here. (*Tearing off his clothes.*)
> *Fool.* Prithee, nuncle, be contented; 'tis a naughty night to swim in.
>
> (III. iv. 105)

This is the furthest flight, not of tragedy, but of philosophic comedy. The autocratic and fiery-fierce old king, symbol of dignity, is confronted with the meanest of men: a naked lunatic beggar. In a flash of vision he attempts to become his opposite, to be naked, 'unsophisticated'. And then the opposing forces which struck the lightning-flash of vision tail off, resolved into a perfect unity by the Fool's laughter, reverberating, trickling, potent to heal in sanity the hideous unreason of this tempest-shaken night: ''tis a naughty night to swim in'. Again this is the process of humour: its flash of vision first bridges the positive and negative poles of the mind, unifying them, and then expresses itself in laughter.

This scene grows still more grotesque, fantastical, sinister. Gloucester enters, his torch flickering in the beating wind:

> *Fool.* . . . Look, here comes a walking fire.
> (*Enter* Gloucester, *with a torch.*)
> *Edgar.* This is the foul fiend Flibbertigibbet: he begins at curfew and walks till the first cock . . . (III. iv. 116)

Lear welcomes Edgar as his 'philosopher', since he embodies that philosophy of incongruity and the fantastically-absurd which is Lear's vision in madness. 'Noble philosopher', he says (III. iv. 176), and 'I will still keep with my philosopher' (III. iv. 180). The unresolved dualism that tormented Troilus and was given metaphysical expression by him (*Troilus and Cressida*, v. ii. 134–57) is here more perfectly bodied into the poetic symbol of poor Tom: and since Lear cannot hear the resolving laugh of foolery, his mind is focused only to the 'philosopher' mumbling of the foul fiend. Edgar thus serves to lure Lear on: we forget that he is dissimulating. Lear is the centre of our attention, and as the world shakes with tempest and unreason, we endure something of the shaking and the tempest of his mind. The absurd and fantastic reign supreme. Lear does not compass for more than a few speeches the 'noble anger' (ii. iv. 279) for which he prayed, the anger of Timon. From the start he wavered between affection and disillusionment, love and hate. The heavens in truth 'fool' (ii. iv. 278) him. He is the 'natural fool of fortune' (iv. vi. 196). Now his anger begins to be a lunatic thing, and when it rises to any sort of magnificent fury or power it is toppled over by the ridiculous capping of Edgar's irrelevancies:

> *Lear.* To have a thousand with red burning spits
>   Come hissing in upon 'em—
> *Edgar.* The foul fiend bites my back.   (iii. vi. 17)

The mock trial is instituted. Lear's curses were for a short space terrible, majestic, less controlled and purposeful than Timon's but passionate and grand in their tempestuous fury. Now, in madness, he flashes on us the ridiculous basis of his tragedy in words which emphasize the indignity and incongruity of it, and make his madness something nearer the ridiculous than the terrible, something which moves our pity, but does not strike awe:

> Arraign her first; 'tis Goneril. I here take my oath before this honourable assembly, she kicked the poor king her father.   (iii. vi. 49)

This stroke of the absurd—so vastly different from the awe we experience in face of Timon's hate—is yet fundamental here. The core of the play is an absurdity, an indignity, an incongruity. In no tragedy of Shakespeare does incident and dialogue so recklessly and miraculously walk the tight-rope of our pity over the depths of bathos and absurdity.

This particular region of the terrible bordering on the fantastic and absurd is exactly the playground of madness. Now the setting of Lear's madness includes a sub-plot where these same elements are presented in stark nakedness, with no veiling subtleties. The Gloucester-theme is a certain indication of our vision and helps us to understand, and feel, the enduring agony of Lear. As usual, the first scene of this play strikes the dominant note. Gloucester jests at the bastardy of his son Edmund, remarking that, though he is ashamed to acknowledge him, 'there was good sport at his making' (I. i. 23). That is, we start with humour in bad taste. The whole tragedy witnesses a sense of humour in 'the gods' which is in similar bad taste. Now all the Lear effects are exaggerated in the Gloucester theme. Edmund's plot is a more Iago-like, devilish, intentional thing than Goneril's and Regan's icy callousness. Edgar's supposed letter is crude and absurd:

> . . . I begin to find an idle and fond bondage in the oppression of aged tyranny . . . (I. ii. 53)

But then Edmund, wittiest and most attractive of villains, composed it. One can almost picture his grin as he penned those lines, commending them mentally to the limited intellect of his father. Yes—the Gloucester theme has a beginning even more fantastic than that of Lear's tragedy. And not only are the Lear effects here exaggerated in the directions of villainy and humour: they are even more clearly exaggerated in that of horror. The gouging out of Gloucester's eyes is a thing unnecessary, crude, disgusting: it is meant to be. It helps to provide an accompanying exaggeration of one element—that of cruelty—in the horror that makes Lear's madness. And not only horror: there is even again something satanically comic bedded deep in it. The sight of physical torment, to the uneducated, brings laughter. Shakespeare's England delighted in watching both physical torment and the comic ravings of actual lunacy. The dance of madmen in Webster's *Duchess of Malfi* is of the same ghoulish humour as Regan's plucking Gloucester by the beard: the groundlings will laugh at both. Moreover, the sacrilege of the human body in torture must be, to a human mind, incongruous, absurd. This hideous mockery is consummated in Regan's final witticism after Gloucester's eyes are out:

> Go, thrust him out at gates, and let him smell
> His way to Dover. (III. vii. 93)

The macabre humoresque of this is nauseating: but it is there, and integral to the play. These ghoulish horrors, so popular in Elizabethan drama, and the very stuff of the *Lear* of Shakespeare's youth, *Titus Andronicus*, find an exquisitely appropriate place in the tragedy of Shakespeare's maturity which takes as its especial province this territory of the grotesque and the fantastic which is Lear's madness. We are clearly pointed to this grim fun, this hideous sense of humour, at the back of tragedy:

> As flies to wanton boys are we to the gods;
> They kill us for their sport. (iv. i. 36)

This illustrates the exact quality I wish to emphasize: the humour a boy—even a kind boy—may see in the wriggles of an impaled insect. So, too, Gloucester is bound, and tortured, physically; and so the mind of Lear is impaled, crucified on the cross-beams of love and disillusion.

There follows the grim pilgrimage of Edgar and Gloucester towards Dover Cliff: an incident typical enough of *King Lear*—

> 'Tis the times' plague when madmen lead the blind. (iv. i. 46)

They stumble on, madman and blind man, Edgar mumbling:

> . . . five fiends have been in poor Tom at once; of lust, as Obidicut; Hobbididance, prince of dumbness; Mahu, of stealing; Modo, of murder; Flibbertigibbet, of mopping and mowing, who since possesses chambermaids and waiting-women . . . (iv. i. 59)

They are near Dover. Edgar persuades his father that they are climbing steep ground, though they are on a level field, that the sea can be heard beneath:

> *Gloucester.* Methinks the ground is even.
> *Edgar.*   Horrible steep.
>   Hark, do you hear the sea?
> *Gloucester.*   No, truly.
> *Edgar.* Why, then your other senses grow imperfect
>   By your eyes' anguish. (iv. vi. 3)

Gloucester notices the changed sanity of Edgar's speech, and remarks thereon. Edgar hurries his father to the supposed brink, and vividly describes the dizzy precipice over which Gloucester thinks they stand:

> How fearful
> And dizzy 'tis to cast one's eyes so low!
> The crows and choughs that wing the midway air
> Show scarce so gross as beetles: half way down
> Hangs one that gathers samphire, dreadful trade! . . .
>
> (IV. vi. 12)

Gloucester thanks him, and rewards him; bids him move off; then kneels, and speaks a prayer of noble resignation, breathing that stoicism which permeates the suffering philosophy of this play:

> O you mighty gods!
> This world I do renounce, and, in your sights,
> Shake patiently my great affliction off:
> If I could bear it longer, and not fall
> To quarrel with your great opposeless wills,
> My snuff and loathed part of nature should
> Burn itself out.
>
> (IV. vi. 35)

Gloucester has planned a spectacular end for himself. We are given these noble descriptive and philosophical speeches to tune our minds to a noble, tragic sacrifice. And what happens? The old man falls from his kneeling posture a few inches, flat, face foremost. Instead of the dizzy circling to crash and spill his life on the rocks below—just this. The grotesque merged into the ridiculous reaches a consummation in this bathos of tragedy: it is the furthest, most exaggerated, reach of the poet's towering fantasticality. We have a sublimely daring stroke of technique, unjustifiable, like Edgar's emphasized and vigorous madness throughout, on the plane of plot-logic, and even to a superficial view somewhat out of place imaginatively in so dire and stark a limning of human destiny as is *King Lear*; yet this scene is in reality a consummate stroke of art. The Gloucester-theme throughout reflects and emphasizes and exaggerates all the percurrent qualities of the Lear-theme. Here the incongruous and fantastic element of the Lear-theme is boldly reflected into the tragically-absurd. The stroke is audacious, unashamed, and magical of effect. Edgar keeps up the deceit; persuades his father that he has really fallen; points to the empty sky, as to a cliff:

> . . . the shrill-gorged lark
> Cannot be heard so far . . .   (IV. vi. 59)

and finally paints a fantastic picture of a ridiculously
grotesque devil that stood with Gloucester on the edge:

> As I stood here below, methought his eyes
> Were two full moons; he had a thousand noses,
> Horns whelk'd and waved like the enridged sea;
> It was some fiend . . .   (IV. vi. 70)

Some fiend, indeed.

There is masterful artistry in all this. The Gloucester-
theme has throughout run separate from that of Lear, yet
parallel, and continually giving us direct villainy where the
other shows cold callousness; horrors of physical torment
where the other has a subtle mental torment; culminating
in this towering stroke of the grotesque and absurd to
balance the fantastic incidents and speeches that immediately
follow. At this point we suddenly have our first sight of Lear
in the full ecstasy of his later madness. Now, when our
imaginations are most powerfully quickened to the grotesque
and incongruous, the whole surge of the Gloucester-theme,
which has just reached its climax, floods as a tributary the
main stream of our sympathy with Lear. Our vision has thus
been uniquely focused to understand that vision of the
grotesque, the incongruous, the fantastically-horrible, which
is the agony of Lear's mind:

> *Enter* Lear, *fantastically dressed with wild flowers.*
>   (IV. vi. 81)

So runs Capell's direction. Lear, late 'every inch a king', the
supreme pathetic figure of literature, now utters the wild
and whirling language of furthest madness. Sometimes his
words hold profound meaning. Often they are tuned to the
orthodox Shakespearian hate and loathing, especially sex-
loathing, of the hate-theme. Or again, they are purely ludicrous, or would be, were it not a Lear who speaks them:

> . . . Look, look, a mouse! Peace, peace; this piece of toasted cheese will
> do't . . .   (IV. vi. 90)

It is certainly as well that we have been by now prepared
for the grotesque. Laughter is forbidden us. Consummate

art has so forged plot and incident that we may watch with
tears rather than laughter the cruelly comic actions of Lear:

> *Lear.* I will die bravely, like a bridegroom.[1] What!
>   I will be jovial: come, come; I am a king,
>   My masters, know you that?
> *Gentleman.* You are a royal one, and we obey you.
> *Lear.* Then there's life in't. Nay, if you get it, you shall get it with run-
>   ning. Sa, sa, sa, sa.
>
> (iv. vi. 203)

Lear is a child again in his madness. We are in touch with
the exquisitely pathetic, safeguarded only by Shakespeare's
masterful technique from the bathos of comedy.

This recurring and vivid stress on the incongruous and
the fantastic is not a subsidiary element in *King Lear*: it is
the very heart of the play. We watch humanity grotesquely
tormented, cruelly and with mockery impaled: nearly all the
persons suffer some form of crude indignity in the course of
the play. I have noticed the major themes of Lear and
Gloucester: there are others. Kent is banished, undergoes the
disguise of a servant, is put to shame in the stocks; Cornwall
is killed by his own servant resisting the dastardly mutilation
of Gloucester; Oswald, the prim courtier, is done to death
by Edgar in the role of an illiterate country yokel—

> . . . keep out, che vor ye, or ise try whether your costard or my ballow
> be the harder . . .   (iv. vi. 247)

Edgar himself endures the utmost degradation of his disguise as 'poor Tom', begrimed and naked, and condemned
to speak nothing but idiocy. Edmund alone steers something
of an unswerving tragic course, brought to a fitting, deserved,
but spectacular end, slain by his wronged brother, nobly
repentant at the last:

> *Edmund.* What you have charged me with, that have I done;
>   And more, much more; the time will bring it out:
>   'Tis past, and so am I. But what art thou
>   That hast this fortune on me? If thou'rt noble,
>   I do forgive thee.
> *Edgar.*   Let's exchange charity.
>   I am no less in blood than thou art, Edmund;
>   If more, the more thou hast wrong'd me.
>   My name is Edgar . . .   (v. iii. 164)

---

[1] This is to be related to *Antony and Cleopatra*, iv. xii. 100, and *Measure for Measure*,
iii. i. 82; also *Hamlet*, iv. iv. 62.

The note of forgiving chivalry reminds us of the deaths of Hamlet and Laertes. Edmund's fate is nobly tragic: 'the wheel has come full circle; I am here' (v. iii. 176). And Edmund is the most villainous of all. Again, we have incongruity; and again, the Gloucester-theme reflects the Lear-theme. Edmund is given a noble, an essentially tragic, end, and Goneril and Regan, too, meet their ends with something of tragic fineness in pursuit of their evil desires. Regan dies by her sister's poison; Goneril with a knife. They die, at least, in the cause of love—love of Edmund. Compared with these deaths, the end of Cordelia is horrible, cruel, unnecessarily cruel—the final grotesque horror in the play. Her villainous sisters are already dead. Edmund is nearly dead, repentant. It is a matter of seconds—and rescue comes too late. She is hanged by a common soldier. The death which Dostoievsky's Stavrogin singled out as of all the least heroic and picturesque, or rather, shall we say, the most hideous and degrading: this is the fate that grips the white innocence and resplendent love-strength of Cordelia. To be hanged, after the death of her enemies, in the midst of friends. It is the last hideous joke of destiny: this—and the fact that Lear is still alive, has recovered his sanity for this. The death of Cordelia is the last and most horrible of all the horrible incongruities I have noticed:

> Why should a dog, a horse, a rat have life,
> And thou no breath at all? (v. iii. 308)

We remember: 'Upon such sacrifices, my Cordelia, the gods themselves throw incense' (v. iii. 20). Or do they laugh, and is the *Lear* universe one ghastly piece of fun?

We do not feel that. The tragedy is most poignant in that it is purposeless, unreasonable. It is the most fearless artistic facing of the ultimate cruelty of things in our literature. That cruelty would be less were there not this element of comedy which I have emphasized, the insistent incongruities, which create and accompany the madness of Lear, which leap to vivid shape in the mockery of Gloucester's suicide, which are intrinsic in the texture of the whole play. Mankind is, as it were, deliberately and comically tormented by 'the gods'. He is not even allowed to die tragically. Lear is 'bound upon a wheel of fire' and only death will end the victim's agony:

> Vex not his ghost: O, let him pass! he hates him
> That would upon the rack of this tough world
> Stretch him out longer.   (v. iii. 315)

King Lear is supreme in that, in this main theme, it faces the very absence of tragic purpose: wherein it is profoundly different from *Timon of Athens*. Yet, as we close the sheets of this play, there is no horror, nor resentment. The tragic purification of the essentially untragic is yet complete.

Now in this essay it will, perhaps, appear that I have unduly emphasized one single element of the play, magnifying it, and leaving the whole distorted. It has been my purpose to emphasize. I have not exaggerated. The pathos has not been minimized: it is redoubled. Nor does the use of the words 'comic' and 'humour' here imply disrespect to the poet's purpose: rather I have used these words, crudely no doubt, to cut out for analysis the very heart of the play— the thing that man dares scarcely face: the demonic grin of the incongruous and absurd in the most pitiful of human struggles with an iron fate. It is this that wrenches, splits, gashes the mind till it utters the whirling vapourings of lunacy. And, though love and music—twin sisters of salvation—temporarily may heal the racked consciousness of Lear, yet, so deeply planted in the facts of our life is this unknowing ridicule of destiny, that the uttermost tragedy of the incongruous ensues, and there is no hope save in the broken heart and limp body of death. This is of all the most agonizing of tragedies to endure: and if we are to feel more than a fraction of this agony, we must have sense of this quality of grimmest humour. We must beware of sentimentalizing the cosmic mockery of the play.

And is there, perhaps, even a deeper, and less heartsearing, significance in its humour? Smiles and tears are indeed most curiously interwoven here. Gloucester was saved from his violent and tragic suicide that he might recover his wronged son's love, and that his heart might

> 'Twixt two extremes of passion, joy and grief,
> Burst smilingly.   (v. iii. 200)

Lear dies with the words

> Do you see this? Look on her, look, her lips,
> Look there, look there!   (v. iii. 312)

What smiling destiny is this he sees at the last instant of
racked mortality? Why have we that strangely beautiful
account of Cordelia's first hearing of her father's pain:

> . . . patience and sorrow strove
> Who should express her goodliest. You have seen
> Sunshine and rain at once: her smiles and tears
> Were like a better way: those happy smilets,
> That play'd on her ripe lip, seem'd not to know
> What guests were in her eyes; which parted thence,
> As pearls from diamonds dropp'd. In brief,
> Sorrow would be a rarity most belov'd,
> If all could so become it.   (iv. iii. 18)

What do we touch in these passages? Sometimes we know
that all human pain holds beauty, that no tear falls but it
dews some flower we cannot see. Perhaps humour, too, is
inwoven in the universal pain, and the enigmatic silence
holds not only an unutterable sympathy, but also the ripples
of an impossible laughter whose flight is not for the wing of
human understanding; and perhaps it is this that casts its
darting shadow of the grotesque across the furrowed pages
of *King Lear*.

IX

THE *LEAR* UNIVERSE

IT has been remarked that all the persons in *King Lear* are either very good or very bad. This is an overstatement, yet one which suggests a profound truth. In this essay I shall both expand and qualify it: the process will illuminate many human and natural qualities in the *Lear* universe and will tend to reveal its implicit philosophy.

Apart from Lear, the protagonist, and Gloucester, his shadow, the subsidiary dramatic persons fall naturally into two parties, good and bad. First, we have Cordelia, France, Albany, Kent, the Fool, and Edgar. Second Goneril, Regan, Burgundy, Cornwall, Oswald, and Edmund. The exact balance is curious. It will scarcely be questioned that the first party tend to enlist, and the second to repel, our ethical sympathies in so far as ethical sympathies are here roused in us. But none are wholly good or bad, excepting perhaps Cordelia and Cornwall. Our imaginative sympathies, certainly, are divided: Albany is weak, Kent unmannerly, Edgar faultless but without virility, there is much to be said for Goneril and Regan, and Edmund is most attractive. There is no such violent contrast as the Iago-Desdemona antithesis in *Othello*. But the *Lear* persons are more frankly individualized than those in *Macbeth*: though the *Lear* universe is created on a highly visionary plane, though all the dramatic persons are toned by its peculiar atmosphere, they are, as within that universe and as related to the dominant technique, clearly differentiated. *King Lear* gives one the impression of life's abundance magnificently compressed into one play.

No Shakespearian work shows so wide a range of sympathetic creation: we seem to be confronted, not with certain men and women only, but with mankind.[1] It is strange to find that we have been watching little more than a dozen people. *King Lear* is a tragic vision of humanity, in its complexity, its interplay of purpose, its travailing evolution. The play is a microcosm of the human race—strange as that

[1] Some of my comments follow closely those of A. C. Bradley.

word 'microcosm' sounds for the vastness, the width and depth, the vague vistas which this play reveals. Just as skilful grouping on the stage deceives the eye, causing six men to suggest an army, grouping which points the eye from the stage toward the unactualized spaces beyond which imagination accepts in its acceptance of the stage itself, so the technique here—the vagueness of locality, and of time, the inconsistencies and impossibilities—all lend the persons and their acts some element of mystery and some suggestion of infinite purposes working themselves out before us. Something similar is apparent in *Macbeth*, a down-pressing, enveloping presence, mysterious and fearful: there it is purely evil, and its nature is personified in the Weird Sisters. Here it has no personal symbol, it is not evil, nor good; neither beautiful, nor ugly. It is purely a brooding presence, vague, inscrutable, enigmatic; a misty blurring opacity stilly overhanging, interpenetrating plot and action. This mysterious accompaniment to the *Lear* story makes of its persons vague symbols of universal forces. But those persons, in relation to their setting, are not vague. They have outline, though few have colour: they are like near figures in a mist. They blend with the quality of the whole. The form of the individual is modified, in tone, by this blurring fog. The *Lear* mist drifts across them as each in turn voices its typical phraseology; for this impregnating reality is composed of a multiplicity of imaginative correspondencies in phrase, thought, action throughout the play. That mental atmosphere is as important, more important sometimes, than the persons themselves; nor, till we have clear sight of this peculiar *Lear* atmosphere, shall we appreciate the fecundity of human creation moving within it. *King Lear* is a work of philosophic vision. We watch, not ancient Britons, but humanity; not England, but the world. Mankind's relation to the universe is its theme, and Edgar's trumpet is as the universal judgement summoning vicious man to account. In *Timon of Athens*, the theme is universalized by the creation of a universal and idealized symbol of mankind's aspiration, and the poet at every point subdues his creative power to a clarified, philosophic, working out of his theme. Here we seem to watch not a poet's purpose, but life itself:

life comprehensive, rich, varied. Therefore the clear demarcation of half the persons into fairly 'good', and half into
fairly 'bad', is no chance here. It is an inevitable effect of a
balanced, universalized vision of mankind's activity on
earth. But the vision is true only within the scope of its own
horizon. That is, the vision is a tragic vision, the impregnating thought everywhere being concerned with cruelty,
with suffering, with the relief which love and sympathy may
bring, with the travailing process of creation and life. In
Macbeth we experience Hell; in *Antony and Cleopatra*,
Paradise; but this play is Purgatory. Its philosophy is
continually purgatorial.

In this essay I shall analyse certain strata in the play's
thought, thus making more clear the quality of the mysterious
presence I have noticed as enveloping the action; and in the
process many persons and events will automatically assume
new significance. The play works out before us the problems
of human suffering and human imperfection; the relation
of humanity to nature on the one hand and its aspiration
toward perfection on the other. I shall note (i) the naturalism
of the *Lear* universe, using the words 'nature' and 'natural'
in no exact sense, but rather with a Protean variation in
meaning which reflects the varying nature-thought of the
play; (ii) its 'gods'; (iii) its insistent questioning of justice,
human and divine; (iv) the stoic acceptance by many persons
of their purgatorial pain; and (v) the flaming course of the
Lear-theme itself growing out of this dun world, and touching
at its full height a transcendent, apocalyptic beauty. These
will form so many steps by which we may attain a comprehensive vision of the play's meaning.

The philosophy of *King Lear* is firmly planted in the soil
of earth. Nature, like human life, is abundant across its
pages. Lear outlines the wide sweeps of land to be allotted
to Goneril:

> Of all these bounds, even from this line to this,
> With shadowy forests and wide champains rich'd,
> With plenteous rivers and wide-skirted meads,
> We make thee lady.   (1. i. 65)

We have the fine description of Dover Cliff:

> The crows and choughs that wing the midway air
> Show scarce so gross as beetles: half way down
> Hangs one that gathers samphire, dreadful trade!

(IV. vi. 14)

From this elevation

> the murmuring surge,
> That on the unnumber'd idle pebbles chafes,
> Cannot be heard so high.

(IV. vi. 21)

And, from below, 'the shrill-gorged lark so far cannot be seen or heard' (IV. vi. 59). Lear is 'fantastically dressed with wild flowers' (IV. vi. 81).[1] And we hear from Cordelia that

> he was met even now
> As mad as the vex'd sea; singing aloud;
> Crown'd with rank fumiter and furrow-weeds,
> With burdocks, hemlock, nettles, cuckoo-flowers,
> Darnel and all the idle weeds that grow
> In our sustaining corn.

(IV. iv. 1)

The references to animals are emphatic. The thought of 'nature' is as ubiquitous here as that of 'death' in *Hamlet*, 'fear' in *Macbeth*, or 'time' in *Troilus and Cressida*. The phraseology is pregnant of natural reference and natural suggestion; and where the human element merges into the natural, the suggestion is often one of village life. The world of *King Lear* is townless. It is a world of flowers, rough country, tempestuous wind, and wild, or farmyard, beasts; and, as a background, there is continual mention of homely, countrified customs, legends, rhymes. This world is rooted in nature, firmly as a Hardy novel. The winds of nature blow through its pages, animals appear in every kind of context. The animals are often homely, sometimes wild, but neither terrifying nor beautiful. They merge into the bleak atmosphere, they have nothing of the bizarre picturesqueness of those in *Julius Caesar*, and do not in their totality suggest the hideous and grim portent of those in *Macbeth*. We hear of the wolf, the owl, the cat, of sheep, swine, dogs (constantly), horses, rats and such like. Now there are two main directions for this animal and natural suggestion running through the play. First, two of the persons undergo a direct return to nature in their purgatorial progress; second, the actions of

---

[1] The stage-direction is Capell's.

humanity tend to assume contrast with the natural world in point of ethics. I shall notice both these directions.

Edgar escapes by hiding in 'the happy hollow of a tree' (II. iii. 2), and decides to disguise himself. He will

> . . . take the basest and most poorest shape
> That ever penury, in contempt of man,
> Brought near to beast: my face I'll grime with filth;
> Blanket my loins; elf all my hair in knots;
> And with presented nakedness outface
> The winds and persecutions of the sky.
> The country gives me proof and precedent
> Of Bedlam beggars, who, with roaring voices,
> Strike in their numb'd and mortified bare arms
> Pins, wooden pricks, nails, sprigs of rosemary;
> And with this horrible object, from low farms,
> Poor pelting villages, sheep-cotes, and mills,
> Sometime with lunatic bans, sometime with prayers,
> Enforce their charity. (II. iii. 7)

The empasis on nakedness open to the winds; on man's kinship with beasts; on suffering; on village and farm life; on lunacy; all these are important. So Edgar throughout his disguise reiterates these themes. His fantastic utterances tell a tale of wild country adventure, in outlying districts of man's civilization, weird, grotesque adventures:

> Who gives anything to poor Tom? whom the foul fiend hath led through fire and through flame, through ford and whirlpool, o'er bog and quagmire . . . (III. iv. 49)

He is 'hog in sloth, fox in stealth, wolf in greediness, dog in madness, lion in prey' (III. iv. 93). He sings village rhymes—'through the sharp hawthorn blows the cold wind' (III. iv. 45, 99). He has another of 'the nightmare and her nine-fold' (III. iv. 124). He gives us a tale of his nauseating diet:

> Poor Tom; that eats the swimming frog, the toad, the tadpole, the wall-newt and the water; that in the fury of his heart, when the foul fiend rages, eats cow-dung for sallets; swallows the old rat and the ditch-dog; drinks the green mantle of the standing pool . . . (III. iv. 132)

'Mice and rats', he tells us, 'and such small deer, have been Tom's food for seven long year' (III. iv. 142). He studies 'how to prevent the fiend and to kill vermin' (III. iv. 163).

He is always thinking of beasts—'the foul-fiend haunts poor
Tom in the voice of a nightingale' and a devil in his belly
croaks for 'two white herring' (III. vi. 32). He sings of the
shepherd and his sheep (III. vi. 44). Lear, in his madness,
talks or sings of little dogs, 'Tray, Blanch and Sweetheart',
that bark at him, and Edgar answers:

> Tom will throw his head at them. Avaunt! you curs!
>> Be thy mouth or black or white,
>> Tooth that poisons if it bite;
>> Mastiff, greyhound, mongrel grim,
>> Hound or spaniel, brach or lym,
>> Or bobtail tike or trundle-tail,
>> Tom will make them weep and wail:
>> For with throwing thus my head,
>> Dogs leap the hatch, and all are fled.   (III. vi. 67)

In the role of poor Tom Edgar enacts the *Lear* philosophy,
expresses its peculiar animal-symbolism, and raises the pitch
of the madness-extravaganza of the central scenes. Here he
acts the appropriate forms which the *Lear* vision as a whole
expresses. His words and actions are therefore most important. So, later, he becomes the high-priest of the *Lear*
religion: a voice, a choric moralizer. He has little personality:
his function is more purely symbolical. Thus his slaying of
the prim courtier Oswald in his guise of a country yokel with
broad dialect (IV. vi.) suggests the antithesis between the
false civilization and the rough naturalism which are the
poles of the *Lear* universe. So, also, his challenge of Edmund
at the end, with the trumpet blast, is strongly allegorical,
suggesting a universal judgement. Now what Edgar suffers
in mimicry, Lear suffers in fact: his return to nature is
antiphonal to Lear's, points the progress of Lear's purgatory,
illustrates it. The numerous animal-references suggest both
Tom's kinship with beasts and his lunacy: animals being
strange irrational forms of life to a human mind, perhaps
touching some chord of primitive mentality, some stratum
in subconsciousness reaching back aeons of the evolutionary
process, now tumbled up in the loosened activity of madness.
The suggestions of Edgar's speeches here form exquisite
and appropriate accompaniment to Lear's breaking mind.

Lear's history is like Edgar's. He, too, falls back on

nature. From the first there is a primitive, animal power about him; from the first he is in sympathy with the elements of earth and sky. There is a pagan ferocity in Lear. 'Blasts and fogs upon thee', he cries to Goneril (i. iv. 323). Again,

> Strike her young bones,
> You taking airs, with lameness! (ii. iv. 165)

and,

> You nimble lightnings, dart your blinding flames
> Into her scornful eyes! Infect her beauty,
> You fen-suck'd fogs, drawn by the powerful sun,
> To fall and blast her pride. (ii. iv. 167)

He prays to 'nature, dear goddess' to convey sterility into Goneril's womb (i. iv. 299). To the heavens themselves he utters that pathetic, noble prayer:

> O heavens,
> If you do love old men, if your sweet sway
> Allow obedience, if yourselves are old,
> Make it your cause; send down and take my part! (ii. iv. 192)

When his daughters prove relentless, he, like Edgar, offers himself to the elements and beasts:

> No, rather I abjure all roofs, and choose
> To wage against the enmity o' the air;
> To be a comrade with the wolf and owl—
> Necessity's sharp pinch! (ii. iv. 211)

Next we find him 'contending with the fretful elements' (iii. i. 4), directly addressing the 'cataracts', 'hurricanoes', the winds and thunder in his magnificent apostrophe to the storm (iii. ii.). He prays it to

> Crack nature's moulds, all germens spill at once
> That make ingrateful man. (iii. ii. 8)

He then reviles the elements as 'servile ministers'; at the end of the play he recollects how 'the thunder would not peace at my bidding' (iv. vi. 104). When he finds Edgar, not only are Tom's mumbling irrelevances correctly focused for his cracking reason, but Tom himself, naked, savage, bestial, symbolizes that revulsion from humanity and the deceptions of human love and human reason which has driven him into the wild night-storm:

> . . . Is man no more than this? Consider him well. Thou owest the worm no silk, the beast no hide, the sheep no wool, the cat no perfume. Ha! Here 's three on ''s are sophisticated! Thou art the thing itself: unaccommodated man is no more but such a poor, bare, forked animal as thou art. Off, off, you lendings! come, unbutton here.
>
> (III. iv. 105)

Notice the suggestion that man's clothes, symbols of civilization, are only borrowed trappings from other forms of nature: man and nature are ever closely welded in the thought-texture here. Lear revolts from man, tries to become a thing of elemental, instinctive life: since rational consciousness has proved unbearable. Hence the relevance of animals, and animal-symbolism, to madness. For madness is the breaking of that which differentiates man from beast. So Lear tries to become naked, bestial, unsophisticated; and later garlands himself with flowers. The Lear-theme is rooted throughout in nature.

Thoughts of nature are also related to human vice. The evil of mankind is often here regarded as essentially a defacing of 'nature', since this is now 'human nature', and human nature is moral. Thus Gloucester thinks Edmund is a 'loyal and natural boy' (II. i. 86). Edmund is asked to 'enkindle all the sparks of nature' to avenge his father's suffering (III. vii. 86). Goneril and Regan are called 'unnatural hags' by Lear. Their acts are a 'deformity', says Albany; and Goneril is a fiend in woman's shape (IV. ii. 60). 'Nature' which 'contemns its origin', says Albany, is self-destructive:

> She that herself will sliver and disbranch
> From her material sap, perforce must wither
> And come to deadly use.   (IV. ii. 34)

Lear wonders at Regan's nature:

> Then let them anatomize Regan: see what breeds about her heart. Is there any cause in nature that makes these hard hearts?
>
> (III. vi. 80)

Earlier he had referred to her 'tender-hefted nature' (II. iv. 174). But Lear himself has been unnatural, as Gloucester suggests:

> This villain of mine comes under the prediction; there 's son against
> father: the King falls from bias of nature. There 's father against child.
>
>   (I. ii. 122)

Goneril and Regan are 'most savage and unnatural', says
Edmund, in pretence of agreeing with his father (III. iii. 7).
It is man's nature to be loving: yet he behaves, too often,
like the beasts. His inhumanity is therefore compared to
animals. Ingratitude in a child is hideous as a 'sea-monster'
(I. iv. 285); Goneril is a 'detested kite' (I. iv. 286); she and
her sister are 'she-foxes' (III. vi. 25); women have turned
'monsters' (III. vii. 102); humanity are in danger of becoming
ravenous as 'monsters of the deep' (IV. ii. 50); Goneril
'be-monsters' her feature (IV. ii. 63). She and Regan are
'tigers, not daughters' (IV. ii. 40); they are 'dog-hearted'
(IV. iii. 47); their 'sharp-tooth'd unkindness' is fixed in
Lear's heart like a 'vulture' (II. iv. 137). Such phrases—
there are others—show how firmly based on thoughts of
nature is the philosophy of *King Lear*. Unkindness is inhuman, and like the beasts. The daughters of Lear are
'pelican daughters' sucking the blood that begot them
(III. iv. 74); they are like the cuckoo in a hedge-sparrow's
nest (I. iv. 238). The animal world may have its own ways:
but mankind, by nature, should be something other than
the beasts. Yet nature seems to create the good and humane
together with the brutal and unnatural, irrespective of
parents:

>   It is the stars,
>   The stars above us, govern our conditions;
>   Else one self mate and make could not beget
>   Such different issues.   (IV. iii. 34)

So, when humanity is cruel as the beasts, it is better to
leave them and return to nature: by comparison the beasts
are less cruel; they are, any way, natural. So Lear, like Edgar,
exposes himself to storm, companion of 'owl' and 'wolf';
and 'taxes not the elements with unkindness' (III. ii. 16), for
they are not his daughters. Those daughters, and Edmund,
are human beings, yet cruel as beasts that have no sense of
sympathy. They are therefore throwbacks in the evolutionary process: they have not developed proper humanity.
They are 'degenerate' (I. iv. 277; IV. ii. 43). This is stressed

implicitly by those phrases quoted above comparing Goneril and Regan to beasts: it is stressed explicitly by Edmund of himself. Edmund is the 'natural' son of Gloucester. His birth symbolizes his condition: and he is animal-like, both in grace of body and absence of sympathy. He is beautiful with nature's bounty and even compasses intellect and courtly manners: he lacks one thing—unselfishness, sympathy. He is purely selfish, soulless, and, in this respect, bestial. Therefore 'nature' is his goddess:

> Thou, nature, art my goddess; to thy law
> My services are bound. Wherefore should I
> Stand in the plague of custom, and permit
> The curiosity of nations to deprive me,
> For that I am some twelve or fourteen moonshines
> Lag of a brother? Why bastard? Wherefore base?
> When my dimensions are as well compact,
> My mind as generous and my shape as true,
> As honest madam's issue? Why brand they us
> With base? with baseness? bastardy? base, base?
> Who, in the lusty stealth of nature, take
> More composition and fierce quality
> Than doth, within a dull, stale, tired bed,
> Go to the creating a whole tribe of fops,
> Got 'tween asleep and wake?   (I. ii. 1)

This is the key to Edmund's 'nature'. He repudiates and rejects 'custom', civilization. He obeys 'nature's' law of selfishness; he does not understand that it is in the nature of man to be unselfish, to love and serve his community, as surely as it is in the nature of the beast to glut his own immediate desire. Edmund's mistake is this. He thinks he has power to carve for.himself, as a solitary unit. He recognizes no fate, but only free will. It is 'the excellent foppery of the world' to put faith in the ruling of the stars, of destiny, or believe in any gods. Man is what he is, by his own choice:

> 'Sfoot, I should have been that I am, had the maidenliest star in the firmament twinkled on my bastardizing.   (I. ii. 147)

He is retrograde from man's advance beyond the immediate desires of the bestial creation.

In *King Lear* the religion, too, is naturalistic. We can distinguish three modes of religion stressed here by the poet. First, the constant references to the 'gods'; second, the thoughts about ethical 'justice'; and, third, the moral or spiritual development illustrated by the persons before us. The 'gods' so often apostrophized are, however, slightly vitalized: one feels them to be figments of the human mind rather than omnipotent ruling powers—they are presented with no poetic conviction. And exactly this doubt, this questioning, as to the reality and nature of the directing powers, so evident in the god-references, is one of the primary motives through the play. The gods here are more natural than supernatural; the good and bad elements in humanity are, too, natural, not, as in *Macbeth*, supernatural. *King Lear* is throughout naturalistic. The 'gods' are mentioned in various contexts where humanity speaks, under stress of circumstance, its fears or hopes concerning divinity: they are no more than this.

Gloucester mentions them often in the latter acts, after his fortunes become tragic. Adversity elicits his definitely religious expressions. In the scene where his eyes are put out (iii. vii) he thrice refers to the 'gods', twice giving them the epithet 'kind'. Yet shortly after he remarks,

> As flies to wanton boys are we to the gods;
> They kill us for their sport. (iv. i. 36)

This, however, is not his usual thought. Before his attempted suicide he gives Edgar a jewel, praying that 'fairies and gods' may 'prosper it' with him (iv. vi. 29); and next speaks his noble prayer commencing: 'O you mighty gods! This world I do renounce . . .' (iv. vi. 35). He is assured by Edgar that his survival is a miracle from 'the clearest gods' (iv. vi. 74). After seeing Lear in madness, Gloucester's sense of the King's sufferings brings home to him his despair's wrongfulness, and he asks forgiveness of the 'ever-gentle gods' (iv. vi. 222). The 'gods' are to Gloucester kind, generous beings: and their kindness and generosity are made known to him through his, and others', sufferings. He becomes, strangely, aware of 'the bounty and the benison of heaven' (iv. vi. 230). His movement toward religion is curiously unrational. Numerous other references to 'the gods' occur. Kent prays that 'the gods' may reward Gloucester's kindness to Lear (iii. vi. 6); ironical enough in view of what happens to him. Cordelia prays to 'you kind gods' (IV. vii. 14); Edgar challenges Edmund as 'false to thy gods' (V. iii. 136); and tells him that 'the gods are just' and plague men with their own vices (V. iii. 172). Albany refers to the 'gods that we adore' (I. iv. 314), and cries 'The gods defend her!' on hearing of Cordelia's danger (V. iii. 258). These phrases do not, as a whole, form a convincing declaration of divine reality: some show at the most an insistent need in humanity to cry for justification to something beyond its horizon, others are almost perfunctory. Even Edmund can say, half-mockingly: 'Now, gods, stand up for bastards!' (I. ii. 22). These gods are, in fact, man-made. They are natural figments of the human mind, not in any other sense transcendent: *King Lear* is, as a whole, preeminently naturalistic. The 'gods' are equivalent in point of reality with 'the stars' that 'govern our conditions' (IV. iii. 34); or the 'late eclipses of the sun' (I. ii. 115) and the prophecies mentioned by Gloucester; or the 'wicked charms' that Edgar was supposed to have been 'mumbling' (II. i. 41).

The evil forces behind nature are here always things of popular superstition, endowed with no such transcendent dramatic sanction as the Ghost in *Hamlet* or the Weird Sisters. As 'the gods' are created by man's change of soul in endurance of pain, so the 'fiends' here are, also, so to speak, home-made. Edgar's fiends are fiends clearly rooted in popular superstition, and they are presented as such. But, though this be their origin, and though they carry no ultimate conviction of any sort as we read, yet their presence serves to heighten the grotesque effects of the poor Tom incidents. Their queer names are a joy. 'Hopdance' croaks in his belly for food (III. vi. 33). We hear that

> The prince of darkness is a gentleman;
> Modo he's called and Mahu. (III. iv. 147)

'Frateretto' is another (III. vi. 8), and 'Smulkin' (III. iv. 144). As Gloucester approaches with a flickering torch, Edgar says:

> This is the foul fiend Flibbertigibbet: he begins at curfew, and walks till the first cock; he gives the web and the pin, squints the eye, and makes the hare-lip; mildews the white wheat, and hurts the poor creature of earth. (III. iv. 118)

Five fiends have been in poor Tom at once; Obidicut, Hobbididance, Flibbertigibbet, Modo, and Mahu (iv. i. 59). He is continually complaining of 'the foul fiend'. Finally there is the glorious fiend he describes to Gloucester, with eyes like 'full moons' and 'a thousand noses' (iv. vi. 70); which description is an exception to my rule, since it surely transcends folk-lore. This is, indeed, the only real fiend in the play: it has a grotesque, fantastic, ludicrous appeal which carries imaginative conviction; but, of course, there is no dramatic reality about him—he is purely a fantasy created by Edgar. Both 'gods' and 'fiends' here are man-made and form part of the play's naturalism. The poet sees them as images in the minds of the dramatic persons, never as direct realities: that is, those persons do not express any consistent, clear, or compelling utterance about their natures. The explicit religion blends therefore with the naturalistic outlook of the whole: gods and fiends are part of man and all are part of nature, merging with animals, elements, earth and its flowers. In *Macbeth*, in *Hamlet*, in *Troilus and Cressida*, there is not stressed this close human-natural relation: but in *Timon of Athens*, *King Lear's* implicit naturalism is rendered explicit. The 'gods' in *King Lear* are, in fact, less potent than natural realities. Witness the compelling beauty, the sense of healing and safety in Cordelia's lines to the Doctor who speaks of 'many simples operative' to 'close the eye of anguish':

> All blest secrets,
> All you unpublish'd virtues of the earth,
> Spring with my tears! be aidant and remediate
> In the good man's distress!   (iv. iv. 15)

Lear himself shows, as I have already indicated, an excessive naturalism in point of religion. His early curses and prayers are addressed to natural objects, or nature personified. The 'heavens' he cries to are natural rather than eschatological: they are, like the earth, 'old'. He invokes 'blasts and fogs', 'nimble lightnings', 'fen-suck'd fogs' to avenge him (p. 183). He wishes 'the plagues that in the pendulous air hang fated o'er men's faults' to punish poor Tom's supposed 'daughters' (iii. iv. 66). These natural deities he prays to execute natural punishment: Regan's young bones are to be struck with lameness, goddess nature is to convey sterility into Goneril's womb. He thinks purely in terms of the natural order. In these speeches his religion is pagan, naturalistic. It is, in fact, nearer primitive magic than religion. He swears by

> the sacred radiance of the sun,
> The mysteries of Hecate, and the night;
> By all the operation of the orbs
> From whom we do exist or cease to be ...   (i. i. 111)

His early gods are classical: Apollo, Jupiter—used, however, purely as oaths; and, once, 'high-judging Jove', with a sense of conviction (ii. iv. 231). In the middle scenes he apostrophizes the elements as living beings. His early primitivism gives place, however, to something more definite in the thought of 'the great gods who keep this dreadful pother o'er our heads', whose 'enemies' are wicked men (iii. ii. 49). Thoughts of morality are being added to his first pagan selfishness. He questions the justice of 'the heavens' towards naked poverty (iii. iv. 28). He thinks of fiends in his madness:

> To have a thousand with red burning spits
> Come hissing in upon 'em—   (iii. vi. 17)

Of women, he says:

> But to the girdle do the gods inherit,
> Beneath is all the fiends'.   (iv. vi. 129)

These are transition thoughts from his early passionate paganism. The return to nature which he endures in the play's progress paradoxically builds in him a less naturalistic theology. At the end, he can speak to Cordelia those blazing lines:

> You do me wrong to take me out o' the grave:
> Thou art a soul in bliss; but I am bound
> Upon a wheel of fire, that mine own tears
> Do scald like molten lead.   (iv. vii. 45)

Now 'the gods themselves' throw incense on human sacrifices (v. iii. 20). He and Cordelia will be as 'God's spies' (v. iii. 17) —here not 'the gods', but 'God's'. Slowly, painfully, emergent from the *Lear* naturalism we see a religion born of

disillusionment, suffering, and sympathy: a purely spontaneous, natural growth of the human spirit, developing from
nature magic to 'God'.

The emergent religion here—the stoic acceptance, the
purification through sympathy, the groping after 'the gods'
—all these are twined with the conception of justice. The
old Hebrew problem is restated: *King Lear* is analogous to
the *Book of Job*. Is justice a universal principle? The thought
of justice, human and divine, is percurrent. The first sentence
of the play suggests that Lear is guilty of bias:

> *Kent.* I thought the King had more affected the Duke of Albany than
> Cornwall.   (i. i. 1)

He is unjust to Cordelia and to Kent in the first act. His
suffering is provisionally seen to be related to injustice of his
own. Edmund, too, has reason to complain of injustice: the
world brands him with the shame of his birth and inflames
his mind. Many of the persons here attempt to execute justice.
Kent punishes Oswald for his impertinence and is himself
punished; Regan and Cornwall sit in judgement on Gloucester, and gouge out his eyes; a servant takes the law into his
own hands and kills Cornwall; Edgar punishes Oswald and
Edmund with death; France and Cordelia raise an army to
right the affairs of Britain. Gloucester does his best to bring
Edgar to justice. Lear is concerned with the more primitive
thought of vengeance, and invokes the heavens and nature
to aid him. His 'revenges' will be 'the terror of the earth'
(ii. iv. 285). The thought of justice burns in his mind during
the storm: now can the gods 'find out their enemies'; hypo-
crites, with 'crimes unwhipp'd of justice' must tremble before
'these dreadful summoners' (iii. ii. 49). He himself, however,
is 'a man more sinned against than sinning' (iii. ii. 60). But
he next thinks of those in ragged poverty: it is well for pomp
to take this tempestuous physic, exposure's misery, that so
the rich may share their wealth and 'show the heavens more
just' (iii. iv. 36). His mind thus beating on 'justice', the old
man's reason breaks and the same thought is expressed now
in lunatic action. He holds his mock-trial of Goneril and
Regan, with poor Tom as 'learned justicer' (iii. vi. 24):

> I'll see their trial first. Bring in the evidence.   (iii. vi. 38)

Tom is the 'robed man of justice' and the Fool his 'yoke-fellow of equity'; and Kent is 'o' the commission'. The 'honourable assembly' proves corrupt:

> Corruption in the place!
> False justicer, why hast thou let her 'scape?   (III. vi. 58)

When we meet Lear again in madness (IV. vi.) we find him still on the same theme. He thinks himself in judicial authority:

> When I do stare, see how the subject quakes.
> I pardon that man's life. What was thy cause?
> Adultery?
> Thou shalt not die: die for adultery! No:
> The wren goes to't, and the small gilded fly
> Does lecher in my sight.   (IV. vi. 111)

He remembers that 'Gloucester's bastard son' was kinder, as he thinks, to his father than his legitimate brother. Lear's mind in madness is penetrating below the surface shows to the heart of human reality—that heart rooted in nature, uncivilized, instinctive as 'the small gilded fly'. The 'simpering dame', apparently pure-minded and virtuous, is yet lecherous at heart:

> The fitchew nor the soiled horse goes to't
> With a more riotous appetite.   (IV. vi. 125)

It is the old problem of *Measure for Measure*: man's ethics, his show of civilization, are surface froth only. The deep instinctive currents hold their old course, in earth, beast, and man. Man's morality, his idealism, his justice—all are false and rotten to the core. Lear's mind has, since his first mad-scene, pursued its lonely orbit into the dark chaos of insanity, and now whirls back, in the fourth act, grotesque and baleful comet, with a penetrating insight into man's nature: whereas his first mad justice thoughts at the mock-trial were born of a primitive desire to avenge himself on his daughters. Now he returns, with a new justice-philosophy. He concentrates on the mockery and futility of human justice:

> Look with thine ears; see how yond justice rails upon yond simple thief. Hark in thine ear: change places; and, handy-dandy, which is the justice, which is the thief?   (IV. vi. 155)

A 'beggar' will run from a 'farmer's dog'. That is the great
image, says Lear, of authority. 'A dog's obeyed in office.'
The beadle lusts himself to use the whore he whips. All is
corrupt:

> Robes and furr'd gowns hide all. Plate sin with gold,
> And the strong lance of justice hurtless breaks.
>
> (IV. vi. 170)

Therefore 'none does offend'. Lear's mind is ever on justice:
tearing at it, worrying it, like a dog with a bone. And these
thoughts of naturalistic psychology hold a profound suggestion: they are a road to recognition of the universal injustice.
For when earthly justice is thus seen to be absolutely non-
existent and, in fact, impossible, the concept of 'justice' is
drained of meaning. How then can we impose it on the
universal scheme? With a grand consistency the poet main-
tains this sense of universal injustice up to the last terrible
moment of the tragedy.

This question of human justice is clearly part of the wider
question: that of universal justice. In the *Lear* universe we
see humanity working at cross-purposes, judging, condemning, pitying, helping each other. They are crude justicers:
Lear, unjust himself, first cries for human justice, then curses
it. But he also cries for heavenly justice: so, too, others here
cry out for heavenly justice. Their own rough ideas of equity
force them to impose on the universal scheme a similar
judicial mode. We, who watch, who view their own childish
attempts, are not surprised that 'the gods' show little sign
of a corresponding sense. According to human standards
things happen here unjustly. The heavens do not send down
to take Lear's part; his curses on Goneril and Regan have
no effect. The winds will not peace at his bidding. Common
servants demand that Heaven shall assert its powers:

> *Sec. Servant.* I'll never care what wickedness I do,
>   If this man come to good.
> *Third Servant.*   If she live long,
>   And in the end meet the old course of death,
>   Women will all turn monsters.   (III. vii. 99)

So, too, Albany cries that if 'the heavens' do not quickly
'send down their visible spirits' to avenge the offences of man

humanity will prey on itself like sea-monsters (IV. ii. 46).
And when he hears of the servant's direct requital of
Gloucester's wrong by the slaying of Cornwall, he takes
it as proof of divine justice:

> This shows you are above,
> You justicers, that these our nether crimes
> So speedily can venge.   (IV. ii. 78)

And again:

> This judgement of the heavens, that makes us tremble,
> Touches us not with pity.   (V. iii. 233)

But there is no apparent justification of the thought: men
here are good or bad in and by themselves. Goodness and
cruelty flower naturally, spontaneously. A common servant
instinctively lays down his life for an ideal, because goodness
is part of his nature; in another, his nature may prompt him
to wrong, and so the captain promises to obey Edmund's
dastardly command with these words:

> I cannot draw a cart, nor eat dried oats;
> If it be man's work, I'll do it.   (V. iii. 39)

His nature as a man, his station in life as a soldier, both seem
to point him to obedience: again the emphasis is on nature
and there is again the suggestion, percurrent in *King Lear*,
of animals and country life. The story of the play indeed
suggests that wrongful action first starts the spreading poison
of evil; and that sin brings inevitable retribution. Lear suffers
a mental torment for his unbalanced selfishness and short-
sightedness—a mental fault; Gloucester loses his eyes, that
'most pure spirit of sense' (*Troilus and Cressida*, III. iii. 106)
in return for his sensual fault:

> The gods are just, and of our pleasant vices
> Make instruments to plague us:
> The dark and vicious place where thee he got
> Cost him his eyes.   (V. iii. 172)

But it is all a purely natural process: there is no celestial
avatar, to right misguided humanity. The 'revenging gods'
do not bend all their thunders against parricides (II. i. 47).
Wrongdoers are, it is true, punished: but there is no sense
of divine action. It is Edgar's trumpet, symbol of natural

judgement, that summons Edmund to account at the end, sounding through the *Lear* mist from which right and wrong at this moment emerge distinct. Right wins, surely as the sun rises: but it is a natural, a human process. Mankind work out their own 'justice', crime breaks the implicit laws of human nature, and brings suffering alike on good and bad. But not all the good persons suffer, whereas all the bad meet their end swiftly. This is the natural justice of *King Lear*. To men, it must seem more like 'fortune' than 'justice'. Kent prays to 'fortune' to 'smile once more' and turn her wheel (II. ii. 180). She does not do so. Lear is 'the natural fool of fortune' (IV. vi. 196). To men the natural justice seems often inconsiderate, blind, mechanic. The utmost antithesis is seen in the grim punishment of Cordelia for her 'most small fault'. But, from an objective view of the *Lear* universe, other facts regarding the universal justice emerge, and we begin to have sight of some vague purpose working itself out in terms of nature and of man.

In *King Lear* we see humanity suffering. It is a play of creative suffering. Mankind are working out a sort of purgatory. The good ones know it; the bad seem not to. The good are sweetened, purified by adversity: the bad, as A. C. Bradley notes, are swiftly demoralized and brutalized by their success, while those who turn their sufferings to profit endure with a fine stoicism. Kent is typically stoical throughout. There is stoic nobility in the Fool's patter of bitter fun. Edgar repeats this stoic theme, voicing the purgatorial philosophy of the play in many contexts. After seeing Lear's madness he finds his own suffering miraculously eased. He speaks a soliloquy, saying that our miseries cease to be woes when we see our betters suffering too; when there is a partnership and fellowship of suffering, then pain is lessened—it becomes 'light and portable' (III. vi. 111–19). He finds his state as poor Tom to hold comfort. To be thus outcast robs chance of power to hurt him:

> To be worst,
> The lowest and most dejected thing of fortune,
> Stands still in esperance, lives not in fear:
> The lamentable change is from the best;
> The worst returns to laughter. (IV. i. 2)

Therefore he welcomes the 'blasts' of 'unsubstantial air'.
Extreme suffering steadies him on the rock of assurance:
uncertainty and fear, worst sting of pain, are lacking. This
quality, indeed, differentiates the *Lear* from the *Macbeth*
mode: *King Lear* shows a suffering from knowledge;
Macbeth, a more ghastly agony of fear. Edgar, however,
next sees his father:

> My father, poorly led? World, world, O world!
> But that thy strange mutations make us hate thee,
> Life would not yield to age.   (IV. i. 10)

He discovers Gloucester's blindness:

> O gods! Who is't can say 'I am at the worst'?
> I am worse than e'er I was.   (IV. i. 25)

He realizes that

> . . . worse I may be yet: the worst is not
> So long as we can say, 'This is the worst'.   (IV. i. 27)

Mankind are here continually being ennobled by suffering.
They bear it with an ever deeper insight into their own
nature and the hidden purposes of existence. 'Nothing
almost sees miracles but misery' (II. ii. 172). In some strange
way the suffering they endure enriches them, brings them
peace. So Gloucester can give his purse to Edgar in disguise,
joying in the thought that his misery makes another happy;
and continuing with a replica of Lear's thought, prays the
heavens to 'deal so still', forcing the rich to share their
superfluity (IV. i. 67). Gloucester moves beyond self-interest,
through suffering, to the nobility and grandeur of his prayer:

> O you mighty gods!
> This world I do renounce, and, in your sights,
> Shake patiently my great affliction off:
> If I could bear it longer, and not fall
> To quarrel with your great opposeless wills,
> My snuff and loathed part of nature should
> Burn itself out.   (IV. vi. 35)

There follows his attempted suicide: finding himself alive,
he fears there is no release from tyranny (IV. vi. 64), but
Edgar cheers him, comforts him, saying that it was 'some
devil' who beguiled him into suicide; that

> the clearest gods, who make them honours
> Of men's impossibilities have preserved thee.
>
> (IV. vi. 74)

He is to 'bear free and patient thoughts'. Then Lear enters
in extravagant madness. Gloucester's sympathy wells up in
the noble phrase:

> O ruin'd piece of nature! This great world
> Shall so wear out to nought.   (IV. vi. 138)

Gloucester and Edgar stand in a kind of reverence before
Lear's anguish: Edgar's 'heart breaks at it' (IV. vi. 146).
When Lear is gone, Gloucester prays for forgiveness from
the 'gentle' gods—strange epithet after the recent incidents:

> *Gloucester.* You ever-gentle gods, take my breath from me;
>   Let not my worser spirit tempt me again
>   To die before you please!
> *Edgar.*   Well pray you, father.
>
> (IV. vi. 222)

Edgar, so often the voice of the *Lear* philosophy, has here,
in leading his father to suicide, in saving him, and in pointing
the moral—in limning his picture of the fiend on the cliff
edge, in urging that the gods have preserved him, in all this
he is, as it were, the high-priest of this play's stoicism, of
endurance which forbids a facile exit in self-murder. He
understands his father's purgatorial destiny, and thus helps
to direct it. He understands and sympathizes, since he
himself is

> A most poor man, made tame to fortune's blows;
> Who by the art of known and feeling sorrows,
> Am pregnant to good pity.   (IV. vi. 226)

Now Gloucester speaks gently of 'the bounty and the benison
of heaven' (IV. vi. 230).

Strange paradox. It is strange, and very beautiful, to watch
this burning purgatory, these souls so palely lit by suffering,
aureoled and splendid in their grief. Each by suffering finds
himself more truly, more surely knows the centre on which
human fate revolves, more clearly sees the gods' mysterious
beneficence. Gloucester is blind—but he knows now that
he 'stumbled when he saw'. We watch humanity, pained and
relieving pain, and finding peace. Gloucester's purgatory was

contingent on his first lending aid to Lear and raising the hate of the adverse party: thus an act of goodness buys the inestimable gift of purgatorial agony. But suicide cheats the high gods of their purpose. Once again, when Gloucester longs for death, Edgar answers:

> What, in ill thoughts again? Men must endure
> Their going hence, even as their coming hither.
> Ripeness is all.   (v. ii. 9)

That is, men must await ('endure') the destined hour of death, directing it no more than they direct the hour of birth: they must await till the harvest of their pain is ripe. Ripeness is all—so Gloucester is matured by suffering, and his death, when it comes, is sweet. He finds his wronged son Edgar:

> . . . his flaw'd heart
> 'Twixt two extremes of passion, joy and grief,
> Burst smilingly.   (v. iii. 198)

The statement of *King Lear* on the suicide-problem which troubled *Hamlet* is, indeed, explicit. Man may not decide his awful entry into the unknown territory of death. That is to thwart 'the gods' of their purgatorial purpose.

With Lear himself, too, ripeness is all. In the scene of his reunion with Cordelia, he wakes to music, like a mortal soul waking to immortality, to find his daughter bright as 'a soul in bliss'; now both find the richness of love more rich for the interval of agony, misunderstanding, intolerance. Cordelia's sincerity was not, perhaps, wholly blameless: both were proud. Now love returns, enthroned: 'misery' has again worked its 'miracle'. All woman's motherly love is caught up in Cordelia's speech:

> Was this a face
> To be opposed against the warring winds?
> To stand against the deep dread-bolted thunder?
> In the most terrible and nimble stroke
> Of quick, cross-lightning? to watch—poor perdu—
> With this thin helm? Mine enemy's dog,
> Though he had bit me, should have stood that night
> Against my fire; and wast thou fain, poor father,
> To hovel thee with swine, and rogues forlorn,
> In short and musty straw?   (iv. vii. 31)

Lear is waked into love: now he is humble, he knows he is 'a foolish fond old man' (iv. vii. 60). He will drink poison if Cordelia wishes it. His purgatory has been this: cruelly every defence of anger and pride that barriers his consciousness from his deepest and truest emotion—his love for Cordelia, whom he loved most, on whom he had thought to set his rest (i. i. 125)—has been broken down. In those middle storm scenes we were aware of his hatred and thoughts of vengeance, together with a new-born sympathy addressed to suffering humanity throughout the world. Then the whirling ecstasies of lunacy: now the healing balm of uttermost humility and love. He humbles himself, not to Cordelia, but to the love now royally enthroned in his heart erstwhile usurped:

> Pray you now, forget and forgive. I am old and foolish.
> (iv. vii. 84)

His purgatory is almost complete; but not yet complete. From him a greater sacrifice than from Gloucester is demanded. He and Cordelia are now prisoners. Cordelia in adversity is a true daughter of this stoic world:

> We are not the first
> Who, with best meaning, have incurr'd the worst.
> For thee, oppressed King, am I cast down;
> Myself could else out-frown false fortune's frown.
> (v. iii. 3)

Lear, at this last moment, touches exquisite apprehensions. Now simple things will please. Formerly a king, intolerant, fierce, violent, whom any opposition roused to fury, now an old man ready to be pleased with simplest things: they will 'talk of court news'; the gods themselves throw incense on such sacrifices; Lear and Cordelia will

> take upon 's the mystery of things
> As if we were God's spies. (v. iii. 16)

God's spies, in truth: since Lear now sees only with eyes of love. Love is the last reality but one in Lear's story: love and God. Not the last. There are still the vague, inscrutable 'gods' of the *Lear* mist, their purposes enigmatic, their actions inscrutable. There remains death. Death and 'the

gods'—if indeed those gods exist. Uttermost tragedy, and
unknowing, senseless 'fortune', has its way at the end. Love
and 'God' exist herein, transcendent for a while, in golden
scenes where Cordelia is bright with an angel brightness.
But they do not last, cannot free Lear finally from the fiery
wheel of mortal life:

> I am bound
> Upon a wheel of fire, that mine own tears
> Do scald like molten lead.   (IV. vii. 46)

On the wide canvas of this play three persons stand out
with more vivid life than the rest: Edmund, Lear, Cordelia.
They correspond to three periods in man's evolution—the
primitive, the civilized, and the ideal. Edmund is a throw-
back in the evolutionary process. He is a 'natural' son of
Gloucester, he is, as he tells us, a son of 'nature'. He is
uncivilized; he rejects civilization because civilization has
rejected him. He is unprincipled, cruel and selfish; but he has
fascination. He has a kind of sex-appeal about him. Goneril
and Regan fall readily before his charm. He is beautiful as
an animal, physically a paragon of animals, with an animal's
lithe grace, a cat's heartless skill in tormenting the weak.
Edmund is not cruel: he, catlike, lacks the gift of sympathy.
He is playing a game. And he has an impudent charm of
conscious superiority and sex-attraction. We cannot resist
his appeal—we are glad that so rich a personality meets his
end with some dramatic colour. His life he has regulated with
a theatrical sense, and he closes it with a touch of fine tragedy:

> Thou hast spoken right, 'tis true;
> The wheel is come full circle; I am here.   (V. iii. 175)

This is a fitting conclusion to the schemes of Edmund; he
is, as it were, always trying to stage a combination of events
in which he shall figure prominently. He has a sense of his
own romantic self-adventure. Witness his exquisite remark
to Goneril before the battle:

> *Goneril.* My most dear Gloucester.
> *Edmund.*   Yours in the ranks of death.
>   (IV. ii 25)

King Lear is a complex of primitive and civilized elements:
he is a selfish, high-tempered, autocratic old man. He is

wrong-headed without being vicious. He deceives himself.
He swerves from sentiment to cruelty: neither are real. He
has in fact 'ever but slenderly known himself' (I. i. 296).
Then comes his purgatory, in the shape of a return to nature,
a knowledge of his animal kinship, a wide and sweeping
sympathy, a tempestuous mental torment on the tempest-
riven heath. In madness thoughts deep-buried come to the
surface: though at first he acts his futile desire for revenge
in his mock-trial, later a finer lunatic apprehension glimpses
profound human truths. His thoughts fix on the sex-inhibi-
tions of civilized man, delving into the truth of man's
civilized ascent. He finds sex to be a pivot-force in human
affairs, sugared though it be by convention. All human
civilization and justice are a mockery. He is all the time
working deep into that which is real, in him or others, facing
truth, though it be hideous. He has been forced from a
deceiving consciousness built of self-deception, sentiment,
the tinsel of kingship and authority, to the knowledge of his
own and others' nature. His courtiers lied to him, since he
is not ague-proof (IV. vi. 108). He wins his purgatorial
reward in finding that which is most real to him, his love
for Cordelia. For the first time he compasses his own reality,
and its signs are humility and love. He falls back on the
simplicity of love: next of death. His purgatory then closes.
This is the movement from civilization, through a return to
nature and a revulsion from civilized man to death, which
is later massively reconstructed in *Timon of Athens*.

   Cordelia, in that she represents the principle of love, is
idealized: Edmund is of the past, Lear of the present,
Cordelia of the future dispensation. She is like 'a soul in
bliss'. Her tears are 'holy water' and her eyes 'heavenly'
(IV. iii. 32): she alone here has both goodness and fascination.
Kent and Albany are colourless, Edgar little more than a
voice: Cordelia is conceived poetically, like Lear and
Edmund. She is a personality, alive, tangible. There is thus
an implicit suggestion of a time-succession about these three.
They correspond to definite layers in the stratified philosophy
of *King Lear*: the bestial and pagan where life was young
and handsome, from which human civilization has emerged;
the superficially civilized, yet far from perfect—the present

dispensation of unrestful, weary, misfeatured man; and, finally, the ideal. The purgatorial progress is a progress to self-knowledge, to sincerity: hence Cordelia's original 'fault' of ill-judged sincerity is one with her significance as a symbol of human perfection. This thought is implicitly stressed in the final speech of the play. She is of the future humanity, suffering in the present dispensation for her very virtue. Nor is this evolution-thought an irrelevant imposition: it is throughout implicit in *King Lear*. The play is a play of naturalism, of spiritual qualities represented as a natural growth. Humanity here is shown as kin to the earth and winds and animals: but some of the persons, being wicked, appear, in shape of men and women, unnatural; whereas the good, by following out their purgatorial pilgrimage, attain to a spiritual harmony in which they feel at home. This is equivalent to the statement that goodness is the natural goal of man, and the aim of evolution. Therefore at the end the danger of evil-doers is crushed. The good forces, not the evil, win: since good is natural, evil unnatural to human nature. Edgar and Albany are left to direct the 'gored state' to health. *King Lear* shows us the spiritual evolution of man: not one age, but all ages, of natural and human progress are suggested in its pages.

In this analysis I have viewed the *Lear* universe objectively. As a whole, the play has a peculiar panoramic quality. We can watch the persons below us, working their own ruin or their own purgatorial liberation. In this sense—as in its naturalism—the play resembles a Hardy novel. But this vision gives birth to one tremendous theme growing out from it. The figure of Lear stands out gigantic; the theme of his madness flames from this bleak world. The violent and extravagant effects of the storm-scene kindle the imagination till it cannot watch, but rather lives within, the passionate event. Then follows the extravaganza of Lear, Edgar, and the Fool, with their variegated play of the fantastic to the sound of thunder, lit by the nimble strokes of lightning. This is purely a phantasma of the mind: Lear's mind, capering on the page with antic gesture, creating the Goneril and Regan phantoms of the mock-trial to shimmer like mirage-figures in the dancing heat of unreason. Lear's mind encloses us here—it is as a gash in the actualized fabric of the play, a rending of objective vision, laying bare the mental torment of Lear: this we do not watch, we live within it. We have a close-up of Lear's mind which becomes our mind: we burn through Lear's purgatorial agony. The effect is curious: the gash becomes bigger than the thing it cuts. It envelopes, encloses us. As we feel Lear's anguish, we know it to be the central thing in the play, the imaginative core and heart of the rest. But then the fire of this ecstatic fantasia dies down through the horror of Gloucester's torture to the pervading colourlessness: all is grey and wan whilst Edgar and Gloucester climb their purgatorial ascent. Again the spark of the imaginatively bizarre burns bright in the comedy of Gloucester's fall, and is quickly lashed into flame at the wind of Lear's entrance, crowned in flowers, ludicrous, terrifying, pitiable, preaching to us of infants who wawl and cry on this great stage of fools, flinging fiery sparks of unextinguishable thought from the catherine-wheel of his spinning mind. Then the white presence of Cordelia, with restorative kiss, and the remediate virtues of earth's simples, the kindly nurse of anguish, sleep, and the strains of music, are all interwoven in the awakening of Lear from the wheel of fire to a new consciousness of love. Nature, human love, music—all blend in this transcendent scene: the agony of this play works up to so beautiful a moment, heavenly sweet, that one forgets the bleak world, the rough and cruel naturalism which gave it birth. The Lear-theme gathers itself through the rush of madness for this crescendo of silent beauty, a sudden blaze of light, in which the sweets of nature, the sweets of humanity, and, thirdly, some more divine suggestion in the strains of music, blend together to create in this natural world something of an unearthly loveliness. Though it does not last, it has yet fired the world and lives on. The naturalism of *King Lear* pales before this blinding shaft of transcendent light. This is the justification of the agony, the sufferance, the gloom. Though once more the shadows close, it has existed, immortal, in its own right, bending to no natural law. From the travail of nature the immortal thing is born; time has given birth to that which is timeless.

These are the vivid, the fiery, things in *King Lear*: the

tempestuous passion, the burning-wheel of mortal agony, the angel peace of a redeeming love; and then death, hideous and grinning—the hanged Cordelia, and Lear's cracked heart: a mockery. As though the whole play in anguish brings to birth one transcendent loveliness, only to stamp it out, kill it. With Gloucester the recognition of his wronged son and death are simultaneous; his heart 'bursts smilingly'. For Lear there is no such joyful end. In face of the last scene any detailed comment of purgatorial expiation, of spiritual purification, is but a limp and tinkling irrelevance. One comment only is justifiable:

> Break, heart; I prithee, break.   (v. iii. 314)

The action has been whirled to the most terrifically agonized ending in Shakespeare. Now we think that golden love was but an oasis in a desert pilgrimage: no continuing city. Pain unbearable before gave place to merciful insanity. Now the last agony of the again gashed, impaled, quivering soul is more mercifully embalmed in death:

> Vex not his ghost: O, let him pass! he hates him
> That would upon the rack of this tough world
> Stretch him out longer.   (v. iii. 315)

There is peace merciful and profound and calm. It is utterly dependent for its serenity and tranquillity on the pain it ends: that pain dependent on the transcendent beauty it has seen strangled. This is the absolute peace of death, of nothingness, where consciousness was late stretched, hideously drawn out beyond endurance, on the rack of a life whose cruelty brings beauty to birth, whose beauty is its most agonizing cruelty. Wherein shall we seek our revelation—in that deathless dream of love, or in this death?

We have found two primary qualities in *King Lear*: the panoramic view of good and bad people working out their destiny; and the fiery, passionate, grotesque Lear-theme which the pangs of this cold world bring to birth. The naturalism of the play travails to produce out of its earthly womb a thing of imaginative and miraculous splendour, high-pitched in bizarre, grotesque, vivid mental conflict and agony: which in turn pursues its rocket-flight of whirling madness, explosive, to the transcendent mystic awakening into love, dropping bright balls of silent fire, then extinguished, as the last tragic sacrifice claims its own, and the darkness closes. This is the sweeping ascent of the Lear-theme, rushing, whistling in air, a sudden visionary brilliance, and many colours across the heavens, expanding petals of jewelled flame; next falling back to earth: a comet-like progress, leaving trails of fire to streak for an instant the dark mid-air which again entombs the *Lear* universe at the end, as man battles on to make more history, to bring to birth another Lear and another miracle of love. But these two modes are not in reality distinct: the one grows from the other, they are interfused, intrinsicate. We cannot untie the knot of the divine twisted with the earthly. Here the emphasis is everywhere on naturalism. No strong religious phraseology or suggestion is maintained throughout: 'the gods' are vague, symbols of groping mankind: imaginative transcendence grows out of the naturalism, is not imposed on it. The symbolic effects are here never contrary to natural possibility. The tempest is fierce indeed—there are 'such sheets of fire, such bursts of horrid flame', that 'man's nature cannot carry the affliction nor the fear' (III. ii. 46). There are 'groans of roaring wind and rain': but there are no 'lamentings heard i' the air, strange screams of death', as in that other more ghastly tempest in *Macbeth*. The animal-symbolism throughout *King Lear* is everywhere natural, rooted in nature, in country life. Here horses do not 'eat each other', nor does 'the mousing owl' prey on the 'towering falcon'. The imaginative effects are strongly emphasized, but always within natural law. In *Macbeth* we find an abnormal actuality subservient to the imaginative vision; in *King Lear* an imaginative vision emergent from a pure naturalism. The two modes are bridged by the animal-symbolism, since these numerous references serve a dual purpose, both insisting on man's kinship with nature—especially, here, nature ugly as a mongrel-cur—and also lending themselves at the same time to the extravagant and bizarre effects of madness. But madness itself is the disjointing of mind by the tug of conflicting principles: the animal and the divine; the past and the future. Man's agony comes in the wrench of futurity from the inertia of animal life. The dual purposes of this animal-symbolism are thus in reality one. This Shakespearian symbolism, here and in *Macbeth* and *Julius Caesar*, is fundamental to our understanding: its peculiar nature tunes our consciousness in each to the exact pitch of the peculiar vision we are to receive.

The naturalism of *King Lear* is agnostic and sombre often, and often beautiful. Human life is shown as a painful, slow struggle, in which man travails to be born from animal-nature into his destined inheritance of human nature and supreme love. Unhappy, his mind torturingly divided in his world; yet, by suffering and sympathy, he may attain to mystic recognition and praise his gods. Here the cruel and wolf-hearted bring disaster on themselves and others: evil mankind is self-slaughterous, self-contradictory. But even they know love and die in its cause. The primary persons, good and bad, die into love. Goneril and Regan, flint-hearted, bend before that universal principle. They die by passion for their Edmund, beautiful as a panther, and as deadly. They, like he, are below humanity: yet they know love. So, too, in the ravenous slaughter of wood or ocean, love rules creation. That universal pulse is strong within the naturalism of *King Lear*, beats equally in the hearts of Goneril and Cordelia. And what of Edmund? He has loved only himself, with a curious consciousness of his own fasci-nation. May that be counted love? Edmund does not dis-close his order for Cordelia's death which would, according to his cunning device, never otherwise have been laid to his charge till, seeing the bodies of Goneril and Regan brought in, his heart is flamed by the tragic pathos of their sacrifice:

> Yet Edmund was belov'd.   (v. iii. 242)

He recognizes love at last, its mystery, its power, its divinity. He knows himself to die aureoled in its unresisted splendour. Now he speaks quickly:

> I pant for life: some good I mean to do,
> Despite of mine own nature. Quickly send,
> Be brief in it, to the castle; for my writ
> Is on the life of Lear and on Cordelia:
> Nay, send in time.   (v. iii. 245)

Again the *Lear* universe travails and brings forth its miracle.
1972: see p. ix above.

X

THE PILGRIMAGE OF HATE: AN ESSAY
ON *TIMON OF ATHENS*

IN this essay I outline the nature of a tragic movement more precipitous and unimpeded than any other in Shakespeare; one which is conceived on a scale even more tremendous than that of *Macbeth* and *King Lear*; and whose universal tragic significance is of all most clearly apparent. My purpose will be to concentrate on whatever is of positive power and significance, regarding the imaginative impact as all-important however it may appear to contradict the logic of human life. My analysis will first characterize the imaginative atmosphere of the early acts and indicate its significance as a setting for the personality of Timon; next, it will show how the subsidiary persons and choric speeches are so presented that our sympathy is directed into certain definite channels; and, finally, I shall point the nature of the second half of the play, contrasting it strongly with the earlier acts and indicating the reversal of symbolic suggestion. Such an analysis will inevitably reveal important facts as to the implicit philosophy, exposing its peculiar universality, and the stark contrast of the partial and imperfect nature of humanity and the world of the senses with the strong aspiration toward infinity and perfection and the ultimate darkness of the unknown embodied in the two parts of the play.

The first acts convey the impression of riches, ease, sensuous appeal, and brilliant display. The curtain rises on a blaze of magnificence and the first persons are the Poet, Painter, Jeweller, and Merchant. In no play of Shakespeare is the opening more significant. Art, wealth, trade are represented, things which stand for human intercourse, progress, civilization, worldly success and happiness. Here poet and painter enjoy leisure to hold forth on their art, and jeweller and merchant await high payment for their wares. In the early acts we are continually reminded of wealth. Ventidius is left 'rich' by his father (I. ii. 4); Lucullus dreams of 'a silver basin and ewer' (III. i. 6); talents are thrown about like pence. Many other coins and fine articles are mentioned: we hear of solidares, crowns, 'money, plate, jewels and such like trifles' (III. ii. 23); of 'jewels' and 'rich jewels'; a 'casket', diamonds, and silver goblets. Timon appears boundlessly rich:

> If I want gold, steal but a beggar's dog,
> And give it Timon, why, the dog coins gold.   (II. i. 5)

We hear that

> Plutus, the god of gold,
> Is but his steward.   (I. i. 287)

Metaphors from metal occur:

> Let molten coin be thy damnation,   (III. i. 56)

and

> They have all been touched and found base metal.
>   (III. iii. 6)

Silver dishes are hurled by Timon at his flatterers:

> Stay, I will lend thee money, borrow none.   (III. vi. 112)

These acts scintillate with the flash of gold coins and rich metals and stones. They delight the imagination's eye and touch, as the glittering proper names delight the ear. These, however, are but elements in a single effect of wealth, ease, refined luxury, and, in the earliest scenes especially, sensuous joy. Feasting is continual and elaborate:

> A banqueting-room in Timon's House. Hautboys playing loud music.
> A great banquet served in; Flavius and others attending . . .   (I. ii)

Visitors are announced by the sound of trumpets. Besides feasting and music, we have images of visual delight meticulously described. The poet looks at the painting:

> Admirable: how this grace
> Speaks his own standing! what a mental power
> This eye shoots forth! how big imagination
> Moves in this lip! to the dumbness of the gesture
> One might interpret.   (I. i. 31)

Timon later praises the same picture. We have a vivid and lengthy description of the poet's symbolical work (I. i. 43–94), and the painter outlines its visual possibilities in his 'condition' of plastic art. Beautiful animals are mentioned, such as 'greyhounds' (I. ii. 198), a 'bay courser' (I. ii. 220), and 'four milk-white horses trapped in silver' (I. ii. 192). All these things, gifts of Fortune to those she wafts to her with her 'ivory hand' (I. i. 71), build up an atmosphere of visual delight. All the senses are catered for: hence, after the feasting and music, there is a mask introduced by a boy-Cupid:

> *Cupid.* Hail to thee, worthy Timon, and to all
> That of his bounties taste! The five best senses
> Acknowledge thee their patron; and come freely
> To gratulate thy plenteous bosom; th' ear,
> Taste, touch, smell, pleased from thy table rise:
> They only now come but to feast thine eyes.   (I. ii. 130)

The emphasis on the 'senses' is apparent. Timon bids his 'music' welcome the maskers. Then (I. ii):

> Music. Re-enter Cupid, with a mask of Ladies as Amazons, with lutes in their hands, dancing and playing.

And,

> The Lords rise from table, with much adoring of Timon; and to show their loves, each singles out an Amazon, and all dance, men with women, a lofty strain or two to the hautboys, and cease.

Timon thanks the maskers and invites them to an 'idle banquet'. We are lost in a riot of display, a gold-mist of romance and pleasures of the senses. The setting is brilliant, the wealth apparently inexhaustible, the pleasures free. We can imagine the rich food and wine, the blare and clash of music, embraces, laughter, and passages of glancing love; the coursing of blood, the flushed cheek, the mask of fair dancers and Cupid.

Timon's world is sensuous and erotic, yet not vicious or ignoble. Even in Flavius' denunciation of Timon's way of life, a grand profusion, an aristocratic brilliance and richness of entertainment yet pleases us:

> So the gods bless me,
> When all our offices have been oppress'd
> With riotous feeders, when our vaults have wept

With drunken spilth of wine, when every room
Hath blaz'd with lights and bray'd with minstrelsy,
I have retir'd me to a wasteful cock,
And set mine eyes at flow.   (II. ii. 167)

And that is the voice of reproof, when the bright day of thoughtless expenditure is done. Whilst it is in act, we are carried away by the magnificence of the effects, and our imaginations are kindled by the vivid pulse of entertainment, feast, friendship, and music. The poetry of the senses is lived before our eyes, yet withal there is refinement, courtesy, aesthetic taste, for this world is lorded by the rich heart of Timon. The early atmosphere of *Timon of Athens* resembles the poetic atmosphere of *Antony and Cleopatra*. In both there is the same kind of atmospheric technique that focuses our vision to the unique differing worlds of gloom of *Macbeth* and *King Lear*; and in both this sensuous blaze is conceived as a setting for a transcendent love. Only by subduing our more independent faculties in abeyance to the imaginative quality of these early scenes shall we receive the play as poetry and know its meaning. A true interpretative faculty in the reader must be the bride of the poet's imagination, since only so can it give birth to understanding. So, by dwelling inwardly on the points I have adduced to indicate the imaginative quality of Timon's setting, our consciousness will be, as it were, tuned to respond to and appreciate the true erotic richness of Timon's soul.

The world of Timon and the soul of Timon are thus interdependent, and our consideration of the total imaginative impact illuminates his personality. Though at first sight there may seem something barbaric and oriental in Timon's generosity and sense of display, yet we are confronted in reality not with barbarism, but humanism. The impressions I have noted do not indicate relics of the past—though the best of a romantic Hellenism and of an Elizabethan aristocracy have contributed something—but an idealized perfected civilization. Timon himself is the flower of human aspiration. His generosity lacks wisdom, but is itself noble; his riches reflect the inborn aristocracy of his heart; his pleasures, like his love of friends, are in themselves excellent, the consummations of natural desire and in harmony with the very spirit of man's upward endeavour towards the reality of art, the joys of civilization, and love universal. Timon's world is poetry made real, lived rather than imagined. He would break down with conviviality, music, art, the barriers that sever consciousness from consciousness. He would build a paradise of love on earth. Now just as Timon's love of sweet things, though not gluttonous nor vicious, is yet eminently a matter of the senses and unrestrained, so his affection for his friends, to which the rest is a setting and a direction of our sympathies, is no pale and sainted benevolence, no skeleton philanthropy nor ice-cold charity. His love, too, is the love not of the saint, but the lover; a rich erotic perception welling up from his soul, warm-blooded, instinctive, romantic and passionate. It is the love of Othello for Desdemona, of Antony for Cleopatra, of Shakespeare for the fair boy of the Sonnets. These we understand; so, too, we form some contact with the self-renouncing, ascetic, all-embracing love of the saint. But Timon's is the passionate, somewhat selfish, love of one lover for another, physical and spiritual, of the senses as of the soul; yet directed not toward one creature or one purpose but expanding its emotion among all men.

Timon is a universal lover, not by principle but by nature. His charity is never cold, self-conscious, or dutiful. He withholds nothing of himself. His praise to the painter (I. i. 161) is sincere appreciation; his jests with the jeweller (I. i. 167) kind and not condescending; his chance of doing good to his servant whose lack of wealth forbids his desired marriage is one of those god-sent adventures in kindness that make the life of Timon a perpetual romance. His heaven is to see the young man's eyes brimming with joy. He hates the least suggestion of insincerity and scorns ceremony:

> Nay, my lords,
> Ceremony was but devis'd at first
> To set a gloss on faint deeds, hollow welcomes,
> Recanting goodness, sorry ere 'tis shown;
> But where there is true friendship, there needs none.
> Pray, sit; more welcome are ye to my fortunes
> Than my fortunes to me.   (I. ii. 15)

He does not doubt that his friends would, if occasion called, reciprocate his generosity, and an excess of emotion at the thought brings tears to his eyes:

> ... Why, I have often wished myself poorer, that I might come nearer to you. We are born to do benefits: and what better or properer can we call our own than the riches of our friends? what a precious comfort 'tis, to have so many, like brothers, commanding one another's fortunes! O joy, e'en made away ere't can be born! Mine eyes cannot hold out water, methinks: to forget their faults, I drink to you.
>
> (i. ii. 105)

There is no shame in this confession of tears: he lives in a world of the soul where emotion is the only manliness, and love the only courage. If, as Shakespeare's imagery sometimes suggests, the lover sees his own soul symbolized in his love, then we can say that Timon projects himself into the world around him; mankind is his own soul; a resplendent and infinite love builds an earthly paradise where it may find complete satisfaction in the inter-communion of heart with heart, and gift with gift. If this transcendent love can be bodied into shapes and forms which are finite; if the world of actuality and sense does not play Timon false—then humanism can thrive without religion, and an earthly paradise is no deceiving dream.

The poet has shown us a supreme lover. Love is presented, for purposes of the play, alone, unmixed with judgement. Timon's generosity is extreme, and his faith child-like. But we are not left free to criticize his acts. Even though we were to remain insensible to the imaginative atmosphere and the hero's lovable personality, the accompanying persons are so drawn as to heighten, not lessen, our respect for Timon; and as the first gold-haze of romance and sensuous appeal thins with the progress of the first three acts, and shapes of personification stand out clear and solid, this element of technique becomes increasingly important. The most striking subsidiary figure is Apemantus. Contrasted with Timon's faith and love, we have a churlish cynicism and disgust. Timon is a universal lover, Apemantus a universal cynic. His mind functions in terms of the foul, bestial, and stupid attributes of man (i. i. 178–249). He makes lascivious jests. He loaths the shape of man powerfully as Timon loves it:

> The strain of man's bred out
> Into baboon and monkey. (I. i. 260)

And,

> What a coil's here!
> Serving of becks and jutting out of bums! (I. ii. 239)

His cynicism is a compound of ridicule, foul suggestion, and ascetic philosophy. Timon shows him a picture:

> *Timon.* Wrought he not well that painted it?
> *Apemantus.* He wrought better that made the painter; and yet he's but a
> filthy piece of work. (I. i. 201)

Thus swiftly are condemned God, man, and man's aspiration and endeavour. The pregnancy of this answer is amazing in its compactness and the poignance of its sting. As he watches the observances of respect, the greetings and smiles attendant on Alcibiades' entry, he comments:

> So, so, there!
> Aches contract and starve your supple joints!
> That there should be small love 'mongst these sweet knaves,
> And all this courtesy! (I. i. 257)

Entertainment is a mockery to him, for his thoughts are centred on the transience of shows, the brittleness of the armour of manners with which civilized man protects the foulness within from the poisoned dart of truth. Therefore he sits apart during the feast, refusing the food of Timon, gnawing roots, drinking water. Masquers enter, and he comments:

> Hoy-day, what a sweep of vanity comes this way!
> They dance! They are mad women.
> Like madness is the glory of this life,
> As this pomp shows to a little oil and root. (I. ii. 139)

He is anxious to warn Timon, feeling that he is too noble for the company that wastes his means:

> ... It grieves me to see so many dip their meat in one man's blood; and
> all the madness is, he cheers them up too. (I. ii. 42)

His respect for Timon is, however, clearly noted:

> Even he drops down
> The knee before him and returns in peace
> Most rich in Timon's nod. (I. i. 61)

Therefore the presence of Apemantus serves many purposes. It points us to the insincerity of Timon's friends and the probable course of events; it shows us that even the cynic cannot help but honour and respect Timon; and it makes us feel how repellent is this very cynicism, which is the opposite of Timon's faith and love. Apemantus thus enlists our respect for Timon, and even at their final meeting, when Timon has left Athens, we are again shown that Timon's hate is not as Apemantus'.

But we are repelled not alone by the churlish philosopher: we are even more repelled by the false friends of Timon. The incident of Lucullus' refusal is exquisitely comic, yet bitterly satiric. Nothing more meanly unpleasant could well be imagined, and yet its truth to human nature cannot be denied. His greed, flattery, hypocrisy, and finally open confession of baseness, are drawn in swift, masterly strokes, culminating in:

'Here 's three solidares for thee; good boy, wink at me, and say thou saw'st me not,' and 'Ha! now I see thou art a fool and fit for thy master.'

(III. i. 47, 53)

Lucius comes off little better (III. ii). Ventidius, whom Timon has generously redeemed from prison, is found 'base metal' (III. iii. 6). And Sempronius, hearing of the failure of other friends of Timon, whom he himself had suggested were more indebted than he, refuses at last angrily on the score of his hurt feelings at being the last to whom Timon sends. Flavius' description of his failure to raise a loan is powerful enough (II. ii. 214–23). All these incidents are clearly presented to indicate the meanness inherent in these specimens of humanity. The dice are heavily loaded. Our judgements have no choice. Neither the friends of Timon nor Apemantus can usurp our sympathy. The poet and painter—whatever they may be as artists—are also depicted as time-servers: towards the end of the play, when they come to Timon to gain his favour, their dialogue with each other exposes their clear hypocrisy. In addition, the short scene between Alcibiades and the Senate (III. v)[1] tends

---

[1] I believe the authenticity of this scene has been questioned. But it has some phrases in the finest Shakespearian idiom. Possibly the text is bad in places. One speech (ll. 24–37) is fairly obviously an instance of prose misprinted as verse. The scene reads rather like a piece of hurried and unrevised work.

further to enlist our dislike of the community in which Timon
lives. It suggests that Athens is suffering from an ingrateful
and effete generation, greedy and mean. Says Alcibiades:

> I have kept back their foes,
> While they have told their money and let out
> Their coin upon large interest, I myself
> Rich only in large hurts.   (III. v. 108)

This reference to the state's greed and the usury 'that
makes the senate ugly' (III. v. 101) serves to link the theme
of Alcibiades with that of Timon's friends. We know, too,
that Timon has put his fortune at the Senate's disposal. He
tells Flavius to go

> to the senators—
> Of whom, even to the state's best health, I have
> Deserv'd this hearing—bid 'em send o' the instant
> A thousand talents to me.   (II. ii. 206)

Later, when they need his help, they confess 'forgetfulness
too general, gross' (v. i. 149); and Alcibiades, speaking to
Timon, talks of

> . . . cursed Athens, mindless of thy worth,
> Forgetting thy great deeds, when neighbour states,
> But for thy sword and fortune, trod upon them . . .   (IV. iii. 93)

The theme of Alcibiades is close-woven with that of Timon,
and both endure ingratitude from the Senate, symbol of the
state of Athens. We feel, in fact, that Timon's personality
alone is responsible for any pleasure we have received in this
Athens. It is a state of greed and ingratitude. The fine flower
of civilization to which I have referred is evidently not in
itself existent here, but purely a projection of Timon's mind.
There are, however, certain persons who appear both good
and rational: all these emphasize Timon's nobility.

It is noticeable, indeed, that references to Timon's nobility
are continual throughout. We hear that he has 'a noble spirit'
(I. ii. 14); he is

> A most incomparable man, breath'd, as it were,
> To an untirable and continuate goodness.   (I. i. 10)

We hear of his 'good and gracious nature' (I. i. 57); his 'noble
nature' (II. ii. 218); his 'right noble mind' (III. ii. 88); that

'he outgoes the very heart of kindness' (I. i. 286) and that

> the noblest mind he carries
> That ever govern'd man.　　　　　　　　　　(I. i. 292)

Timon's words 'unwisely, not ignobly have I given' (II. ii. 184) hold finality. Such references are scattered throughout the play and their effect on us is powerful, even though they be sometimes spoken by insincerity. But the next group of persons to be noticed are evidently sincere: they are (i) the 'Strangers' who play a purely choric part, and (ii) Timon's Servants. It is to be observed that these, who alone express a balanced and rational view, all love and honour Timon, and remark on this instance of his betrayal as significant of a universal and fundamental human truth. I have noted that Timon is a universal lover: again we are directed to the universality of the theme here presented. Three Strangers, who have heard Lucius' refusal, comment thereon:

> *First Stranger.* Do you observe this, Hostilius?
> *Second Stranger.*　　　　　Ay, too well.
> *First Stranger.* Why, this is the world's soul; and just of the same piece
> 　　Is every flatterer's spirit. Who can call him
> 　　His friend that dips in the same dish? for, in
> 　　My knowing, Timon has been this lord's father,
> 　　And kept his credit with his purse,
> 　　Supported his estate; nay, Timon's money
> 　　Has paid his men their wages: he ne'er drinks,
> 　　But Timon's silver treads upon his lip;
> 　　And yet—O, see the monstrousness of man
> 　　When he looks out in an ungrateful shape!—
> 　　He does deny him, in respect of his,
> 　　What charitable men afford to beggars.
> *Third Stranger.* Religion groans at it.　　　　　(III. ii. 71)

The purpose and effect of this as expressing the meaning of the play's movement need no comment. It is the same with Timon's servants. Flaminius has discovered Lucullus' baseness, and thrown back the offered bribe. Lucullus leaves him and he soliloquizes:

> May these add to the number that may scald thee!
> Let molten coin be thy damnation,
> Thou disease of a friend, and not himself!
> Has friendship such a faint and milky heart,
> It turns in less than two nights? O you gods,

I feel my master's passion! this slave,
Unto his honour, has my lord's meat in him:
Why should it thrive and turn to nutriment,
When he is turn'd to poison?
O, may diseases only work upon't!
And, when he 's sick to death, let not that part of nature
Which my lord paid for, be of any power
To expel sickness, but prolong his hour! (III. i. 55)

This speech occurs when the action is working up to its tremendous climax, and embodies the tremor heralding eruption. Here civilization is beginning to assume a hideous guise, and man's form to appear as the painted outside to an inward filth. We feel the damming up of some mighty current, the impetuous and curbless love which is in Timon —and we are more than half aware of its awful impending release. This speech, and the similar one of the Servant at III. iii. 27–42, serve to direct our minds in sympathy toward the future hate of Timon. One only of his servants dares to criticize the master they all love: Flavius. His dialogue with Timon in Act II is supremely beautiful in the large-hearted simplicity and faith of master and servant:

> *Flavius.* Heavens, have I said, the bounty of this lord!
> How many prodigal bits have slaves and peasants
> This night englutted! Who is not Timon's?
> What heart, head, sword, force, means, but is Lord Timon's?
> Great Timon, noble, worthy, royal Timon!
> Ah, when the means are gone that buy this praise,
> The breath is gone whereof this praise is made:
> Feast-won, fast-lost; one cloud of winter showers,
> These flies are couch'd.
> *Timon.*   Come, sermon me no further:
> No villainous bounty yet hath pass'd my heart;
> Unwisely, not ignobly, have I given.
> Why dost thou weep? Canst thou the conscience lack,
> To think I shall lack friends? Secure thy heart;
> If I would broach the vessels of my love,
> And try the argument of hearts by borrowing,
> Men and men's fortunes could I frankly use
> As I can bid thee speak. (II. ii. 174)

Flavius, in his great love for Timon, throughout the play draws us too in faith to his master, even when his words most clearly limn his faults. And in soliloquy after Timon's retirement from Athens, his love wells up in a noble eulogy of his lord:

> Poor honest lord, brought low by his own heart,
> Undone by goodness! Strange, unusual blood,
> When man's worst sin is, he does too much good!
> Who, then, dares to be half so kind again?
> For bounty, that makes gods, does still mar men.
> My dearest lord, bless'd, to be most accurs'd,
> Rich, only to be wretched, thy great fortunes
> Are made thy chief afflictions.   (iv. ii. 37)

The intrinsic and absolute blamelessness of Timon's generosity is emphasized. Timon's 'fault' is essential love, essential nobility, unmixed with any restraining faculty of criticism. He is spontaneous in trust and generosity. 'Every man has his fault', says Lucullus, 'and honesty is his' (iii. i. 30). The heart's-gold of Timon is alloyed with no baser metal of intellect.

The faithfulness of Timon's Servants stands as a major theme in the drama. After the final failure, and Timon's retirement to the woods, they meet, not as servants to the same lord, but rather as disciples to a loved and world-crucified master. It is significant that, though cast adrift in poverty, it is the loss of their lord, and the iniquity of his friends, that grieve them most:

> *First Servant.*   Such a house broke!
> So noble a master fall'n! All gone! and not
> One friend to take his fortune by the arm,
> And go along with him!
> *Second Servant.*   As we do turn our backs
> From our companion thrown into his grave,
> So his familiars to his buried fortunes
> Slink all away, leave their false vows with him,
> Like empty purses pick'd; and his poor self,
> A dedicated beggar to the air,
> With his disease of all-shunn'd poverty,
> Walks, like contempt, alone.   (iv. ii. 5)

It is as though the spirit of Timon's former love and generosity has settled among them as an everlasting bond of love. We begin to know that we have been watching something more than the downfall of a noble gentleman:

> *Third Servant.* Yet do our hearts wear Timon's livery;
> That see I by our faces; we are fellows still,

Serving alike in sorrow: leak'd is our bark,
And we, poor mates, stand on the dying deck,
Hearing the surges threat: we must all part
Into this sea of air.
Flavius.   Good fellows all,
The latest of my wealth I'll share amongst you.
Wherever we shall meet, for Timon's sake,
Let's yet be fellows; let's shake our heads, and say,
As 'twere a knell unto our master's fortunes,
'We have seen better days'. Let each take some;
Nay, put out all your hands. Not one word more:
Thus part we rich in sorrow, parting poor.   (IV. ii. 17)

'Nay, put out all your hands'. . . . The still poetry of deepest
emotion, the grandest simplicity of the human soul, these
do not sound their noblest notes in this play till the pages
thereof are become 'rich in sorrow': and then they touch
a music, as in this speech, of a more wondrous simplicity and
a more mighty and heart-quelling beauty than anything in
King Lear or *Othello*. This, however, is to forestall. This
scene occurs after the shadow of eternity has overcast the
drama.

Enough has been said to indicate the nature of the technique that loads and all but overcharges the first part of this
play with a clear honour and love of Timon's generosity and
free-hearted soul; that indicts an overplus of humanity with
the uttermost degree of despisal; that leaves us in the naked
knowledge of the inevitable ignition and the dynamite of
passion that thunders, reverberates, and dies into silence
through the latter acts. The poet unfalteringly directs our
vision: to ignore the effect of these massed speeches condemning Timon's friends and all but deifying Timon is to
blur our understanding, to refuse the positive and single
statement of this the most masterfully deliberate of Shakespeare's sombre tragedies. Then shall we fail before the deep
music of the two final acts. But if yet more definite indication
be needed, it is to be found in the Poet's early speech, a
unique Shakespearian introduction to his own play:

I have, in this rough work, shaped out a man,
Whom this beneath world doth embrace and hug
With amplest entertainment . . .   (I. i. 44)

It is all there, a clear description of the play's theme. Even the peculiar universality is clearly noted, especially in the next lines:

> . . . my free drift
> Halts not particularly, but moves itself
> In a wide sea of wax: no levell'd malice
> Infects one comma in the course I hold;
> But flies an eagle flight, bold and forth on,
> Leaving no tract behind.   (I. i. 46)

This is manifestly not true of Shakespeare's Poet, who has composed his poem for Timon alone, but profoundly true of Shakespeare himself. Again:

> Sir, I have upon a high and pleasant hill
> Feign'd Fortune to be thron'd: the base o' the mount
> Is rank'd with all deserts, all kind of natures,
> That labour on the bosom of this sphere
> To propagate their states: amongst them all,
> Whose eyes are on this sovereign lady fix'd,
> One do I personate of Lord Timon's frame,
> Whom Fortune with her ivory hand wafts to her;
> Whose present grace to present slaves and servants
> Translates his rivals.   (I. i. 64)

The sequel is as the action of *Timon of Athens*. *Timon of Athens* is as a parable, or an allegory; its rush of power, its clean-limned and massive simplicity, its crystal and purposive technique—all these are blurred and distorted if we search for exact verisimilitude with the appearances of human life. It is sublimely unrealistic. But if we recognize its universal philosophic meaning, it is then apparent in all its profundity and masterly construction. We are here judging the chances of the spirit of perfected man to embrace Fortune and find love truly interfused in this 'beneath world': to build his soul's paradise on 'the bosom of this sphere'. Timon is the archetype and norm of all tragedy.

Now creditors swarm round Timon in his own hall, greedy for the gold which to Timon is alone rich as the symbol of the heart's blood and pulse of friendship:

> *Timon.* The place which I have feasted, does it now,
>   Like all mankind, show me an iron heart?   (III. iv. 84)

They press round him, insistent:

> *Timon.* Cut my heart in sums.
> *Titus.* Mine, fifty talents.

Timon. Tell out my blood.
Lucius' Servant. Five thousand crowns, my lord.
Timon. Five thousand drops pays that. What yours?—
 and yours?
First Varro's Servant. My lord,—
Second Varro's Servant. My lord,—
Timon. Tear me, take me, and the gods fall upon you!

(III. iv. 94)

This is all we see of the transition: when next Timon appears
the iron of enduring hate has entered his soul. True, he has
one more banquet; invites his friends to it; withholds his
rage till he has made one speech of withering scorn—then
volleys the titanic fury of his kingly nature in hate sovereign
as tremendous as his sovereign love. There is no tragic movement so swift, so clean-cut, so daring and so terrible in all
Shakespeare as this of Timon. We pity Lear, we dread for
Macbeth: but the awfulness of Timon, dwarfing pity and
out-topping sympathy, is as the grandeur and menace of the
naked rock of a sky-lifted mountain, whither we look and
tremble. Deserting Athens, he steps from time into eternity.
The world of humanity tilts over, and is reversed. We see
now, not with the vision of man, but henceforth with that
of the aspiring spirit of love that has scorned mankind for
ever. Timon will tolerate no disorder, within and without
his mind, like Lear, torn betwixt love and loathing, division
which is madness. The chaos which his imprecations are to
call on man will be as a concord within the soul of him
whose love is reversed, and who is no longer of this world.
Thus Timon preserves the grander harmony of loneliness
and universal loathing, and fronts his destiny, emperor still
in mind and soul, wearing the imperial nakedness of hate.
This unswerving majesty holds a grandeur beyond the barbaric fury of Othello, or the faltering ire of Lear. The heart's-
gold in Timon has seen the ingrateful and miserly greed
that would coin for use the infinity of a great soul's love.
So Timon leaves Athens.

His long curses are epics of hatred, unrestrained, limitless,
wild. The whole race of man is his theme. His love was ever
universal, now his hate is universal, its theme embraces every
grade, age, sex, and profession. He hates the very shape, the
'semblable' of man (IV. iii. 22). Timon's love, itself an infinity

of emotion, was first bodied into finite things; finite humanity, the sense-world of entertainment and art—and those symbols and sacraments of love: gifts. Of all these he was patron, friend, lover. Then he too, though gigantic in his love, was yet a confined, individualized, and lovable personality, like Othello. One knew him, a friend. But his love, itself infinite, has proved itself 'a slave to limit'[1]: generosity was dependent on the limits of wealth, his faith in man on the limitations of human gratitude. Unwise, no doubt—supreme love is unwise: an element of judgement would borrow something of its rich worth. The poet has shown us a supreme love, dissociated from other qualities, and this love, trusting finite symbols of itself, has failed disastrously. It now appears as a naked force, undirected towards any outward manifestations, diffused and bodiless, no longer fitted to the finite, a thing inhuman, unnatural, and infinite. Timon, naked and fierce-eyed, is no longer personal, no longer one of mankind. He is pure passion, a naked rhythmic force, a rush and whirl of torrential energy loosed from any contact or harmony with temporal and confining limits, a passion which

> . . . like the current flies
> Each bound it chafes.   (I. i. 23)

There is thus less imaginative unity in *Timon of Athens*: rather a strongly marked duality. The latter part of the play is contrasted with and related logically to the beginning. In *Hamlet* we see the tragic superman incongruously set in a normal social unit and working chaos therein; in *Macbeth* and *King Lear*, he is given a world of the same nature as himself, a single visionary universe woven in the pattern of imagination's truth. Here there is a curious time-sequence. The hero is first a resplendent man among men, superhuman,

---

[1] 'This is the monstruosity in love, lady, that the will is infinite and the execution confined, that the desire is boundless and the act a slave to limit.' (*Troilus and Cressida*, III. ii. 85); the typical Shakespearian thought that the infinity of love is in conflict with actuality, or the reflection of actuality in the mind, intellect. Hence the thought, a little further on, expressed by Cressida:
> . . . to be wise and love
> Exceeds man's might; that dwells with gods above.   (163)
With which we might compare *Timon of Athens*, IV. ii. 41: '. . . bounty, that makes gods, does still mar men'. Troilus tries unsuccessfully to enclose love's mystery in his mind, Timon to embody it in acts.

perhaps, but not inhuman: now he becomes inhuman. We need not question Timon's Athens: save for Timon himself, prince-hearted and lord of love, it is the world we know, first sensuous and attractive, then trivial, poor-spirited, dishonest. Timon alone, with his shadow Apemantus, is in his latter hate of the anti-social and wayward nature of Hamlet and Lear. In *Timon of Athens* we are given a logical exposition of the significance of earlier plays. The hero's passion is clearly juxtaposed and related logically to a normal human society. The play is in two firmly contrasted parts. During the second our universe changes with the change in Timon, and after the brilliance of Athens the shadow of an infinite gloom broods over the desert solitudes where Timon communes with his hate. Mankind are then dim spectres only, and Timon's passion alone reality. The nature of that passion demands further attention.

The contrast between the first and the second parts is clearly a contrast of the sense-world and the finite with the spiritual and the infinite. Timon's hate expresses itself in aversion from all kinds of moral wholeness and physical health—that is, with all finite forms. They have been proved false coin. Hence he declaims disease, vice, confusion on men:

> Son of sixteen,
> Pluck the lined crutch from thy old limping sire,
> With it beat out his brains! Piety, and fear,
> Religion to the gods, peace, justice, truth,
> Domestic awe, night-rest, and neighbourhood,
> Instruction, manners, mysteries, and trades,
> Degrees, observances, customs, and laws,
> Decline to your confounding contraries,
> And let confusion live! Plagues incident to men,
> Your potent and infectious fevers heap
> On Athens, ripe for stroke!   (IV. i. 13)

So, too, he repeatedly prays Phrynia and Timandra to spread disgusting disease among men, and Alcibiades to paint the ground with man's blood (IV. iii). There is no hideous crime or ghoulish dishonour or ravaging disease that Timon would not imprecate passionately on his race. His former world of health and pleasure has been destroyed by one thing: the exposure of the rottenness of its love. That love-dream killed, his eyes are opened to all forms of human frailty, moral, physical, social. This movement suggests that the loss of love alone is responsible for all the ills that flesh endures: mankind without love he would wish to disintegrate, to rot. Any form of human organism or political or social order incites his hate, and he calls down wholesale disintegration on mankind. Only by remembering his former pleasures taken in finite and sensible symbols of love, can we see the unity of his curses: he is violently antagonized by human health, bodily or social. No finite thing in humanity escapes his hate. Hence his curses against the moral order: since morality is a spiritual essence satisfactorily bodied into finitude and actuality. The infinity of his passion can now tolerate no such cramping or channelling of itself, and all finite forms are anathema. But there is more than negative logic in his philosophy. Timon's original force of soul is ultimate. First infused into love of man, thence driven, it expresses itself, first in a positive and passionate aversion from all finite forms—that is, he must love or hate. Second, we have clear signs of the reality toward which this primary energy is directing him: the infinite and ineffable to which he is bound. There is a swift movement toward infinity. From the gold-haze of the mystic dream of a universal love on earth have emerged stark contours of base ingratitude: then the outward world of man and its shapes swiftly vanishes, and the inward world of infinite spirit takes its place, first expressing its nature by aversion from the other mode of life, then turning towards all that is vast, inhuman, illimitable, void.

The course is direct. There is no tragic conflict, and therefore no dramatic tempest-symbolism occurs to heighten our imagination of storm and stress: Timon's curses will not ring weak. Nor is there any divagation from his inhuman quest. In the concluding scenes we are aware of two modes in the utterance of Timon: passionate hate, and a solitary contemplation of the infinite, the two interfused or alternate; and of three orders of dramatic persons—(i) pale ghosts of mankind, linking us to the world we have left; (ii) Timon; and (iii) a wild ocean, a breadth of nature, the great earth and its sun and moon, agents interacting in a cosmic drama mightier than man's puppet-play, yet finally dwarfed too by the grander soul of Timon, unsatiated in thought by the farthest limits of the material universe. I shall therefore note shortly, first, the visits of Apemantus and Flavius to Timon, and next, the poetic suggestion—contrasted strongly with the early sensuous and finite appeal—of these latter acts: the vast symbols, the far-flung imaginations. In these scenes the Shakespearian poetry takes on a mighty and compulsive rhythm, a throb and pulse unknown in other plays. As Timon severs all contact with the finite world and, like some majestic liner, cleaves the dark seas of infinity, we voyage too, put off from land on the big loom of that leviathan, to leave safe coasts and plough forward into the unknown, bosomed on the swell and heave of ocean, by the lode-star of a titanic love.

Apemantus comes to Timon, the philospher of hate to the prophet of hate. The incident points the difference between them, and is important. Apemantus first advises Timon to return to mankind, to turn flatterer himself. He points out that this life of hardship serves no purpose of revenge, and that nature will be no less cruel than men. Will the bleak air, the trees, the creatures hardened in nature's battle with a cruel heaven, come to Timon's bidding, and flatter? Timon angrily bids him depart. Apemantus shows signs of desiring friendship:

Apemantus. I love thee better now than e'er I did.
Timon. I hate thee worse.
Apemantus.　　　　Why?
Timon.　　　　Thou flatter'st misery.　　　　(IV. iii. 234)

Which turns a shaft of light inward on Apemantus' meanness. Timon reveals him to himself as a flatterer like the rest: a man to whom loathing is an enjoyment, not a terrible destiny; who comes to receive the bounty of Timon's hate as others to receive of his wealth; who was now hoping to join Timon in a dilettante festival of cynicism. Hence Apemantus is lashed into anger and spite—then, recovering himself, he defends his philosophy as compared with Timon's passion. He points out that to adopt the hard life which Timon has embraced from a considered philosophy would be well enough, but that Timon does it 'enforcedly'. His own, however, is a 'willing misery', which 'outlives incertain

pomp' (IV. iii. 243), and is thus the highest good, since
contented poverty is richer than the wealthiest discontent.
If Timon's misery is unwilling, there is nothing for him but
death. Apemantus states the case with an admirable logic.
Timon answers that Apemantus' philosophy is born of the
marriage of poverty and a mean spirit. Had he been favour-
ably placed by fortune, he would have lived luxuriously and
in vice—have 'melted down' his youth with lust: but,
having been 'bred a dog', he has evolved a philosophy out
of envy. Apemantus has no cause to hate, since he has not
been flattered and deceived. But with Timon, once the
centre of man's supposed love, it is different:

> But myself,
> Who had the world as my confectionary,
> The mouths, the tongues, the eyes and hearts of men
> At duty, more than I could frame employment,
> That numberless upon me stuck as leaves
> Do on the oak, have with one winter's brush
> Fell from their boughs and left me open, bare
> For every storm that blows.   (IV. iii. 260)

If Apemantus had not been born 'the worst of men', he too
would have been knave and flatterer. Timon, too, speaks
truth. Apemantus and Timon hate with a difference: one,
because he is less than mankind—the other because he
is greater. Hence Timon is particularly disgusted with
Apemantus, who apes, and enjoys, the bitter passion of
his own enduring soul.

This dialogue is most important for our understanding
of the essential meaning of the play. The two hates are
juxtaposed. Apemantus upholds the worth of his as a thing
of judgement, systematized into a way of life. To Timon that
is abhorrent, and witnesses a gross nature. Now Apemantus
is right when he tells Timon that death is the only hope
left for him. Apemantus has scorned humanity, but lives
on with them, feeding his scorn; he continues 'vexing'
men, which is, says Timon, 'a villain's office or a fool's'
(IV. iii. 238); and he enjoys doing it, which proves him a
'knave' (IV. iii. 239). Apemantus has hated life, yet loves to
live. But for Timon, who has uncompromisingly broken
from mankind, and whose sweeping condemnation includes

not only humanity and the beasts of nature (iv. iii. 329) but even sun and moon (iv. iii. 442): for Timon there is, as Apemantus points out, only death. Apemantus confesses that the universal destruction he would like to see he would yet postpone till after he himself is dead (iv. iii. 396); and Timon's final curse on Apemantus is to fling back on him his own command to Timon: 'Live and love thy misery' (iv. iii. 398); that is, continue to be Apemantus—than which there is no bitterer imprecation. From these considerations the difficulties of this dialogue will be made clear. Timon's especial loathing and Apemantus' vulgar rage are both inevitable. Apemantus sees himself in his meanness, as a creature less than those he has loved to despise. But Timon is weary of curses. He turns away and speaks to himself:

> I am sick of this false world, and will love nought
> But even the mere necessities upon't.
> Then, Timon, presently prepare thy grave;
> Lie where the light foam of the sea may beat
> Thy grave-stone daily. (iv. iii. 378)

In the other visit to be noticed, Timon's hate is pitted against something of a very different kind. Flavius, Timon's steward, comes to remind us of the reality of faithfulness and love. Yet even here Timon loses no jot of grandeur. At first he refuses to see, then to recognize, his faithful servant. Finally, he is forced to realize that in simple love his steward is again offering his service to the ruin of his old master:

> Had I a steward
> So true, so just, and now so comfortable?
> It almost turns my dangerous nature mild.
> Let me behold thy face. Surely, this man
> Was born of woman.
> Forgive my general and exceptless rashness,
> You perpetual-sober gods! I do proclaim
> One honest man—mistake me not—but one;
> No more, I pray—and he's a steward.
> How fain would I have hated all mankind!
> And thou redeem'st thyself: but all, save thee,
> I fell with curses. (iv. iii. 499)

The beauty of this incident is the beauty of a blade of grass beneath the architrave of a cathedral. The finite virtue of simple humanity is asserting its right to stand within the vaulted silences of the eternal which scorns all limit, all failure. Timon stays for a moment his onward passionate adventure, pauses to proclaim one honest man: though the edifice of his creed of hate be a mighty thing, the blade of grass, rooted in the strength of a mightier, splits one stone of the foundation. But Timon, with an afterthought, suspects Flavius of mean motives. Reassured, he shows him his gold, and gives him wealth with the terrible injunction that he, too, is to hate mankind:

> Look thee, 'tis so! Thou singly honest man,
> Here, take: the gods out of my misery
> Have sent thee treasure. Go, live rich and happy;
> But thus condition'd: thou shalt build from men;
> Hate all, curse all, show charity to none,
> But let the famish'd flesh slide from the bone,
> Ere thou relieve the beggar; give to dogs
> What thou deny'st to men; let prisons swallow 'em,
> Debts wither 'em to nothing; be men like blasted woods,
> And may diseases lick up their false bloods!
> And so farewell and thrive.   (IV. iii. 532)

Timon is again left alone in his solitary pride of soul. He lives in a cave 'near the sea-shore'. He is now a naked son of earth, and speaks to the Bandits a solemn knowledge of nature's kinship with man's wants:

> Why should you want? Behold, the earth hath roots;
> Within this mile break forth a hundred springs;
> The oaks bear mast, the briers scarlet hips;
> The bounteous housewife, nature, on each bush
> Lays her full mess before you. Want! Why want?
>
> (IV. iii. 423)

He, who aspires only to the infinite, chafes at the limitations of the physical, and yet again finds solace in thought of the earth's vastness, in one of those grand undertones of harmony that characterize the tremendous orchestration of this play:

> That nature, being sick of man's unkindness
> Should yet be hungry! Common mother, thou
> Whose womb unmeasurable and infinite breast
> Teems, and feeds all; whose self-same mettle,
> Whereof thy proud child, arrogant man, is puff'd,
> Engenders the black toad and adder blue,
> The gilded newt and eyeless venom'd worm,

With all the abhorred births below crisp heaven
Whereon Hyperion's quickening fire doth shine;
Yield him, who all thy human sons doth hate,
From forth thy plenteous bosom, one poor root!

(IV. iii. 177)

His thoughts are already set beyond the world of man, in the silence of eternity: yet he is not himself beyond the world of nature, he is, incongruously, hungry. As in this speech, Timon's utterance is often addressed with a deep recognition and intimacy toward the vast forces, the stillness, the immensities of nature, clear springs which the intellect of man has muddied. These are innocent, they wake responses in him. He addresses sun and earth as his co-equals, peers of his unsatiated and universal soul:

O blessed breeding sun, draw from the earth
Rotten humidity; below thy sister's orb
Infect the air!   (IV. iii. 1)

'Thou sun, that comfort'st, burn!' he cries (v. i. 136); and, at the end, 'Sun, hide thy beams! Timon hath done his reign' (v. i. 228).

We are nevertheless reminded that these vast forces are yet not friends of Timon: not with them will he find any but a temporary purge and solace to his pain. Says Apemantus:

What, think'st
That the bleak air, thy boisterous chamberlain,
Will put thy shirt on warm? will these moss'd trees,
That have outliv'd the eagle, page thy heels,
And skip where thou point'st out? will the cold brook,
Candied with ice, caudle thy morning taste,
To cure thy o'er-night's surfeit? Call the creatures
Whose naked natures live in all the spite
Of wreakful heaven, whose bare unhoused trunks,
To the conflicting elements expos'd,
Answer mere nature; bid them flatter thee . . .   (IV. iii. 222)

Timon also expresses the thought that the animal-kingdom is no better than man's civilization—as ruthless as human nature, as devouring and cruel. He catalogues the beasts in the speech commencing:

. . . If thou wert the lion, the fox would beguile thee: if thou wert the
lamb, the fox would eat thee . . .   (IV. iii. 330)

He knows that sun and moon and sea and earth live, like men, by perpetual interaction, thieving, and absorption; that if he attributes personality to nature, his curses must be levelled against earth and sky, his indictment must include the whole cosmic mechanism:

> *Alcibiades.* How came the noble Timon to this change?
> *Timon.* As the moon does, by wanting light to give:
> But then renew I could not, like the moon;
> There were no suns to borrow of.   (IV. iii. 66)

Or again,

> The sun 's a thief, and with his great attraction
> Robs the vast sea; the moon 's an arrant thief,
> And her pale fire she snatches from the sun;
> The sea 's a thief, whose liquid surge resolves
> The moon into salt tears; the earth 's a thief,
> That feeds and breeds by a composture stolen
> From general excrement.   (IV. iii. 442)

This sweep of the fanciful imagination is profound: it involves the knowledge that the meanest of man's vices owes its viciousness to man's moral ascension. Timon cannot impose the laws of his generous soul on the unthinking mechanism of the universal scheme. Not on the breast of nature, nor in contemplation of the solar fire mated to earth or sea, can he find that to which he moves. He ranges the planetary spaces of the night and finds no home: nowhere but within the spaceless silence of the deeper night of death will he be at peace. He is thus retrogressing swiftly through the modes of being. They are, in order: chaos, or the primal night; the stellar, mundane, natural and human worlds; culminating in man's civilization. Here, starting in the first scene with the four symbolic figures of civilization, we fall back swiftly on nature, earth, sun and the ultimate void of that infinity, undisciplined to form, whose only symbol can be some suggestion of formlessness, immensity, chaos; whose favourite symbol in Shakespeare is always the sea. Timon knows the end to which he aspires. It is so clear—so implicit in the whole allegorical movement—that no cause of death is given or needed:

> Then, Timon, presently prepare thy grave;
> Lie where the light foam of the sea may beat
> Thy grave-stone daily.   (IV. iii. 380)

And:

> Come not to me again: but say to Athens,
> Timon hath made his everlasting mansion
> Upon the beached verge of the salt flood;
> Who once a day with his embossed froth
> The turbulent surge shall cover: thither come,
> And let my grave-stone be your oracle.   (v. i. 219)

The void of death, darkness; the Shakespearian 'nothing' which brings Timon 'all things' (v. i. 193). The dark sea which is infinite formlessness, infinite depth, the surge and swell within the soul of man, the deeps beyond intellect, or sight, or sound. It is this surge that has throbbed within the poetry of tremendous symbols, this tide of emotion that breaks and sobs in Timon's passion when, his active hate subdued, he speaks the language of a soul beyond the world of manifestation and tuned to its own solitary music; the psalmody of earth and sun and the wide sea of eternal darkness beating on the rocks of creation.

We are given no chance to sentimentalize Timon's hate. Its nobility derives solely from its utter reversal of love. It is thus not a spiritual atrophy, a negation, a cold vacuum of the soul, like the pain of Hamlet, but a dynamic and positive force, possessing purpose and direction. Therefore, though impelled to its inevitable death-climax, the tragic movement of this play leaves us with no sense of the termination of the essential Timon: its impact on the imagination is rather that of a continuation, circling within and beyond the mysterious nothing of dissolution, in a new dimension congruous with the power and the passion which have forced him toward death. The especial reality of Timon is this of powerful, torrential movement to freedom: which freedom from all that we call 'life' is so necessary and excellent a consummation to the power and the direction of Timon's passion, that it can in no sense be imagined as a barrier or stoppage. It is rather as though the rushing torrent, so long chafed by the limits of its channel, breaks out into the wide smoothness of the living sea. The death-theme in *Timon of Athens* is of the greatest importance, the crowning majesty of the play's movement. Timon speaks to the Senators:

> Why, I was writing of my epitaph;
> It will be seen to-morrow: my long sickness
> Of health and living now begins to mend,
> And nothing brings me all things.   (v. i. 190)

The nothingness of death becomes 'all things' to Timon who passionately desires that 'nothing'. No conceivable symbol of desire will now serve that love, therefore in desiring death it desires nothing but its own unsatiable love: there it will, as it were, turn back within its own richness. Timon, embracing this ineffable darkness with joy, is already outside himself, viewing his own tragedy, as we do, with objective delight. And so he looks toward death, and imagines his end, and sees it, as we do, to be good—to hold the gift of 'all things'. Consciousness that derives joy from the death of consciousness is already, as we who watch, outside the dying and the death. It is but another aspect of the living power of Timon, the vivid, dynamic, swift force of passion which is in him: the heat of it unsatiated by the mode called 'life' has been excruciating, an expanding, explosive essence prisoned, and in death it will burn the enhampering body to fling backward its invisible brilliance in the illumination of 'all things'. 'Health and living' have been to Timon as a 'long sickness'. In so far as we have been aware of this reversal of significance during the action, we shall know that we have long walked with Timon in death. Life and death have interchanged their meaning for him, and he now utters that paradox which is at the heart of all tragedy.

Therefore the grand death-speeches at the close come not as a super-added adornment, a palliative, but rather as a necessary and expected continuation, consummation, satisfaction. They are not to be analysed as solitary units of philosophic utterance, but as living thought precipitated by the momentum of the tragic theme as a whole, gaining their impact from the force that has driven Timon from ease and luxury to nakedness among the naked beasts and trees and planets of the night, and beyond these to the unbodied and immortal nakedness of death. We have watched a swift unwrapping of fold on fold of life's significances—civilized man, beasts, the earth, the objective universe itself, till we reach the core of pure and naked significance, undistorted by any symbol, in the nothingness of death. Yet at every step in Timon's history we have been aware, not of a lessening, but of an increase of his grandeur; that is, at every stripping of the soul of Timon we have known that what was taken is but another rag, what remains, the essence, the reality. For Timon, at the end, is pure essence of significance, beyond the temporal, in touch with a conquering knowledge of his furthest destiny. Nothing will be proved the largesse of all things. So he cries:

> Graves only be men's works and death their gain!
> Sun, hide thy beams! Timon hath done his reign.   (v. i. 227)

Again is emphasized the completeness with which Timon's love is reversed. It is not alone a turning away from mankind: rather a passionate turning inward from all forms and shapes of actuality, all manifestation, from the cosmic scheme. He would wish the race to die out, the sun blackened, the glass of time exhausted. Only the rhythm of the tireless beat of waves, the crash and the whispering retraction, these alone signify some fore-echoing of the thing which is to receive Timon. This is only the last step, into the cold night of death, of the movement we have been watching all along. It is truly spoken that

> Timon is dead, who hath outstretch'd his span.   (v. iii. 3)

His hate of man was ever but one aspect, or expression, of the turning inward of his soul toward death, and since he flung back titanic curse on Athens, his being has been centred not in time but throughout the otherness of eternity.

Yet there is one symbol that persists throughout both parts of the play and this has important meaning: gold. Gold-symbolism is throughout recurrent, and impressions of gold and riches are woven close within the texture of thought and emotion. Timon's nature is essentially one of richness. Everyone is amazed, from the start, at the richness of his personality and the generosity and wealth in which it manifests itself. Instances of this are frequent: I have quoted some. Men are 'rich in Timon's nod' (i. i. 63); 'Plutus, the god of gold, is but his steward' (i. i. 288). Throughout the play richness of heart and actual gold are associated or con-

trasted. A jewel is made more valuable by Timon's wearing
it (I. i. 173). In wasting Timon's riches, his flatterers 'dip
their meat' in his 'blood' (I. ii. 42). At the pivotal moment
of the play (III. iv.), Timon cries, 'Tell out my blood!' They
'cut' his heart 'in sums'. 'Five thousand drops' of his heart's
blood will pay his debt of five thousand crowns. The contrast
is ever between gold and the heart's blood of passionate love
of which it is a sacrament: the association, of the metaphoric
value of gold and the value of love; or conversely, of hardness
and the callousness of ingratitude—mankind is 'flinty', of an
'iron heart', to Timon, since these are metals possessing
hardness without value. His flatterers prove 'base metal'
(III. iii. 6). The 'hearts' of Timon's servants wear his 'livery'
(IV. ii. 17), though payment and outward shows are at an
end; and Flavius, 'whilst he has gold', will serve Timon's
'mind' (IV. ii. 50). These ideas are deeply embedded throughout. Now the gold-symbolism continued into the last two
acts serves a double purpose. First, it remains to Timon a
symbol of mankind's greed:

> Earth, yield me roots!
> Who seeks for better of thee, sauce his palate
> With thy most operant poison! What is here?
> Gold? yellow, glittering, precious gold? No, gods,
> I am no idle votarist: roots, you clear heavens!
> Thus much of this will make black white, foul fair,
> Wrong right, base noble, old young, coward valiant.
> Ha, you gods! why this? what this, you gods? Why, this
> Will lug your priests and servants from your sides,
> Pluck stout men's pillows from below their heads:
> This yellow slave
> Will knit and break religions, bless the accurs'd,
> Make the hoar leprosy ador'd, place thieves
> And give them title, knee and approbation
> With senators on the bench . . .   (IV. iii. 23)

Second, it draws men to him as of old, and suggests the
continued richness and nobility of his nature, the native
aristocracy of his heart. Even in hate he reacts on man for
good, not ill. The Bandit speaks:

> He has almost charmed me from my profession, by persuading me
> to it.   (IV. iii. 457)

He is still a prince among men, the desired of men, a fate he
cannot escape. The 'yellow, glittering, precious gold' which

he finds endues him still with superiority and power and enables him to aid the army levied against Athens, thus constituting an important link between the hate of Timon and the avenging ardour of Alcibiades.

Timon, in love or hate, bears truly a heart of gold. He is a being apart, a choice soul crucified. He has a mind 'unmatched' (iv. iii. 525). He is one

Whose star-like nobleness gave life and influence   (v. i. 68)

to the world that has driven him without its walls. Sun-like he used to 'shine' on men (iii. iv. 10). The issues for which a Timon contends are the issues not of Athens but of humanity. He is a principle of the human soul, a possibility, a symbol of mankind's aspiration. His servants know that his loss is as the loss of a golden age. A bright spirit has been on earth, spirit of infinite and rich love and bounty, and its wings have been soiled by mortality. Timon, who 'flashed a phoenix', is left a 'naked gull' (ii. i. 31). The elected of the heavens has been scorned of man. So the poetry of this play is large and deep, immeasurably grand, and pregnant of human fate. When Timon lifts his voice to Heaven proclaiming 'one honest man' (iv. iii. 506), his words hold an echo no less universal than Abraham's prayer to Jehovah to spare the iniquitous city, if ten just men be found therein; when Timon's servants part to wander abroad separated, they are as disciples of the Christ meeting after the crucifixion.[1] Of these thoughts the poetry is indeed most worthy. It is loaded with a massive, compulsive emotion, in comparison with which the words of Hamlet, Troilus, Othello, and even Lear, are as the plaintive accents of children. A mighty rhythm of a race's longing, of human destiny unalterable and uncomplained, sounds through the whole play, and wakes an unearthly majesty of words in the symphonic harmonies of the final acts. There is no turning aside, no

---

[1] The analogy is obvious and suggested by other passages. We have:
  There's much example for 't; the fellow that sits next him now, parts bread with him,
  pledges the breath of him in a divided draught, is the readiest man to kill him: 't has
  been proved.   (i. ii. 48)
and   Who can call him
  His friend that dips in the same dish?   (iii. ii. 73)
Another New Testament reference occurs at iv. iii. 475-6.

regret in all the passion of Timon, but it

> flies an eagle flight, bold and forth on,
> Leaving no tract behind—   (I. i. 50)

until, in the poetry of the latter half of the play, the mind
is a-voyage on unfathomed and uncharted seas, whose solid
deeps of passion but wanly and waveringly reflect the vastest
images that man can dream. In this recurrent solemnity of
utterance more grand for its massive and fathomless simplicity, we joy in that we listen not to the accents of mortality
but to those of the spirit of a race. Therefore, though Flavius
saves mankind from utter condemnation by one act of faith,
we know that the organ notes of implacable hatred cannot
so be stilled, since by them alone the soul of Timon pursues
its course. He is no 'idle votarist' (IV. iii. 27):

> Hate all, curse all, show charity to none.   (IV. iii. 534)

The profoundest problems of racial destiny are here symbolized and fought out. In no other play is a more forceful, a more irresistible, mastery of technique—almost crude
in its massive, architectural effects—employed. But then no
play is so massive, so rough-hewn into Atlantean shapes
from the mountain rock of the poet's mind or soul, as this
of Timon. 'I have in this rough work shap'd out a man . . .'
It is true. No technical scaffolding in Shakespeare has to
stand so weighty and shattering a stress. For this play is
Hamlet, Troilus and Cressida, Othello, King Lear, become
self-conscious and universal; it includes and transcends them
all; it is the recurrent and tormenting hate-theme of Shakespeare, developed, raised to an infinite power, presented in
all its tyrannic strength and profundity, and—killed. Three
acts form the prologue. Our vision thus with infinite care and
every possible device focused, we await the onrush of a
passion which sums in its torrential energy all the lesser
passions of those protagonists foregone. Timon is the
totality of all, his love more rich and oceanic than all of theirs,
all lift their lonely voices in his universal curse. Christ-
like, he suffers that their pain may cease, and leaves the
Shakespearian universe redeemed that Cleopatra may win
her Antony in death, and Thaisa be restored to Pericles.

The individual soul has been scorned by the community.

But the fault is not venial to the heavenly justice. Alcibiades, too, has been banished. A man of blood and war (I. ii. 79–83), strong-handed, with an army at his command, he comes on Athens, accusing. He is youth and strength armed against old age, dotage, greed. This is clearly pointed in many passages (III. v. 95–116; v. iii. 8; v. iv. 13). He is the new generation coming on the old, effacing a worn-out and effete civilization, bringing retribution for its crimes, restoring harmony and health:

> Sound to this coward and lascivious town
> Our terrible approach.
> *Enter Senators on the walls.*
> Till now you have gone on and fill'd the time
> With all licentious measure, making your wills
> The scope of justice; till now myself and such
> As slept within the shadow of your power
> Have wander'd with our travers'd arms and breath'd
> Our sufferance vainly: now the time is flush,
> When crouching marrow in the bearer strong
> Cries of itself 'No more': now breathless wrong
> Shall sit and pant in your great chairs of ease,
> And pursy insolence shall break his wind
> With fear and horrid flight.   (v. iv. 1)

The crime of Athens is this: they have preferred the gold of coins to the gold of love. They have slaughtered love: Timon is dead. Him, who was civilization's perfected flower, their civilization has ruthlessly slain. Too late, the terror-struck Senators sent legates to the naked Timon of the woods, imploring forgiveness and aid. They 'entreat him back to Athens' (v. i. 146). Let him come back and forgive and all will be well. For he is a soul greater than the warrior Alcibiades, and can match a nobler strength and a more beautiful, against the enemies of Athens. Once before his 'sword and fortune' (IV. iii. 95) saved ingrateful Athens from her foes, but now Alcibiades' purpose is 'in part for his sake moved' (v. ii. 13): they know that he is the symbol of their sin, that he alone has called down divine wrath on their city. The rich gold of Timon's heart has equipped and paid Alcibiades' soldiers, Timon's curse has breathed immortal fire into his army, and set Heaven's lightning on his sword:

Be as a planetary plague, when Jove
Will o'er some high-viced city hang his poison
In the sick air.   (iv. iii. 109)

Alcibiades fights invulnerable in the immortal armour of
a Timon's curse; and when the Senate know Timon to be
dead, they cast themselves on Alcibiades' mercy:

First Senator.   Noble and young,
When thy first griefs were but a mere conceit,
Ere thou hadst power or we had cause of fear,
We sent to thee, to give thy rages balm,
To wipe out our ingratitude with loves
Above their quantity.
Second Senator.   So did we woo
Transformed Timon to our city's love
By humble message and by promis'd means:
We were not all unkind, nor all deserve
The common stroke of war.   (v. iv. 13)

They claim that those who committed these wrongs are
dead; that Athens, its buildings, customs, institutions, long
planted in past centuries, ought not to suffer for one
iniquitous generation. Time is old since Alcibiades and
Timon left Athens.

Alcibiades grants their prayer, moves down to them. He
assumes dictatorship as Heaven's minister on earth, to right
the balance of a civilization grown effete in idle prosperity.
We are brought to the knowledge that humanity progresses
by conflict alone, and that too much prosperity, though it
make one Timon, yet kills a state. Alcibiades is the stern
and merciful bearer of the heavenly command, who alone,
at this moment, has the sovereign right to speak of Timon's
faults. A soldier shows him Timon's epitaph:

Alcibiades. These well express in thee thy latter spirits:
Though thou abhorr'dst in us our human griefs,
Scorn'dst our brain's flow and those our droplets which
From niggard nature fall, yet rich conceit
Taught thee to make vast Neptune weep for aye
On thy low grave, on faults forgiven. Dead
Is noble Timon: of whose memory
Hereafter more.   (v. iv. 74)

An infinite, undying grief, for that lost infinity of love. But
Timon has refused the limitations of man. He has hungered

for infinity and scorned all that is partial, ephemeral, limited in space, time, or any ethical code. These, his faults, are passed. Though throughout the play we have been forced to centre all our sympathies on Timon, at this last moment, when, as is customary in Shakespeare, the individual tragedy is thrown into relation with the ebb and flow of generation on generation, and human time rolls on, we see the two parts of this play, the shapes of the finite and the phantoms of the infinite, as complementary aspects of the eternal and ever-present interaction in which are both man and God. Therefore Alcibiades knows that Timon's quenchless thirst of absolute love on earth is a 'fault', that neither man, nor his civilization, nor perhaps his God, are creatures alone of good or of evil, but find their being in the constant interplay of both, the dissolution and the rebuilding, war and peace, the rebirth of the new from broken shards of the old:

> Bring me into your city,
> And I will use the olive with my sword,
> Make war breed peace, make peace stint war, make each
> Prescribe to other as each other's leech.
> Let our drums strike. (v. iv. 81)

The earthly paradise is a delusion, and Timon's kingdom, if indeed it be existent, is not of this world.

ADDITIONAL NOTE (1947–8)

Since writing this I have produced and acted in *Timon of Athens*, and plan to do so again (December, 1948); and have also developed my general reading of it for other purposes. Such experiences, including in particular the visualization of its two parts in terms of Nietzsche's Apollonian and Dionysian principles, together with a comparison of Timon with both Byron's Sardanapalus and Nietzsche's 'superman', have increased my respect for this central work. I do not, of course, deny certain roughnesses due probably—as my original note on p. 214 suggests—to lack of revision: and for a careful discussion of this particular problem, see Prof. Una Ellis-Fermor's article in the *Review of English Studies*, July 1942; also Prof. Peter Alexander's *Shakespeare: his Life and Art* (1938).

Timon is always well *above* his own curses. His attitude to Alcibiades' warring is ironic (IV. iii. 105; v. i. 179, 194) and his most violent accents charged internally with the love and pity which he scorns (as at IV. iii. 112–27; 536–8; v. i. 176–8). His force is the more frightening for being the scorn (v. iv. 75–7) of a superhuman virtue.

1974: See my *Christ and Nietzsche* (1948) and p. ix above. Also my forthcoming study, *Shakespeare's Dramatic Challenge*.

XI

SHAKESPEARE AND TOLSTOY

IN this essay I attempt to show how a comparison with Tolstoy, who, with Goethe, is of all modern writers most nearly comparable with Shakespeare, reveals a striking similarity of spiritual experience. I shall draw upon *The Varieties of Religious Experience* (Longmans, Green & Co., 1925; originally 1902) for my facts concerning Tolstoy. William James writes:

> In Tolstoy's case the sense that life had any meaning whatever was for a time wholly withdrawn. The result was a transformation in the whole expression of reality. When we come to study the phenomenon of conversion or religious regeneration, we shall see that a not infrequent consequence of the change operated in the subject is a transfiguration of the face of nature in his eyes. A new heaven seems to shine upon a new earth. In melancholiacs there is usually a similar change, only it is in the reverse direction. The world now looks remote, strange, sinister, uncanny. Its colour is gone, its breath is cold, there is no speculation in the eyes it glares with. (p. 151.)

A quotation from *Hamlet* would really be more apposite here than this from *Macbeth*. This passage, and others from the chapter entitled 'The Sick Soul', inevitably recall Hamlet's:

> I have of late—but wherefore I know not—lost all my mirth, foregone all custom of exercises; and indeed it goes so heavily with my disposition that this goodly frame, the earth, seems to me a sterile promontory; this most excellent canopy, the air, look you, this brave o'erhanging firmament, this majestical roof fretted with golden fire, why, it appears no other thing to me than a foul and pestilent congregation of vapours. (II. ii. 313)

Hamlet inaugurates the period of pained thought in the sequence of Shakespeare's plays. It is an embodiment, in terms of drama, of exactly that state which William James calls 'The Sick Soul'. Now Sir Sidney Lee in his *Life of William Shakespeare* has an interesting passage with reference to the cause of the shadow that overcasts Shakespeare's work at this period:

> A popular theory presumes that Shakespeare's decade of tragedy was the outcome of some spiritual calamity, of some episode of tragic gloom in his private life. No tangible evidence supports the allegation. The

external facts of Shakespeare's biography through the main epoch of his tragic energy show an unbroken progress of prosperity, a final farewell to pecuniary anxieties, and the general recognition of his towering genius by contemporary opinion. The biographic record lends no support to the suggestion of a prolonged personal experience of tragic suffering. Nor does the general trend of his literary activities countenance the nebulous theory. Tragedy was no new venture for Shakespeare when the seventeenth century opened . . . ultimately tragedy rather than comedy gave him the requisite scope for the full exercise of his matured endowments, by virtue of the inevitable laws governing the development of dramatic genius. To seek in the necessarily narrow range of his personal experience the key to Shakespeare's triumphant conquest of the topmost peaks of tragedy is to underrate his creative faculty and to disparage the force of its magic. (*A Life of William Shakespeare*, XIX, p. 417)

That is the view of orthodox Shakespeare commentary. I feel that many modern commentators would subscribe to it, unreservedly. But the issue is by no means clear, as usually stated. The argument appears to presuppose a necessary causality linking spiritual experience to external conditions, a relation which may well not exist, and is certainly often not apparent. 'The external facts', 'the biographic record', are offered to disprove the possibility of 'some spiritual calamity', or 'a prolonged period of tragic suffering': which is manifestly a misuse of biographical facts, and rests on an inadequate valuation of the mysterious workings of the soul. Now, even though it could be proved that Shakespeare was not suffering from a conscious melancholy during the writing of *Hamlet*, that he was not in a state of conscious mystic vision when he wrote *The Tempest*, the significance of the series bounded by these plays would in no sense be impaired. They might reflect a previous rhythm of spiritual experience rising from the 'unconscious mind'; or they might be divinely inspired. We do not fully understand the nature of what Sir Sidney Lee here names 'the creative faculty'; we cannot say whence arises 'the force of its magic'. One cannot safely dogmatize about the causality of spiritual experience or artistic composition. It is, however, interesting to compare Tolstoy's account of his extreme pain, its circumstances, its symptoms: wherein we shall be reminded of both the Problem Plays of Shakespeare and Sir Sidney Lee's references to Shakespeare's worldly prosperity at the time when they were being written.

Tolstoy, like the Shakespeare of 1600, was not a young and inexperienced man when sickness entered his soul. He, too, had already written tragic literature during happier days. He, too, was prosperous. This is his account:

> ... All this took place at a time when so far as all my outer circumstances went, I ought to have been completely happy. I had a good wife who loved me and whom I loved; good children and a large property which was increasing with no pains taken on my part. I was more respected by my kinsfolk and acquaintances than I had ever been; I was loaded with praise by strangers; and without exaggeration I could believe my name already famous. Moreover, I was neither insane nor ill. On the contrary, I possessed a physical and mental strength which I have rarely met in persons of my age. I could mow as well as the peasants, I could work with my brain eight hours uninterruptedly and feel no bad effects.
>
> And yet I could give no reasonable meaning to any actions of my life. And I was surprised that I had not understood this from the beginning. My state of mind was as if some wicked and stupid jest was being played upon me by some one. One can live only so long as one is intoxicated, drunk with life; but when one grows sober one cannot fail to see that it is all a stupid cheat. What is truest about it is that there is nothing even funny or silly in it; it is cruel and stupid, purely and simply.
>
> (p. 153)

Those last words express admirably the quality of that insistent pain and disgust that rings through certain passages of Shakespeare. This is not a strained comparison: Tolstoy's words form an exactly appropriate comment on these plays. We think of Hamlet's bitterness to Ophelia, of Thersites, Apemantus. It will be clear, too, that Shakespeare's material success can in no sense be adduced to disprove the personal nature of the pain in *Hamlet*: Tolstoy's words about his reasons for happiness might have been spoken by the Shakespeare Sir Sidney Lee gives us. Reasons have little to do with spiritual harmony and peace of mind.

According to my interpretation of the Shakespeare Progress, the pain expressed in *Hamlet* is subjected to a careful and penetrating examination in the next plays, *Troilus and Cressida* and *Measure for Measure*. Each is pregnant with intellectual vitality: *Troilus and Cressida* is rich in metaphysical analysis beyond any previous play of Shakespeare, and *Measure for Measure* reveals a studied commentary on man's moral nature reaching both back to the teaching of Jesus and forward to the most modern of psychological theories.

These two plays witness a depth of thought, a striving, and a determination which make the following parallel from Tolstoy's experience of particular value to the interpreter of Shakespeare:

> 'But perhaps', I often said to myself, 'there may be something I have failed to notice or comprehend. It is not possible that this condition of despair should be natural to mankind.' And I sought for an explanation in all the branches of knowledge acquired by men. I questioned painfully and protractedly and with no idle curiosity. I sought, not with indolence, but laboriously and obstinately for days and nights together. I sought like a man who is lost and seeks to save himself—and I found nothing. I became convinced, moreover, that all those who before me had sought for an answer in the sciences have also found nothing. And not only this, but that they have recognized that the very thing which was leading me to despair—the meaningless absurdity of life—is the only incontestable knowledge accessible to man. (p. 155)

So Macbeth cries:

> . . . it is a tale
> Told by an idiot, full of sound and fury,
> Signifying nothing. (v. v. 26)

I do not suggest by this quotation that Shakespeare—or his poetic genius—was in any sort of spiritual pain during the writing of *Macbeth*: if ever man was in an ecstasy of divine joy it was the Shakespeare of the great tragedies, which are in the nature of answers to *Hamlet*. The tragedies include and master the tortured thought of *Hamlet*; since their perfected form, their power of passion, their death-mysticism, throw the thought-content into relation with infinite vistas of significance. This quotation says what *Hamlet* in parts makes us feel; also, what Macbeth feels. But the reader to whom those lines are true absolutely, and not merely relatively to their context, is not receiving the message of supreme poetic tragedy.

William James writes of the phenomenon of Tolstoy's 'absolute disenchantment with ordinary life, and the fact that the whole range of habitual values may, to a man as powerful and full of faculty as he was, come to appear so ghastly a mockery' (p. 156). So also to a man of Shakespeare's mental and spiritual stature, we may well, in face of his written work, believe that the pain—if there were a corresponding conscious pain—was tremendous: the nausea of Hamlet, the railing of Thersites, the volcanic curses of Timon, would surely tell their own story. The hate-theme, as I have elsewhere named it, is of supreme importance for our understanding of Shakespeare. In exact proportion to the erotic perception of poetry, just as Timon's disillusioned hate is the measure of his original love, it came near to shattering Shakespeare's dramatic technique in *Hamlet*, and is a thing of torment and unrest until it is mastered by the cleansing power of tragedy, and finally interpreted in the allegory of *Timon of Athens*.

'It must be confessed', says William James, 'that it is hard to follow these windings of the hearts of others, and one feels that their words do not reveal their total secret.' But it is exactly on this point that I would claim that the work of a great poet, when it reveals a rhythm of spiritual development across a span of years, is of extreme interest and value, not alone to the man of letters, but to the metaphysician and the theologian: for the poetic faculty is exactly this—the power to express with clarity the darkest and deepest truths of the mind or soul. In proportion as we admit Shakespeare to be a great poet, we must admit his works to be a revelation, not of fancy, but of truth. I shall now attempt a brief statement of Shakespeare's progress from intellectual search to the emotional significance of tragedy, as related to the corresponding movement of Tolstoy's mind or soul as described by William James. The two movements are similar, the especial mark of each being the introduction of the concept of infinity: a concept explicit in Tolstoy's self-revelation, and implicit in Shakespearian tragedy.

This was Tolstoy's solution:

> . . . Tolstoy, pursuing his unending questioning, seemed to come to one insight after another. First, he perceived that his conviction that life was meaningless took only this finite life into account. He was looking for the value of one finite term in that of another, and the whole result could only be one of those indeterminate equations in mathematics which end with $0 = 0$. Yet this is as far as the reasoning intellect by itself can go, unless irrational sentiment or faith brings in the infinite. (p. 184)

This is the exact curve taken by the developing genius—conscious or unconscious—of Shakespeare when he advanced beyond the plays of pain to the plays of profundity and grandeur. It must be noted that the symptoms of spiritual sickness come first in a tragedy, *Hamlet*: but they tend to destroy its tragic significance and leave it not grandly tragic but rather distressing and painful. *Hamlet* is not a play of tragic form; it lacks the sense of unalterable movement. The poet continued with two plays of intellectual analysis: and there, in *Troilus and Cressida* and *Measure for Measure*, we are not confronted with a movement toward death; the persons are left alive. But in the supreme tragedies there are two new elements. First, there is a sense of titanic passion, direction, and power in the delineation of the protagonist, which certainly was not apparent in the oscillating incertitude of *Hamlet*; second, there is the death-climax. The grandeur and essential optimism of the true Shakespearian tragedy is due to these two elements: passion and death. And both equally 'bring in the infinite'. Death was not wanted in *Troilus and Cressida*: its reverberations would awake suggestions of infinity which, in a play of that analytical texture, would be out of harmony. So, too, passion, or emotion, is, as Shakespeare's phraseology continually suggests, of an infinite significance set beyond the reach of intellect.[1] All that hell of hatred at man's infirmity and the painted gloss of his civilization, the nausea and the disgust —all this sickness of the soul is rendered significant in the tragic harmonies of *Timon of Athens*. Seen from the reverse side, from the angle of the soul of Timon bound passionately toward death as to a positive good, the hate-theme, so painful in Hamlet, so repellent in Thersites, becomes at once but a potentiality of the unrestful and aspiring soul of the

---

[1] The essential 'infinity' of love—and, indeed, of any passion or emotion—is recurrently suggested in Shakespeare. It is considered incapable of inclusion in shape of intellectual thought or action. Wide space metaphors are thus used, as in *Antony and Cleopatra*, I. i. 16–17; but more often we find sea-metaphors. In *Twelfth Night* love 'receiveth as the sea' (I. i. 11) and 'is all as hungry as the sea' (II. iv. 102); Othello's thwarted love becomes vengeance 'like to the Pontic sea' (III. iii. 454); and Juliet says

> My bounty is as boundless as the sea
> My love as deep. (II. ii. 133)

The association is most clearly pointed in *The Two Gentlemen of Verona*:

> A thousand oaths, an ocean of his tears
> And instances of infinite of love
> Warrant me welcome to my Proteus. (II. vii. 69)

The sea-symbol of infinity is often related to the tempest-symbol of tragedy, sea-storms continually symbolizing tragic passions. It is this infinity of the soul which Timon reaches in the 'nothing' of death. Hence his sea-shore grave.

protagonist who, scorning all that is partial, all that is limited, embraces a union with infinity in death. The optimism of Shakespearian tragedy is, no doubt, irrational: but it is potent. Rooted in a sense of death as a supreme good, death as a consummation and evaluation of passion, and passion as a justification of death, it is not nihilistic, but, in the finest sense of the words, philosophic and mystic. Especially in *Timon of Athens*, during the final scenes, we scale the silences of eternity. Terrible and sombre, yet irresistibly grand, the death-mysticism of the play is compelling, and leaves a memory, not of pain, or hate, but profundity and infinite significance. It is as though, by throwing a death-in-time into sharp contrast with a soul-life-out-of-time, the poet reveals the finite as silhouetted against the infinite. Thus 'irrational sentiment' (for Shakespeare) and 'faith' (for Tolstoy) 'brings in the infinite', and the mind recognizes, along the fringes of the consciousness, the awakening light of an impossible revelation.

Tolstoy, after his conversion, continued to reject the superficialities of civilization, and his attitude shows a remarkable likeness to that of the poet, as given in the utterances of Timon. Tolstoy lived the very history that Shakespeare traced out for him three centuries earlier. This was what Tolstoy thought:

> I gave up the life of the conventional world, recognizing it to be no life, but a parody on life, which its superfluities simply keep us from comprehending. (p. 185)

To quote William James's comment:

> Tolstoy was one of those primitive oaks of men to whom the superficialities and insincerities, the cupidities, complications, and cruelties of our polite civilization are profoundly unsatisfying, and for whom the eternal veracities lie with more natural and animal things. (p. 186)

So, too, Timon, after his retiring to the woods in nakedness, speaks to the Bandits:

> *Banditti*. We are not thieves, but men that much do want.
> *Timon*. Your greatest want is, you want much of meat.
>   Why should you want? Behold, the earth hath roots;
>   Within this mile break forth a hundred springs;
>   The oaks bear mast, the briers scarlet hips;

The bounteous housewife, nature, on each bush
Lays her full mess before you. Want! Why want?
First Bandit. We cannot live on grass, on berries, water,
As beasts and birds and fishes.   (IV. iii **421**)

'Tolstoy', says William James, 'did not reach pure happiness again.' He 'had drunk too deep of the cup of bitterness ever to forget its taste.' He concludes:

For Tolstoy's perceptions of evil appear within their sphere to have remained unmodified. His later works show him implacable to the whole system of official values: the ignobility of fashionable life; the infamies of empire; the spuriousness of the Church, the vain conceit of the professions; the meannesses and cruelties that go with great success; and every other pompous crime and lying institution of this world. To all patience with such things his experience has been for him a permanent ministry of death.   (p. 187)

To point the analogy, rather the exact correspondence, further is unnecessary. This passage might have been written of Timon: it is a perfect précis of his great speeches. Timon, too, curses the whole of civilization (IV. iii.): the 'learned pate' that 'ducks to the golden fool'; the 'lawyer' who 'pleads false title'; 'the flamen that scolds against the quality of the flesh and not believes himself', and the 'counterfeit matron', whose 'habit' only is honest and herself a 'bawd'. Timon, too, knows that

Religious canons, civil laws are cruel;
Then what should war be?   (IV. iii. 60)

—that gold 'will knit and break religions' (IV. iii. 34), that if one man's a flatterer,

So are they all; for every grise of fortune
Is smooth'd by that below.   (IV. iii. 16)

Therefore Timon, like Tolstoy, severs himself from civilization:

Therefore, be abhorr'd
All feasts, societies, and throngs of men.   (IV. iii. 20)

For Timon, too, his experience has been 'a permanent ministry of death'; and he, like Tolstoy, dies on the cold breast of nature apart from mankind.

Above all, we find in both Shakespeare and Tolstoy a violent, exaggerated sex-satire. It is as though the extreme erotic idealism of the artist's mind stimulates a repressed sex-instinct into virulent, unruly force. In the work of Shakespeare it is reflected as an almost unhealthy horror of sexual impurity, an unnecessarily savage disgust at the physical aspect of sex unless hallowed by a spiritual and faithful love. The insistence of this element in the work of Shakespeare is most important. It is a raging and turbulent thing throughout. If we compare this strain in Shakespeare —so consistently related to the hate-theme—with the hatred of sexual impurity in *Resurrection* and *The Kreutzer Sonata*, we shall see how closely akin were these two great men on a matter deep in the soul of each: for of each it is true, as Mr. Masefield has said of Shakespeare, that 'sex ran in him like a sea'.

I have shown how the rhythm of the spirit of Shakespeare's plays from *Hamlet* to *Timon of Athens* is paralleled by the experience of Tolstoy. The mind of Tolstoy, unlike the genius of Shakespeare, advanced no further.

XII

SYMBOLIC PERSONIFICATION

THE theme of *Timon of Athens* is closely connected with that of *Othello*. The comparison is interesting and important. In both plays we have a protagonist compact of generosity, trust, nobility. Both possess the same richness of soul, something of the same flood and swell of passion's music, a similar Oriental sense of display. At the crisis each swerves from passionate love to its opposite with a similar finality. Indeed, Othello's words,

> No, to be once in doubt
> Is once to be resolved,   (III. iii. 179)

are even truer of Timon than of himself. In both, toward the end, a massive harmony of words builds a serenity which grows out of the violent revulsion and loathing. Towards the close of each play we are struck with grand imagery of sun and moon and earth.

In *Othello* the poet expresses dramatically the destructive force of cynicism and un-faith directed against that Love to which man aspires, and in whose reality he attempts to build his happiness. Ultimately, in so far as *Othello* expresses a universal truth, it must be considered to suggest the inability of love's faith to weather the conditions of this world. Raising the three chief persons to a high pitch of transcendental meaning, we see Othello as a symbol of noble mankind, Desdemona as a divinity comparable with Dante's Beatrice,[1] and Iago as a kind of Mephistopheles.[2] This

---

[1] This is not a rash statement. The Provençal troubadours are the fathers of modern European romantic literature. With them chivalric romance merged into the cult of the Virgin. So, too, with our modern novelists, and the everlasting love-theme. Its appeal is wide and deep, touching not alone the heart but the soul: every romancer is a troubadour and his theme of love a symbol of divinity.

[2] If we consider the first part of *Faust* and *Othello* we find that the imaginative equivalence of Mephistopheles and Iago is very close: save for a few tricks of Goethe's Devil, the one is no more supernatural in personality than the other. The spectator or reader accepts both with the same kind of acceptance, and Mephistopheles' conjuring tricks demand little more credulity than Iago's intricate devices: his conversation with Cassio, for instance, staged to deceive Othello. Mephistopheles and Iago are conceived with approximately the same degree of realism: but the Weird Sisters in *Macbeth* are conceived as wholly supernatural beings and serve to point the difference clearly.

meaning is not obvious in *Othello*: but it is seen to be implicit
on the analogy of other plays. This general theme, in *Othello*
projected into definite persons and events, is the very theme
to be expressed later in *Timon of Athens*. There a change has
taken place. *Othello's* figures are first men and women, and
only second symbols; the plot is first a story, second a
philosophic argument. In *Timon of Athens* the reverse obtains.
Timon is first a symbol, second a human being; the play is
primarily an argument or parable, only secondarily forced,
as it best may, to assume some correspondence with the
forms and events of human affairs. Othello is an individual,
in love with an individual. Timon is a creation of superhuman grandeur, a universalized and gigantic principle of
generosity, nobility, love; loving, not an individual, but all
men. He is a universal lover. The universal philosophy
beneath the particularized persons and plot of *Othello* is thus
retold more self-consciously in *Timon of Athens*: in a certain
sense—depending on our expectance of what pure art
should be—retold philosophically rather than artistically; or,
put more truly perhaps, directly rather than artificially.
Timon thus replaces Othello; the love of Timon, or perhaps
its symbol, the men of Athens—that is, mankind—replaces
Desdemona; Apemantus replaces Iago. The triangle is complete. The underlying statement implicit in *Othello* becomes
explicit in *Timon of Athens*.

Iago is fundamentally kin to the 'churlish philosopher'
Apemantus. Apemantus represents a philosophic principle,
an especial attitude to life. It is practically the equivalent of
Iago's attitude. Apemantus, like Iago, is 'nothing if not
critical'. Though he does not himself influence Timon, the
philosophy of which he is the exponent certainly does,
possessing him as Iago's scheme possesses Othello. Apemantus, in the universalized and philosophic drama of *Timon of
Athens*, is exactly analogous to Iago in the play of individual
persons and intricate action. The root principle of both is
cynicism. Both win the same kind of victory. That is, though
they superficially ruin the hero, they do not finally degrade
his soul. Nor is it a difference of primary importance that
Iago is shown to have lied, and Apemantus is proved correct.
If we regard the hero's love as the pivot reality, we shall,

having regard to the philosophic, universal nature of *Timon of Athens*, see that Timon's love is not shown to be at fault. In both plays a great love is violently wrenched from its symbol by different means: both heroes follow their own love to death. *Timon of Athens*, in fact, explains the meaning of *Othello*: it asserts the inability of any finite symbol to hold an infinite love in a world where a cynical philosophy, and the facts that philosophy derive from, exist. This statement is projected into a human plot first: later it is retold, as it were, more self-consciously. The main difference lies in the fact that *Timon of Athens* possesses a more significant and extended falling action. Othello drops in a trance, raves, murders; then recovering himself, it is true, shows the exotic richness of his soul in the final scene, expresses there his grandest poetry, reaches out to the silver beauty of the cold, unseeing bodies of the night sky, to the 'chaste stars', and moon:

> It is the very error of the moon;
> She comes more near the earth than she was wont,
> And makes men mad. (v. ii. 107)

But it is a poor correspondence to those latter scenes where Timon's soul voyages 'bold and forth on' to the furthest reaches of a human experience, till we lose knowledge of his end in the darkness of eternity. Yet in both plays love is an infinity, a vast sea of passion, precipitate and uncontrollable. In both the tragic reversal of love is terrifying in its swiftness and tameless, irrevocable strength. In *Othello* each figure of the triangular scheme is carefully individualized, puppets of the drama whose interplay is wrought on the web of human intrigue: Iago's individuality deriving, however, chiefly from its negation of human reality and human definition within a setting where these are significant. In *Timon of Athens* there are again three forces: Timon, the transcendent lover; mankind, the bride of his soul; and Apemantus, the devil of cynicism. Yet here the plot is not one of action and incident, but is moved purely by the interacting qualities and thoughts of human nature; played out, not in Venice or Cyprus or, in truth, if we read the play aright, in Athens, but on the wide stage of 'this beneath world', on the breast of that 'common mother', earth, beneath the eyes of the revolving sun and moon; a dramatic movement which swims majestically through two whole acts within the moveless spaces of the eternal. The consummate artistry of *Othello* develops into the mighty parable of *Timon of Athens*.

Othello and *Timon of Athens* are together concerned with the recurrent Shakespearian hate-theme: the one is the most concretely projected into human symbols, the other the most universal and profound dramatic statement of this Shakespearian philosophy. But these are not the only plays thus concerned. *King Lear* illustrates the same problem. Lear himself builds all his happiness in his three daughters' love: one he distrusts unjustly, like Othello—as to the others, he is disillusioned, like Timon. Instead of the swift reversal of love to its other aspect of hate, the greater part of *King Lear* plays on that mutual territory of madness due to the tension of two opposing principles forcing in opposite directions, till the reason snaps, leaving a hideous vision of the horrible and grotesque. The plot of *King Lear* is, fundamentally, the plot of *Timon of Athens* and *Othello*. Here Lear, Cordelia, and Edmund—persons outstanding with vivid significance from the rest—replace Othello, Desdemona, Iago. Now *Troilus and Cressida* also turns wholly on this theme of love disillusioned. Here the later theme of *King Lear* is viewed from a more purely intellectual, metaphysical standpoint: as in *King Lear*, the hero's mind is distraught by a knowledge of incompatibilities that leave no 'rule in unity itself'. Thersites in this play forecasts Apemantus, possessing the same philosophical, inactive quality, since *Troilus and Cressida*, like *Timon of Athens*, appeals to a region of the mind philosophic rather than strictly dramatic. We recognize an underlying relationship between Apemantus and Thersites on the one hand, and Iago and Edmund on the other. The former are expressions of cynicism in language and dramatic comment; the latter express their cynicism in actions, directly influencing the course of the drama. The former are passive, the latter active. Their essential similarity is, however, important. Finally in *Measure for Measure* the same triple symbolism is represented, with certain modifications, by the Duke, Isabella, and Lucio. In each of these plays we see the same three figures recurring. They are representative of (i) noble mankind, (ii) the supreme value of spiritual love, and (iii) the cynic. In each, the hero's nobility is suggested by a reference to his soldiership, which seems to be a necessary qualification for the Shakespearian hero, war being a positive value second only to love. That is true, too, of *Hamlet*.

These considerations throw back light on the play that preludes all these later symbolizations of the hate-theme. *Hamlet* is of all Shakespeare's plays the most baffling. We can consider Hamlet as a man of noble nature and fine sensibility, agonized by a merciless convergence of cruel events; as a creature of loathing and sickly neurotic disgust at the thought of love's infidelity; as a symbol of death due to his ghost-converse and ghost-mission. All these are legitimate comments. There is a quality in the supernatural mystery and death-atmosphere of the play which alone of these greater plays makes contact with the nightmare evil of *Macbeth*. For it should be clear that *Julius Caesar*, which preludes this succession, though, as I show elsewhere, it expresses the *Macbeth* rhythm, is on too erotic and brightly optimistic a plane to draw level with *Macbeth* in respect of evil atmosphere and power. *Hamlet* is pre-eminently the first of the plays to express vividly that mode of cynicism and hate which I have called the hate-theme. Love-cynicism and death-horror are powerful in the play. Hamlet is nauseated by Gertrude's unfaithfulness—justly: he cynically rejects Ophelia—unjustly. Hamlet thus contains the germ of *Troilus and Cressida*, *Othello*, and *Timon of Athens*. Many other themes of later plays occur in *Hamlet*. Hamlet's mind and Ophelia's, like Lear's, are wrenched and distraught to madness by an unbearable knowledge: also the comic utterances, resultant from the extreme tension of pain, which Hamlet speaks after the Ghost has left him, forecast the grotesquely comic element of *King Lear*. The death-speeches of *Measure for Measure* continue the meditations of Hamlet, and the agony of Angelo in temptation is a replica of Claudius' prayer. *Hamlet*, in fact, contains the essence of all these later plays, crammed into it, unrestfully heaving to be free and find their consummate expression. Here is the truest reason for the extreme difficulties and the extreme fascination of the play.

One more important point is to be observed: there is no person to correspond to Thersites, Iago, Edmund, Apemantus. There is no dramatic representative of cynicism in conflict or comparison with the hero. The play lacks its Mephistopheles. Even though the Ghost be considered an equivalent, he soon disappears and is, anyway, too remote: as for Claudius, he is the very antithesis of the cynic. I have shown, too, that, properly regarded, Hamlet is far from being a wholly lovable personality. One side of his nature at least —and it assumes power as the play progresses, thus forecasting the tragic movements to follow—is bitter and inhuman as Apemantus, and, like Apemantus, poignant in the cynic sting of its wit. He has, too, Iago's devilish cunning in action: he tortures Claudius as Iago tortures Othello. The truth emerges that Hamlet is both hero and villain in his own drama. In *Othello* most clearly of all since *Othello* is most evidently a human story, the hero and villain are directly opposed in a drama of action and intrigue; in *Timon of Athens* they are juxtaposed as philosophical principles, human potentialities rather than human beings. From this view, *King Lear* and *Troilus and Cressida* tend toward the *Othello* and *Timon of Athens* types respectively. But in the solitary figure of Hamlet, incommensurable with those persons in whose community he is set, there are confined both these principles. He is, from the viewpoint of transcendental interpretation, both noble mankind and devil.[1] His own madness is, in truth, 'poor Hamlet's enemy' (v. ii. 253). He torments himself as well as others. The poet's mind, aware of a certain rhythm of human life associated with love, disillusion, and despair, in the later plays splits these forces of his own consciousness into appropriate dramatic figures, playing them off against each other, thereby respecting the

---

[1] Hence arises that antic, elfish, Puck-like quality in Hamlet vividly present from the play-scene onward: some actors will emphasize this more than others. It is worth noting that in a repertory company Hamlet, Iago, and Apemantus will probably be best played by one leading actor, and Claudius, Othello, and Timon by another. It has been stated that Iago should appear as a bluff soldier—as he seems to Othello. I think this wrong and that it is better to sacrifice realism and let Iago show something of his serpentine nature throughout in dress and bearing. We accept the duping of Othello: but it is always helpful to assist the visual imagination in pointing an all-important spiritual quality.

peculiar form and technique of drama. But in the single figure of Hamlet he has attempted to reflect the totality of his creating mind, and it is in respect of this that Hamlet himself more truly mirrors the personal—that is, the whole —creative mentality of the poet than any one of the other tragic heroes or villains I have noticed in this essay. Here we are close to the secret not only of the technical difficulty, the puzzlement of the play: at the same time we touch the source of the perennial fascination, the shifting lights of good and evil, the amazing vitality, of its protagonist. In so fully reflecting the whole of the poet's mind, Hamlet has, in fact, become too human to be properly dramatic. He has the mystery of reality about him. He has, as it were, started from his context with a life more real than art; as though a cinematograph figure began to walk out of the pictured sheet instead of across it—which would be supremely interesting, but most disconcerting. In so far as we fix our attention on the universe of the whole play, and on that alone —which is the natural interpretative approach—Hamlet will appear superhuman among men and women: in so far as we forget the claims of art—that is, the claims of the unique piece of work in its totality—and concentrate on the protagonist alone, we see a man alive among puppets.

These greater plays of Shakespeare, with the one towering exception of *Macbeth*, thus turn all fundamentally on the same axis. Attention to this substratum of pervading unity focuses for us the poles of reference by which Shakespearian tragedy in this genre of the hate-theme must be analysed. The mind of the dramatist is concerned with certain vital problems—in which conjugal happiness is the supreme good —to the exclusion of others: to that mind in composition and to ours in reading, these problems must be regarded not merely as important, but, within the confines of our immediate attention, all-important. They assume universality. This Shakespearian drama is set within the framework of a love-convention, partly personal to the author, partly a convention of the modern world: one which has, moreover, a profound and universal psychological appeal. This convention necessarily limits the universe of each drama, which then itself automatically becomes truly universal in signifi-

cance. In so far as we see the action of each play as a perfect
and complete statement within its own limits, we are forced
to know it as a universal statement. Therefore it is by no
fantasy of exaggeration that in interpretation the free-hearted
hero ultimately becomes mankind; the villain, creature of
cynicism, becomes the Devil, Goethe's prince of negation;
and the loved one becomes the divine principle, Dante's
Beatrice. These three figures persistently recur, in the various
dresses and habiliments of Shakespeare's drama. Each of
these tragedies drives the theme to a similar close. Nor do
these symbols die with *Timon of Athens*: they reappear, in
different form. In *Antony and Cleopatra*, a play pitched
throughout on a note of visionary splendour and dazzling
consciousness of love which is most nearly comparable of
all past plays to the erotic spiritualized world of *Julius
Caesar*, the cynic reappears, pale reflex of Apemantus, in the
common-sense rough commentary of Enobarbus: but here
his worse fault is his desertion of his master at the hour of
trial—he is comparable with Peter rather than Judas in the
Christian tragedy. And himself he gives us a fine description
of Cleopatra, the principle and queen of love:

> The barge she sat in, like a burnish'd throne,
> Burn'd on the water . . .   (II. ii. 199)

Again, in the Final Plays, Pericles and Leontes lose their
loved ones, the brothel-scenes in *Pericles* and the jealousy
of Leontes reflecting the earlier hate-theme. But there is no
dramatic figure of cynicism till in *Cymbeline* the triangle is
again complete: Posthumus, Iachimo, Imogen. In these
plays the old theme is violently set in motion on the old lines,
then just as violently reversed. Remembering the Shakespearian convention within which the plot-figures function
and have their being, we shall be prepared to see a profound
significance in these later plot-formations. For, within the
limits of its convention, poetic drama reflects a truth not
itself limited but universal. Finally, in the all-inclusive statement of *The Tempest*, the three figures are seen to be three
modes of the poet's mind: there Prospero has mastered, and
controls, both Ariel and Caliban.

XIII

THE SHAKESPEARIAN METAPHYSIC

I NEXT shortly outline a rough metaphysic which emerges from a consideration of these plays as imitations of life.

Two groups must be contrasted: first, plays of the hate-theme, that is: *Hamlet, Troilus and Cressida, Othello, King Lear, Timon of Athens*; second, plays analysing evil in the human mind: the Brutus-theme in *Julius Caesar, Hamlet*, and *Macbeth*. The division cannot be absolute: Hamlet's mental agony has much of the abysmal and bottomless nightmare fear of *Macbeth*; *Measure for Measure*, being related to both sex and temptation, touches both groups. But I shall first notice the two kinds primarily in their difference, laying no emphasis on those points where they blend with each other and are seen to be ultimately two aspects of one reality: at the extremes it will be clear that the divergence is both rigid and important. I shall first make some general remarks to clarify the points at issue with reference to the *Macbeth* evil.

Our understanding of *Macbeth* is assisted by attention to a scene in *Richard II*. The Queen speaks:

> ... yet again, methinks,
> Some unborn sorrow, ripe in fortune's womb,
> Is coming towards me, and my inward soul
> With nothing trembles ...   (ii. ii. 9)

Bushy answers:

> Each substance of a grief hath twenty shadows,
> Which shows like grief itself, but is not so;
> For sorrow's eye, glazed with blinding tears,
> Divides one thing entire to many objects;
> Like perspectives, which rightly gazed upon
> Show nothing but confusion, eyed awry
> Distinguish form: so your sweet majesty,
> Looking awry upon your lord's departure,
> Finds shapes of grief, more than himself, to wail;
> Which, look'd on as it is, is nought but shadows
> Of what it is not.   (ii. ii. 14)

We remember Macbeth's 'Nothing is but what is not'. The Queen's mental state is a confused and blurred vision, a mysterious and dark foreboding in the soul, causing fear: the similarity to the *Macbeth* universe is evident. The Queen answers:

> It may be so; but yet my inward soul
> Persuades me it is otherwise: howe'er it be,
> I cannot but be sad; so heavy sad
> As, though on thinking on no thought I think,
> Makes me with heavy nothing faint and shrink.   (II. ii. 28)

There is more play on the word 'nothing' finishing with the Queen's:

> . . . nothing hath begot my something grief;
> Or something hath the nothing that I grieve.   (II. ii. 36)

The Queen's state of foreboding and fear is justified. Ill news is announced, and she cries: 'Now hath my soul brought forth her prodigy'; she is a 'gasping new-delivered mother'. So, too, in *Macbeth* the Weird Sisters prophesy truth. In this speech we should note that it represents a state of fear, nameless, associated with the parallel concepts 'nothing' and 'soul' which are, indeed, almost interchangeable in Shakespeare;[1] confusion on the plane of actuality, as noted by Bushy; and prophecy, rationally untrustworthy, yet empirically justified. As in this passage, the 'soul' in Shakespeare is often regarded as 'prophetic'.[2] Macbeth, too, endures fear and a sense of abysmal deeps of the soul's 'nothing' (p. 153) related to action resulting in disorder in the actual world—in other words, crime; prophecy, too, is closely interwoven throughout the endurance of Macbeth's evil. It is true that the Queen's fears are not connected with a guilty conscience as seem to be those of Gertrude in *Hamlet*:

> To my sick soul, as sin's true nature is,
> Each toy seems prologue to some great amiss . . .   (IV. v. 17)

---

[1] Bassanio refers to the consummation of his soul's desire as 'a wild of nothing, save of joy' (*The Merchant of Venice*, III. ii. 183). The poet makes 'shapes' out of 'airy nothing' (*A Midsummer Night's Dream*, v. i. 16). The incoherence of madness is a 'nothing' which is 'more than matter' (*Hamlet*, IV. v. 173). Dreams are 'nothing' (*Romeo and Juliet*, I. iv. 96–100). See also *Cymbeline*, IV. ii. 300. Both 'nothing' and 'soul' are, of course, the 'unconscious mind' of psychology (see also *The Crown of Life*, p. 82).

[2] Cp. *Romeo and Juliet*, III. v. 54; *Hamlet*, I. v. 40; Sonnet cvii:
> Not mine own fears, nor the prophetic soul
> Of the wide world dreaming on things to come . . .

or those called down on Tarquin by Lucrece:

> Let ghastly shadows his lewd eyes affright;
>   And the dire thought of his committed evil
>   Shape every bush a hideous shapeless devil.
>
> (*The Rape of Lucrece*, 971)

But the difference is superficial. In *Richard II* the relation between the mental state and the outer world is independent of the individual's actions; in *Hamlet* and *The Rape of Lucrece* it succeeds crime; in *Macbeth* it preludes and accompanies crime. Only by letting our vision of metaphysical references be blurred by a disproportionate attention to the guilt-factor shall we fail to see an essential and profound kinship; in fact, a unity. Therefore a close attention to the Queen's speech serves to emphasize those points I have noticed in my analysis of *Macbeth*.

A further comparison throws the *Macbeth* vision into stronger relief. *Macbeth* is, as I observe elsewhere, a repetition of the Angelo-theme in *Measure for Measure*. The stories show similar rhythms of original surprise and self-conflict in the hero, a swift and overpowering victory of temptation, a resultant agony of loneliness, guilt, and fear, followed by a rapid excess of crime, culminating in an open condemnation and failure which brings peace. But Angelo's words in temptation are less profound than Macbeth's. His will-power seems to be actively engaged in opposing temptation, and he cannot understand why his 'heart' should be so much stronger than his 'words' of prayer. He is at a loss:

> When I would pray and think, I think and pray
> To several subjects. Heaven hath my empty words;
> Whilst my invention, hearing not my tongue,
> Anchors on Isabel: Heaven in my mouth,
> As if I did but only chew his name;
> And in my heart the strong and swelling evil
> Of my conception.   (II. iv. 1)

Angelo's speech is more superficial than Macbeth's. It shows us a consciousness of conflict in which a will-power is pitted against a stronger emotion: it is a clear picture of what most of us know. The *Macbeth* revelation, however, goes deeper. It suggests in highly imaginative language the true nature of evil—the dissociation from all external phenomena of the individual soul. There seems here no room for the will-concept. The poet makes his dramatic person aware of the deepest channels of his own being. In a sense, we can say that the persons of dramatic poetry at its intensest are always made to do this: they utter, not those things of which humanity is normally aware, but the springs of action, the deep floods of passion, the essence of human reality—all which the normal self-consciousness of individuality tends to blur and veil. Angelo is thus conceived self-consciously, like a real man: his words might almost be spoken by any one, and are readily intelligible. Macbeth's, however, are very difficult. 'Will-power' seems to have vanished.[1] The hero explains for us the true nature of his experience, which in real life he would not have known. In these respects the tragedy of *Macbeth* tends to answer the psychological problem of *Measure for Measure*; and the similar one of Claudius in *Hamlet* (III. iii. 36–72). Claudius endures a conflict exactly analogous to Angelo's. Both engage in the same kind of futile struggle. In *Macbeth* the poet goes deeper. He here relates the temptation-theme as a whole to such scattered single speeches in earlier works as I have quoted above from *Richard II* and *The Rape of Lucrece* and builds a whole play, as it were, out of those earlier flashes of insight. Which, moreover, is the normal Shakespearian process. The supreme plays are always explications in imaginative detail on a big scale of experiences which are worded, with just the same quality, colour, and profundity, in scattered metaphors, speeches, or incidents, in his earlier work. *Macbeth* especially is often forecast. For instance, again in *The Rape of Lucrece*, we have:

> O, deeper sin than bottomless conceit
> Can comprehend in still imagination!   (701)

It is just that power of 'bottomless conceit' which the *Macbeth* vision adds to the psychological analysis of *Measure for Measure*.

---

[1] 'Will' clearly finds no place in the passionate world of the great tragedies. To say that Shakespeare chose heroes lacking in will-power is less valuable than to say that poetic-tragedy is concerned only with those deeper springs of action which the will-concept tends to blur. Failure to resist temptation is generally interpreted as lack of 'will-power'. This is, indeed, the word's most frequent use: 'will' is a thing most generally known by its absence, and hence it is fundamentally unreal.

Ghastly 'shapes' and 'forms' are seen by the inward eye of the mind in evil. They are often considered as unreal, yet they may be powerful of effect. Messala speaks over Cassius' dead body:

> O hateful error, melancholy's child,
> Why dost thou show to the apt thoughts of men
> The things that are not?   (*Julius Caesar*, v. iii. 67)

We hear of

> ... moody, moping and dull melancholy,
> Kinsman to grim and comfortless despair,
> And at her heels a huge infectious troop
> Of pale distemperatures and foes to life.
>   (*Comedy of Errors*, v. i. 79)

It is a kind of madness and like madness is 'cunning' in 'bodiless creation' (*Hamlet*, III. iv. 137). Indeed, the delirium quality of *Macbeth* makes contact with the insanity-theme of *King Lear*, the 'evil' and 'hate' modes touching at this point. What the tortured mind sees is often the 'very painting' of 'fear' as in *Macbeth* (III. iv. 61). Or we may find a nightmare-state of prophecy, related to blood and disorder and turbulence in the actual world:

> ... I have dream'd
> Of bloody turbulence, and this whole night
> Hath nothing been but shapes and forms of slaughter.
>   (*Troilus and Cressida*, v. iii. 10)

Above all, this consciousness is a state of fear: fear which is contrasted with its opposite—love:

> Fears make devils of cherubins; they never see truly ... O, let my lady apprehend no fear: in all Cupid's pageant there is presented no monster.
>   (*Troilus and Cressida*, III, ii. 72–9)

It is here suggested that perfect love is a state of security. And yet love, too, can induce a state of inward tremor imaginatively twin to Macbeth's first anguished encountering of evil:

> Even such a passion doth embrace my bosom:
> My heart beats thicker than a feverous pulse;
> And all my powers do their bestowing lose,
> Like vassalage at unawares encountering
> The eye of majesty.   (*Troilus and Cressida*, III. ii. 35)

The same *Macbeth* similarity is apparent in another love-speech:

> . . . there is such confusion in my powers,
> As, after some oration fairly spoke
> By a beloved prince, there doth appear
> Among the buzzing pleased multitude;
> Where every something, being blent together,
> Turns to a wild of nothing, save of joy,
> Express'd and not express'd.
>
> (*The Merchant of Venice*, iii, ii. 178)

The states of extreme evil and supreme love have a definite imaginative similarity. They stand out from other modes in point of a certain supernormal intensity, a sudden, crushing, conquering power, a vivid and heightened consciousness. In these respects they seem to transcend the hate-mode, except where that touches madness. *Macbeth* and *Antony and Cleopatra* are supreme in point of imaginative transcendence.

The hate-theme in Shakespeare is necessarily related to love. It is dependent on the failing of love's reality. Hamlet, Troilus, Othello, Lear, Timon, all endure essentially the same pain with reference to love, though in Hamlet this is included within the wider death-consciousness. They see their ideal drained, so to speak, of spiritual significance. The flame of love's faith is extinguished, there is an odour of oil and smoke. The bestial elements of man assume disproportionate significance as the spiritual is denied. Hence the animal references in Othello's paroxysm, Lear's madness, and in *Timon of Athens*. The flesh, no longer irradiated by the divinity of love, becomes essentially unclean. Sex is foul. Man is an animal aping something he has no right to claim as his. In every instance the hero suffers through a wrenching, a drawing out, of something deep within him: his love, bodied into a symbol, is banished thence and it is as the banishment of his own soul from himself. For the soul has perfect reality only when it is projected into some 'shape' or 'form'. This is, indeed, suggested by Ulysses' dialogue with Achilles, in *Troilus and Cressida*, which has profound implications. The dialogue runs as follows:

> *Ulysses.*   A strange fellow here
> Writes me: 'That man, how dearly ever parted,

How much in having, or without or in,
Cannot make boast to have that which he hath,
Nor feels not what he owes, but by reflection;
As when his virtues shining upon others
Heat them and they retort that heat again
To the first giver.'
Achilles.   This is not strange, Ulysses.
The beauty that is borne here in the face
The bearer knows not, but commends itself
To others' eyes; nor doth the eye itself,
That most pure spirit of sense, behold itself,
Not going from itself; but eye to eye oppos'd
Salutes each other with each other's form;
For speculation turns not to itself,
Till it hath travell'd and is mirror'd there
Where it may see itself. This is not strange at all.   (III. iii. 95)

This implies a system of symbolism which should be considered in relation to Troilus's speech on love at II. ii. 61–5
—a speech which I have already analysed. On the plane of
(i) human intercourse, and (ii) sense-perception, the subject
has no knowledge of his own reality apart from an object.
Man cannot 'of himself' know his own qualities 'for aught'
till he sees them reflected in others (III. iii. 118). Regarding
love as the supreme and most intense expression of (i)
human intercourse and (ii) sense-perception, we find this
dialogue to imply that the lover sees his own soul in his
beloved: a thought equivalent to Troilus's statement, and
recurrent in other passages of Shakespeare.[1]

The Shakespearian hero suffers an agonizing incertitude
at the expulsion of his love or soul from its symbol. Hamlet
dies in this agony, this incertitude; Troilus projects his soul
into war and revenge, directed against the Greeks, symbols
of his hate; Othello finds his ideal again too late, and follows
it to death; Lear endures agony till his love-soul regains a
temporary home in Cordelia. Timon alone makes no terms
with actuality. His infinity of love banished once, he scorns
to project it into any finite 'shape', but lets it pursue its
lonely derelict course: that is, lets it express itself as
pure negation, pure hate. This is, in brief, the nature of
the hate-theme expressed in terms of a metaphysic of sym-

---

[1] *Troilus and Cressida*, III. ii. 155; *Romeo and Juliet*, II. ii. 164; *Twelfth Night*, I. v. 290;
Cymbeline, v. v. 264; *Love's Labour's Lost*, IV. iii. 316; Sonnets, xxii, 6; xxxi, 14; cix, 4.

bolism suggested by numerous passages of Shakespeare: which metaphysic is also necessitated by the Shakespearian evil. There are thus two primary uses of 'soul' in Shakespeare. First, the Shakespearian lover sees his 'soul' reflected in his loved one; second, the victim of evil endures a hideous vision of the abysmal 'nothing' of his own soul. This is the 'bottomless conceit' that comprehends blackest evil. Now if we construct a rigid scheme based on these suggestions, and will admit a dualism of (i) soul or spirit and (ii) actuality and the manifest world of sense, then we may view with clarity three important kinds of Shakespearian thought or vision. We can say that good is love and exists when the actual burns with a spiritual flame kindled, or recognized, or supplied by the regarding soul; it tends to be immediate and intuitive.[1] We can next observe that the Shakespearian hate, as expressed recurrently in what I have called the 'hate-theme', is an awareness of the world of actuality unspiritualized, and shows a failure to body infinite spirit into finite forms and a consequent abhorrence and disgust at these forms. It tends to originate in a backward time-thinking, the recurrent plot-symbol being the failing of love's vision in the temporal chain of events. And, thirdly, the Shakespearian evil is a vision of naked spirit, which appears as a bottomless chasm of 'nothing' since it is unfitted to any external symbols; which yet creates its own phantasmal shapes of unholy imagination and acts of disorder and crime, making of them its own grim reality; which is concerned not only with the backward temporal sequences of manifestation as they normally appear, but looks forward and has forbidden knowledge of futurity, trades in half-truths and truths of prophecy; an inmost knowledge of the time-succession which, though not wholly false, is yet poisonous;

---

[1] This intuitive and timeless nature of love's integrity is expressed finely in *Troilus and Cressida*, IV. v. 165:

> What's past and what's to come is strew'd with husks
> And formless ruin of oblivion;
> But in this extant moment, faith and troth,
> Strain'd purely from all hollow bias-drawing,
> Bids thee, with most divine integrity,
> From heart of very heart, great Hector, welcome.

The Gospel Command to take no thought for the morrow is an analogy on the plane of universal love.

a sight of that spiritual machinery which man cannot properly understand and into which he penetrates at his peril.

Our three modes of love, hate, and evil may be rendered firmly distinct on this basis of a dualistic opposition of 'actuality' and 'spirit'. That this dualism is not meaningless may be seen from Macbeth's reaction to the Weird Sisters' prophecies. Futurity has meaning only as an activity of 'mind' or 'spirit'. In seeing into the future, Macbeth views the 'spiritual' dissociated from the 'actual'.[1] In Shakespearian phraseology, which is here remarkably consistent and copious, spiritual essences are 'born' into 'shapes' by 'time'.[2] Human birth,[3] and also artistic creation[4], are the result of a union between earthly and divine elements. Thus Macbeth's vision of the future is a knowledge of the essence, without a clear image of the 'shape'. 'Thoughts' are 'unveiled in their dumb cradles' (*Troilus and Cressida*, III. iii. 201). The process is described in *Troilus and Cressida*:

> Sith every action that hath gone before,
> Whereof we have record, trial did draw
> Bias and thwart, not answering the aim,
> And that unbodied figure of the thought
> That gave't surmised shape.   (I. iii. 13)

[1] The implications of this are similar to those of Coleridge's statement that the Weird Sisters represent 'the imaginative dissociated from the good'. For the concept of 'the good' is ultimately dependent on human and temporal actuality. Therefore the Weird Sisters represent 'the imaginative dissociated from all human and temporal symbols'.

[2] The time-shape association occurs at: *Troilus and Cressida*, I. iii. 385; *Hamlet*, III. i. 131 and IV. vii. 149–50; *Love's Labour's Lost*, IV. iii. 378; *2 Henry IV*, III. ii. 362. The time-birth association is copious: *Pericles*, IV. Pro. 45; *The Winter's Tale*, IV. Chor. 8, 27; *Othello*, I. iii. 377 and 410; *Antony and Cleopatra*, II. ii. 10 and III. vii. 81; *Hamlet*, III. i. 175; *Romeo and Juliet*, II. Pro. 2; *Cymbeline*, I. iv. 136; *Macbeth*, I. iii. 58 and II. iii. 65. The whole value of this image is emphasized in:

> I have a young conception in my brain;
> Be you my time to bring it to some shape.
> (*Troilus and Cressida*, I. iii. 312)

'Shape' is also used in Shakespeare for one element of the finished result of artistic composition.

[3] The dualistic nature of human birth is suggested at *Twelfth Night*, v. i. 246–8; *Othello*, II. i. 64; *The Merchant of Venice*, v. i. 64–5: in these the body is considered as clothing to the soul. The implications of this are put clearly in *Romeo and Juliet*:

> Since birth and heaven and earth, all three do meet
> In thee at once.   (III. iii. 119)

[4] The thought is developed in *A Midsummer-Night's Dream*, v. i. 12–17, and *Richard II*, v. v. 1–11. In the latter, the brain-soul opposition must be equated with the intellect-intuition opposition of Bergson's system, in which intellect is eminently practical and evolved in order to use material shapes.

The prophecy-theme in *Macbeth* is of this kind. Macbeth's fault is that he interprets prophecies too readily into his own blundering 'shapes' of actuality. His first crime deliberately puts prophecy into immediate action, instead of waiting for it to be born naturally; his later ones rest on assurances which, when they materialize, turn out to be different from what he expected. Now the three modes of evil, hate, and love can be said to be symbolized dramatically in the three life-visions of *Macbeth*, *King Lear*, *Antony and Cleopatra*. I have shown that the first two can be related respectively to the two concepts, spirit and actuality. Each by itself is inadequate, and the fulness of vision results in the love-mode where spirit and actuality are one. Three small incidents, connected with sleep, in these plays further illuminate their qualities.

Macbeth speaks to the Doctor:

> *Macbeth.* How does your patient, doctor?
> *Doctor.*   Not so sick, my lord,
>   As she is troubled with thick-coming fancies,
>   That keep her from her rest.
> *Macbeth.*   Cure her of that.
>   Canst thou not minister to a mind diseas'd,
>   Pluck from the memory a rooted sorrow,
>   Raze out the written troubles of the brain,
>   And with some sweet oblivious antidote
>   Cleanse the stuff'd bosom of that perilous stuff
>   Which weighs upon the heart?
> *Doctor.*   Therein the patient
>   Must minister to himself.   (v. iii. 37)

The *Macbeth* experience is essentially one beyond the actual, beyond all natural laws. Compare this with *King Lear*. Cordelia, too, talks to a Doctor:

> *Cordelia.*   What can man's wisdom
>   In the restoring his bereaved sense?
>   He that helps him take all my outward worth.
> *Doctor.* There is means, madam:
>   Our foster-nurse of nature is repose,
>   The which he lacks; that to provoke in him,
>   Are many simples operative, whose power
>   Will close the eye of anguish.
> *Cordelia.*   All blest secrets,
>   All you unpublish'd virtues of the earth,
>   Spring with my tears!   (iv. iv.8)

In *King Lear* the ill is natural; the remedy is natural. In *Macbeth* the evil is supernatural; and there is no remedy but an equivalent supernatural power of grace, as described at length by Malcolm, speaking of the good King of England, and his 'miraculous work' of healing (IV. iii. 147). Finally, we may observe a somewhat similar incident in *Antony and Cleopatra*. Cleopatra describes to Dolabella her dream of Antony:

> I dream'd there was an Emperor Antony:
> O, such another sleep, that I might see
> But such another man! (v. ii. 76)

She describes her wondrous dream, and concludes:

> *Cleopatra.* Think you there was, or might be, such a man
>   As this I dream'd of?
> *Dolabella.*   Gentle madam, no.
> *Cleopatra.* You lie, up to the hearing of the gods.
>   But, if there be, or ever were, one such,
>   It's past the size of dreaming: nature wants stuff
>   To vie strange forms with fancy; yet, to imagine
>   An Antony, were nature's piece 'gainst fancy,
>   Condemning shadows quite.
>
>   (v. ii. 93)

These three incidents form microcosms of their respective worlds. They point (i) the transcendental unreality of the *Macbeth* experience, (ii) the pure realism or naturalism of *King Lear*, and (iii) the transcendental realism of *Antony and Cleopatra*. The third is thus the sum of the first two. The three modes are related to evil, hate, and love; or fear, knowledge, and recognition of reality in the widest and profoundest implications of the word.

I use so rigid a scheme purely to clarify our knowledge of the relations existing between different plays: it is a useful and indeed necessary basis of commentary. But in thus relating and subduing the *Macbeth* experience of evil to a monistic system it will be evident that I have contradicted my statement in analysis of *Macbeth* that the evil it projects imaginatively is an absolute evil. Nevertheless it may seem safest in so difficult a matter to sacrifice logical consistency to clarity. While we have regard to the *Macbeth* experience, we have so powerful an intuition of evil that no word of less violent impact than 'absolute' is completely satisfactory; but, from a balanced view of the whole of Shakespeare's work, that evil is best regarded as relative. It is, so to speak, absolute whilst it lasts, which is, perhaps, equivalent to denying it any absolute reality. Within the *Macbeth* universe —and within that universe only—the evil has its undisputed way—for a while. The bark is tempest-tossed, but cannot be finally lost: in the last act the sickening eclipse is lifted, and Macbeth himself emerges, as I have noticed, unafraid. A further consideration all but resolves our difficulty. The absolute reality of the evil is contingent on the objectivity of the Weird Sisters. Now they are clearly conceived as objective. They appear on the stage alone, cannot be considered as purely figments of Macbeth's or Banquo's mind. They are objective, however, only in the sense that the other persons and events are objective: but these other persons and events have slight individual meaning independent of the *Macbeth* vision as a whole. The whole play is cast in a uniquely visionary, unrealistic mould: it represents a spiritual, not an actual, reality. It is the most subjective of Shakespeare's tragedies. Either we can say that the whole *Macbeth* universe reflects the mental experience of the protagonist— a technical device to make us feel his personal experience; or, better still, we can regard the play as throughout a single imaginative creation of Shakespeare's mind, expressive of one aspect of the poet's soul rather than imitative of humanity, a vision in which Macbeth, Banquo and his Ghost, the Weird Sisters, the air-drawn dagger, Duncan's horses (which eat each other), and the poetry of darkness so emphatic, possess all an equivalent, personal, lyric reality. Whichever view we adopt, we see that, though the Weird Sisters are conceived objectively, they possess this objectivity only within an intensely subjective universe. They are real in relation to a universe itself unreal. Their objectivity is conditional only. Again, we are brought to the knowledge that the evil is absolute only within certain limits, either within the limits of the *Macbeth* vision with all its technical machinery, or within the limits of time, as I observe above: it is absolute whilst it lasts. This is probably the proper road to solution of the question of evil in its widest application: we may say that it has a 'conditional reality'.

In conclusion, it may be observed that the two modes of hate and evil are only provisionally distinct. This appears from a short examination of *Hamlet*, *Macbeth*, and *Timon of Athens*. *Hamlet* foreshadows *Macbeth* in: (i) The supernatural machinery which early influences the protagonist; (ii) the quality of Hamlet's melancholy, fixed in something negative yet powerful; and (iii) the process by which his mental state forces him to express himself in actions of blood and destruction. *Hamlet* also foreshadows the hate-theme of *Troilus and Cressida*, *King Lear* and *Timon of Athens*. Also the death-consciousness of Hamlet is to be related to the death-mysticism implicit in the following tragedies. I conclude that the *Hamlet* experience in its totality contains the essence of all these later plays. The tragedies of the hate-theme are not independent of the death-theme. The death-conclusions of *Othello* and *King Lear* are important: they throw the problem of the drama into relation with the mystery of eternity. *Macbeth* starts where these plays leave off—Macbeth endures an awareness of 'nothing', a death-consciousness, and we see a positive and active symbolism of his experience in his acts of destruction. An awareness of essential nothingness produces acts of nihilism. In *Timon of Athens* all these elements receive coherent, allegorical form, with a strong emphasis on hate and death. Since Timon withdraws from humanity the word 'evil' is unsuitable. Here hate is shown as the revulsion from actuality of a noble, loving soul: disillusioned and thwarted, Timon aspires to the 'nothing' of death. In *Hamlet* the sequence of plays to follow is already implicit: *Timon of Athens* is in the nature of a retrospect.

Again, we may consider both modes as representing essentially a severance of the individual from his environment. In this state of disharmony the protagonist concentrates attention either (i) on the outer things he has lost or (ii) on his own starved soul. Or we may say that in *King Lear* outer disorder (Gloucester's speech about the 'late eclipses' supports this) reacts on the protagonist, disrupting his mind; whereas in *Macbeth* the disorder in the protagonist's mind disrupts the state. We are thus regarding two aspects of a single reality: their relation is most closely welded in *Hamlet*, and most clearly exposed in *Timon of Athens*.

XIV

TOLSTOY'S ATTACK ON SHAKESPEARE
(1934)

I

THE proper study of Shakespeare's work is only beginning. Appreciation has been granted in full
measure; praise has reverberated down the centuries; but
understanding has kept no pace with applause. And, indeed,
applause has often been misdirected. The splendours of
Shakespeare are vast and inexhaustible; but there are some
elements in his work which are not, which, by its very
nature, cannot be, the fine pieces of realistic exactitude to
which his idolaters have raised them. The Shakespearian
world does not exactly reflect the appearances of human
or natural life. The events in his world are often strange to
the point of impossibility. Whoever knew the sun go out?
What man has ever acted as did King Lear, what woman
as Hermione? Shakespeare has been praised to excess for
'characterization'. The term is vague. If however we take it
in its most usual and popular sense, as photographic verisimilitude to life, depending on clear differentiation of each
person in the play or novel, we find 'characterization' not
only not the Shakespearian essence, but actually the most
penetrable spot to adverse criticism that may be discovered
in his technique. Thence two great minds have directed their
hostility: Tolstoy and Bridges. Here I shall show that those
attacks on Shakespeare, often perfectly justifiable within
limits, are yet based on a fundamental misunderstanding of
his art; but that such misunderstanding is nevertheless
extremely significant and valuable, since it forces our appreciation and interpretation from excessive psychologies of
'character', which run to waste over a wide expanse of theory,
into legitimate channels of inquiry into the true substance
and solidity of Shakespeare's dramatic poetry. We shall then
see, too, that Tolstoy's further objection to Shakespeare's
lack of any religious essence in his work is also quite without
foundation.

Shakespeare is a great poet. We have, misled by nine-teenth-century romantic criticism, regarded him rather as a great novelist. The position is put trenchantly by Professor Barker Fairley while reviewing my Shakespearian interpretations in *The Canadian Forum*. I quote from his fine statement:

> ... For although I was brought up in the view that Shakespeare was primarily interested in character I never quite believed it, because it never enabled me to read Shakespeare with the deep satisfaction that I have learned to expect from great poetry. Lacking any clue to the universal values which I felt must be discoverable in him I always came away hungry and dissatisfied from my study of him. And it seemed to confirm me in this private suspicion of mine about Shakespeare that all other great poets manage with so few characters.

We shall find a closely similar expression by Tolstoy of his failure to derive satisfaction from Shakespeare equivalent to that he has 'learned to expect' from other poets. Professor Barker Fairley mentions Homer, Dante, and Aeschylus, and observes that if we make Shakespeare's power depend on characterization we align him rather with Tolstoy and Balzac than with them:

> Surely it is for the story-tellers and the recorders to multiply character and for the poets to reach beyond these individual variations into the philosophic invariables.

Again:

> Yet we go on as before, treating Shakespeare as the student of personality, the multiplier of character. Why do we do it? Because we have nothing to put in its place. Finding ourselves incapable of coping with the dark depths that lurk behind the tragedies, unable to see clearly or to move clearly in them, baffled and confused by them, we retreat again into the dramatic daylight and content ourselves with what we can see there. This is what the orthodox view of Shakespeare amounts to; it is a *pis aller*, a second best, a confession of defeat. We may make a virtue of it and talk of the divine inexplicability of Shakespeare, of the all-seeing poet too wise for philosophy, and what not, and all we mean is that when we try to enter the dark cellarage of his mind our little candles blow out and we withdraw in fear and confusion.

That appears to me to be an admirable exposition of the whole matter. We have not understood Shakespeare. And our error has been this: a concentration on 'character' and realistic appearances generally, things which do not constitute Shakespeare's primary glory; and a corresponding and dangerous, indeed a devastating, neglect of Shakespeare's poetic symbolism. Hence our age-long inconscience of those twin pillars which support the architecture of the Shakespearian universe: 'tempests' and 'music'.

II

Tolstoy was genuinely pained and perplexed by his inability to appreciate Shakespeare. My quotations will be drawn from the essay 'Shakespeare and the Drama' in the fine volume *Tolstoy on Art* (O.U.P.), a massive collection of some of the most masculine, incisive, and important criticism that exists; all, whether we agree or disagree, of so rock-like an integrity and simplicity that its effect is invariably tonic and invigorating, and often points us directly, as in this essay on Shakespeare, to facts before unobserved, yet both obvious and extremely significant. Tolstoy sincerely tried to like Shakespeare:

> My perplexity was increased by the fact that I have always keenly felt the beauties of poetry in all its forms: why then did Shakespeare's works, recognized by the whole world as works of artistic genius, not only fail to please me, but even seem detestable? (p. 394).

Tolstoy found Shakespeare's works 'insignificant and simply bad'; they induced in him 'repulsion, weariness, and bewilderment' (p. 394). Nobly he appears to have read, and re-read them, 'several times over' in Russian, English, and German (p. 394). Always with the same result. He is definite in his conclusions that Shakespeare is a poor writer. Shakespeare is 'a man quite devoid of the sense of proportion and taste' (p. 437); his plays are compositions 'having absolutely nothing in common with art or poetry' (p. 439); they are 'works which are beneath criticism, insignificant, empty, and immoral' (p. 447); and again, Shakespeare is an 'insignificant, inartistic, and not only non-moral but plainly immoral writer' (p. 463).

Where a mind like Tolstoy's can so violently oppose the approbation of the centuries there is something curiously wrong. Nor is it merely a question of Tolstoyan prejudice.

Robert Bridges, generally acknowledged as a fine poet
and critic, reacted to Shakespeare in a precisely similar
fashion. I quote from the 1927 edition (O.U.P.) of his 1907
essay *The Influence of the Audience on Shakespeare's Drama*.
Bridges regarded Shakespeare as a genius prostituting his
art to please his public. Hence:

> . . . Shakespeare should not be put into the hands of the young without
> the warning that the foolish things in his plays were written to please the
> foolish, the filthy for the filthy, and the brutal for the brutal; and that, if
> out of veneration for his genius we are led to admire or even tolerate such
> things, we may be thereby not conforming ourselves to him, but only
> degrading ourselves to the level of his audience, and learning contamina-
> tion from those wretched beings who can never be forgiven their share
> in preventing the greatest poet and dramatist of the world from being
> the best artist.   (p. 28)

True, Bridges at every turn admits the supreme power and
ability of Shakespeare, and is at pains to find reasons for his
faults. He has the advantage, which Tolstoy had not, of
receiving the Shakespearian poetry as no foreigner can ever
quite receive it. But he is unequivocal in his dislikes:

> Exasperation is the word that I should choose to express the state of
> feeling which the reading of the *Othello* induces in me . . . (p. 24)

Elsewhere Bridges complains of Shakespeare's carelessness,
disregard of improbabilities in plot-texture, faults of 'characterization', and want of taste. Here are a few of his phrases:
'bad jokes and obscenities' (p. 2), 'extreme badness of passages' (p. 2), 'scenes which offend our feelings' (p. 4), 'disgusting utterance' (p. 5), 'disgusting detail' (p. 7), 'blurr'd
outline' (p. 13), and so on. It is all just like Tolstoy, who
continually complains of Shakespeare's vulgarity. Tolstoy
refers to his perplexity, his search for a resolution of the
difficulty. In somewhat the same strain Bridges writes of
Shakespearian tragedy that 'the pleasure attending our surprise gratifies us, and our critical faculty is quieted by the
reflection that there must be a solution, and that it is natural
enough that we should not hit upon it at once' (p. 17). But
both were finally sure of themselves. Shakespeare was con-
victed of numerous faults. No defence was forthcoming; and
'realistic' criticism was loosed on the twentieth century.

It is time to reverse such criticism. First, we must observe its place in the history of Shakespearian study. It is plainly a reaction from the extravagant praise and rhetorical appreciation that so long and so loud sounded throughout the nineteenth century. Tolstoy quotes a passage from Swinburne:

> I am not minded to say much of Shakespeare's Arthur. There are one or two figures in the world of his work of which there are no words that would be fit or good to say. Another of these is Cordelia. The place they have in our lives and thoughts is not one for talk. The niche set apart for them to inhabit in our secret hearts is not penetrable by the lights and noises of common day. There are chapels in the cathedral of man's highest art, as in that of his inmost life, not made to be set open to the eyes and feet of the world. Love and Death and Memory keep charge for us in silence of some beloved names. It is the crowning glory of genius, the final miracle and transcendent gift of poetry that it can add to the number of these and engrave on the very heart of our remembrance fresh names and memories of its own creation.

Such writing necessarily provokes a reaction. We should observe, too, how the critic here has said nothing whatsoever beyond what might have been understood from his opening sentences. Yet as the rest of the passage vitiates even those, which asserted that nothing was to be said about Arthur or Cordelia, the total resultant is one of sheer vacancy. This is an extreme instance; but it is typical of a tendency in nineteenth-century commentary. Such 'romantic' critics praised extravagantly, and either ignored the necessity to think out their meanings or, in trying to do so, actually misunderstood themselves. They felt the Shakespearian grandeur; they understood, or thought they understood, the Shakespearian persons; and therefore they often assumed that the Shakespearian grandeur was almost wholly a matter of 'characterization', and realistic description of human life. Tolstoy saw that they were wrong. And Tolstoy's violent attack on Shakespeare is primarily aroused, not by Shakespeare, but by the Shakespearian commentators. He refers to their 'long foggy erudite articles' (p. 458). The critics 'began to search Shakespeare for non-existent beauties, and to extol them' (p. 455): which is often true. The essay continually returns to the extravagant praise lavished on Shakespeare: praise which Tolstoy rightly saw to be either mere froth and sentiment, or definitely wrong. He can even afford Shakespeare himself a little praise:

> If people now wrote of Shakespeare that, for his time, he was a great
> writer, he managed verse well enough, was a clever actor and a good
> stage-manager, even if their valuation were inexact and somewhat exag-
> gerated, provided it was moderate, people of the younger generations
> might remain free from the Shakespearian influence.   (p. 462)

He can admit Shakespeare's 'masterly development of the
scenes' (p. 455). But he cannot, and will not, admit Shakespeare's eminence in characterization, in which, if we limit
the term to Tolstoy's meaning, he is quite right; nor his
eminence as a comprehensive and exact artist in a wide and
detailed sense, in which he is, with Bridges, quite wrong.
So Tolstoy quotes numerous examples of romantic panegyric.
His conclusion is:

> And really the suggestion that Shakespeare's works are great works of
> genius, presenting the climax both of aesthetic and ethical perfection, has
> caused and is causing great injury to men.   (p. 459)

Misguided as he may be in his whole contention, Tolstoy
is nevertheless correct in his feeling that the Shakespearian
commentary he knew was often quite out of touch with the
facts.

These masses of doubtful commentary had, indeed, clearly
influenced him. He looked in Shakespeare for the qualities
most usually praised and found them non-existent. The
actual fact, namely that Shakespeare's idolaters had continually passed over the poet's most important qualities, did
not occur to him. It could hardly have done so. Where an
English poet, Bridges, was baffled, we could hardly suppose
Tolstoy to have succeeded. Both, writing about the same
time, and similarly, though independently, reacting from
romantic criticism, bring forward precisely the same objections: poor characterization, impossible events, exaggeration,
vulgarity. Applying the hackneyed opinions to Shakespeare,
they found that these qualities refused to fit: Tolstoy therefore rejects Shakespeare wholesale; Bridges those elements
that repel him.

His essay, Tolstoy tells us,

> is the result of repeated and strenuous efforts, extending over many years,
> to harmonize my views with the opinions about Shakespeare accepted
> throughout the whole educated Christian world.   (p. 393)

Which shows how closely he was influenced by the commentators. From the commentators he advanced to Shakespeare, and found therein numerous extraordinary events
which the commentators had done nothing to explain. His
attack on Shakespeare is thus at root a healthy attempt to
break free from the 'hypnotism', as he calls it, of romantic
criticism. Lear's division of his kingdom he finds absurd.
Gloucester's attempted suicide he finds absurd. He concludes that 'Shakespeare's characters continually do and
say what is not merely unnatural to them but quite
unnecessary' (p. 437). Now *King Lear* is undoubtedly a
strange play. While we expect normal occurrences therein
we shall certainly fail to receive its statement. Incongruity
is everywhere. Lear's original action is incongruous, as
Gloucester clearly and incisively observes; and the sequent
action shows a whole world of incongruous events, bizarre,
fantastic. At the climax, we have Gloucester's mock-suicide.
The pattern of the whole must be grasped before we can
understand the significance of the parts. Looking for normal
human events, Tolstoy was baffled. We can hardly blame
him, directed, as he was, by a century of European commentary that stressed mainly Shakespeare's consummate
skill in characterization, and tended to neglect his daring
flights of symbolism, his bold strokes of allegory, his amazing power of bodying forth in terms of humanity, beasts,
and elements a central dynamic idea whose ultimate mystery
is by these expressions carried over to us but never bound
rigidly to any law of 'characterization', 'realism', 'observation', or any other of those elements of art so often taken
to be its only purpose and essence. Not that the Shakespearian imagination is purely subjective. Rather it fuses the
power originating in the poet's soul with the appearances
he observes. Fusing thus 'expression' with 'imitation', the
poet accomplishes his 'creation': which process, the process
of all poets, is always exquisitely balanced and harmonized
in Shakespeare. Tolstoy, expecting rather the novelist's skill
tending more towards 'observation' and 'imitation', is perplexed by Shakespeare. We may notice in passing that
Tolstoy's own aesthetic theory in his essay 'What is Art?'
concentrates rather on the inwardness of art, the 'feeling'

of the artist. His novels strike us, however, primarily by their realism and objectivity. They appear real as life itself, in a sense that Shakespeare's work does not. But, whether in his early practice or later theory, Tolstoy presents a rock-like simplicity. And this grand simplicity in his soul is baffled and repelled by the infinite complexities of the Shakespearian art. He could never have liked Shakespeare, because of his intellectualism, subtlety, and complexity; and yet without the misguided commentary to which he looked for help he would probably not have hated, and might even, within limits, have admired him.

So *King Lear* is condemned for being unnatural: 'this unnatural scene' (p. 399), 'the struggle does not result from a natural course of events' (p. 420), 'equally unnatural is the secondary and very similar plot' (p. 420), 'full of unnatural occurrences' (p. 405). 'Unnatural' indeed. The whole play is concerned with this matter of 'nature' and 'unnatural' events. Often as Tolstoy insists on the unnatural occurrences in *King Lear*, he does not do so so often, nor so powerfully, as the poet himself. As usual, the 'fault' observed by the critic is essential to the Shakespearian vision.

Similarly, Bridges objects that *Macbeth* presents no clear motive for the protagonist's crime. For which he blames Shakespeare:

> If he had any plain psychological conception, we should expect the drama to reveal it; but his method here is not so much to reveal as to confuse. (p. 14)

Again:

> Now this veiled confusion of motive is so well managed that it must be recognized as a device intended to escape observation. That the main conception of the play is magnificent is amply proved by the effects obtained; but they are none the less procured by a deception, a liberty of treatment or a 'dishonesty', which is purposely blurred. The naturalness is merely this, that in nature we cannot weigh or know all the motives or springs of action; and therefore we are not shock'd at not being able to understand Macbeth; the difficulty indeed is one main source of our pleasure, and is intended to be so: but this is not nature, in the sense of being susceptible of the same analysis as that by which the assumptions of science would investigate nature. (p. 15)

This passage calls for two criticisms. First I shall speak of Bridges' reference to Shakespeare's 'intentions'.

We should observe here the recurrence of the 'intention' concept: 'intended to escape observation', 'purposely blurr'd', 'and is intended to be so'. This is ever the sign of false criticism, criticism which has forgotten the primary fact of artistic composition, namely, that it derives not from 'consciousness' nor 'unconsciousness' in the usual sense, but rather from a third mode, neither the one nor the other, for which we have no proper word. We may, of course, talk metaphorically of the 'purpose', meaning the thought-direction, of the art-form itself; or the 'purpose' of one part, as contributing this or that to the whole; but never, except in definitely psychological analysis of the poet himself, of the 'intention' or 'purpose' in the poet's mind as distinct from or modifying the thing intended or purposed. Therefore to assert here that such and such an effect is 'intended to escape observation' means nothing relevant whatsoever. It cannot quite mean that such a power to elude observation is the proper and natural purpose of such an effect, since then there could scarcely be any complaint. Rather Bridges means that the poet 'intended' this. And how, indeed, can anyone know such a thing? And what difference does it make if we do? In exactly the same way Tolstoy, misled by the usual cliches of Shakespearian commentary, flounders into 'intentions':

> Such is the introduction. Not to speak of the vulgarity of these words of Gloucester, they are also out of place in the mouth of a man whom it is intended to represent as a noble character. (p. 397)

How do we know this? Why should Gloucester be 'intended' to be a noble character? Therefore, continues Tolstoy,

> ... these words of Gloucester's at the very beginning of the piece, were merely for the purpose of informing the public in an amusing way of the fact that Gloucester has a legitimate and an illegitimate son. (p. 398)

'Purpose'. So, too, Bridges often thinks he has found Shakespeare's 'purpose' of pleasing a vulgar audience. Many writers have likewise played games with Shakespeare's 'intentions'. The attempt is quite unnecessary, success always impossible, and, if achieved, would be necessarily irrelevant if not meaningless. Next I shall remark on another aspect of Bridges' criticism of *Macbeth*.

The matter of Macbeth's temptation, it is argued, is not treated scientifically. Bridges realizes that we cannot say it is 'unnatural' as depicted by the poet, since 'in nature we cannot weigh or know all the motives or springs of action'. All we can say is, that it 'is not nature, in the sense of being susceptible of the same analysis as that by which the assumptions of science would investigate nature'. That is, presumably, the *Macbeth* problem is less easily analysed than a real human problem of the same kind. Which is partly true, since a real problem would present, probably, a deceptive appearance of simplicity. But motive is always vague, a complex woven of conscious desire, semi-conscious promptings, opportunity, and, in addition, certain unknown quantities which any analysis will falsify. *Macbeth* penetrates below the veils of 'causality' and 'intention', and all such surface concepts by which we attempt to simplify the complicated interactions of appearances. It is true that 'we cannot weigh or know all the motives or springs of action. . .'. With consummate art the poet has forced us to pierce below such ready assurances as we habitually use; has forced us to forgo the comfortable 'assumptions of science'. And this very vagueness, irrationality, and mystery that baffles Bridges in the first act vitalizes the whole play, reiterated and reinforced by numerous events, actions, speeches, and metaphors throughout. The play presents a vision of essential evil in all its irrationality. Again, the critic has attacked the poet for his profundity, regarding as an ugly blot the very signature of his genius.

There is no question of blame. Writing when he did, Bridges could not be expected to read the deeper meanings in Shakespeare. His very complaints, like Tolstoy's, are a step towards understanding. Tolstoy and Bridges suffered from clear thinking: which differentiates them from their predecessors. It is for us to make a further advance. The analytic critic of Shakespeare will henceforth know that he must first grasp the vitalizing ideas behind the phenomena of the plays: otherwise his criticism will be vapid.

In the same way Bridges was insensitive to the vitalizing idea in *Measure for Measure*. 'The pardon of Angelo', he says, 'will hardly find an advocate' (p. 7). And yet the play imperatively demands such a conclusion, as certainly as the Parable of the Prodigal Son. The play is soaked in Christian ethics from start to finish, as I have shown in my detailed analysis. *Measure for Measure* presents a kind of thesis. It has a very clear ethical plan. But the poet's compressed dramatic method has continually baffled critics who look only for 'characterization', though the characterization, when understood in terms of the plot, is here probably more careful and exact than elsewhere in Shakespeare. All Bridges' objections to Angelo are quite meaningless once the pattern is grasped. He even makes definitely false statements, induced by the wrong focus of his critical vision. Angelo, he says, is not a 'passionate' man: 'there is no passion in his calculating lust' (p. 11). Again:

> His temperament does not, I think, tally with the notion of the sudden outburst of an uncontrollable animal instinct which had been artificially repressed. (p. 11)

Let us quote Shakespeare:

> What, do I love her,
> That I desire to hear her speak again,
> And feast upon her eyes? What is't I dream on?
> O cunning enemy, that, to catch a saint,
> With saints dost bait thy hook! Most dangerous
> Is that temptation that doth goad us on
> To sin in loving virtue: never could the strumpet,
> With all her double vigour, art and nature,
> Once stir my temper; but this virtuous maid
> Subdues me quite. Ever till now,
> When men were fond, I smiled and wonder'd how.
> (*Measure for Measure*, ii. ii. 177)

And yet, 'there is no passion in his calculating lust'. Again:

> When I would pray and think, I think and pray
> To several subjects. Heaven hath my empty words;
> Whilst my invention, hearing not my tongue,
> Anchors on Isabel: Heaven in my mouth,
> As if I did but only chew his name;
> And in my heart the strong and swelling evil
> Of my conception. (ii. iv. 1)

Is this not passion? But his final forgiveness is inevitable. The critic who does not like the last act of *Measure for Measure* will not be easily convinced by argument. He has so completely missed the whole point of the play. What are we to say to some one who returns from a performance of *King Lear* complaining that for his part he could see nothing funny in the conclusion? The problem is the same. No Shakespearian play will reveal its riches to anyone who refuses first to accept, and try to understand, it, fitting all minor discrepancies in with the main pattern, building the unity in his own mind which the poet has built on paper. There will then be little to complain of. But it is curious that the one play of Shakespeare which concentrates most on 'character' and ethical principles generally should be the one most usually attacked on these grounds.

Both Tolstoy and Bridges attack mainly Shakespeare's characterization. Their respective remarks on *King Lear*, *Macbeth*, and *Measure for Measure* are typical. It is clear, moreover, that they in each instance failed to see, I will not say what the poet 'intended', but what the work of art itself intends. They inspect as through a glass wrongly focused and see only a blurry chaos; they then proceed to assert that this chaos was 'intended' by the poet.

Although I have suggested the profound psychology that underlies the strangeness of *Macbeth*, there is clearly a sense in which Shakespeare's persons do not appear as 'natural' as Tolstoy's. We have at least the unusual pleasure of recognizing that the critic can here himself produce what he finds lacking in the subject of his hostility. Many very strange, all but impossible, things happen in Shakespeare. Tolstoy concentrates chiefly on *King Lear*—which is very refreshing since, for some reason, *King Lear* has never properly stood the brunt of the ignorant attacks levelled from time to time on *Measure for Measure*, *Timon of Athens*, *Troilus and Cressida*, and *Hamlet*; and surely it is as extraordinary as any.

> Then, curiously enough, to the very spot on the open heath where he is comes his father, blind Gloucester, led by an old man, and he too talks about the perversities of fate in that curious Shakespearian language. . . .
>
> (p. 409)

A remarkable coincidence. No one can deny that this is a purely arbitrary stroke of art or artificiality. The play is crammed with them. There is 'Gloucester's jump' as Tolstoy calls it—usually passed over by commentators as a perfectly natural event. As Tolstoy points out, the whole matter of Edmund's plot and Gloucester's rejection of Edgar is 'unnatural'. Moreover, the similarity between plot and sub-plot is itself surely a coincidence:

> The fact that the relation of Lear to his daughters is just the same as that of Gloucester to his sons, makes one feel even more strongly that they are both arbitrarily invented and do not flow from the characters or the natural course of events.   (p. 420)

This is undeniable. Nor is all this solely due to the necessities of dramatic art. Tolstoy quotes from the old play, *Leir*, to show how it is better than Shakespeare's in this respect. He makes his point clearly, and is, from his own view of art, here, however, irrelevant, perfectly correct. Similarly, he shows how the original tale of *Othello* has been, as it were, deliberately made more unnatural by Shakespeare. He writes of Iago's motives very much as Bridges of Macbeth's:

> There are many motives, but they are all vague; in the romance there is one motive and it is simple and clear.   (p. 431)

Tolstoy and Bridges are ever in close agreement.

Bridges likewise observes Shakespeare's habit of altering the clear reasons for things which he finds in his 'source':

> For instance, in *The Merchant of Venice*, the love of Antonio for Bassanio, which in the absence of explanation appears romantic, is merely carried over without its motive from the old story, in which Antonio is Bassanio's godfather, and adopts him and loves him as his own son. Again, Antonio's melancholy with which Shakespeare opens his play so well, using it as an interesting attraction and another romantic trait—very valuable as preparation for his conduct—is develop'd from a hint in the novel, where Antonio is sad on account of Bassanio's ill-successes. And this is an example of the greater interest of such a mood when unaccounted for, since in the original story it is of no special value.   (p. 20)

Bridges is often, as here, on the point of seeing the solution: namely, that we must accept Shakespeare's people before we understand them; and that, if we do this, we find our understanding not only of them, but of actual life, immeasurably enriched. Again:

> It would seem from such instances that Shakespeare sometimes judged conduct to be dramatically more effective when not adequately motived. In *The Winter's Tale* the jealousy of Leontes is senseless, whereas in the original story an adequate motive is developed.   (p. 21)

But *Othello* was altogether too much for Bridges, as for Tolstoy, who, however, thought it not the best but the 'least bad' (p. 429) of Shakespeare's plays. Both critics agree that the play is thoroughly weak in mechanism. 'The whole thing is impossible' (p. 23), says Bridges. It induces in him 'exasperation':

> . . . and seeing how cleverly everything is calculated to this effect, I conclude that it was Shakespeare's intention, and that what so hurts me was only a pleasurable excitement to his audience, whose gratification was relied on to lull their criticism.   (p. 24)

Exactly: 'gratification' must 'lull' our 'criticism' before we stand any chance of understanding. Certainly, *Othello* witnesses a sequence of amazing improbabilities; but if they appear harsher than elsewhere—as they do to Bridges— this is because the persons are more clearly differentiated and realized as individuals distinct from their world than are those in *King Lear* or *Macbeth*. Nor is there here the usual power of dominating atmosphere to force our too unwilling 'suspension of disbelief'. The 'better' Shakespeare's 'characterization', the cruder his plot may sometimes appear.

I shall now attempt a clarification. If my arguments seem to lead to complexity and excessive intellectualization, I reply that such qualities are forced by Tolstoy's attack. It would be easy enough to defend Shakespeare with the same dogmatic simplicity as Tolstoy uses: but that would scarcely resolve our difficulty.

Tolstoy himself will help us:

> That a great mastery in the presentation of character is attributed to Shakespeare arises from his really possessing a peculiarity which, when helped out by the play of good actors, may appear to superficial observers to be a capacity to manage scenes in which a movement of feeling is expressed. However arbitrary the positions in which he puts his characters, however unnatural to them the language he makes them speak, however lacking in individuality they may be, the movement of feeling itself, its increase and change and the combination of many contrary feelings, are often expressed correctly and powerfully in some of Shakespeare's scenes.
>   (p. 435)

That is valuable. Shakespeare's power is not merely representative. He does not show us people acting or speaking as people ordinarily do. For one thing, his persons usually speak blank verse: which would be intolerable in real life. To understand Shakespeare, one must make this original acceptance: to believe, first, in people who speak poetry; thence in human actions which subserve a poetic purpose; and, finally, in strange effects in nature which harmonize with the persons and their acts; the whole building a massive statement which, if accepted in its entirety, induces a profound experience in the reader or spectator. Tolstoy, concentrating here on 'characters', sees that a single person in the drama may well express variations of feeling, complex and contradicting emotions. This is just what poetry can do better than prose. In this way the poetic dramatist strips the appearance from human affairs, laying bare the essence. Into that naked world of burning thought and quick-changing emotion, that psychic world half-known to ourselves and carefully obscured from our neighbour, to that world the poet directs our experiencing minds. What Tolstoy observes in single persons is, however, even more true of the whole Shakespearian art-form. The thoughts and emotions of the protagonist are usually, in Shakespeare's greater plays, the substance not only of him, but of his world. He is really one with his world. He speaks unnaturally, perhaps: his world is usually, in varied ways, unnatural. And Tolstoy sees that 'the movement of feeling' is, in a sense, true, though the language be unnatural: in the same way, if we have regard to the whole art-form, 'the movement of feeling' is true, though the events be unnatural. Again, the Shakespearian world is not the world we habitually see. Yet it is the world we experience: the poignant world of primal feeling, violent subterranean life, and wayward passionate thought, controlled, denied, hidden often, then up-gushing to surprise ourselves; the inner world we experience, the world we live and fear, but not the world we normally see; nor the world we think we understand.

Therefore Hamlet, as Tolstoy will tell us, is no true 'character'. He cannot be. 'Character' in the ethical sense is the result of co-ordinating and controlling varied impulses. Men do this in different ways, expressing some, repressing others. Hence they present different 'characters' to the world, and thus we have 'character' in its literary sense. The essence of objective 'characterization' is 'differentiation'; and dif-ferentiation involves limitation. If the 'character' be not properly limited and defined, he is the less precisely drawn as a 'character'. In actual life we do well to hide and repress certain instincts. Nevertheless such dangerous impulses may be the very substance of art, for there is certainly a close relation between repressed emotions or thoughts and artistic expression, and the literary art-form is usually compact of such impulses. These are often split into different 'charac-ters': the more strictly each is limited and defined the less universally poetic he will be as a unit, and the more perfect as a 'character'. But the quintessentially poetic figure may have a full share of these impulses. Hamlet is such a figure. He is more than protagonist: he is a play in himself. He expresses many impulses, good and evil, and thus is one of Shakespeare's most universal single creations. As men are not different in the instincts and desires they possess, but only in those they express, the deeper we go in human under-standing, the less ultimate meaning we must attribute to differences of character between man and man; and if much of the poetry of life is to be confined in one person, as it is in Hamlet, his 'character' will automatically cease to exist. So madness, or rather frenzied sleep, disturbs Ahab, in *Moby Dick*, so that he rises from his bed. Melville writes:

> This latter was the eternal, living principle or soul in him; and in sleep, being for the time dissociated from the characterizing mind, which at other times employed it for its outer vehicle or agent, it spontaneously sought escape from the scorching contiguity of the frantic thing, of which, for the time, it was no longer an integral.   (*Moby Dick*, xliv)

The word 'characterizing' is significant. Hence Hamlet has no 'character', as Tolstoy saw:

> But as it is accepted that Shakespeare, the genius, could write nothing bad, learned men devote all the power of their minds to discovering extra-ordinary beauties in what is an obvious and glaring defect—particularly obvious in *Hamlet*—namely, that the chief person of the play has no char-acter at all. And lo and behold, profound critics announce that in this drama, in the person of Hamlet, is most powerfully presented a perfectly new and profound character, consisting in this, that the person has no character; and that in this absence of character lies an achievement of genius—the creation of a profound character! And having decided this, the learned critics write volumes upon volumes, until the laudations and

explanations of the grandeur and importance of depicting the character
of a man without a character fill whole libraries.   (p. 434)

Exactly. Tolstoy sees the truth. But there is more to say.

In Shakespeare it is usual to find what is first a recurrent
idea or image, or set of images, later expanded into a whole
play. The same happens with poetic style in general. The
whole business of poetic drama is to present persons speaking
the soul-language of poetry, but otherwise more or less
correspondent with real life. We are shown a visionary life
where humanity ceases to be comparatively dumb. Art always
discloses the inner flame of reality:

> Transparent Helena! Nature shows art,
> That through thy bosom makes me see thy heart.
> (*A Midsummer-Night's Dream*, ii. ii. 104)

This is a matter of style, irrespective of plot. But, as though
this were not enough, in Shakespeare's greater tragedies the
same process is reflected in the plot too. The hero, or his
world, suffers a rough tearing away of all superficial coverings, leaving the spirit exposed: thus there is created an
opportunity by which the protagonist (in *Hamlet*) or his
whole world (in *Macbeth*) becomes, as it were, doubly
poetic. So the process by which an image may develop
into a play is paralleled by this process by which poetry
itself—which is largely a revelation of 'soul' or 'spirit'
—is expanded into plots where the persons endure, in
their actuality, a similar unique disclosure. In this sense,
too, Hamlet is quintessentially poetic. Therefore we may
say that even if he had a 'character' before the action, events
—especially the sepulchral revelation of the Ghost—so tear
the superficial coverings of life from his eyes; tear also the
superficial consciousness from his mind; that they leave him
a naked soul, confronting the naked soul of mankind. And
in this consists his especially intense tragic poetry. Similarly
in *Julius Caesar* and *Macbeth* reality is ript open and naked
spirit exposed, flaring its fires through Rome, glaring its
hideous torment in Scotland. Or in *King Lear*, deceptive
appearance is agonizingly withdrawn, a deceptive consciousness dethroned, and Lear himself reaches self-knowledge
through the fantastic leaping devils of lunacy, knowledge

of his own soul. In all these plays there is a violent, extravagant, lurid spirit-world of some sort exposed; and in *Timon of Athens*, too, the tinsel glitter of civilization and humanism is withdrawn, leaving mankind naked to the imprecations of the naked Timon.

All these plays present a vision which deliberately looks deeper than 'character' even in the more poetic sense by which we speak of the 'characters' in *Henry IV*; deeper than character or any realistic experience. And we must note that in so far as the artist plumbs thus deep in his soundings, he tends to create sombre plays, tragic plays, plays instinct with elements black, fearful, evil, and spirits of nightmare fantasy. The protagonist may be shown as mad. Psychologically, we may say that the artist is liberating the deeper instincts most habitually unrecognized and repressed. But such instincts may yet again be blended with brighter essences and create again new beauty as profound as these yet less terrible; and such art will immediately appear more realistic. Beyond a certain point, evil, being hostile to life and therefore unnatural, must, in any extreme vision, have an extraordinary and unnatural expression; whereas what is good for life is, at an extreme, necessarily more life-like. *Antony and Cleopatra*, blending tragedy with romance, is more nearly correspondent to actual affairs than are the sombre plays: its theme is love, and the love-instinct is good; and what is most good tends to be most life-like, and needs no violent plot and symbolism such as we find in *Macbeth* or *Hamlet*. Such life-likeness will be far from photographic: it is still intensely poetic, containing all elements exposed in those sombre statements, yet mating them afresh to human and natural actuality in terms of emotional and intellectual language far from any normal speech. So numerous variations are played on 'characterization' in Shakespeare. In *Othello* and *Coriolanus* the persons are very firmly differentiated and fairly 'natural'; in *Timon of Athens*, firmly differentiated but scarcely 'natural' in the usual sense; in *Antony and Cleopatra* 'natural' but not very solidly differentiated; in *King Lear*, and still more in *Macbeth*, often both 'unnatural' (in the sense of 'remarkable' or 'strange') and slightly differentiated. But in all these greater plays the whole

vision is primary: human realism, sometimes natural, sometimes unnatural, only exists in vassalage to this poetic vision.
And so Hamlet especially, who is formed as a person of the
visionary substance which vitalizes the greater tragedies, has
no 'character'. He is more than 'literary': he is like a real
person with a real person's potentiality for all things, in
which he resembles Cleopatra. The persons surrounding
him are nearer 'characters' in the literary sense: they are well
differentiated. Hamlet is universal. In him we recognize
ourselves, not our acquaintances. Possessing all characters,
he possesses none.

It is really not surprising that Tolstoy should have
found fault with Shakespeare's 'characterization'. In his
sense, it clearly does not exist:

> If the characters utter whatever comes to hand and as it comes to hand
> and all in one and the same way as in Shakespeare, even the effect of
> gesture is lost; and therefore whatever blind worshippers of Shakespeare
> may say, Shakespeare does not show us characters.   (p. 424)

Tolstoy would have all the persons speak differently, according to their own 'characters'. Shakespeare's persons make
utterance from a height where all men speak alike: the height
of universal experience, refracted often in human terms,
voiceless save by poetry.

III

I shall next show more clearly how both Tolstoy and
Bridges have failed to appreciate Shakespeare primarily
through neglect of his imaginative and symbolic effects, due
to the excessive emphasis placed on Shakespeare's characterization throughout nineteenth-century commentary.

It is strange that Shakespeare's most subtle symbolic
effects should expose him to charges of vulgarity and grossness. Both critics find Shakespeare guilty of excessive vulgarity and exaggeration. For example, Bridges writes:

> And this provides an ample account of the next fault that offends my
> feelings, that is what may be called brutality, which, though often
> mingled with the indelicacy already spoken of, must be distinguished
> from it.   (p. 4)

He remarks on 'the extravagant grossness of Leontes' language to Hermione', and asserts that 'the coarse terms in which Claudio repudiates Hero enfeeble the plot of *Much Ado About Nothing*'. I have already sufficiently indicated how the horrors of sex-loathing are necessary to the patterning of many plays; indeed often, as in *Troilus and Cressida* and *Hamlet*, are primary themes. It is the same with Leontes. And, as for *Much Ado About Nothing*, Claudio's behaviour very considerably modifies our idea of Claudio as a person in the play. It is dramatically dynamic. Probably the critic means that Claudio's words are out of place in a person whom it is 'intended' to represent as a gentleman. So Bridges finds Shakespeare's dialogue 'pitched in extravagant tones' (p. 6). And Tolstoy says the same:

> In Shakespeare everything is exaggerated: the actions are exaggerated, so are their consequences, the speeches of the characters are exaggerated, and therefore at every step the possibility of artistic impression is infringed.
>
> (p. 438)

It will be obvious that this and all the complaints about characterization are due to a single cause: a failure to focus imaginatively the proper poetic pattern to be inspected. Most of the difficulties are swiftly resolved by any competent imaginative interpretation.

Bridges is repelled by a speech in *The Tempest:*

> . . . in proximity to Prospero's romantic cell there is a 'filthy-mantled pool' which is the occasion of a disgusting utterance in the mouth of the delicate Ariel.   (p. 5)

Ariel's remark as to how the pool 'o'erstunk' the feet of his victims may seem unpleasant. Possibly, it does not suit Ariel. I could say that I thought it harmless, but that would be merely my own opinion. What does matter, however, is this: we should be more ready to receive the poet's message. 'Characterization' may not here be primary. There may be something else we ought to consider. The 'filthy-mantled pool' is symbolically of considerable importance: a fitting punishment for the coarseness, the lust and villainy and greed, of the delinquents. Just as Falstaff is tipped into the Thames mud and later has his fat body tormented by gnomes and fairies, these suggesting that spiritual element his lust has wronged, so Caliban and Trinculo and Stephano are likewise chased and punished by Ariel and Prospero's spirits, and left in a bog. And in Ariel's words we have a reminder that their filthy punishment is to be related to their own uncleanness, their essential earthiness and lack of spirit-beauty. His phrase is appropriately vivid. Now clearly, whether or not Bridges would have been satisfied with this explanation, he shows no signs that he has even considered it. Nor could we expect him to have done so.

The poet's vision is thus often wronged by a critical intelligence which does not see the vitalizing plan and purpose beating in the incidents and persons, without some sympathy with which those incidents and persons themselves appear unreal and often vulgar. Bridges necessarily finds *The Winter's Tale* impossible. Clearly, his method could not begin to understand it. For what scheme of 'characterization' could ever account for Hermione's extraordinary behaviour? It is amusing to see the realistic critical intelligence at work on a poet's vision of immortality as though it were a newspaper account of a street event. Nor is it surprising that 'tempests', too, come under the shadow of this criticism:

> And how easy it would have been to have provided a more reasonable ground for Othello's jealousy. If in the break of the second act his vessel had been delay'd a week by the storm, those days of anxiety and officious consolation would have given the needed opportunity, and the time-contradictions might also have been avoided.   (p. 23)

How easy, indeed. And how easy to accept the play as it is without making dream pictures of what it might be. And what if the tempest is here far more important than any 'reasonable' grounds for jealousy, or time-contradictions? The *Othello* tempest is presented as powerless to hurt or delay the lovers: that is its place in *Othello*. It is to be contrasted with the tempests of passion that follow. By the time he came to *Othello* the poet might at least be allowed to put his tempest where and how he chose. He had surely had enough practice by then. Why attempt to rewrite the drama and alter the symbolic effects? Such is the method of false criticism.

Tolstoy also comes up against tempests. There is a tempest in *King Lear* as well as in *Othello* and the other plays; and this tempest worried Tolstoy. It was a 'coarse embellishment.' He writes:

> Act III begins with thunder, lightning, and storm—a special kind of storm such as there never was before, as one of the characters in the play says. (p. 405)

Again,

> Lear walks about the heath and utters words intended to express despair: he wishes the winds to blow so hard that they (the winds) should crack their cheeks, and that the rain should drench everything, and that the lightning should singe his white head and thunder strike the earth flat and destroy all the germs 'that make ingrateful man'. The Fool keeps uttering yet more senseless words. Kent enters. Lear says that, for some reason, in this storm all criminals shall be discovered and exposed. Kent, still not recognized by Lear, persuades Lear to take shelter in a hovel. The Fool thereupon utters a prophecy quite unrelated to the situation, and they all go off. (p. 405)

It is easy to sneer at Tolstoy's lack of insight. But can the 'characterization' school of criticism answer Tolstoy's objections here or elsewhere? And can any school of criticism defend the Fool's soliloquy? It is strange that the disintegration of Shakespeare has paid such respectful disregard to *King Lear*. It certainly is not the least 'unnatural' of the plays. Tolstoy found the language quite untrue to human nature:

> No real people could speak, or could have spoken, as Lear does—saying that, 'I would divorce me from thy mother's tomb' if Regan did not receive him, or telling the winds to 'crack your cheeks', or bidding 'the wind blow the earth into the sea', or 'swell the curled waters 'bove the main', as the Gentleman describes what Lear said to the storm. . . . (p. 423)

Observe how Tolstoy continually returns to the tempest. His powerful mind penetrates to the heart of his subject: his conclusions may be wrong, but his error is worth more than most critics' truth. Again:

> Instead of the unnatural expulsion of Lear during a tempest and his roaming about the heath, in the old play Leir with Perillus during their journey to France very naturally come to the last degree of want. (p. 427)

Shakespeare's imaginative effects repelled and worried Tolstoy, as they should repel and worry any clear-thinking critic who has not properly understood their nature:

> The artificiality of the positions, which do not arise from a natural course of events and from the characters of the people engaged, and their incompatibility with the period and the place, is further increased by the coarse embellishments Shakespeare continually makes use of in passages meant to be specially touching. The extraordinary storm during which Lear roams about the heath, or the weeds which for some reason he puts on his head, as Ophelia does in *Hamlet*, or Edgar's attire—all these effects, far from strengthening the impression, produce a contrary effect.
>
> (p. 421)

Again Tolstoy selects for attack matters of primary importance. For Lear's crown of flowers holds a deep significance. It is the crown of his purgatory. It is a symbol with many relations. It touches the crown of thorns of the Crucifixion. And yet its flower-sweetness also suggests and prepares us for the child-like innocency of Lear's latter state, when he is reunited in love with Cordelia. In this it resembles Ophelia's crown of flowers. It is 'fantastic'—witness Capell's direction: 'Enter Lear fantastically dressed with wild flowers'. Or, as Tolstoy puts it, 'just then, Lear enters, for some reason all covered with wild flowers' (p. 413). This, with the crown described by Cordelia, suggests the 'fantastic' madness that he has endured, and also the wild-simple nature which he reaches after the loss of his kingship, leaving civilization for love and nature's simplicity. And then again, the crown reminds us of Cleopatra's diadem of love, or Cassius' wreath, suggesting victory through and in suffering and tragedy. So various may be the content of a symbol; so exquisite is the Shakespearian imagination. Similarly we could write on Ophelia's crown, or Edgar's nakedness. But all this is missed by the specialists in 'characterization'.

In the same way the fine 'sun' and 'moon' symbolism of *Othello* was missed by Tolstoy:

> A man who is preparing to murder some one he loves cannot utter such phrases, and still less after the murder can he say that the sun and moon ought now to be eclipsed and the globe to yawn, nor can he, whatever kind of a nigger he may be, address devils, inviting them to roast him in sulphur, and so forth.   (p. 430)

And here, again, Tolstoy is worrying at a truth. Othello's language is decorative, excessively so; and we cannot understand the play properly without attending to this quality. Othello himself is compact of romance, highly-coloured, rich, exotic; and his words are in a style unique in Shakespeare. They often border on the sentimental, luxuriating in emotion:

> If he really suffers from grief and remorse then, when intending to kill himself, he would not utter phrases about his own services, about a pearl, about his eyes dropping tears *as fast as the Arabian trees their medicinal gum*, and still less could he talk about the way a Turk scolded a Venetian, and how *'thus'* he punished him for it. (p. 430)

There is justice in Tolstoy's complaint. Yet he misses the power of Shakespeare's symbols, the 'sun' and 'moon' whose light shines or dims in Shakespeare according to love's fortunes on earth; he misses the power of the 'jewel' in Shakespeare's love-poetry, and the fine importance always given to warrior-service, such as Othello's, throughout the plays. These, the imaginative effects and what Professor Barker Fairley has well called the 'philosophic invariables', are not being received. However Tolstoy and Bridges both continually worry at the important, the significant, points; irritated by them, as though semi-consciously aware of the true Shakespearian excellences, yet powerless to focus their beauty.

So Shakespeare is put down as a writer pandering to vulgar tastes:

> 'But one must not forget the times in which Shakespeare wrote', say his belauders. 'It was a time of cruel and coarse manners, a time of the then fashionable euphuism, that is, an artificial manner of speech—a time of forms of life strange to us, and therefore to judge Shakespeare one must keep in view the times when he wrote.' (p. 438)

So writes Tolstoy, here stating admirably the main thesis advanced by Bridges, and followed by modern commentary. Failing to find any inherent unity in the art-form, the critic has to overstep the limit of aesthetic commentary and try to account for the artistic essence in terms of its 'causes', its 'circumstances', its supposed inartistic 'purposes'. Thus our modern 'realistic' criticism of Shakespeare came into being: aptly, it soon developed into disintegration, such pseudo-realism and pseudo-scholarship, if carried far, being essentially disintegrating and destructive.

IV

Tolstoy indicts Shakespeare on two main charges. First, his poor characterization and unnatural effects generally; and, second, his lack of the religious essence. Granted the Shakespeare given to him by the commentators, we cannot easily blame him. I have answered the charge against 'characterization'. I have already partly answered Tolstoy's second point; but I offer a few more remarks thereon.

Following the commentators, Tolstoy finds Shakespeare's ethic intolerable. He quotes Gervinus at length and Brandes. Both these consider themselves able to say just what Shakespeare thought wrong and what he thought right. Their conclusions appear extremely rash, though Tolstoy here agrees with them:

> . . . And any one who reads attentively the works of Shakespeare cannot but acknowledge that the attribution of this view of life to Shakespeare by those who praise him is perfectly correct.   (p. 445)

Elsewhere, however, Tolstoy complains that Shakespeare's work shows no coherent thought at all. Indeed, he quite fails to find any sort of satisfactory religion, philosophy, or any unity whatsoever, in the Shakespearian universe: 'The characters utter whatever comes to hand and as it comes to hand' (p. 424). We have a fine emphasis on the importance of religion to the drama:

> Art, especially dramatic art which demands for its realization extensive preparations, expenditure, and labour, was always religious, that is to say, its object was to evoke in man a clearer conception of that relation of man to God attained at the time by the advanced members of the society in which the art was produced.
>
> So it should be by the nature of the matter, and so it always had been among all nations: among the Egyptians, Hindus, Chinese, and Greeks—from the earliest time that we have knowledge of the life of man. . . .
> (p. 452)

Tolstoy observes how the decline of the Miracle and Morality plays synchronized with the rediscovery of Greek models, which were favoured by dramatists who should have worked out for themselves a new Christian drama; and how afterwards eighteenth-century writers in Germany, becoming wearied by the French classical school, yet still admiring the

Greek tragedians, looked for something of the same sort to copy:

> These men, not understanding that the sufferings and strife of their heroes had a religious significance for the Greeks, imagined that it was only necessary to reject the inconvenient law of the three Unities, and without containing any religious element corresponding to the beliefs of their own time, the representations of various incidents in the lives of historic personages and of strong human passions in general would afford a sufficient basis for the drama.   (p. 454)

Goethe praised Shakespeare. His work satisfied the demands of the moment. Shakespearian idolatry was born in Germany, and quickly overspread Europe. Such is Tolstoy's account. So Shakespeare was praised for work from a religious point of view quite chaotic:

> To make their praise of the whole of Shakespeare more convincing they composed an aesthetic theory, according to which a definite religious view of life is not at all necessary for the creation of works of art in general, or for the drama in particular.   (p. 456)

How far Tolstoy is exactly right in his historical details need not concern us. But his main position is clear enough. He cannot accept as a great poet a writer who has no religious centre, background, or framework for his art.

'Religion' is a vague term, but definition is here hardly necessary. Tolstoy uses it in a wide sense and we may do the same, taking its content to range from an exact orthodoxy to an individual's philosophy of life. And clearly Shakespeare presents us very definitely with just such a variable religion-philosophy compound as Tolstoy seems to require. He is an admirable example of the exact kind of writer Tolstoy in theory admired:

> By 'the religious essence of art', I reply, I mean not an external inculcation of any religious truth in artistic guise, and not an allegorical representation of those truths, but the expression of a definite view of life corresponding to the highest religious understanding of a given period: an outlook which, serving as the impelling motive for the composition of the drama, permeates the whole work though the author is unconscious of it. So it has always been with true art, and so it is with every true artist in general and with dramatists especially. Hence, as happened when the drama was a serious thing, and as should be according to the essence of the matter, he alone can write a drama who has something to say to men—something highly important for them—about man's relation to God, to the universe, to all that is infinite and unending.   (p. 457)

This is the true Shakespeare that eluded Tolstoy; the Shakespeare that emerges from attention to his imaginative qualities. Here is the Shakespeare Tolstoy rightly derived from the would-be laudatory commentators:

> But when, thanks to the German theories about objective art, an idea had been established that, for drama, this is not wanted at all, then a writer like Shakespeare who in his own soul had not formed religious convictions corresponding to his period, and who had even no convictions at all, but piled up in his plays all possible events, horrors, fooleries, discussions, and effects, could evidently be accepted as the greatest of dramatic geniuses.
> (p. 457)

Tolstoy's attack forcibly insists on a truth that we must realize in our study of Shakespeare. It is essential with such a writer to understand that axis on which his work revolves: otherwise we necessarily find chaos. And the great writer, as Tolstoy says, is not chaotic.

The drama has, indeed, fallen from its high origin. The problem is crucial to-day, and depends on our understanding of Shakespeare. Whilst Shakespeare's plays are allowed to stand insouciantly regardless of all ultimate questions, then we can safely continue to deny any necessary religious content to the greatest dramatic poetry; since no one will readily deny to Shakespeare at least an honourable place in dramatic history. Once, however, we see that Shakespeare is an artist fit to stand by Dante in point of religious apprehension, then the case for the religious message and purpose of the drama becomes unanswerable.

We must attend to the true interpretation of Shakespeare. Then we shall recognize the deeper meanings of his romantic comedies, their dreamland melodies set beyond the stormy seas of misfortune. And we must observe the blending of that music with the tempestuous passions of the tragedies. We must understand the disorder-philosophy of the Histories, the death-forces in *Hamlet* and *Macbeth* embattled against life, the Christian ethic of *Measure for Measure*, the purgatorial vision of *King Lear*, the accomplished paradise of *Antony and Cleopatra*.[1] And beyond those we shall be directed to the birth and resurrection dramas of the Final Plays; recognizing therein true myths of immortality caught

[1] See my essays on *Antony and Cleopatra* in *The Imperial Theme*.

from the penetralium of mystery by one of the few greatest writers of the world.

Tolstoy understood and trenchantly stated the modern problem:

> The life of humanity only approaches perfection by the elucidation of religious consciousness (the only principle securely uniting men one with another). The elucidation of the religious consciousness of man is accomplished through all sides of man's spiritual activity. One side of that activity is art. One part of art, and almost the most important, is the drama.
>
> And therefore the drama, to deserve the importance attributed to it, should serve the elucidation of religious consciousness. Such the drama always was, and such it was in the Christian world. But with the appearance of Protestantism in its broadest sense—that is to say, the appearance of a new understanding of Christianity as a teaching of life—dramatic art did not find a form corresponding to this new understanding of religion, and the men of the Renaissance period were carried away by the imitation of classical art. This was most natural, but the attraction should have passed, and art should have found, as it is now beginning to find, a new form corresponding to the altered understanding of Christianity. (p. 459)

What 'new form' did Tolstoy expect? Probably a strictly ethical drama, concerned, not with theology, poetic symbolism, death and resurrection, that world of high and creative imagination proper to great art, but rather with the fine simplicities of goodness, human sacrifice, human labour, human love. A drama of ethic and characterization.

One cannot deny the rugged beauty of Tolstoy's gospel. But it is not enough; not enough for a great religious drama. Such drama will be not merely ethical, but metaphysical too, often theocentric, always intensely symbolical. It must body forth in terms of human action and the varied melodies of speech the emotions that surge in man, the grief that wrings his soul, the joy that lights his laughter; and it must suggest the supernatural forces that prompt his little act, the purposes unseen which man serves alike with sun and star and waving corn. It will rend the veil which shrouds the ultimate mysteries of birth and death, so that graves wake their sleepers at its command. Persons both satanic and divine will inter-thread its story, the multitudinous seas sound their war in the tempests of its action, the wrath of its gods thunder from heaven to earth; while all eternities shall linger in its music.

XV

HAMLET RECONSIDERED (1947)

PRELIMINARY NOTE

This essay, a rough preliminary draft of which I have had by me for a number of years, is intended to supplement, though not to replace, those already written (including my 'Rose of May' in *The Imperial Theme*). I hope all the essays will be read in conjunction. It is not, however, supposed that they exhaust the latent meanings of *Hamlet*; and I would draw the attention of my readers to Mr. Roy Walker's very important study in imaginative interpretation, *The Time is Out of Joint*, being published by Andrew Dakers (which I had the privilege of seeing in typescript). Though our approaches are basically similar, and our material in places overlaps, the clashes are, on the whole, comparatively few: an additional witness, if such be needed, of the play's peculiar and inexhaustible wealth.

I

MY former essays on *Hamlet* have for long seemed to me both inadequate and, in their emphasis, misleading. I here offer a restatement, intended, however, less to contradict than to extend and expand my earlier remarks, whilst enlisting for new attention certain scenes and speeches hitherto unjustly neglected.

I challenged the obvious reading of Hamlet as wholly—or almost wholly—sympathetic and Claudius as a thorough stage villain. To that challenge I still, in general, adhere, with this reservation; that the obvious reading is, as it were, assumed and supposed to be modified, not dispelled, by the new remarks. We all know that Hamlet starts as an admirable young man of high ideals and excellent intentions, that Claudius is a criminal opportunist, Gertrude a woman of the world and Ophelia a weakling. But this is not the whole truth. Suppose, in the war of 1914–18, one man volunteers for service and returns a mental and moral wreck, while a friend of his stays at home and builds up, by profiteering, a sound business. In 1935 the one has behind him a criminal career, the other is a respected member of society radiating health and happiness. We assume that volunteering for service is, for purposes of our parable, a high moral action:

yet it leads to evil. Both men appear later before the gates of Heaven. What should St. Peter do?

Such problems call naturally for dramatic exploitation. Absolute honesty was satirised in Molière's Alceste, in *Le Misanthrope*; and somewhat similarly Ibsen's Gregers in *The Wild Duck* spreads misery in the name of his 'claims of the ideal'. The possibility of evil conditioning social good is the theme alike of Ibsen's *Pillars of Society* and Shaw's *Major Barbara*. Here is Undershaft, Shaw's successful munition magnate:

> I moralized and starved until one day I swore that I would be a full-fed free man at all costs; that nothing should stop me except a bullet, neither reason nor morals nor the lives of other men. I said, 'Thou shalt starve ere I starve'; and with that word I became free and great. I was a dangerous man until I had my will: now I am a useful, beneficent, kindly person. That is the history of most self-made millionaires, I fancy. When it is the history of every Englishman we shall have an England worth living in.

We are reminded of Claudius. The problem is not, strictly speaking, ethical: it is rather the problem of ethics, or morality. Is morality autonomous? Are morals good? We are plunged into a realm beyond morality, beyond good and evil; into Nietzsche's world; though it would be a foolishness to equate the thoughts of Shaw's ironic comedy with the Nietzschean profundity. It is that very profundity to which *Hamlet* introduces us.[1]

These complexities my former essays related to the more final opposition of life and death. The play is shadowed by death, and this we ignore at our peril. Whatever else we find within the play a primary emphasis, in interpretation or production, must be allowed to the imaginative weight of the Ghost scenes, the Graveyard, the final group of dead bodies, Hamlet's soliloquy—and clothes; to the poetic realization of death as a living presence. Whatever else we discover, these, the imaginative, poetic and dramatic, solidities must be preserved.

Such are the difficulties in whose toils Hamlet and the other persons—to say nothing of the poor would-be com-

---

[1] My references to Nietzsche are elucidated in my study of *Thus Spake Zarathustra* in *Christ and Nietzsche*.

mentator—are caught. The drama aims to penetrate beyond
good and evil by relating the opposition to life and death,
using a complex design in which the positive of one opposition is alined with the negative of the other, so sharply
stimulating our sense of incongruity and dissatisfaction.

In my earlier essays I rather rashly—and this is symptomatic of what I do find wanting in them—stated that on
certain occasions Hamlet showed 'utter loss of control'; but
this is surely a matter best left to the individual reader, actor
or producer. The unsatisfactory nature of my own statements
was brought home to me whilst acting the part, when my
emphases fell differently; and differently too during performances in different productions. Shakespeare has been at
great pains, as Bridges puts it in *The Testament of Beauty*, to
set Hamlet 'gingerly'—excellent word!—on the knife-edge
dividing sanity from madness. The variations of that delicate
balance, which may here or there tilt one way or the other
on different readings, are not to be arbitrarily defined.

But why should Shakespeare do this? The recurrence of
mad themes in great literature, and especially in drama, or
works of dramatic quality, is obvious: in Greek and Elizabethan drama, in Dostoievsky, in Melville, in *Journey's End*
(which I take to be a more important work than is usually
supposed). Madness or semi-madness may be used—and
this is especially clear in Stanhope—for dramatizing a profound insight. The poet, by projecting and mastering mad
themes in literature, is able to make certain daring explora-
tions without risking personal insanity. His art is at once an
adventure into and a mastery of the demonic, Nietzsche's
'Dionysian' world. Now Hamlet the man has often enough
been felt to reflect, in some especial sense, the poet himself,
the artistic temperament as such; and if this be so, it is quite
natural that he should be shown in a state of variously controlled insanity. Here, as in other matters, the play tries to
strike a peculiarly subtle balance. So, like many a poet or
dramatist (e.g. Byron, Shaw), Hamlet attacks society by wit
and buffoonery, as well as by actual play-production, in
order to make an all but impossible relation or reference
where disparity is clear and the time 'out of joint' (I. v. 188).
Hamlet suffers for his profundity, for his advance, pre-

maturely hastened by his ghost-converse, beyond normality and mortality. He is on the way to superman status in the Nietzschean sense.

II

We must next proceed to some highly complex analyses. Many readers must have wondered why, though the play is certainly profound, though Hamlet is himself supposed to be a profound thinker, yet, when we actually consider the speeches concerned, there seems little peculiarly difficult or deep. The words are simple, the events easy to follow. Yet somehow the whole, and even Hamlet's own speeches, remain inexhaustibly baffling. Part of the reason we have already attributed to the peculiar countering of imaginative and ethical principles: but there is more to notice. Certain key speeches remain to be considered. As thought, the thinking in these is, superficially at least, simple; but it reflects something other, beyond thought; it reflects, or discusses, a state of being, and that state is not simple, nor the speeches, if carefully inspected, easily understood. Just as we are here pushed beyond morality, beyond good and evil—though the play never properly succeeds in advancing beyond life and death—so we are at times pushed, as it were, to a thinking beyond thought.

We are to concentrate now on the middle action starting with the Players' entry. This scene with the Players at first appears very dubiously organic. It cannot be adequately placed by a reference to Hamlet's 'character' and the nature of his hobbies; not, anyway, without a more profound insight than is usual into the function of hobbies in general and this in particular. The play before the King as normally understood has a melodramatic plot interest only. We shall observe its deeper implications; but these alone can scarcely justify this lengthy introduction.

The Player's long Hecuba speech (II. ii. 498), rich in epic remembrance of a famous action concerned with the cruelty of 'fortune', acts on Hamlet, as does Fortinbras' army later, facing him with the world of high endeavour and noble suffering to which he is not tuned. The Player's rant and tears suggest not an unreal emotion, but rather the use and unleashing of real emotion where artistic emotion was more properly in order. Hamlet is not therefore impressed by the Player's art, though he is an admirer of the lines themselves. His own speaking, according to Polonius, showed 'good accent' and 'discretion' (ii. ii. 498) and he is later to give the Players a lesson in declamation. Polonius is a sensitive critic: he it is who objects to the speech's length and, noting the man's tears, calls it off; though Hamlet tactfully ('He's for a jig or a tale of bawdry or he sleeps', ii. ii. 530) does his best throughout to support his friend. Possibly the account of the boy actors is supposed to underline the quality of these older travelling players: the typical 'old actor' being superceded by these peculiarly young upstarts.[1]

In his soliloquy Hamlet feels inferior, not to the artist, but to the man who feels too passionately to be a good artist:

> What's Hecuba to him or he to Hecuba
> That he should weep for her?   (ii. ii. 593)

So he feels inferior; as later he feels inferior before Fortinbras. 'Am I a coward?' he asks (ii. ii. 606). From the standpoint of good art he has no reason to feel inferior, since his speaking is better than the Player's. He is, too, half-way to a state higher than Fortinbras'; but such claims to worth do not, in practice, prevent people like Hamlet—Prufrock is a modern example—from feeling inferior. After praising the Player's outburst he allows, or perhaps rather forces, himself, to express his own feelings, which stream out in a succession of vulgar adjectives:

> Bloody, bawdy villain!
> Remorseless, treacherous, lecherous, kindless villain!
>   (ii. ii. 616)

The facile alliteration and jingle underline the words' superficial quality, and, as later in the Graveyard scene, Hamlet is annoyed at his own rant. What he wants is something more than curses and less, for a reason the play never, except perhaps once ('Is't not perfect conscience to quit him

---

[1] Some of the dialogue concerning the battle of the theatres is doubtfully organic. Mr. Roy Walker sees in the Players' supercession by children a reflection in miniature of the play's central problem. Certainly the contrast of 'rapiers' and 'goose-quills' supports such a reading.

with this arm?'—v. ii. 67), defines, than bloodshed. Towards
the end of his soliloquy he finds it: the play before the King.
His speaking was artistic speaking and this is pre-eminently
the artist's solution. All art is a means of relating the higher,
beyond-thought, super-state to the lower, normal, consciousness of society. It is approach, attack, and love, all in
one. Hamlet becomes therefore a critic of society resembling
Molière, Voltaire, Swift, Ibsen, Shaw, using art for his
purpose, aiming to attack from within, to raise a fifth column
in the soul of his antagonist, to awake conscience:

> I have heard
> That guilty creatures, sitting at a play,
> Have, by the very cunning of the scene,
> Been struck so to the soul that presently
> They have proclaim'd their malefactions;
> For murder, though it have no tongue, will speak
> With most miraculous organ. I'll have these players
> Play something like the murder of my father
> Before mine uncle. I'll observe his looks.
> I'll tent him to the quick. If he but blench
> I know my course . . .   (ii. ii. 625)

He wonders if such promptings as the Ghost's are indeed
trustworthy. He wants to bring truth to light:

> The play's the thing
> Wherein I'll catch the conscience of the King!   (ii. ii. 641)

Let 'King' stand for government, for society, the world
over and 'the play' for dramatic art, so consistently concerned
with sin and conscience, at all times and places. We begin
to see why this couplet echoes and re-echoes in us with a
more than melodramatic meaning. ·

It might be argued that Hamlet's is not the highest kind
of art; that it serves a detective function, is at the best
propagandist and satiric. But something similar works
within all great drama, the 'detective' function there ex-
ploring the depths of the unconscious, the soul, of the
audience. There is no ultimate distinction. Elsewhere Hamlet's view of drama is perhaps Jonsonian rather than Shakespearian. He sees it as eminently a social reflection:

> They are the abstracts and brief chronicles of the time. After your death
> you were better have a bad epitaph than their ill report while you live.
>   (ii. ii. 555)

As a thinker, Hamlet is, in all these passages, still tangled in the web of good and evil, though he has glimpses, as we shall see, of something more important. To his mother he preaches directly, moving after the play from stage to pulpit.

To return. When, after the first Players' scene, we next meet Hamlet, we find him, as never elsewhere, in a serene, backwater, mood, entirely in his own world, whatever that may be. He is unhampered by contact with others: remember his earlier sigh of relief at 'Now I am alone . . .' (ii. ii. 583). But this time he does not, as before, consider his immediate contacts and purposes: his thoughts are at once less hampered and more universal. Here, if anywhere, we should get the real Hamlet.

This soliloquy (iii. i. 56–88) at first seems reasonably clear, but difficulties multiply on close inspection. Commentators differ as to whether Hamlet's

> To be, or not to be; that is the question

refers to the proposed killing of Claudius or to the killing of himself. Hitherto I have supported the latter reading, but I now think that both are somehow included, or rather surveyed from a vantage not easy to define. Let us leave the opening until we have studied the remainder.

The thinking is enigmatic and its sequences baffling; and our analysis cannot avoid complexity. It will be the more easily followed if we remember the root dualism of the play: that of (i) introspection, deathly melancholia, and a kind of half-willing passivity and (ii) strong government (the King), martial honour (Fortinbras) and lively normality (Laertes). Synthesis appears impossible. There seems to be no *middle path*. Our soliloquy attempts the synthesis by means of a confused and ambiguous phraseology. Hamlet considers

> Whether 'tis nobler in the mind to suffer
> The slings and arrows of outrageous fortune,
> Or to take arms against a sea of troubles
> And, by opposing, end them.   (iii. i. 57)

The first lines suggest the universal problem of man's tragic destiny, but the last two at least seem to indicate an actual contest: such sea-imagery is associated elsewhere in Shakespeare with the repelling of armed invasion.[1] 'Take arms' therefore hints the idea of hostile action as opposed to passive endurance, though one cannot be sure that suicide, as a violent reply to fortune, may not be present also. One could argue that, since 'slings and arrows' are metaphorical, 'take arms' may be so too; and that 'sea of troubles' in close association with 'fortune' suggests a universal problem that could not be adequately met by direct action, with 'suicide' as a necessary corollary constituent to the meaning. The phraseology is at once inclusive and enigmatic, and enigmatic precisely because it is inclusive of incompatibles, since hostile action is the direct opposite of suicide; self-slaughter, in terms at least of life, being the one ultimate and absolute retreat. It is this absolute distinction that normally confuses Hamlet and such as he (the pacifist to-day is an example), since there appears to be no proper middle way; yet here it would appear that Hamlet's mind is thinking somehow outside, or above, this apparently vital distinction. His phraseology is abnormal; and it is to grow more so.

Next, he meditates on death, not necessarily as a result of suicide—which it is at least arguable that he has not yet considered—but purely as a general philosophic speculation, considering carefully its possibilities of peace and pain, and moving on explicitly to suicide as the obvious solution to human ills could one be sure of a dreamless sleep. This forms the main body of our soliloquy and is easy to understand, being typical enough of our death-shadowed protagonist. But we are finally returned, in a most peculiar manner, to the world of fine action: from deathly and explicitly suicidal meditation, but with no sense whatever of contrast, to the Fortinbras values. The phraseology is again enigmatic. Fear of the future life 'puzzles the will' of the would-be suicide. The phrase is clear; yet, in view of Hamlet's central problem throughout, we cannot avoid a semi-conscious reference to worldly action. Next, we hear that 'conscience does make cowards of us all.' Now 'conscience' may mean (i) conscience in the modern sense, as 'Catch the conscience of the King'

---

[1] See also *Richard II*, ii. i. 62; *King John*, ii. i. 24; *Pericles*, iv. iv. 43; v. i. 195; *Cymbeline*, v. iv. 96. See *The Crown of Life*, p. 194.

(II. ii. 642), 'How smart a lash that speech doth give my
conscience' (III. i. 50), 'They are not near my conscience'
(v. ii. 58), and 'Is't not perfect conscience' (v. ii. 67). There
may be a harking back to the earlier suicide soliloquy and
its thought of 'the Everlasting' fixing, 'his canon 'gainst
self-slaughter' (I. ii. 132). But conscience in this play is
highly honoured (as at I. v. 87), and only dubiously to be
related to cowardice. Some commentators read (ii) 'conscience'='excessive self-consciousness'; that is, the fault of
'thinking too precisely on the event' (IV. iv. 41), the very
words by which Hamlet contrasts his own indecision with
the valour of a Fortinbras ('coward' occurs in both contexts).
So we have suicide directly related to Fortinbras' military
ardour. Can Hamlet mean that if he were as true to his own
longings as a Fortinbras is to his, he would kill, not others,
but himself? Or merely that his conscience, in the religious
sense, precludes suicide? Or both? And now things get
swiftly worse; for next we hear that, through this failure in
courage, 'the native hue of resolution is sicklied o'er with
the pale cast of thought.' The image (cp. Fortinbras' 'lawless
resolutes' at I. i. 98) contrasts the chubby face of youthful
ardour with the sickly introspection of the ascetic. But what
on earth has this rosy-cheeked boy to do with suicide?—
for it is he, not the other, who is expected to take the plunge.
Every line now, by careful gradation, is directing our
thoughts more and more clearly from suicide towards the
incompatible ideal of strong worldly action among men:
'pale cast of thought' quite inevitably belongs to 'thinking
too precisely on the event' (IV. iv. 41). Lastly we are told
that this is how

> enterprises of great pith and moment
> With this regard their currents turn awry,
> And lose the name of action.   (III. i. 86)

No one can conceivably suppose that suicide is here intended.
The 'enterprises' concerned (cp. *Julius Caesar*, II. i. 133; it
is a usual word) are clearly of the same genre as the activities
(called 'enterprise' at I. i. 99) of a Fortinbras (e.g. his invasion
of Poland).

We have then a sequence of abnormal thinking holding
in solution, as it were, the jarring opposites of our play.

It starts from what at least seems thought of strong action ('take arms', 'oppose'), proceeds through death and suicide, and thence returns imperceptibly, yet through an increasing tilting of the balance, to a final emphasis on strong action. The central thought is suicide. Suicide is the one obvious fusion—the best Hamlet can reach at this stage—of the opposing principles of fine action and death-shadowed passivity, will and suffering, sanity and madness. It is the ultimate passivity, being self-negating; yet, being a deed, it is an acted, a lived, a violent and challenging passivity. It is a cool and carefully willed plunge into the irrational, the Dionysian, whose approaches, mixing with affairs, make madness, crime, tragedy. It is thus an attempt to take Nirvana by storm, and so innately paradoxical, raising natural fears of a possible fallacy ('Perchance to dream'). We can at least see how naturally suicide-thinking here, as in Dostoievsky's *Possessed*, may be felt as the one perfect act of the integrated man; and also how it rises naturally from a bedding of confused and paradoxical phraseology; though we, like Hamlet, shall suspect the fallacy in so negative a deed. In these terms, however, we can, provisionally, find one sort of synthesis between the values of a Hamlet and those of a Fortinbras: since both self-slayer and soldier possess an integration on the border-line of life and death. The suicide, like Fortinbras, 'makes mouths at the invisible event' exposing 'what is mortal and unsure' (IV. iv. 50) to the worst death can offer. Through him life deliberately uses its own energy to contradict—more, to contra-act, itself. In such terms, not unlike those, and yet how different!—since there there is a positive aim—of *Antony and Cleopatra*, we approach a synthesis of life and death.[1]

So Hamlet's mind, set 'gingerly' between such extremes —we might also call them the extremes of extraversion and introversion, of masculine and feminine—is here in placid, wandering thought voyaging through his own problems and

---

[1] Shakespeare's thinking on suicide is variously important. It may be given either approval or disapproval. Our present passage should be compared with Edgar's 'Men must endure (i.e. wait for) their going hence, even as their coming hither' since 'ripeness is all' (*King Lear*, v. ii. 9), and also with the life-death fusion through suicide of *Antony and Cleopatra*, where all the positives dominate. Observe that the life of Christ would be less perfect without a willed self-sacrifice of life itself.

in his reverie half-glimpsing, or rather through enigmatic phrases and suicide thoughts half-creating, the synthesis of his agonising incompatibles. For once these extremes inter-shade, they are fluid and run into each other, like dreams. This is a lonely reverie but, like Richard II's reverie in prison,[1] a creative state, like poetry. It is an approach. To what? Here we can attempt a definition of the opening.

'To be' can scarcely just mean 'to act'; nor, surely, does Hamlet mean anything so simple as 'to live or die' and nothing more. He might mean 'to exist or not to exist after death', but that makes no proper opening to a speech certainly concerned deeply with this thought but containing others that tend to interrupt the sequence such an opening demands: if this be its whole meaning, then it is a poor opening. Probably all these meanings are somehow contained; but can we not find something more precise to say about them? After all, these are probably the most famous words in Shakespeare. Well, you may say, was it not an opening that just occurred to Shakespeare by chance and which he, like ourselves, recognized as neat without looking deeper? Very probably something of the sort did happen. But what we have to do is to interpret, not Shakespeare's intention, but our own sense of this being the perfect opening to the central speech in the most discussed work in the world's literature. Is it not likely to hold some great thought? What, then, can it mean? What must it mean? 'If a thing', says the philosopher, 'may be, and must be, it is'.

Hamlet is here in momentary possession of his own universe, surveying those opposite approaches to his goal, of fine action and endurance, or of both—if it may be possible—in one, with which, from start to finish, the play is mainly concerned. And the goal itself, what is that? 'To be': that is, not merely to live, to act, to exist, but really *to be*; to be, as an integrated and whole person, not in the modern psychological but in the Nietzschean sense. A super-state is indicated, a marriage of the twin elements, masculine and feminine, in the soul, whereby the personality is beyond the antinomies of action and passivity; a lived poetry blending

---

[1] Richard's important soliloquy is studied in my 'Note on *Richard II*' in *The Imperial Theme*.

consciousness and unconsciousness, like Keats' 'might half-slumbering on its own right arm'. In this state one is beyond fear of death since life and death have ceased to exist as antinomies. So Hamlet defines his major problem and proceeds, from a height, or depth, half enjoying in a dreamlike confusion the state he aspires to, to survey those different approaches through time and eternity that are open to him. He does not wholly succeed. The one clear emerging solution, suicide, felt as a way out from a bad life to a possibly unpleasant death, is rightly suspect. After all, the state indicated is an all but impossible integration, the Christ-state. It is no less than the final goal of the race; and that is precisely why the opening line echoes and re-echoes from generation to generation with an ultimate authority.

Whilst in this mood—not 'state', since he does not securely possess the integration he glimpses—he is confronted suddenly by the girl he loves, Ophelia. Now Nietzsche's Zarathustra, and therefore also, presumably, his Superman, is, like Christ, necessarily unmarried, since the higher integration is a marriage within the personality that positively precludes marriage. Hamlet is in a super-sexual, monastic, mood and Ophelia is discovered at her devotions. We may recall the subtle tempting of Angelo[1]:

> O cunning enemy, that, to catch a saint,
> With saints dost bait thy hook!
>
> (*Measure for Measure*, ii. ii. 180)

A host of conflicting emotions necessarily swirl in Hamlet now. He wishes to be remembered in her prayers, he denies his love, he urges her to enter a nunnery, he rejects human life, sex and procreation wholesale. Much of it is forced by his temporary beyond-marriage integration; but one watches a swift decline, not unlike that of Isabella. Super-sexual care of a loved weakling swiftly becomes (something similar happens in his interview with his mother) neurotic infra-sexual cynicism and ends in behaviour like madness: the dialogue is admirably devised to underline Hamlet's utter failure to live the synthesis he dreams. It is, pretty nearly, unactable: at least, the actor can do little more than go

---

[1] The conception of Angelo is clearly implicit in that of Hamlet: in both idealism leads on to a most unidealistic violence.

through the paces required: the text, if properly understood, is too powerful for dramatic exposition.

When we next meet Hamlet he has recovered his balance and is addressing the Players (III. ii. 1). The speech is not, as one might think, an inessential. Shakespeare is not taking time off from the exigencies of drama to have a fling on his own. Shakespeare's own interests are certainly being used, but they are used for a purpose relating to the inmost nature of the drama he is composing.

Here Hamlet is again, and more precisely so than before, the artist.[1] In artistic terms he enjoys full possession and expression of the super-state for which he was recently groping in creative reverie. Remember that his speaking earlier was good, though the Player's was not. He has now been giving the Players a lesson:

> Speak the speech, I pray you, as I pronounced it to you, trippingly on the tongue. But if you mouth it, as many of your players do, I had as lief the town-crier spoke my lines . . .   (III. ii. 1)

Here, if nowhere else, Hamlet knows what he is talking about, and the flow of his prose style is correspondingly assured. Now Hamlet's advice outlines in terms of stage artistry the conditions in which the play's major conflicts might be resolved. The Players are to control their passions; they are to attain repose. The most violent actions on the stage must be graceful and temperate:

> Nor do not saw the air too much with your hand, thus; but use all gently; for in the very torrent, tempest, and, as I may say, whirlwind of passion, you must acquire and beget a temperance, that may give it smoothness. O, it offends me to the soul to hear a robustious, periwig-pated fellow tear a passion to tatters, to very rags, to split the ears of the groundlings . . .   (III. ii. 4)

The same is true of style in any game, of skill in any craft. Hamlet's phrases mirror, moreover, a truth of life-as-art. It is the same with any artistic theory of worth: point by point references of Pope's *Essay on Criticism* to the art of living are profoundly revealing. In living, as in art, creative action matures not from bluster and violence, but from repose.

---

[1] For my previous remarks on Hamlet's importance as aesthetic theorist and social dramatist, see variously *The Burning Oracle*, p. 44; *The Olive and the Sword*, p. 43; *The Crown of Life*, pp. 207, 221; *Christ and Nietzsche*, p. 223 (composed, 1940).

'Controlled emotion' does not quite describe that repose, since it suggests a dualism: it is precisely Hamlet's efforts at self-control that witness his inability to live his own artistic wisdom. The art of life is not an ethic; ethic, like technical rules, is a makeshift. The repose, or poise, required corresponds again to Keats' definition of poetry as 'might, half-slumbering on its own right arm'; in life it will suggest a trust in beneficent powers to do their share—Keats' 'negative capability'—without over-straining, impatience and anxiety in oneself, the trust expressed later in 'There's a special providence in the fall of a sparrow' (v. ii. 232); in acting, it is the power of the thing left unsaid, the gesture not made. It will always be partly unconscious and instinctive. The beginner at golf is usually guilty of 'thinking too precisely on the event'; but not so the expert, whose thought is embedded in, sunk in, dissolved throughout, the living action, mind and body functioning as a unit. So it is with the actor: the action is to be suited to the word, the word to the action (III. ii. 20), far more exactly than by any conscious planning; and so too, with 'word' assuming a deeper significance, in the wholly dedicated, saintly, life. But such a life is not necessarily passive. The actors are specifically warned that they be 'not too tame': they are to pursue the tight-rope course between nature and artificiality, to set their art 'gingerly' between the extremes of romantic and classic. The same note was struck by Hamlet in his praise of the play which was 'caviare to the general', characterized by 'modesty' and lack of affectation, 'an honest method, as wholesome as sweet, and by very much more handsome than fine' (II. ii. 466–75). What we are stressing is nothing new: it is the old doctrine of the Tao;[1] the 'nothing too much' of ancient Greece; it conditions the creation of Nietzsche's Superman, a creature of superb repose, yet 'terrible' in 'goodness'; it is given fullest incarnation in the life of Christ, in whom passivity and a listening in to Divine purpose becomes positive and challenging activity, with victory maturing from death. In terms of dramatic art Hamlet's speech outlines, as his 'To be, or not to be' soliloquy groped after, the one positive to

[1] See a most interesting article concerning Confucius most relevant to our present discussion, in *The Wind and the Rain*, by Mr. F. Sherwood Taylor (Autumn 1946).

which the unresolved conflicts of this and all such dramas point.

There is, of course, more in the speech, some of it less widely significant. The necessity of truth to nature—'a mirror up to nature'—is, as in Pope, central, while the image of one of 'nature's journeymen' strutting and bellowing may be ironically applied to Hamlet himself within the artistry of life, at least during the middle action.

Hamlet is continually feeling, through various approaches, towards this elusive ideal. Here is an earlier expression:

> What a piece of work is a man! How noble in reason; how infinite in faculty; in form, in moving, how express and admirable; in action how like an angel; in apprehension how like a god! The beauty of the world, the paragon of animals. And yet, to me, what is this quintessence of dust? Man delights not me.   (ii. ii. 323)

The words make no claim to any supernal insight; yet the phrase 'in action how like an angel' is especially relevant.[1] It suggests a certain athletic grace and poise that, if grouped with other such passages in Shakespeare, especially the description of 'young Harry' light as 'feathered Mercury' leaping on his horse as an angel 'dropped down' from Heaven (*I Henry IV*, iv. i. 104), help to define, pictorially, our aim. Nietzsche's Superman is likewise an angelic person, created by the descent of 'grace' to the visible order. To Hamlet his own father was such a gracious figure:

> See, what a grace was seated on this brow!
> Hyperion's curls, the front of Jove himself,
> An eye like Mars to threaten and command;
> A station like the herald Mercury
> New-lighted on a heaven-kissing hill;
> A combination and a form indeed
> Where every god did seem to set his seal,
> To give the world assurance of a man.   (iii. iv. 55)

Such pictorial glimpses of man transfigured play an important part in Hamlet's story.

His feeling after human perfection may, however, be presented more inwardly, more psychologically. Directly after his address to the Players there follows immediately and most aptly—the sequence of Shakespeare's thought from

---

[1] See my 'Notes on the Text of *Hamlet*', Note B.

art to life is beautifully clear[1]—Hamlet's carefully phrased address to Horatio, whom he considers 'as just a man' as his own 'imagination' has encountered:

> Dost thou hear?
> Since my dear soul was mistress of her choice
> And could of men distinguish, her election
> Hath seal'd thee for herself; for thou hast been
> As one, in suffering all, that suffers nothing;
> A man, that fortune's buffets and rewards
> Has ta'en with equal thanks; and bless'd are those
> Whose blood and judgement are so well commingled
> That they are not a pipe for Fortune's finger
> To sound what stop she please. Give me that man
> That is not passion's slave, and I will wear him
> In my heart's core, ay in my heart of heart,
> As I do thee.   (iii. ii. 67)

Horatio (whether rightly or not need not concern us—he is being used very obviously for this purpose) is defined as a man well on the way to integration. 'Fortune's finger' recalls 'the slings and arrows of outrageous fortune' (iii. i. 58) in Hamlet's soliloquy. Notice the emphasis on invulnerable suffering. Notice, too, that Horatio does not control his passions: rather his 'blood' (i.e. virility, passion) and 'judgement' are (as in the art of acting) 'commingled', a marriage of elements, as in Nietzsche, being indicated. On the stage of life Horatio uses all 'gently'. Kipling's *If* offers a similar insight:

> If you can dream, and not make dreams your master;
> If you can think—and not make thoughts your aim;
> If you can meet with triumph and disaster,
> —And treat those two imposters just the same . . .

Such a person will, we are told, be 'a man':

> And, what is more, you'll be a man, my son.

For 'man' we must clearly read, or understand, 'superman', as also, pretty nearly, in Hamlet's description of his father as a 'combination' of god-like faculties which 'give the world assurance of a man' (iii. iv. 62). Man, as yet, has not fulfilled the purposes of God, or Nature: he is only on rare occasions what he was meant to be, or become. So, too, Brutus is described in terms of a synthesis of faculties

[1] Mr. Roy Walker has independently observed this interesting transition. *The Wheel of Fire*

recalling Hamlet's speech to Horatio (himself 'more an antique Roman, than a Dane'—v. ii. 355), and ending with an emphasis on 'man':

> His life was gentle, and the elements
> So mixed in him that Nature might stand up
> And say to all the world, 'This was a man'.
>
> (Julius Caesar, v. v. 73)

That is, Nature could for once boast of her handiwork. True, these speeches are not explicitly transcendental; but they are very valuable pointers. Certainly Hamlet feels his father as, pretty nearly, a superman:

> He was a man; take him for all in all;
> I shall not look upon his like again.   (I. ii. 187)

Why not? Except that to Hamlet his own father is, partly through love—for love always has precisely this trans-figuring quality—felt as an earnest, a symptom, of what humankind should be; man not as he, 'this quintessence of dust' (II. ii. 328), is to our normal awareness, but as, given the right occasion and speaking the language of the gods, or of Shakespeare, he may appear, sometimes, on the stage; and may be expected to appear, one day, in full actuality, on the stage of Earth—or Heaven.

Hamlet's play before the King is provisionally successful, but leads nowhere. Neither here, nor in his move from stage to pulpit to sermonize his mother where, as in his dialogue with Ophelia, a noble super-sexual idealism degenerates swiftly into infra-sexual neurosis, does he appear really effectual. He can compose a stinging, satiric and ironic play; but he cannot live that wholeness reflected by the art itself as opposed to its obvious content; that wholeness reflected by his address to the Players. He is not—who is?—a 'man' in this highest sense. The play's central paradox, whereby the good person is a continual threat to a reasonably normal society, reaches a climax in these violent yet ineffectual scenes. Hamlet in life cannot act creatively.[1] He looks back,

---

[1] Observe that Hamlet, in the manner of the neurotic, expends great energy without directing it wisely; just as the over-swinging of a golf tyro represents not a superabundance but a misplacing of energy, since his club, *at the moment of impact*, is not as forceful as he thinks. 'Style' in any game or art is the right use and timing of energy and emphasis, not a repudiation of them. Hence 'over-acting' is a dangerous term. Good acting cannot be too powerful.

is critical, shows little love. His play is satiric and Jonsonian; his philosophy death-ridden and Websterian; his sex disgust Swiftian and Manichean. He is sunk deep in the knowledge of good and evil and clogged by ethic. Only in reverie, artistic theory and occasional mind-pictures of transfigured man, does he glimpse a resolution. That is, he does not attain to the Shakespearian health which puts him into action and surveys his failure, nor to the New Testament freedom from the Law. That is why he cannot move through society with the assurance of a Christ, or a St. Francis; and nothing else, it might seem, would serve his turn. He cannot even get as far as his cousins Timon and Prospero; he cannot rise beyond what Nietzsche calls 'the avenging mind'. He is left divided, all but insane, spasmodic. More: he is ill-mannered which, as we shall see, is perhaps worse.

Our play thus indirectly attacks ethics. Hamlet may purpose well, he may try to control himself, he may will the good; but, though he has intuitions of a supreme excellence, he cannot in life 'suit the action to the word, the word to the action' in perfect reciprocity. We are necessarily baffled, since it is hard to reconcile ourselves to the utter inadequacy of such good intentions. Hamlet can indeed rouse the King's and his mother's conscience, but cannot help them to advance; since conscience alone is, like Pope's 'reason', 'a sharp accuser but a helpless friend' (*Essay on Man*, ii. 154). The point is, if your state of being is harmonious, your deeds are creative, on one plane or another ('His can't be wrong whose life is in the right', 'Whate'er is best administer'd is best', *Essay on Man*, iii. 306; iii. 304). Observe how Timon, whilst urging them to excesses, most amusingly reforms the Bandits. While, however, your own state remains divided, your highest idealism, even an idealism willing the super, the undivided, state, may lead to evil; and there appears to be no short cut. In all this Hamlet is a symbol of man, with his highest idealism and best art, in our era, yet trammelled still in concepts of the Law, justice and death. The result is a multiplicity of murders. The Christian position—that is, the positives of Christ and St. Paul—though not here explicitly surveyed (as they are in *Measure for Measure*), are insistently suggested.

I would therefore not retract what I have elsewhere said concerning the evil in Hamlet, except to admit a certain exaggeration and to remind myself and my readers that we are judging him by a very high standard; by the standard, indeed, of Christ. And so paradoxical is this world of ours that it remains true that to have glimpses of the highest good and fail of its attainment may well land you in a worse mess than anything normal people can experience. That is why Christ regards the admirable and necessary Pharisees as 'whited sepulchres'; why the fine artist may yet be an intolerable person; and why—conversely—Nietzsche is found to interlace his idealism with satanic phrases. It may really be necessary, in thought at least, to work *through* the evil, as Hamlet is shown working through it, indeed perhaps even in some mysterious fashion taking the responsibility of crime on himself in an impossible situation. The beyond-ethic problem cannot be simple. True, we can change the meaning of our words. We can say, and it is partly true, that Hamlet is good throughout; that his faults (bitterness, disgust, cruelty, unjust murders) are forced on him by a bad society, are reflections of it and therefore not properly faults. Yet from that standpoint we can say as much for many wrongdoers, since such people are, to a profound judgement, likely enough to be the superiors of their more normal and less adventurous brethren. But whilst we use words in their usual sense we must surely see guilt in Hamlet's behaviour; a guilt directly related to the inadequacy of his good. He cannot take the final step.

He is himself strongly, at this point, aware of his own limitations, as his soliloquy after meeting Fortinbras' captain shows (IV. iv. 32–66). He is, too, aware that it is less a line of action than a state of being that is at issue (cp. Pope's 'His (i.e. faith) can't be wrong whose life is in the right' and Shelley's 'Which makes the heart deny the *yes* it breathes' at *Prometheus Unbound*, III. iv. 150):

> Rightly to be great
> Is not to stir without great argument,
> But *greatly* to find quarrel in a straw
> When honour's at the stake.   (IV. iv. 53)

Hamlet here sees the futility of Fortinbras' enterprise, yet admires his soul-state. He provisionally accepts the Renaissance values of 'honour' and 'divine ambition', admiring the 'delicate and tender prince' so inflated by immediate life in terms of 'honour' (to the Renaissance mind a mediator, a lightning-conductor, of forces beyond commonsense) that he 'makes mouths at the invisible event' and willingly risks wholesale slaughter ('fortune, death and danger') for a mere 'fantasy'. Fortinbras' lively being exists beyond the life-death antinomy; and it is true that many a death-daring soldier may be nearer the superman status than many an artist. Hamlet certainly regards Fortinbras' actions as possibly true expressions of God's purpose:

> Sure, He that made us with such large discourse,
> Looking before and after, gave us not
> That capability and god-like reason
> To fust in us unus'd . . .   (iv. iv. 36)

When Hamlet acknowledges that 'incitements of my reason and my blood' impel him to a revenge which he admits is perfectly easy, 'reason' covers imagination and intuition; it is wisdom, finest apprehension (cp. 'in apprehension, how like a god' at ii. ii. 326).[1] As against this we have Hamlet's own 'thinking too precisely on the event' (i.e. on the outcome), which has only 'one part wisdom and ever three parts coward' (cp. 'conscience does make cowards of us all' and 'pale cast of thought' at iii. i. 83–5). Through the concept of 'honour' the Renaissance made its own terms with the religion-war antinomy; 'honour' was at once religion and a 'way' in the Gospel and Confucian sense. So Hamlet, who is a Renaissance gentleman, sees to his 'shame'

> The imminent death of twenty thousand men
> That for a fantasy and trick of fame
> Go to their graves like beds . . .   (iv. iv. 60)

Hamlet is not consciously beyond the current valuations of Renaissance society. To him Fortinbras is in a state of grace.

---

[1] See my 'Notes on the Text of *Hamlet*', Note B.

III

In my former essays I showed how Hamlet's macabre originality is contrasted with the hum-drum world of Polonius' advice to Laertes and the King's efficiency and general importance as King; on which I might have quoted Rosencrantz' explicit and important statement:

> The single and peculiar life is bound
> With all the strength and armour of the mind
> To keep itself from noyance; but much more
> That spirit upon whose weal depend and rest
> The lives of many. The cease of majesty
> Dies not alone, but like a gulf doth draw
> What's near it with it; it is a massy wheel,
> Fixed on the summit of the highest mount,
> To whose huge spokes ten thousand lesser things
> Are mortis'd and adjoin'd; which, when it falls,
> Each small annexment, petty consequence,
> Attends the boisterous ruin. Never alone
> Did the king sigh, but with a general groan.   (III. iii. 11)

This fine speech, in the style of *Troilus and Cressida*, cannot be written off as sheer flattery: certainly no Elizabethan would have understood it as such. I have also shown (in my essay 'Rose of May' in *The Imperial Theme*) how, when Hamlet's stock is at its lowest after sparing the King (in hopes of his greater damnation),[1] murdering Polonius, tormenting his mother and shocking everyone with his gruesome speeches on death, the dramatist ranges against him all the conventional values: Fortinbras' army, Ophelia's pathetic madness and flowery death, the King's kindly phrases and royal deportment, Laertes' avenging ardour; whilst especially noting the King's crisp dialogue with Laertes on the latter's entry, suggesting that they can do business since they speak the same language, are of the same world; and here we have another at first sight superfluous scene that demands our present attention.

I refer to the King's unnecessarily elaborated discussion with Laertes concerning the Norman, Lamond, and his excelling horsemanship:

---

[1] Hamlet's thoughts here, by pushing revenge to its logical and hateful conclusion, make an ironical comment on the nature of revenge as such.

King.   Two months since
Here was a gentleman of Normandy:
I've seen myself, and served against, the French,
And they can well on horseback; but this gallant
Had witchcraft in't; he grew unto his seat,
And to such wondrous doing brought his horse,
As he had been incorps'd and demi-natur'd
With the brave beast. So far he topp'd my thought,
That I, in forgery of shapes and tricks,
Come short of what he did.
Laertes. A Norman was't?
King. A Norman.
Laertes. Upon my life, Lamond.
King. The very same.
Laertes. I know him well; he is the brooch indeed
And gem of all the nation.
King. He made confession of you;
And gave you such a masterly report
For art and exercise in your defence . . .   (iv. vii. 81)

Observe here the characterizing of Lamond's horsemanship as a perfect unity, a magical skill beyond technique which baffles all attempts at definition. It is an athletic analogue to Hamlet's speech to the Players; and both suggest, as does 'style' in any game or art, a prefiguring of some potentiality in life. We may recall young Harry's horsemanship described in angelic terms.

Now the King and Laertes enjoy a world of accepted values from which Hamlet is cut off: or we can say that they, like Fortinbras, make the contact through 'honour' and horsemanship that Hamlet seeks through reverie and art. His ghost-converse has jerked Hamlet beyond the world of military ambition, though he is himself a good fencer (iv. vii. 103; v. ii. 220) and might have been a good soldier (v. ii. 411); beyond court life, codes of honour, pleasure in travel (like Laertes'). So, after the grim middle action and its talk of worms and death, our contrasting series of bright, life-charged incidents reaches a climax in this pure dialogue of club-room conversation, the quintessence of healthy-mindedness. This is the wider world (suggested by the name Lamond) beyond the prison ('Denmark's a prison', ii. ii. 253) of thought, from which Hamlet's introspective and idealistic agony shuts him. The King and Laertes have almost for-gotten, for a moment, the occasion, the King expanding his description quite unnecessarily. The two are happy in recognition of their own world reflected in each other. It is a relief to the audience; its lucid contemporary realism gives a reference to the whole play, it forms an apt preliminary to what follows. For soon we return to Hamlet again—in a graveyard; from noble action to suicide and damnation (in the Priest's speech, v. i. 248–60), the balanced opposites of Hamlet's soliloquy; from the fine flowers of chivalry and courtesy to the skull.

Hamlet's sea-adventures (which I have previously compared to Stavrogin's voyage into the far north) may be allowed (though the text itself gives no explicit warrant for it) to serve vaguely some symbolic purpose: certainly he comes back a subtly changed man. His graveyard meditations show a new repose. True, he is thinking of death and that is easy stuff for him; it is the more complex business of life that gets him down. However, his words on Yorick show perhaps his only words in the play of really convincing love. Though this repose is temporarily shattered by his tussle with Laertes, it returns in his dialogue with Horatio and his banter—it is no worse, a mild, good-natured ragging—of Osric. Here, as in the graveyard, there is a vein of refined, suave, courtly satire to be distinguished from his earlier disgust: he is above his antipathies.

We are approaching the play's conclusion. How should we ourselves, if we had the choice, end it? Were Hamlet to rouse himself and, imitating Laertes and Fortinbras, prove active for immediate revenge, we should say that here was a satisfying melodrama, if no more. If he were to remain bitter like Timon and embrace a tragic end, we should approve the artistic logic. Were he to show signs of developing the magic powers of a Prospero, we should note a too-rapid development of his mystic propensities, but might accept the philosophic implications, whilst taking pleasure in seeing the student prove a match for the politician. If he returned with a sense of artistic superiority, washed his hands of the whole nasty business and confined himself to writing a Ph.D. thesis at Wittenberg on satiric literature; or, better still, set himself to compose explosive dramas calculated to terrify all the kings of Europe, we, to-day, should be very pleased with him indeed. Some of us, of religious leanings, might like him to turn Christian, take the load of evil on himself, transmute it in silent endurance and lend all his efforts to creating peace: such is the solution which Shakespeare appears to survey in *Measure for Measure*. But he does none of these. Instead, he accepts the wager and, in obedience to his mother's advice, proceeds to offer Laertes an official apology (probably for both the murder of Polonius and his graveyard attack), even going so far as to confess, in all seriousness and at great length (v. ii. 239–58), that he has been sadly afflicted with madness. Nothing could more clearly support my earlier contention that Hamlet is, or has been, in relation to his society, thoroughly abnormal and dangerous. What has happened? Hamlet has himself realized this. He has always admitted, though instinctively untuned to them, the courtly values of his society. Here, without somehow ceasing to be himself, he respects, outwardly at least, the people he has hitherto scorned. Laertes answers with a provisional acceptance of the apology, whilst making some highly technical reservations concerning the need to hand over the case to 'elder masters of known honour' (v. ii. 262) before a final commitment. 'Honour', with its manifold technicalities, bulks large; and Hamlet, one feels, subscribes, even contributes, to the dominating courtliness. But now, as never before, he calmly and confidently means to execute the Ghost's command: 'The interim is mine' (v. ii. 73).

On his return, Hamlet's words witness a new poise. His manners too have changed. Social conventions are a ritual to which man submits his personal instincts; they are a way of attuning one to necessities beyond one's conscious egotism. They are a kind of acting, an attempt if not to live at least to express something of the artistic grace and balance. Thus Hamlet's words on Osric are, though satiric, yet courtly. Hearing of his mother's advice that he use some 'gentle entertainment' to Laertes, he answers: 'She well instructs me' (v. ii. 218). His letter to the King (iv. vii. 42) showed perhaps a certain irony ('High and mighty', 'beg leave to see your kingly eyes'); but his use later of 'your Grace' (v. ii. 275) rings true; so does his instinctive 'good

Madam' (v. ii. 304) to the Queen during the fencing. The stage tradition of elaborate salutes to the throne before the match is therefore sound. Our chief persons enter on this last occasion in a ritualistic, one might almost say a dreamlike, state, as though half-consciously submitting their quarrel to some higher court of appeal. To each other, they are polite; the harmonious quality of their engagements is preluded by Hamlet's and Laertes' embracing of friendship under the King's personal direction, with the stately occasion marked by the King's signals of drum and cannon. True, all these effects, including Hamlet's manners, are superficial, since on both sides hostility lurks beneath; but that is, precisely, the whole point of manners; and it is expressly this superficiality, this acted conventionality, that is here so important, for only within its frame can a conclusion be reached. Hamlet is at last willing to stop being profound. The 'time' is no longer 'out of joint'; a relation has been established.

What, on Hamlet's side, does this mean? He has attained humility before his society, the world as it is; that is, therefore, before the King as King. Surely the reader has been struck, during our talk of beyond-ethic possibilities and compulsions, by the thought that, failing a kingdom of heaven on earth, morals are an essential? Law and order must be preserved. The second-best is needed to avoid disaster. But Hamlet has pushed beyond the second-best; and what is he to do? What are others, such as he, Nietzscheans, to do? Art and reverie are not enough. Is there not a second-best for them to *live* by? There is. It is simple. It is love; love of a very simple and realistic kind; a love which is humility before not God's ideal for the race but God's human race as it is, in one's own time and place. Hamlet has somehow reached it and hence his new courtesy before men and acceptance before God:

> Not a whit, we defy augury; there's a special providence in the fall of a sparrow. If it be now, 'tis not to come; if it be not to come, it will be now; if it be not now, yet it will come. The readiness is all. Since no man has aught of what he leaves, what is't to leave betimes? Let be.
>
> (v. ii. 232)

Hamlet has accepted not only his surroundings, but himself. We may suppose that he now knows himself neither saint nor soldier, but a Renaissance gentleman of finely tuned sensibility; and that is saying a lot. He now knows intuitively that he will do the work before him; and mark what happens. As soon as he attains this state of being, the contact formerly missing is at once established and *everything falls into line for him*. The actual duel sums up, as I have shown elsewhere, the play's general quality of indecision and oscillation, of insecure balance—remember the importance of our balanced opposites in Hamlet's reverie and the stress on balance in the address to the Players—of actions returned 'on the inventors' heads' (v. ii. 399), in sharp and significant play; it is at once ritual and symbol. Then Hamlet gets his one perfect opportunity: first, he catches the King at a moment of extreme and patent crime—always his desire—with victims, dead and dying, littered all around; second, the King is accused in public by someone else; thirdly Hamlet has himself been worked up to sudden, instinctive action, which he has always found easy; and lastly he is already, and knows it, on the brink of that 'felicity' (v. ii. 361) of death to which he has long been more attuned than to life. There is thus a suicidal quality in his revenge, which recalls the blend of suicide and fine action in his soliloquy. By a pretty irony the King's plot has been developed to make Hamlet's action easy and inevitable. Hamlet has won this success by humility and acceptance. In his own, Renaissance, terms, he has attained to his Kingdom of Heaven and all the rest is at once added: 'To be, or not to be: that is the question'.

So we work up to the formal conclusion; the dead bodies, Hamlet on the throne, prince now among the dead; the new life in Fortinbras, military and young; and between, as mediator, Horatio. This formality, together with the effect here and earlier (at 1. iv. 6) of sounds, I have discussed in my *Shakespearian Production*.

IV

It is true that this conclusion is not one which an age that regards *Henry V* as a pot-boiler and *Henry VIII* as an enigma will most readily appreciate; but I believe that it is good for us to observe it. We must remember that the courtly values of the Renaissance touched the hem at least of religion, as that text-book of contemporary idealism, Castiglione's *Il Cortegiano*, shows. Their importance in *Hamlet* as a standard of reference is clear from Ophelia's speech attributing to Hamlet 'The courtier's, soldier's, scholar's, eye, tongue, sword' (III. i. 160). In its conclusion, moreover, *Hamlet* only the more clearly shows itself to be, what it is generally supposed, the hub and pivot of Shakespeare's whole work in its massed direction: for both the Duke in *Measure for Measure* and Prospero return finally to take up their ducal responsibilities, and Shakespeare himself concludes his great sequence of more personal works with the nationalistic and ritualistic *Henry VIII*.

Fortinbras dominates at the end, as he did in Horatio's early speech.[1] The psychological action is framed in steel and given a warrior setting: such is the background for the working out of some hints, both in Hamlet's unease and Claudius' preference of diplomacy to warfare (in his dealings with Fortinbras), of the beyond-warrior integration. Hints: for the greatest drama can offer no more. For what is involved? No less than the attempt to lift the old revenge-theme, rooted in drama from Aeschylus to O'Neill, rooted too in our ways of life, in our courts of justice and international relationships, indeed, in the very structure of our thought, beyond its stark oppositions; to heave over human affairs from the backward time-consciousness of Nietzsche's 'avenging mind' into the creative inflow. Such an attempt involves finally the will to fuse Church and State, the Sermon on the Mount with international action; it is a will towards the Nietzschean synthesis, Ibsen's 'Third Empire'. This troubled theme is, as in Aeschylus, pushed to a ritualistic close; raised, that is, from intellect to life, from thought to being, and there we must leave it.

That these deeper issues were not planned out by Shakespeare is likely enough; it is probable that he could not have planned them. The poet, as such, does not think thoughts;

---

[1] The importance of Fortinbras' various entries has been neatly emphasized by Mr. Francis Berry in *Young Fortinbras* (*Life and Letters*, February 1947). See also Mr. Berry's poem *The Rival Princes* in *The Galloping Centaur* (1952).

he makes them; though it may be for us to think the thoughts which he has made. The meanings here discussed are not insisted on by the poetry; they emerge only to a sensitive and listening enquiry. They are rather suggested than said. But that is no reason why we, with due care, should not proceed to say them: it is our business to say them.

ADDITIONAL NOTE (1948)

My reading of 'To be or not to be' has important analogies in Ibsen. Falk, the poet in *Love's Comedy*, is a Hamlet-figure who discards poetry for action, aiming to 'live' poetry, to 'be' rather than to 'write'. *Peer Gynt* studies a superficial self-realization. Variations on 'Be thyself' are played by or with reference to the Troll King, the Boyg, the Sphinx (who holds the answer to man's 'enigma' since 'he is himself'), the drowning Cook, the Priest (in his Graveyard sermon), the Button Moulder and the Thin Person (or Devil); and continually by Peer, whose philosophy of the 'Gyntish self' occurs at iv. i. The true self, or being, is beyond ethic: wickedness may be a better qualification than nonentity and Peer tries to convict himself of crime to escape dissolution (v. vii; x). *Brand* is even more incisive, concentrating on wholeness of being, on 'all or nothing':

> To be seems worthy no man's strife;
> To breathe is still your best endeavour.   (i.)

Compare Hamlet's

> What is a man
> If his chief good and market of his time
> Be but to sleep and feed?   (iv. iv. 33)

Ibsen's life-work may, like Shakespeare's and Nietzsche's, be discussed, if not defined, in terms of 'self-realization'. More: this quest for integration, of man or society, is the central drive of Western drama.

APPENDIX

TWO NOTES ON THE TEXT OF *HAMLET*
(1947)
NOTE A
Horatio's Speech on Ancient Rome
Hamlet, i. i. 113–26

THE investigations of historical scholarship have of late done much to increase our knowledge of the Elizabethan age. They have also done something to clarify the problems posed by Shakespeare's work in general and his text in particular; but here they have, I think, done less than is usually supposed. Both popular and scholarly editions appear nowadays to take delight in departing from what had almost become the traditional and accepted readings; and in these notes I shall discuss a couple of important passages in *Hamlet* that have, it would seem, suffered from an over-enthusiastic enquiry. Here I must cross swords with the leading textual editor of our day, whose labours for the New Cambridge Shakespeare have met with so wide a popularity and so just an approbation. Many of the questions raised by Professor Dover Wilson's various introductions, emendations and notes I am incompetent to discuss; but sometimes I may be forgiven for feeling that the uninformed student can steady himself on ground that quivers dangerously beneath the tread of scholarship.

Directly before the Ghost's second entry in the opening scene of *Hamlet* Horatio recalls (i. i. 113) the portents that preceded the assassination of *Julius Caesar*:

> In the most high and palmy state of Rome,
> A little ere the mightiest Julius fell,
> The graves stood tenantless and the sheeted dead
> Did squeak and gibber in the Roman streets.
> *As stars with trains of fire, and dews of blood,*
> *Disasters in the sun*; and the moist star
> Upon whose influence Neptune's empire stands
> Was sick, almost to Doomsday, with eclipse.
> And even the like precurse of fierce events,
> As harbingers preceding still the fates
> And prologue to the omen coming on,
> Have heaven and earth together demonstrated
> Unto our climatures and countrymen—
> But soft! Behold! Lo! where it comes again.

It will be clear that the italicized words are unsatisfactory; syntactically, they appear to constitute an adjectival phrase without its noun. It has sometimes been supposed that a line has been dropped; which would, very easily, account for the grammatical hiatus. There is, however, a tendency to expect of an editor more than is humanly possible: given a 'crux', he has to solve it. But surely the text may be wrong; as a matter of hard fact, a line may have been dropped; and if so, nothing can be done about it, beyond composing a satisfying substitute.

Professor Dover Wilson is less timid. He elects to transfer bodily the four lines 'As stars . . . eclipse' to the end, so that his text reads:

> In the most high and palmy state of Rome,
> A little ere the mightiest Julius fell,
> The graves stood tenantless, and the sheeted dead
> Did squeak and gibber in the Roman streets,
> And even the like precurse of fierce events,
> As harbingers preceding still the fates
> And prologue to the omen coming on,
> Have heaven and earth together demonstrated
> Unto our climatures and countrymen,
> As stars with trains of fire and dews of blood,
> Disasters in the sun; and the moist star,
> Upon whose influence Neptune's empire stands,
> Was sick almost to doomsday with eclipse.
> —But soft! Behold! Lo! where it comes again . . .

There, then, are our alternatives.

I submit that this rearrangement cannot be allowed. I am willing enough to believe, since so high an authority is satisfied, that such an error could have been perpetrated by the compositor; I base my judgement on other considerations, on the words themselves. Let us briefly attempt simple paraphrases of the two variants.

The first says: 'A little before Julius Caesar died, the graves opened and the dead walked the streets; there were also portents in the skies, such as comets, bloody rain, sun-spots and an eclipse of the moon. Now portents just like these in the sky and on the earth have appeared to our own people in the past.—But here it comes again!'

Let us turn to the second version. This reads: 'A little before Julius Caesar died, the graves opened and the dead walked the streets. Now portents just like these in the sky and on the earth have appeared to our own people in the past; such as comets, bloody rain, sun-spots and an eclipse of the moon—But here it comes again!'

The structure of meaning is ruined. The phrase 'heaven and earth *together*' makes no proper sense when so far the ghosts alone have been mentioned; nor is it properly amplified by the following reference to sky-portents only. Nor is it reasonable to say, in effect, 'We have known similar things to ghosts, such as comets and eclipses'; they are not similar enough. Finally the past 'was' following the perfect 'have demonstrated' jars the syntax.

How comes it that such an authority as Professor Dover Wilson puts forward a theory so easily shown to be unsatisfactory? Here is his statement:

> 'My rearrangement, following a suggestion by Gerald Massey (*Secret Drama of Shakespeare's Sonnets*, 1872, sup. p. 46), who notes that lunar eclipses are not mentioned in Plutarch, restores the sense.'
>
> (*Hamlet*, New Cambridge Shakespeare, p. 144)

There is here a serious error. Lunar eclipses cannot be found in Plutarch, though the sun is dimmed; but neither can one find 'stars with trains of fire' or 'dews of blood' in Plutarch, both of which are referred to in *Julius Caesar*. Mr. Kenneth Muir has now (in *Notes & Queries*, 7 February, 1948) very helpfully taken the matter in hand and concludes that Shakespeare seems to have used two or more classical sources (from Vergil, Ovid, Lucan and Plutarch) in both *Julius Caesar* and *Hamlet*, with the result that neither solar nor lunar disturbances can be called intruders in Shakespeare's Rome, since the sun is eclipsed in Vergil and Lucan and dimmed in Ovid and Plutarch, and the moon has blood-spots in Ovid (all with reference to Julius Caesar's death). Consequently, no good reason exists for lifting these portents, together with the comets and bloody rain (which are in Ovid, Lucan and *Julius Caesar*), to a non-Roman context.

What of this other context? In reference to the lines 'As stars . . . eclipse' we have (pp. 144–6) the following note:

> Shakespeare is referring to contemporary events. Solar eclipses were visible in England on February 25, 1598, July 10, 1600 and December 24, 1601; and lunar ones on February 11 and August 6, 1598 (and again in November 1603). The year 1598 was thus rich in eclipses . . .

Astrologers, we are told, predicted that the eclipse of July 1600 pointed to an event somewhere between January 20, 1601 and July 12, 1603; so that Essex' rising was considered a fulfilment of the omen. Hence, we are to suppose, Horatio's words: 'And even the like . . . countrymen'.

This suggestion is, surely, unacceptable. Horatio and the others are discussing the reason for the Ghost's appearance. The speech has clear dramatic point. He says such things have been known to happen before to his own countrymen. How can we suppose him to step out of his dramatic context and address the audience with the implied remark: 'Our own recent portents during the reign of Elizabeth have been fulfilled by Essex' rebellion'? This is a tense, opening, scene; it is atmospherically the most important Ghost scene in Shakespeare; everything depends on riveting the audience's attention and keeping it riveted. The Ghost has appeared once, for a moment or two only. We await its return. Can the dramatist intend to switch our thoughts to our own place and time *immediately before* the Ghost's second appearance? And does not the other, correct, version serve admirably to whet our attention for this second entrance?

It might be argued that we could leave England out of it; that Shakespeare, remembering contemporary Elizabethan portents, offers them to Horatio, who may then be supposed to refer to contemporary Danish portents. But were the portents contemporary, they would not easily fit Horatio's argument. To what could they refer? Not very well to the old King's death, since this could not serve as a studied comparison, an analogy, to the present portent, which is the old King himself. They would themselves have to be grouped with the present portent as possible precursors of an unknown future: it would not be easy to be certain that they were fulfilled already. But this ruins the point of the comparison. What Horatio means is: 'Such portents as this we have just seen have regularly proved to be true warnings in the past'. 'Harbingers preceding still the fates' means 'forerunners with a consistent regularity time and again ('still') having foreshadowed what was later found to happen'. If it means less than that there is little point in the speech. It cannot therefore refer to a single event such as Essex' rebellion. This is made fairly clear by the plural 'fierce events' and quite clear by the plural 'climatures', the latter indicating, with a certain intentional *vagueness*, various countries and almost certainly various occasions. How many such 'fierce events' could Horatio possibly have known prophesied and later fulfilled in his own life-time? No. The lines do not refer to contemporary or recent events in either Elizabethan England or Horatio's Denmark. The most we can possibly concede is that recent portents in England may have helped Shakespeare to devise such a speech; but in saying that we have said nothing.

Nor can we leave these arguments with so vague an acquiescence, since it is the contemporary reference that prompts Professor Dover Wilson to transfer the four lines. Lunar eclipses do not fit ancient Rome (though they are, roughly, covered by one of Shakespeare's probable sources); they do fit the year 1598; therefore the lines containing the lunar reference must be taken from their Roman context and placed in a context of contemporary reference. That is the argument. 'Climatures and countrymen' are to mean 'England and Englishmen.' That, we have seen, is dramatically impossible, and we are forced to suppose Shakespeare to be referring to ancient events in Denmark. Since he knows little of Danish legends, he allows them an eclipse of the moon as well as supplying them with comets, bloody rain (both taken from *Julius Caesar* or its Roman sources) and sun-spots. But if Shakespeare can so freely invent Danish portents, why may he not add just one lunar eclipse to those of ancient Rome? On Professor Dover Wilson's showing lunar eclipses may well have been in his mind, since he had himself recently seen one.

But it is not really necessary to suppose such an influence at work. The moon plays a part in Shakespeare's disorder-symbolisms (drawn at first from legendary sources) as early as *Richard II*, where we hear that 'the pale-faced moon looks bloody on the earth' (II. iv. 10) and *King John*, with its description of 'five moons' in the sky (IV. ii. 182). In Sonnet xxxv we have 'clouds and eclipses stain both moon and sun'. As his work matures such portents become a normal literary and dramatic stock-in-trade, always ready for a suitable occasion, and with the moon regularly playing its part, as in Othello's

> Methinks it should be now a huge eclipse
> Of sun and moon, and that the affrighted globe
> Should yawn at alteration.   (v. ii. 98)

And

> It is the very error of the moon;
> She comes more near the earth than she was wont,
> And makes men mad.   (v. ii. 107)

The moon is important in *Macbeth* in Hecate's speech (III. v. 23) and in the Weird Sisters'

>   . . . slips of yew
> Sliver'd in the moon's eclipse.   (IV. i. 27)

The witch Sycorax in *The Tempest* was

> one so strong
> That could control the moon, make flows and ebbs,
> And deal in her command, without her power.   (v. i. 269)

The moon plays a prominent part in the superstitions and folk-lore of all ages.
In *A Midsummer-Night's Dream* we hear how the moon, called—as in *Hamlet*
—the 'governess of floods',

> Pale in her anger, washes all the air
> That rheumatic diseases do abound.   (ii. i. 103)

This fairy play is throughout dominated by thoughts of the moon.

Of course, sometimes contemporary events may be indicated, as in Sonnet
cvii, with moon = Queen Elizabeth:

> The mortal Moon hath her eclipse endur'd
> And the sad augurs mock their own presage . . .

We could, perhaps, admit a possible undertone of contemporary reference in
Gloucester's speech beginning:

> These late eclipses in the sun and moon portend no good to us . . .
>   (*King Lear*, i. ii. 115)

This speech, together with Edmund's following soliloquy of ironic comment,
could conceivably be spoken direct to the audience without altogether dis-
turbing dramatic propriety. Both are in the nature of a generalized commentary, chorus-work; but to read anything similar into Horatio's lines is
impossible. The dramatic tension just snaps.

Besides, is it not extremely rash to read 'disasters in the sun' as 'eclipses'?
'Disasters' may mean just 'portents'. If it means 'sun-spots', then Shakespeare
has, in his use of sources, either criss-crossed spots and eclipse with reference
to sun and moon in a manner natural to poetic composition (see my note on
p. 343); or borrowed sun-spots (as weather-signs) from a Vergilian passage
preceding the portents (*Georgics*, i. 441). Whatever the meaning, the vague
word more nearly suggests Shakespeare's Roman sources than an actual and
recent eclipse; and there is accordingly little enough to suggest a contemporary
reference.

Again, can we afford to remove the comets and bloody rain from Rome?
Both occur in *Julius Caesar*. Remember Calphurnia's

> When beggars die there are no comets seen:
> The Heavens themselves blaze forth the death of princes . . .
>   (ii. ii. 30)

And Casca's

> But never till to-night, never till now,
> Did I go through a tempest dropping fire . . .   (i. iii. 9)

And again Calphurnia's

> A lioness hath whelped in the streets,
> And graves have yawn'd and yielded up their dead;
> Fierce fiery warriors fought upon the clouds,
> In ranks and squadrons and right form of war,
> Which drizzled blood upon the Capitol.   (ii. ii. 17)

Here the graves opening and bloody rain are juxtaposed, exactly as in Horatio's speech; what right have we to separate them? Shakespeare's imagination was keenly impressed by these peculiarly fantastic horrors preceding Julius Caesar's death; and *for this very reason* Horatio chooses for his argument this—to a Renaissance poet—all but central act in history. Is it likely that he would be content to leave the great occasion with no more than a reference to ghosts, while transferring its quite exceptional event of bloody rain to Denmark? Is he not bound here to refer to these Roman portents properly? Does he not in fact do so? Why, then, transfer the lines and rob the description of its impact?

The lunar eclipse may not be in *Julius Caesar*; but neither did bloody rain fall on Elizabethan England. One tiny imprecision—if such indeed it can be called—must not be removed to make way for a large discrepancy. Notice that, to avoid any too dangerous an exactitude, the later portents are left vague: the same sort of thing, we are told, has been seen in the heavens and upon earth by our people; that is all.

What, then, is our conclusion? That a line has been dropped. We have no choice but to suppose, or compose, the missing link. Here is a reasonable substitute: 'Distemper'd portents quarter'd in the skies'. The speech now reads:

> In the most high and palmy state of Rome,
> A little ere the mightiest Julius fell,
> The graves stood tenantless and the sheeted dead
> Did squeak and gibber in the Roman streets;
> Distemper'd portents quarter'd in the skies—
> As stars with trains of fire, and dews of blood,
> Disasters in the sun; and the moist star
> Upon whose influence Neptune's empire stands
> Was sick, almost to Doomsday, with eclipse.

The lines run smoothly enough.

It has been my purpose here to save a notable speech from misunderstanding. I hope, too, that my arguments may serve to suggest that historical scholarship has its own, peculiar, dangers. It is often asserted that our greater writers must be read in the light of their particular periods; that historical research should be brought to the illumination of poetry and the settling of textual difficulties. It has for long been my aim to counsel a different course; to assert the paramount necessity of reading any great writer primarily in the light which he himself generates. Whatever sources or influences lie behind the imaginative composition, that composition is only of highest worth in so far as it has assimilated and transmuted those sources and influences. It stands independently of its origin; and if we forget that we end by ignoring the very quality in the work which justifies our anxious attention.

NOTE B

HAMLET'S SPEECH ON MAN

(II. ii. 323–9)

FOR many years now the academic world has been seriously divided on the punctuation of this important passage. I have myself contributed to the discussion, directly or indirectly, in various letters to *The Times Literary Supplement* (17 January, 1929; 10 September, 1931; 14 September and 26 October, 1946); whilst also further reprinting and developing the substance of earlier letters in *The Imperial Theme* (p. 332) and *The Shakespearian Tempest* (App. A, 'The Shakespearian Aviary', pp. 308–19). My present note will unavoidably repeat some of my already published material; but the controversy is as keen as ever, and my own arguments have as yet met with little obvious response. My letter of 14 September, 1946, raised one, violent, reply which may be read as symptomatic of the reaction, in many quarters, to what is admittedly a new approach. It appears therefore necessary to return once more to the defence.

Our choice lies between the punctuation of the Folio and that of the Second Quarto. Here are the two possible readings, both modernized for my purpose:

(i) The Folio:
What a piece of work is a man! How noble in reason; how infinite in faculty; in form and moving, how express and admirable; in action how like an angel; in apprehension how like a god!

(ii) The Quarto:
What a piece of work is a man! How noble in reason; how infinite in faculties, in form and moving; how express and admirable in action; how like an angel in apprehension; how like a god!

The Folio reading is, as it were, traditional; it will be found in any ordinary modern, or last century, text; but Professor Dover Wilson, in his important and influential edition in the New Cambridge Shakespeare, strongly supports the Quarto. Actors nowadays tend to use the Quarto reading and it is likely that future editors will do likewise.

Professor Peter Alexander, whose Shakespearian investigations have always proved most significant, supports what may be called the 'Folio' reading, whilst arguing that both texts are correct, but that the Quarto pointing, in its original form, bore a significance nowadays misunderstood, the intended sense being that of the Folio. To avoid the subtleties involved in Professor Alexander's theory, ably set forth in his British Academy Lecture 'Shakespeare's Punctuation', I have, for my purposes, modernized both quotations, which I shall refer to simply as 'Folio' and 'Quarto'. My purpose here is once again to defend the Folio.

First, I cannot see that 'infinite', as the Quarto would have it, can properly apply to the *singular* 'form', nor to 'moving'; whereas it fits 'faculty' perfectly. As for the Folio 'in form and moving, how express and admirable', the balanced phraseology precisely relates 'express' to 'form' and 'admirable' to 'moving';

whereas the Quarto refers 'express' directly to the vigorous word 'action'. Now I suggest that 'express' is most unlikely to cohabit with 'action'. Professor Dover Wilson takes it to mean 'direct and purposive' (*Hamlet*, p. 176). Are there Shakespearian analogies for such a use? Surely the adjective carries a sense far nearer to that implied by its derivation, a sense still held by the verb, denoting an imprint, static rather than dynamic, as at *Paradise Lost*, VII, 527, where man, in a most significant phrase, is said to have been created 'in the image of God express' (cp. also *Paradise Lost*, VIII, 440–1 and x. 67). Milton's use suggests its natural affinities with such a concept as 'form'; indeed, 'form' and 'pressure' occur together in *Hamlet* in direct reference to human behaviour both at I. v. 100 and, in close association with 'feature', 'image' and 'body', at III. ii. 28, while 'form' is again used in Hamlet's highly relevant description of his father as a figure of majesty and poise at III. iv. 60. We have Ophelia's 'glass of fashion and the *mould* of form' at III. i. 162 (with 'form' again at III. i. 168, in association with 'feature'). Without valour man's 'noble shape' is but 'a form of wax' (*Romeo and Juliet*, III. iii. 125). Man's physical shape is a kind of imprint. 'Nature's copy', we are told in *Macbeth* (III. ii. 38), is 'not eterne'; where the reference is to man's physical being as opposed to his immortal soul (Shakespeare here thinking, as often elsewhere, in terms of a conventional dualism). *The Winter's Tale* has two valuable examples:

> Behold, my lords,
> Although the *print* be little, the whole matter
> And *copy* of the father; eye, nose, lip . . .   (II. iii. 97)

Again,

> Your mother was most true to wedlock, prince;
> For she did *print* your royal father off
> Conceiving you.   (v. i. 124)

So, too, one must not '*coin* Heaven's *image* in *stamps* that are forbid' (with reference to illegitimate children, *Measure for Measure*, II. iv. 46). The metaphor has an honourable lineage: Aeschylus uses it in *The Choephoroe*. We may also remember Morocco's

> They have in England
> A *coin* that bears the figure of an angel
> *Stamped* in gold, but that's *insculp'd* upon;
> But here an angel in a golden bed
> Lies all within.   (*The Merchant of Venice*, II. vii. 55)

The 'angel' of the coin is St. Michael slaying a dragon, a St. George figure. Angels to Shakespeare were definitely active beings; and this particular reference conveniently leads us on.

Consider the phrases 'In action how like an angel; in apprehension, how like a god.' The Quarto's 'How like an angel in apprehension' robs angel of *active* significance whilst relating it directly to a faculty for which Shakespeare's angels show no aptitude; though it is this very association that Professor Dover Wilson regards as a support for the Quarto. But angels are, in Shakespeare, active beings, as on the coin—well known to every Elizabethan—expressly

called an 'angel' because of its St. George imprint. In Shakespeare's most
extended passages on angels, these beings are visualized as athletic, sometimes
as riding, with a strong sense of the word's derivation (Greek *angelos* =
messenger; they are messengers from God to man). Here is a neat and vivid
example from the Balcony scene of *Romeo and Juliet*:

> She speaks.
> O speak again, bright angel; for thou art
> As glorious to this night, being o'er my head,
> As is a winged messenger of Heaven
> Unto the white up-turned wondering eyes
> Of mortals that fall back to gaze on him,
> When he bestrides the lazy-pacing clouds
> And sails upon the bosom of the air.   (II. ii. 25)

The angel is explicitly Heaven's 'messenger' and is imagined as a *riding* figure.
Here is a more concrete example of riding, with 'angel' associated with
'Mercury', the messenger of the gods (i.e. the classical equivalent to 'angel'):

> I saw young Harry with his beaver on,
> His cuisses on his thighs, gallantly arm'd,
> Rise from the ground like feather'd Mercury,
> And vaulted with such ease into his seat,
> As if an angel dropp'd down from the clouds,
> To turn and wind a fiery Pegasus
> And witch the world with noble horsemanship.
>   (*I Henry IV*, IV. i. 104)

The Dauphin's praise of his horse as a wondrous Pegasus at *Henry V*, III. vii.
11–44, is also indirectly relevant, in view of its imaginative tonings, to our
present argument. Such impressions of aerial movement work tumultuously
within a far more complex speech spoken by Macbeth, when agonized by the
proposed murder of Duncan:

> his virtues
> Will plead like angels, trumpet-tongued, against
> The deep damnation of his taking off:
> And pity, like a naked new-born babe,
> Striding the blast, or Heaven's cherubin, hors'd
> Upon the sightless couriers of the air,
> Shall blow the horrid deed in every eye
> That tears shall drown the wind.   (*Macbeth*, I. vii. 18)

We have a complex of half-visualized but appallingly potent beings. The
'angels', the allegorical 'pity' and 'Heaven's cherubin' are all closely akin; they
blow trumpets, ride aerial steeds, inspire emotion. The tempestuous whirl
leaves us with a sense of most violent activity.

These three are probably our most striking poetic passages concerning
angels; and the angels are all active. Where in *Cymbeline* Jupiter descends
riding on an eagle he is clearly functioning as an angel, that is, as a messenger
of God to man; as is Ariel, too, at his Harpy appearance. Christian and

classical mythology are, of course, always likely to be mixed in Shakespeare. We find, for example, a directly relevant passage in terms of classical deities only in Hamlet's description of his father:

> See what a grace was seated on this brow;
> Hyperion's curls; the front of Jove himself;
> An eye like Mars to threaten and command;
> A station like the herald Mercury
> New-lighted on a heaven-kissing hill;
> A combination and a form indeed
> Where every god did seem to set his seal,
> To give the world assurance of a man.　　(*Hamlet*, III. iv. 55)

Notice how Mercury, the specifically angelic (i.e. messenger) deity, stands out from the others in point of visual grace, or poise, felt as one with a superbly executed action. Such, then, are Shakespeare's angels, culminating with Ariel in *The Tempest*, whose athleticism is positively ubiquitous.

I cannot therefore follow Professor Dover Wilson's statements: 'To a thinking Elizabethan angels were discarnate spirits whose only form of action was "apprehension"'; and 'To make Hamlet compare human action to that of an angel is, therefore, to make him talk nonsense' (*Hamlet*, p. 176). I cannot help feeling that Professor Dover Wilson's great and invaluable Elizabethan learning has somehow here debarred him from the simple, the unlearned, approach.

It may be—it has been—argued that these examples do not suffice to prove the major issue. On principle I never consult a concordance; but every relevant Shakespearian passage I know can be used in the Folio's support. Angels are regularly felt as beauteous and especially graceful creatures, of fine action and graceful poise. They may be associated with a lady, but more often suggest a young man; they resemble courtiers; their gifts are physical, not intellectual; they do not think. Here are some examples. Hamlet, seeing the Ghost, calls to 'angels and ministers of grace' to 'defend' him, as guards (I. iv. 39); and repeats the thought on his second encounter, calling on 'heavenly guards' to 'hover' above him in protection (III. iv. 103). They move swiftly, as messengers should, and therefore Lennox in *Macbeth* prays that 'some holy angel' may 'fly' to the English court to unfold Macduff's mission before he arrives (III. vi. 45). Aristocratic 'reverence' is in *Cymbeline* 'that angel of the world' (IV. ii. 248); that is, the mediator between God and man, a descending grace, the phrase growing from the philosophy of Ulysses' speech on order in *Troilus and Cressida*. Claudius prays to angels to assist his action ('bow, stubborn knees') in prayer, to get to work on him, to 'make assay' (*Hamlet*, III. iii. 69); their singing lifts Hamlet to his rest (*Hamlet*, v. ii. 374); they are always *doing* something. They can sing and move at once:

> There's not the smallest orb which thou behold'st
> But in his motion like an angel sings,
> Still quiring to the young-eyed cherubins.
> 　　　　　(*The Merchant of Venice*, v. i. 60)

The angel is felt as both singing and moving, in serene flight. Angels are athletic, artistic and eminently gracious creatures. Aeneas describes the Trojans to

Agamemnon as people of angelic grace:

> Courtiers as free, as debonair, unarm'd,
> As bending angels; that's their fame in peace:
> But when they would seem soldiers, they have galls,
> Good arms, strong joints, true swords; and, Jove's
> accord,
> Nothing so full of heart.   (*Troilus and Cressida*, I. iii. 235)

For 'bending angels' compare the ladies (like 'Nereides') on Cleopatra's barge who 'made their bends adornings' (*Antony and Cleopatra*, II. ii. 216). Angels are, indeed, to Shakespeare very much like young Renaissance gentlemen, equally ready, as this *Troilus* passage suggests, for the arts of either peace or war: the thought is that of *Henry V*, III. i. 3–17, a play where Henry with 'the port of Mars' (I. Pro. 6) is, like Hamlet's father (III. iv. 57), an all but angelic figure; and of *Cymbeline*, IV. ii. 171–81, where the description of the royal boys as *both* gentle and fierce is peculiarly fine. Elsewhere in *Cymbeline*, when the royal boys, with Belarius, have mysteriously saved the day for Britain, functioning as mysterious heaven-sent warriors like the 'Angels of Mons', we hear that it is 'thought the old man and his sons were angels' (v. iii. 85). But the comparison applies too to the gentle, graceful, appearance of Imogen, dressed as a boy:

> By Jupiter, an angel! or, if not,
> An earthly paragon. Behold divineness
> No elder than a boy!   (III. vi. 42)

The term 'angel' suggests therefore to Shakespeare both masculine strength and semi-feminine grace: an almost bi-sexual excellence is suggested. That is the point of 'in action, how like an angel'.

Whenever man moves exquisitely (we may remember Hamlet's address to the Players) he is angelic; when he is over-fleshly, cumbered by the heavier, ungracious elements, he is the reverse. The humour of Titania's love-encounter with Bottom in *A Midsummer-Night's Dream* depends precisely on the contrast of a graceful fairy-queen and an awkward excessively corporeal (remember his name) man; and hence, waked by his rude singing and seeing his lumbering, uncourtly, movements—he is specifically *walking up and down*—she brings out the laughter-catching: 'What angel wakes me from my flowery bed?' (III. i. 135). The same contrast occurs in *Measure for Measure*, where thought of ungainly action leads on in the poet's mind directly to a contrast with 'angels':

> . . . but man, proud man,
> Drest in a little brief authority,
> Most ignorant of what he's most assur'd,
> His glassy essence, *like an angry ape*,
> Plays such *fantastic tricks* before high Heaven
> As make the *angels* weep; who, with our spleens,
> Would all themselves laugh mortal.[1]
>   (*Measure for Measure*, II. ii. 117)

---

[1] That is, laugh themselves to death.

A ludicrous, Caliban figure is intended, whose ungainly and uncomely actions appropriately raise the angels' revulsion and distress; rather as bad technique in a clumsy performer awakes anguish in the expert. The angels weep: they are very human, and here (as in our *Macbeth* passage quoted above) associated with emotion. These graceful and lively people are emotional types: but I know of no instance of a Shakespearian angel thinking.

We have seen that 'angels' may be said to resemble the bi-sexual charm of masculine youth. Thus when in Sonnet CXLIV the poet contrasts his fair friend and dark mistress as his good and bad spirits, the emphasis falls naturally on the young man as 'angel'—'the better angel is a man right fair'—and the woman as 'spirit'; she is called his bad angel once, whereas he is called angel four times, within the one sonnet. The association of 'angel' with the loved youth is eminently natural, since angels are not only athletically assured but beautiful and radiant:

> Angels are bright still, though the brightest fell;
> Though all things foul would wear the brows of grace,
> Yet grace must still look so.   (*Macbeth*, IV. iii. 22)

'Brows' = face: observe the strong emphasis on appearance. Even more physically vivid are the 'Six Personages' of Queen Katharine's Vision, whose elaborately described *bending* and other movements recall earlier passages, and whose 'bright faces' cast a 'thousand beams' like 'the sun' (*Henry VIII* IV. ii. 83–9). Angels are pre-eminently good to look on:

> Thou art like the harpy,
> Which, to betray, dost with thine angel's face,
> Seize with thine eagle's talons.   (*Pericles*, IV. iii. 46)

Shakespeare's angels are not, then, 'discarnate spirits' at all; and if any lingering doubt be left, a remark of the Duke in *Measure for Measure* should dispel it:

> Twice treble shame on Angelo
> To weed my vice and let his grow!
> O what may man within him hide,
> Though angel on the outward side!   (III. ii. 291)

There is a pun on 'Angelo': the name is ironical, suggesting the *appearance* of goodness. Shakespeare's angels are outwardly, not inwardly, conceived.

In suggesting that 'to a thinking Elizabethan' angels were discarnate intelligences, Professor Dover Wilson has his eye on Thomas Aquinas. But was Shakespeare a 'thinking Elizabethan'? He was primarily a stage-poet. Now a poet, as we have observed before, does not think thoughts; he rather makes them; though it may be our business to think the thoughts he makes. In making thoughts a poet may be very simple-minded, and I suggest that the coin called an angel had more fertilizing value for Shakespeare than all the labours of medieval scholasticism. However, to let that pass, there is, on Professor Dover Wilson's own ground, more to be said. Apart from the fact that Shakespeare always visualizes angels as lively and beauteous young people, there is philosophic justification for the Folio, though, in view of our quotations, this scarcely concerns us.

In *A Preface to Paradise Lost* Mr. C. S. Lewis devotes a chapter to 'The Mistake about Milton's Angels'. He explains that there were two main approaches to these matters:

> The great change of philosophic thought in that period which we call the Renaissance had been from Scholasticism to what contemporaries described as Platonic Theology. Modern Students, in the light of later events, are inclined to neglect this Platonic Theology in favour of what they regard as the first beginnings of the scientific or experimental spirit; but at the time this so-called 'Platonism' appeared the more important of the two. Now one of the points in which it differed from Scholasticism was this: that it believed all created spirits to be corporeal.

'Thomas Aquinas', however, 'had believed that angels were purely immaterial' though they could assume materiality on occasion. His angels 'could not eat'; but this, says Mr. Lewis, 'is the view which Milton goes out of his way to controvert'.

Now I am not arguing that Shakespeare was a Platonic Theologian in this sense, nor that he had ever thought seriously about the matter. I prefer merely to study his text, and to remember that to the popular imagination angels have always been visible creatures; in the Bible, in Gregory the Great's 'Angels not Angles', in the Angels of Mons. It may, however, be worth observing that the poet as opposed to the philosopher must necessarily be drawn to the 'Platonic' view, since poetry likes what is visual and concrete and eschews, if it does not abhor, the abstract; it is itself a continual incarnation and its spirits are naturally incarnate spirits. Much as I respect the learning of such justly eminent scholars as Professor Dover Wilson and Mr. C. S. Lewis, I maintain that no such learning drawn from outside the poetic world of Shakespeare weighs anything when balanced against that world itself. However, for those who wish to interpret Shakespeare in such terms, I suggest that Mr. Lewis's chapter—which is not itself of course concerned with Shakespeare at all—may serve, at least, to clarify the argument.

And now for 'apprehension'. We have to choose between 'how like an angel in apprehension' (Quarto) and 'in apprehension how like a god' (Folio). But 'apprehension' is in Shakespeare a god-like rather than an angelic quality. It denotes the ability to grasp the mysterious, to extend consciousness beyond space and time, and is to be closely associated with Shakespeare's many references to swift (i.e. intuitive or emotional) thought. Thus the 'seething brains' of lovers and madmen 'apprehend' more than 'cool reason' (i.e. logical, realistic thinking) can 'comprehend'; the contrast of 'apprehend' and 'comprehend' being further related on directly related to 'strong imagination' as the apprehending faculty (*A Midsummer-Night's Dream*, v. i. 4–22). The speaker is here sceptical; but, while referring in general to 'the lunatic, the lover and the poet' as 'of imagination all compact', he surveys a wide range of intuitive thought. 'Apprehension' normally contains all the various potentialities of our 'imagination': it may give birth to mysterious foreboding (*Troilus and Cressida*, iii. ii. 78); it may be associated with wit (*Much Ado about Nothing*, iii. iv. 67); it is to be contrasted with dullness—'If the English had any apprehension (i.e. imagination) they would run away' (*Henry V*, iii. vii. 150); it can deal in evil, unclean, intuitions (*Othello*, III, iii. 139). It is nevertheless man's finest faculty. When Gaunt urges Bolingbroke in banishment to dominate his surroundings as a 'wise man' by the power of imagination ('Suppose the singing birds musicians'), that is, in Milton's phraseology, to realize that 'the mind is its own place' capable of turning Hell to Heaven, Bolingbroke answers that 'the apprehension of the good' will merely increase his suffering (*Richard II*, I. iii. 275–301). Apprehension is thus a noble, supremely human and so all but superhuman, attribute. When Caesar says of the world

> 'tis furnish'd well with men,
> And men are flesh and blood and apprehensive . . .
> (*Julius Caesar*, III. i. 67)

the word, as the context shows, means something excessively fine; what we should call 'spiritual'. All the stars are, he says, fire, yet one only constant; all men are finely made ('flesh and blood') and finely tuned ('apprehensive'); tuned, that is, to spheres beyond themselves; but only one, himself, remains steadfast and 'unassailable'. 'Apprehension' thus distinguishes man from the beasts; it is a spiritual, a god-like, faculty.

Being an imaginative quality, 'apprehension' is necessarily associated with Shakespeare's 'swift', that is intuitive, thought:

> But his evasion, wing'd thus swift with scorn,
> Cannot outfly our apprehensions.
> (*Troilus and Cressida*, II. iii. 124)

But here we meet a subtle difficulty. Professor Dover Wilson himself enlists one of Shakespeare's many swift-thought references to support the Quarto 'How like an angel in apprehension'. He adduces Hamlet's

> Haste me to know it, that I, with wings as swift
> As meditation or the thoughts of love,
> May sweep to my revenge. (I. v. 29)

But this is no image of an angel thinking; it is a comparison of angelic wings to thought; especially *emotional* thought. The winged being is not the thinker, but the thought. Here is a more concrete embodiment:

> Love's heralds should be thoughts,
> Which ten times faster glide than the sun's beams,
> Driving black shadows over lowering hills:
> Therefore do nimble-pinion'd doves draw love,
> And therefore hath the wind-swift Cupid wings.
> (*Romeo and Juliet*, II. v. 4)

Cupid is as swift as thought; but that is not to say that Cupid thinks. Usually the thought concerned in these passages is of violent quality, and scarcely an equivalent to the graver, because more inclusive, faculty of 'apprehension'. Swift thought may be a matter of tragic passion, at *Antony and Cleopatra*, IV. vi. 35; of maddened conscience, at *Troilus and Cressida*, v. x. 29; of wit and mockery, at *Love's Labour's Lost*, v. ii. 262: or of general mental distress, at *I Henry VI*, I. v. 19. Thought as such may be considered swift, without further implications (as at *Henry V*, Pro. III. 1–3; Pro. v, 8, 15, 23; *King Lear*, III. ii. 4). The swiftness of love may be raised from the realm of intuition to the realm of event. Love's passage is felt as an uncapturable lightning at *A Midsummer-Night's Dream*, I. i. 143–9 and at *Romeo and Juliet*, II. ii. 119. The night of love's enjoyment in *Troilus and Cressida*

> flies the grasps of love
> With wings more momentary-swift than thought.
>
> (IV. ii. 13)

These delicate, angelic, realities are extremely difficult to control and place. Man responds without quite knowing what they are: 'apprehension' is his faculty of awareness.

Two Shakespearian passages deliberately investigate such heightened psychic activity in terms of (i) drink and (ii) love. Falstaff describes the brain under the drink-consciousness as 'apprehensive, quick, forgetive, full of nimble, fiery and delectable shapes' (*II Henry IV*, IV. iii. 107); full, that is, of angel-like, active, essences; itself (the brain) being 'forgetive' (cp. 'in the quick forge and working-house of thought', *Henry V*, v. Pro. 23), being itself in control, master of its shop. But the most important speech of all, singing the praise of love itself as highest wisdom and supreme power, is Biron's in *Love's Labour's Lost*. It is all there and closely related to poetry itself, love-born and contrasted with the 'slow arts' of study:

> But love, first learned in a lady's eyes,
> Lives not alone immured in the brain:
> But, with the motion of all elements,
> Courses as swift as thought in every power,
> And gives to every power a double power,
> Above their functions and their offices.   (IV. iii. 327)

So the lover's faculties become newly sensitive; his valour is Herculean; his artistry superb. The passage is, of course, a noble exaggeration. It is a hymn to a possibility, a potentiality, wherein the higher intuitions of love are fully incorporated and lived, so creating a superhuman life.

Such powers necessarily elude man, but his gift of 'apprehension' at least makes contact with them. Apprehension is awareness of the angelic beauties in all their agility and grace; but even so, the thinker is not himself that agility. The swift being resembles, but does not accomplish, the act of thought:

> Be Mercury, set feathers to thy heels,
> And fly like thought from them to me again.
>
> (*King John*, IV. ii. 174)

If, then, thought be like an angel, to what shall we compare the thinker? Clearly God. The god, so to speak, thinks the angel. This is the very relation of Prospero (compare 'prosperous gods', *Timon of Athens*, v. i. 188) to Ariel:

> *Prospero*. Come with a thought!—I thank thee—Ariel, come!
> *Ariel* (*entering*): Thy thoughts I cleave to. What's thy pleasure?
>
> (*The Tempest*, IV. i. 164)

A very neat exposition of what lies behind the creation of Ariel occurs in Sonnets XLIV and XLV, where the poet as lover plays many variations concerning his own thoughts, which, like Ariel's, he sends out to his love, though, being himself composed partly of heavier elements than these 'present-absent', space-negating, essences, he deplores his own substantiality:

> For nimble thought can jump both sea and land,
> As soon as think the place where he would be.
> But ah! thought kills me that I am not thought . . .   (XLIV)

Again, the thinker is not the thought; the philosopher may well lack something of youthful agility; and so it is Prospero's business always to 'apprehend', imagine and plan, but Ariel's, as angel, to act.[1]

'In apprehension how like a god!' makes, therefore, perfect Shakespearian sense. We remember Hamlet's thought that if man's sole activities are to 'sleep and feed' he is no better than a 'beast':

> Sure, He that made us with such large discourse,
> Looking before and after, gave us not
> That capability and god-like reason
> To fust in us unused.   (IV. iv. 36)

Here 'reason', if we remember the context (Fortinbras' mad yet noble enterprise), though not to be limited to intuition, yet certainly contains the intuitional, emotional quality covered by 'apprehension' and is later carefully distinguished from 'thinking too precisely on the event' (IV. iv. 41); that is, from the reason of pure rationalism; though it is, too, really rather Hamlet's 'apprehension 'of Fortinbras' nobility with which we are concerned, Fortinbras himself being more active (and angelic). Here 'god-like reason' is contrasted with 'bestial oblivion' (IV. iv. 40): it is that which links man to the gods. Such too, is the 'noble and most sovereign reason' (III. i. 166) whose loss in Hamlet raises Ophelia's lovely lines—'like sweet bells jangled, out of tune and harsh'. Gods alone can master and possess in steady wisdom the swift uncapturable agonies of intuition. Therefore

> to be wise and love
> Exceeds man's might; that dwells with gods above.
> (*Troilus and Cressida*, III. ii. 163)

It is, however, through approach to such inclusive wisdom that men become god-like. The over-ruling wisdom of the Duke in *Measure for Measure*, a

---

[1] For a relevant piece of scholastic thought directly applicable in its latter half to both Prospero and Ariel compare the following (italics mine):

Of the angels there are, according to Dionysius, three hierarchies comprising each three orders. . . . Now regarding their natures and offices, we may say that the Seraphim excel all others in that they are united with God himself; 'the Cherubim know the divine secrets'; and the Thrones know immediately the 'types of things in God'. Dominations appoint those things which are to be done; Virtues give the power of execution and *rule over corporeal Nature in the working of miracles*; Powers order how what has been commanded can be accomplished, *and coerce evil spirits*. Principalities and Archangels are the leaders in execution, and *Angels simply perform what is to be done.*—W. C. Curry, *Shakespeare's Philosophical Patterns*, p. 70.

precursor of Prospero, is naturally compared to 'power divine' (v. i. 370). Cerimon is such another, remarking

> I hold it ever
> Virtue and cunning were endowments greater
> Than nobleness and riches; careless heirs
> May the two latter darken and expend,
> But immortality attends the former,
> Making a man a god.   (*Pericles*, iii. ii. 26)

Shakespeare sees man as god-like in relation to certain definite faculties. The Quarto's 'How like a god' is, as an uncompromising and unqualified statement, surely suspect: man is god-like not absolutely but in his one faculty of 'apprehension'.[1]

We must keep the whole speech before us. Our excerpt starts with 'What a piece of work is a man!' Hamlet sees man as a created being. Moreover, the lines continue, after 'In apprehension how like a god', with 'The beauty of the world, the paragon of animals'. Throughout, as the speech's opening lines on earth and firmament make clear, Hamlet is envisaging man as a wondrous upstart from nature, a triumph of creation. Now the Quarto 'How like a god!' (meaning clearly how like God in comparison with 'angel') makes a transcendent climax which the concluding phrases ('The beauty of the world', 'the paragon of animals') tend to destroy; a climax, too, inherently unsuitable to the whole speech, concerned with man as part of creation. In the Folio, however, they merely complete, with a balanced phraseology, the natural meaning of what precedes, 'the beauty of the world' referring mainly to man's angelic outside, while 'paragon of animals' suits rather that faculty of divine imagination (in the Coleridgean or Shelleyan sense) that distinguishes him from the animal creation.

My contention is that Hamlet, in surveying man's various attributes, characterizes, by his comparison of man to an angel, all those excellences of outward beauty, grace, poise, artistry and valour that are elsewhere his concern; but, by his comparison of man's 'apprehension' to a god, advances to a more inward consideration (rather as in the move from his address to the Players to his speech to Horatio), characterizing here rather his own potentialities at their best; while his tragedy lies in his inability to harmonize his own god-like faculties with the angelic world of fine action and gracious behaviour; though, as we have seen, there is, in the final act, a synthesis.

I may therefore be excused for once again returning to this defence. To assure fairness, I conclude by quoting Professor Dover Wilson's own best piece of evidence, adduced in his recent review of Professor Alexander's lecture (*Review of English Studies*, January, 1947, p. 78). Professor Dover Wilson quotes from Pater's translation of Pico della Mirandola's *Oratio de Hominis Dignitate*:

> It is a commonplace of the Schools that man is a little World, in which we may discern a body mingled of earthly elements and ethereal breath,

---

[1] Perhaps the clearest exposition of Shakespeare's general meaning will be found in Marlowe's famous lines from *Tamburlaine*:

> Our souls, whose faculties can comprehend
> The wondrous architecture of the world . . .

and the vegetable life of plants, and the sense of the lower animals, and reason, and the intelligence of angels, and a likeness to God.

I cannot myself accept this as evidence. Even though we grant, which is far from probable, that this passage was a 'source' of Shakespeare's lines, yet surely we know that such a poet uses his sources not for direct transcription but for re-creation; that his mind is at every instant vigorously at work 'in the quick forge and working-house of thought', modifying and re-distributing; and that, given such a speech for regrafting, he will quite certainly change the detail to suit his own artistic, or other, instincts.[1] How steady Shakespeare's imaginative correspondences are my quotations, here and elsewhere, have shown. Why should the chain of correspondences be broken on this solitary occasion? I have not referred to a concordance: but is there, I may with some confidence ask, any passage in Shakespeare that conflicts with my argument?

It is not my intention to attack Elizabethan scholarship, as such; least of all the enthusiastic, and indeed infectious, scholarship of Professor Dover Wilson, who has probably done more than anyone else in our generation to make the Elizabethan age a lively reality to scholar and public alike. But in that very wealth of knowledge, so lightly carried and happily expressed, lies a danger: the danger, on occasion, of letting scholarship dominate, rather than serve, the literature it handles. And yet it is, I well realize, no slight reversal for which, here and elsewhere, I am contending. I suggest that it may be positively dangerous to read a great writer in the light of his age; it is safer, to my mind, to read the age in the light of the great writer. For what, after all, do we mean by historical 'scholarship' or 'learning' as applied to literature? Inevitably, I think, we refer to either (i) second-hand information and deduction or (ii) second-rate books. But neither must take precedence over the immediate and present fact of the living, first-rate, text. We must be wary of interpreting the higher in terms of the lower which it so far outspaces.

---

[1] For analysis of the subtleties involved in a poet's use of his 'sources' see J. Livingston Lowes' *Road to Xanadu* and W. F. Jackson Knight's *Roman Vergil*. 'In general, as with Coleridge', writes my brother of Vergil, 'nothing at all was ever reproduced entirely without alteration' (III. 79). These two studies are directly relevant both here and also to the matter of multiple sources discussed in Note A above.